The
First
85...

a Memoir
by
Jim Freund

The First 85 . . . .

ISBN: 9798616447067

ACKNOWLEDGMENTS AND DEDICATION

I've received useful suggestions on various chapters of the book from a number of people, for which I'm very grateful. I particularly wish to thank my former law partner, Jon Lerner, for reviewing the chapters about my years at Skadden; my sons, Erik and Tom, for helping with the material on themselves, their mother, their grandparents, and their daughters; and my wife, who read the whole thing and offered helpful suggestions throughout.

I'm most indebted here to my good friend, John Doyle, who pored over the entire manuscript at two stages of the process and applied his superb editing skills to offer detailed commentary that sharpened the prose, eliminated redundancies, suggested additions and deletions, and kept the story flowing.

Needless to say, all these good people are exonerated from responsibility for any factual errors, misguided opinions, omissions or excesses in these pages, for which I take full responsibility.

My thanks to Joe Azar, a peerless illustrator, whose cover expertly captures my mood, interests, and achievements at this juncture of my life. You can also see Joe's talents reprised on the covers of six of my other books (back page) and on a special page of the Appendix. Joe has a unique talent of illustrating in vivid pictorial terms just what I've been trying to get across in words.

I doubt I'd have been able to take on and complete this project without the significant everyday help of my versatile assistant Raymond on all aspects, but especially in the complex task of assembling the numerous photo pages.

Finally, I dedicate this memoir to Barbara Fox, my wonderful wife and the principal support for this needy octogenarian. Barbara, if you want to know in detail how I feel about you, please refer to my numerous paeans in Chapter 18 and elsewhere.

June 2020   Jim Freund

TABLE OF CONTENTS

TABLE OF CONTENTS

1. OVERTURE

Some months ago, after struggling to write this memoir over the better part of several years, I finally got around to asking myself the obvious question – *why* am I doing it?

I could easily conjure up rationalizations galore to answer that question, but I'm too long in the tooth to play such self-serving games. What it came down to, I realized, is simply this: an 85-year-old guy who's writing his own memoir must consider his life to have been worthwhile – a fitting subject to explore, and to preserve its more notable contours in print.

"In the end," said Margaret Atwood perceptively, "we'll all become stories." How true . . . . I feel I have something to say, and no one else is going to say it for me. So I want to get it down now while my brain is still functioning and my ability to recall events and string together words hasn't yet faded.

I then posed to myself the natural follow-up question: for *whom* am I writing the book? My answer points to several constituencies:

- First, it's for myself – to collect and record my memories and evaluate my behavior while the raw materials are still relatively intact.
- Second, it's for members of my family – including the unborn ones who may some day develop an interest in their "silent generation" ancestor.
- Third, it's for my friends and acquaintances of a lifetime, with whom I've kept in touch over the years – both on a personal basis and through my annual year-end updates – and who (I'd like to think) have some interest in what I might relate.

Of course, no one is forced to read the whole thing. Princeton classmates may turn to that chapter but pass up my legal career, while lawyer colleagues might review the Skadden Arps section without caring much about the college years. But friends who view me through a particular lens might be willing to consider other less familiar angles. I received a lot of positive feedback about the chapter I sent out in 2018 detailing my Navy service, along these lines – "Hey, Jim, I hadn't known anything about that part of your life and found it interesting."

So, that's the audience I'm writing the book for. It's *not* aimed at people who don't know me. Still, if readers should want to recommend it to friends, they're certainly welcome aboard, and copies will be available on Amazon.

* * *

A memoir depends on memory. Not the *where-did-I-put-the-car-keys* type of memory, but rather the recall of persons and events that may date back many decades.

My memory is by no means photographic, but it's pretty good for identifying high (and low) points, which this exercise has certainly tested. I was able to rely in part on some contemporary written material, such as the daily diary I kept during my 1952 cross-country journey (explored in Chapter 5). The chapters on high school and college (4 and 6) make use of articles in the student newspapers, now available digitally. The Navy experience (7) incorporates references from a cruise book I authored. The chapters on my Skadden law practice (13 through 17) and retirement (19 through 21) contain much information derived from books and articles that I wrote, or in some instances were written about me.

Memory works best on past incidents that achieve anecdotal status, and I've incorporated a number of such tales into this memoir. I'm aware that these stories may have become a bit gilded over the years,[*] but the essence of what occurred remains unaltered.

Recently, a friend brought to my attention an article entitled *Speak, Memory*[**] that raises questions on this point, claiming that "some of our most cherished memories may never have happened – or may have happened to someone else . . . ." The distinction is said to be between "historical truth" and "narrative truth." But fear not – even the author of the article admits that "aberrations of a gross sort are relatively rare, and that, for the most part, our memories are relatively solid and reliable." That's how I feel about mine.

* * *

---

[*] See, for instance, a possible such embellishment in the matter of the nutty sailor related in Chapter 7.

[**] Oliver Sacks, The New York Review, 2/21/13

The bulk of the years I've spent on the planet have been mainly positive and joyful experiences. The first couple of decades – 1934 through 1956, childhood through high school and college – were terrific. The three decades I spent practicing law and doing deals at Skadden Arps – 1966 through 1996 – were exciting and productive (except for a little tail-off at the end). My lengthy retirement – 23 years from 1997 to the present – has been richly rewarding. And the most important people in my life – two parents, two wives, two sons, two granddaughters – have all played a major part in contributing to the good vibes I've felt.

Did you notice, though, that there's a decade missing from this tabulation? It's the period from mid-1956 (after graduation from Princeton) to early 1966 (when I arrived at Skadden Arps). That span, which featured three separate activities of roughly three years each, I've long regarded as neither constructive nor joyous. These consisted of:

- Three mostly unpleasant years in the U.S. Navy aboard an icebreaker that bounced back and forth from the Arctic to the Antarctic – no women, no booze, occasional frostbite, and too many polar bears and penguins;

- As bad as that was, I disliked even more the three depressing years at Harvard Law School that followed (which found me wishing I were back in the vicinity of the South Pole);

- Three-plus seemingly wasted years at my first law firm – a well-meaning, competent, but uninspired legal backwater, where too often the highlight of the day was a two-hour, beer-drenched lunch at a nearby tavern.

To be sure, those years weren't totally bleak. I had no disabling diseases or other serious physical problems. I met my first wife, Barbro, at the end of my Navy service, married her during my third year of law school, and spent three pleasant years with her in NYC while at my first law firm. I made some good friends, enjoyed a lot of laughs, and saw some interesting parts of the world. But for various reasons, I disliked each of the endeavors I was engaged in; and taken in concert, these cast a pall over the entire decade.

I had prospered in high school and thoroughly enjoyed myself in college, which combined to produce a sense of self-confidence as to what I could ultimately achieve, even though I had no idea in what sphere it would take place. The subsequent dismal decade, however, challenged my faith in myself. I compiled a spotty record of accomplishment during those ten years – nothing to give assurance that I would ultimately succeed. I hadn't been beaten down, but I'd certainly climbed no heights. I fretted about perhaps having to settle for a lot less in the way of lifetime achievements than I'd looked forward to.

In this memoir, I've tried to re-examine those discouraging years – to analyze my negative feelings about them, to evaluate whether that viewpoint was well-founded. I searched for whether those years contained some hidden values that enhanced the five succeeding decades.

When we are going through seemingly negative periods and events, it's not easy to assess with any accuracy where things stand. Let's face it – we're all like blind men fondling small portions of an elephant. As the decades pass, however, the view backward in time can often become more balanced.

Take my naval experience, for instance. In retrospect, this formed a helpful insulation between college and career. In contrast to today's undergraduates who face tremendous pressure to get into graduate school or land a good job, this enabled me to enjoy Princeton thoroughly and defer all career decisions to the privacy of my stateroom.

By the way, it's lucky that I took this extra time to make my decision. Becoming a lawyer never occurred to me in college. It evolved while I was in the Navy, defending AWOL seamen in many a court martial held on our icebreaker. In fact, I applied to Harvard Law School from the Antarctic.

Or consider law school. It took me a long time to acknowledge any benefit I received from Harvard. Ultimately, I came to appreciate it as force-feeding the importance of hard work and willpower, which has stood me in good stead during the rest of my life. In particular, if I hadn't absorbed the concept of deferred gratification while at Harvard, I would never have been able to endure the tough task of cranking out the dozen books I've authored over the years.

Even my years at that first unexciting New York law firm I now recognize as a pleasant transitional idyll during the early years of my career and first marriage. It also positioned me to seize a prime professional opportunity when it arose.

So, here's the lesson I've learned. Don't assume the accuracy of your current perspective, especially when it appears hopelessly negative.

4

Not only may good things be in store later on, but they may well be percolating under the surface at that very moment.

* * *

Let me introduce one of the recurring themes of this memoir by relating a story about something that happened during the spring of my junior year at Princeton.

A competition was announced to select who would be the on-campus correspondent for the Princeton Alumni Weekly (PAW) during our upcoming senior year. It was a good gig – you wrote periodic essays on subjects of your own choosing; they were published in a magazine distributed to many thousands of alumni; and PAW actually paid you for the effort. I signed up for the competition, as did perhaps a half-dozen other juniors.

The process to choose a winner consisted of us each writing two sample essays and then being interviewed separately by the PAW editor. I considered myself an accomplished writer and gave some real attention to the essays I submitted, which I thought were pretty good.

The interview was scheduled to take place on a certain Saturday morning. That Friday night I went out with my buddies on a tour of several town taverns, drank too much beer, became loaded, rolled around in the mud, and got little sleep at whatever place I ended up. Awakening Saturday morning with a throbbing hangover, I didn't return to my room to change out of my soiled bar-hopping clothes, failed to shower or shave, and arrived at the interview in a disheveled and partially comatose state.

Later, when I sobered up, I realized that my lack of respect for the interview – an insult I assume none of the other candidates duplicated – had dashed any chance I might have had to win the competition. Needless to say, I didn't get the PAW job.

Upon learning the bad news, I couldn't help wondering *why* I'd acted in that fashion. Here was something, after all, that I really wanted to be chosen for. Why did I screw up my chances of being selected?

The answer didn't take long to hit me. I realized it was to protect myself from the ignominy of losing the competition based on the quality of the writing samples I'd provided. My disastrous interview enabled me to assign it the blame for suffering defeat in a competition I might well have won (or so I was able to tell myself) on the basis of my writing skills. In effect, I had created the very condition that caused me to fail, out of a misguided demand of personal ego. I had purposely screwed up to avoid being judged on my literary merits.

It was a real epiphany for me. Never again did I allow myself to become another self-fulfilling prophecy statistic. From then on, the gospel I preached to all who would listen was not to provide oneself with excuses for failure.

I tell this tale here to illustrate one theme of this memoir. There are a number of insights that I've chosen to live by (or, if I'm unable to live up to some, at least to recognize my shortcomings). I have often arrived at these insights as a result of a mistake I've made or an adverse experience I've endured, such as that disastrous PAW interview. Some of these mishaps that ultimately led to keener judgments are explored in the book.

We're all bound to make mistakes. But in my view, the key is not to look back on them. George Marshall put it this way: "When a thing is done, it's done. Look forward to your next objective." I like the way Hugh White characterized mistakes as "lessons of wisdom," and counseled that "The past cannot be changed. The future is yet in your power." The idea of "lessons of wisdom" is a useful way of defining experience – but remember to hark to Mark Twain's caution:

> "We should be careful to get out of an experience only the wisdom that is in it – and stop there; lest we be like the cat that sits down on a hot stove-lid. She will never sit down on a hot stove-lid again – and that is well; but also she will never sit down on a cold one anymore."

* * *

I feel fortunate to have had a number of interests beyond my career as a lawyer. These really came to the fore in the several decades after retirement. My three principal activities have been music, photography and writing – utilizing the ear, the eye and the brain.

Some people, assessing the breadth of these interests, have referred to me as a "Renaissance man". When I hear someone say that, my invariable response is, "It's tough to be a Renaissance man – you have to work like hell to keep one step ahead of being a dilettante."

In this memoir I attempt to evaluate myself in terms of my varied pursuits. I've tried to be candid. Where I think I'm good, I say so – as the octogenarian cabaret singer Marilyn Maye puts it, "At my age, I'm too old to be humble." Where I'm lacking, I talk about that also. Knowledgeable readers may well have differing opinions, but I think you're entitled to know how I feel about it.

* * *

I've addressed my life more or less chronologically by the events that occurred, but interspersing at various points along the way the key characters – my father and mother, first wife, sons, and Barbara, my nonpareil wife for the past 35 years.

I set great store by what I call *Sheer Happenstance* –the vagaries of fate that impact all of us, and our voluntary decisions that lead to relationships and outcomes which wouldn't have occurred without those choices, but then make all the difference. These have infused my life and, for the most part, have proved to be positive. I'll be calling attention to them at various points in the narrative – but rarely to rue or regret the choices made along the way.

By analogy, there's a terrific lyric by Alan and Marilyn Bergman to a Michel Legrand song, *On My Way to You,* that touches all the right bases of this lifetime journey in terms of ultimately finding the love of your life. I find that if you change the words, "love" and "you" to "the positive opportunity", it admirably expresses my own viewpoint in terms of other choices and occurrences encountered along the way.

I relive the roles I've played,
the tears I may have squandered;
the many pipers I have paid
along the roads I've wandered.
Yet all the time I knew it,
Love was somewhere out there waiting.
Though I may regret a step or two,
If I had changed a single day,
what went amiss or went astray,
I may have never found my way to you.
I wouldn't change a thing that happened
on my way to you."

* * *

I had almost completed the text for this memoir when the coronavirus erupted. Notwithstanding its obvious significance, which touches so many aspects of our lives, I have decided not to let it intrude on the memories and reflections of a lifetime, which are related in my pre-coronavirus voice. I have, however, added an Afterword at the end of the text to offer some observations on the pandemic, as well as on the absence in these pages (notwithstanding my strong aversion to the current Administration) of my views on such matters as politics, critical events (wars, recessions, natural disasters), foreign affairs, and the like.

* * *

Well, that's enough introduction. Let's dive right in now, beginning with a brief look at the year 1934, in the depths of the Great Depression....

2. THE EARLY YEARS (1934-1947)

The nation's birthrate hit its lowest mark in 1934, the year I was born. From then until my debut as a teenager in September 1947, the U.S. struggled through the Great Depression and World War II – not exactly fertile ground for a youngster to flourish in, but for me, very pleasant years to grow up.

My memory of those years is that I had a fine childhood. I was healthy, bright, active and athletic. There were no siblings to dilute the loving parental attention I received as an only child. My folks, although not wealthy, saw to it that all my material needs were met, supplemented by summer camp and special trips. I made good friends and had lots of family around; we lived for most of that period in a modest but comfortable apartment on Manhattan's Riverside Drive; and three of those years were spent at Hunter College Elementary School, then considered a "model school."

* * *

I was born on July 26, 1934 at St. Joseph's Hospital in Far Rockaway, NY.* At that time, my parents were living next to my paternal grandparents in Woodmere, Long Island. Less than a year later, Mom and Dad moved to a small Manhattan apartment building near 106th Street and West End Avenue, where we stayed for several years.

I have almost no memories of life in that first NYC home. But there is one event that sticks in my mind, perhaps courtesy of my mother's propensity to reminisce. We lived on the building's top floor, and the summer sun beat down on the roof mercilessly, transmitting all that heat into our apartment. (There was no such thing as apartment air conditioning back in those days.) It got so hot that at least on one night we took blankets and pillows over to Central Park and slept on the grass.

Dad had purchased an inexpensive home movie camera which he and Mom used sparingly around our apartment, sometimes in Riverside Park, and mostly out at Long Beach, L.I., where we spent time during the

---

* For what it's worth, my birthdate was two months after the birth of the famed Dionne quintuplets in Canada – an occurrence that, back in those limited diagnostic years, may well have caused some pre-delivery concerns for my parents

summers. Although the low quality clips jump all over the place – perhaps in my parents' effort to conserve expensive film – they do provide relevant glimpses of my life at that time.

I see this little blond kid trying to run from the beach into the ocean with his father always catching him just before he hits the waves. In fact, I seem to always be in motion – running or riding a tricycle or swinging in a playground. With the onset of winter, I'm pictured on a sled with my mother, throwing snowballs at my father.

There I am standing at a train door with the conductor, and then at the wheel of a fire truck next to a fireman. We celebrated my birthday every July with a party in Long Beach, the kids all decked out in cone-shaped hats held on by rubber bands tucked under the chin.

A number of clips take place beneath a Christmas tree, encircled by a Lionel model railroad with a train chugging along. I'm climbing all over my father. You can see the strong bond between us, even when we don boxing gloves and go at each other. Mom is knitting in one of the shots – a craft she continued to excel at into her post-centennial years. The three of us look very happy.

My grandparents appear in some of these early movies. Although they were then a lot younger than I am now, they look so much older – or am I just flattering myself? My mother's parents, Julius and Esther Coleman, lived near us at 98th Street and Broadway. My father's parents, Emanuel and Mollie Freund, lived on 70th Street and Amsterdam Ave. My mother's sister and her husband, Debbie and Murray Tillman, lived on 72nd St. near West End Avenue. My father's sister and her husband, Ruth and Mel Cahn, lived on the West Side at 108th St. with their daughter Judy (who, both then and today, is my close cousin). I was on good terms with all my relatives, but I don't remember any of them (except for Mom and Dad) as influential figures in my life.

After a few years in that first apartment, we moved to 300 Riverside Drive at 102nd St. where we lived for about a decade. I enjoyed being right next to Riverside Park with the Hudson River just beyond, although on cold winter days the west wind came blasting up the block in gusts strong enough to knock over a little guy.

Most memories from that time have faded, but I can place in time two of my earliest recollections. First, there was a Japanese restaurant in the building next to ours where Mom and I often ate dinner when Dad was "on the road." One day we found the doors shuttered and the restaurant closed.

Only later did I figure out that its closing must have related to the December 7, 1941 Japanese attack on Pearl Harbor. For all I know, the restaurant staff was interred, as were so many Nisei from the West Coast.

Second was the day in 1945 that I heard on the street of President Roosevelt's death. When I went upstairs to tell my mother, she reacted angrily – ("You must never joke about serious things like that!") and refused to believe me until it was eventually confirmed.

I have a vision of myself – possibly in knickers – on 102nd Street which sloped upward to West End Avenue, playing what we called "stoopball" with my local buddies. It consisted of bouncing a Spaldeen rubber ball off the stoop of one of the street's brownstones. (But then what happened? – I can't remember the rules of the game.) What I do recall is that periodically a lookout would spot a gang of Irish or Italian teenagers from Amsterdam and Columbus Avenues, heading down our block toward Riverside Park. These were tough guys, not averse to shaking us down for the nickels and dimes in our pockets, so we usually retreated indoors until they passed through.

Here's another incident in that vein (but with a twist) which occurred a few years later. We were in Central Park – four or five white kids – when we were accosted by four or five black kids, a little bigger and more menacing. "Give us your money!" demanded their leader.

We weren't about to resist. (Had we been cautioned to fold at such times by our parents, or were we just chicken to duke it out? – I can't recall.) We dug some change out of our pockets and handed the coins over to their leader. When he'd received all that was coming, the leader and his foot soldiers took off running.

All of them, that is, except one boy, who stayed behind. We wondered what he was after. "I just want you guys to know," he stammered, "that this wasn't my idea. I'm sorry about it."

He lingered. Were we supposed to excuse him for robbing us? I wasn't sure, nor were my pals, so we said nothing. After a short while and without another word, he walked away slowly in the direction his leader had gone . . . .

The landlord of 300 Riverside Drive, who lived in the building, had a daughter my age – my friend, Jane. One spring, I was invited to a birthday party she was having in their apartment.

A few weeks earlier at Easter time, my parents had presented me with two baby chicks that I kept in the bathtub and played with for hours. As I prepared to go to Jane's party, my mother gave me strict instructions: "Don't say anything about the chicks!"

I was confused. "Why not?" I asked. "Because," she replied, "our lease says we can't have little animals like that running around the apartment – and I don't want Jane's father, who's our landlord, to find out we're in violation."

I didn't really understand what the fuss was all about, but I gave a pledge of silence and went to the party. When I came back home, Mom quizzed me. "Were you a good boy who didn't say anything about the chicks?" To which I replied, "Yes I was. But guess what, Mom – Jane's dad gave her a present of two ducklings for her birthday, and we played with them in their bathtub."

Another recollection that sticks in my mind involves my maternal grandparents, who I liked very much. At times when my parents wanted an evening off, they would leave me with them. And on occasion, Esther and Julius would take me to the movies at the Riverside Theatre on Broadway and 96th Street, near their apartment.

My enduring memory of those movie excursions is entering the theatre in the middle of one of the two movies on the bill (no one ever checked starting times), walking down the aisle, and hearing Esther identify where we should sit – "Over here, the next row, a couple of seats in . . ." – in a very loud voice that echoed around the theater. Then, within a few minutes of being seated, Julius would fall into a deep slumber and begin to snore in an ear-piercing tone that lasted throughout the movie, to the anguish of everyone in the area. All this was very embarrassing for a little kid.

* * *

I had a brief stint in some kind of nursery school near our house but don't remember any kindergarten. I spent the first two grades at P.S. 54, at 104th Street and Amsterdam Avenue. I have almost no memory of those years, or of anyone in my class, but later on my mother was fond of telling about one incident.

It occurred early in World War II. In the middle of a school day, based on some apparently flawed national security intelligence, an emergency was declared to deal with an anticipated air raid on New York

City by one of the Axis powers. The administrators of P.S. 54 panicked, closed the school, and told all the kids to get home quickly. The problem for me, however, was that up to then I'd always been picked up at school by Mom or a maid at the end of the day, which was still hours away.

When Mom somehow found out what was happening, she rushed to the school, saw immediately that it was closed, and realized there was no little Jimmy around. Panicking, she raced the half-dozen or so blocks to our apartment – hoping against hope that I'd made it by myself, hadn't been run over by a car or trolley, and wasn't traumatized by the experience. When she opened the door to our apartment, there I was, dressed up in my cowboy outfit – chaps, ten-gallon hat, holsters and all – twirling two toy pistols and shouting, "Let 'em come!"

I must have suffered from headaches in my early school days, which Mom attributed to the agonizingly slow pace in the classroom – her implication being that I was the smart kid held back by a bunch of nincompoops. So I was taken out of P.S. 54 to spend the third grade at Walden School, a small private school on 88th Street and Central Park West.

* * *

My class at Walden consisted of six boys and about that many girls. It was a very liberal school that kept its distance from traditional education. For instance, we called the teachers – even the school principal – by their first names. One of my classmates was Dick Eisner, a lifelong friend with whom I still play octogenarian tennis almost every week. He stayed at Walden another five years before joining me at Horace Mann.

"I had no grammar when I got to HM," Dick told me recently. "I didn't know about nouns and pronouns. They didn't believe in cursive writing – we had to print everything. And there was little or no homework nor any foreign language taught."

But I enjoyed myself there. We did have some math; we read a few books; there was art and a shop period; and we spent a lot of time on projects. I remember one that I think involved cocoa production, for which we built a little straw hut in the classroom. I also recall the kids running a store at lunchtime, where goods and coins changed hands.

This was in the middle of World War II, but neither Dick nor I recall the conflict ever being discussed. I do remember six-man touch football games in Central Park; and I'll never forget late afternoons in Dick's apartment a few blocks from school, where a ping pong table took up the bulk of his bedroom.

* * *

My mother wasn't happy with Walden's informality; and when my father received a draft notice which presaged an imminent drop in family income, she decided to take me out of private school and back into the public school system. (As it turned out, Dad's draft notice was later rescinded.)

But not just to any public school. Somehow she secured an open place for me in the fourth grade of Hunter College Elementary School (HCES), located at 69th Street between Park and Lexington Avenues. I've been told that HCES was generally considered to be the best public elementary school in the city. There was competition to be admitted to HCES; they say you needed an IQ of 135 or better to get in. Whether or not that was the case, the kids there seemed pretty bright, and the teachers treated us accordingly. I don't recall suffering any headaches for slow pacing at Hunter, where I spent the next three years (4th through 6th grades, from September 1943 to June 1946).

We had about fifty kids in our grade, split into two classes. One of my classmates was Bill Silver, who later in life became a close friend. Three guys I remember with some nostalgia were Danny Josephthal, a good pal; Marty Heyert, who was much more knowledgeable about politics and other current events than the rest of us; and Palmer Hughes, who had an encyclopedic knowledge of sports.

Palmer and I were both athletic and competed in various sports venues. We became fascinated by the lure of someone running a four-minute mile, which wasn't attained until 1954 by England's Roger Bannister.* One day after school we decided to do something about it.

---

* Not to name-drop, but in later life I became friendly with Roger's son Thurstan and spent a memorable night with both of them some years ago before Roger passed away.

14

We were in Palmer's apartment, which was at one end of a long narrow hall. We measured the length of the hall (walking the distance heel-toe heel-toe), corrected for our feet being less than a foot long, and divided the result (let's say, 200 feet back and forth) into the 5,280 feet of a mile. We figured out that if we ran back and forth about 26 times, it would constitute close to a mile.

And so we ran a relay, scampering from one end to the other – pushing off the end door and doubling back, sweating profusely, clocking ourselves with my stopwatch. Although it's unlikely that we came anywhere within hailing distance of the elusive four minute goal, I recall feeling fulfilled at the climax – did this augur my much later adult affinity for taking on challenges?

Our teachers were Miss Brennan and Miss Burgess, and Dr. Brumbaugh was the principal. Wilma Classon (neé Fagin), who was in my HCES class and helped me recall those years, said I shouldn't forget Anna Curtis Chandler, the woman who showed us slides of masterworks in a tiered room during the art appreciation hour. Students from Hunter College became involved with us, assisting on projects that had been assigned. (Some have suggested they were using us as research guinea pigs.)

We studied math, English, social science – the usual curriculum. During recesses, we went up to the open roof and kicked a ball around. After school, I played sports in Central Park and Riverside Park under the supervision of a group called Winters, before they deposited me back home in the late afternoon.

World War II was in full force my first two years at HCES, and a loud air raid alarm system went off occasionally from the rooftop. We all wore laminated ID tags around our necks – I still have mine – to enable the authorities to identify us after a catastrophe. Periodically, we crumpled under our desks, butt down on a linoleum square – pulling our legs up, wrapping our arms around them, and keeping our head down until the all-clear sounded.

My clearest war memory, though, was of a different nature. Bubble gum, which we were all fond of, was in very short supply during those years. My Uncle Mel, whose business was supplying products to small stationary stores city-wide, somehow came up with a box of 100 wrapped pieces of penny bubble gum, which he gave as a present to his sole nephew.

In my first (and perhaps only) burst of business entrepreneurship, I marketed the penny gum among my classmates for prices up to and including a dollar apiece – the kids were delighted to get them regardless of cost. Some would chew a piece all day and evening, put it on the bedpost overnight, and resuscitate the lump the next morning by rapid chewing to extend the pleasure for another day.

At one of the first boy-girl parties in the 6th grade, I remember us playing the then popular racy game of "spin the bottle." The boy spinner and the girl to whom the bottle pointed would get up from the circle of kids and go into the closet for an awkward kiss . . . . Such a fond memory . . . .

When the 6th grade concluded in 1946, the boys had to find another venue, although the girls could continue on at Hunter Junior High School. I always thought of it as a graduation, although for the girls going onward I believe it was called a "recognition".

Now skip ahead to 1996, fifty years after we graduated (or the girls were "recognized"). Several of us organized an HCES Class of 1946 reunion, which I volunteered to hold at the West Side townhouse where we lived at the time.

Stephen Langenthal, with the help of others, managed to track down many classmates, including numerous women whose last names had changed. They came from everywhere (including Mexico, the south, and the west coast). It turned out to be a remarkable evening.

Bill Silver arranged for our 1946 class picture to be blown up to a huge size, and we hung it on the wall. Each person also had a small photo of himself or herself at age twelve, to be pinned to a lapel or dress. Some classmates were recognizable, but others had completely changed in appearance. (One girl, whom I recalled as being much taller than all of us back then, must have stopped growing right after school, because she was one of the smallest persons at the party.) The personalities of many attendees were similar to what we remembered, although others had changed notably in the intervening five decades.

Barbara produced a food menu appropriate to 1946 – mac 'n' cheese, hot dogs, chocolate ice cream, and such. I played piano selections of songs popular back then, which people sang with gusto – many not even needing the lyric books I'd prepared. The evening's highlight came when we all gathered in the living room, sitting in chairs and on the floor, swapping tales from the old days in an atmosphere of general merriment.

One topic did engender a lot of discussion. In each of our HCES classes, the desks had been arranged so as to produce two large groupings – the A group and the B group. One fellow, who was at the "B" table, said he'd always been worried that this represented a determination from on high as to his capability – that the kids at the B table weren't as smart as the kids at the A table. I had a vague memory of having been at the A table, but couldn't recall ever hearing even a rumor regarding that kind of qualitative judgment. The living room proceeded to erupt in a spirited debate on the subject, though no general consensus was reached.

* * *

After HCES, word had it that the best public school around was PS 6 at 85th Street and Madison Avenue. A number of the East Side boys, who resided in the appropriate district, were planning to go there. We lived on the West Side, but my mother (and several other parents) lobbied the authorities to let their kids join the migration, and these efforts proved successful.

I enjoyed my seventh grade year at PS 6, although most of my memories have faded. One noticeable change from Walden and HCES, whose enrollments were all white, was that two of the boys in our class were black. I can picture playing ball in the school's courtyard – especially the time we ousted a younger kid from the basketball court, only to have him re-emerge ten minutes later with his big brother and cousin, causing us to quickly wilt. I visualize us at lunchtime, romping down to the Automat near Lexington Ave., changing our quarters into nickels to dial up some hearty food choices.

One particular memory I've long held was of a teacher, back from a trip to the Far East, passing around a piece of jade she'd acquired for the class to fondle. When I told this recently to seventh grade classmate Bill Kaufmann – whose friendship I've renewed in recent years – he not only remembered the same event but even came up with the teacher's name (Miss Childs). I'm saving for Chapter 20 an important moment in my musical life that occurred one night in Bill's apartment.

As the school term ended, my mother's initiative once more came into play. Somehow she engineered my admittance to the single place still open in the eighth grade of Horace Mann School. Mom had a wonderful knack for advancing my education, which I didn't adequately acknowledge back then but am so grateful for today.

Speaking of Mom, and because religion was such a crucial factor in her life, this seems an appropriate juncture for some reflections on that subject.

* * *

My heritage on both sides of the family was Jewish. My maternal grandparents immigrated from Europe as young adults. My paternal grandparents, whose forebears were also European, were both born here; and I learned recently that my grandfather's mother was born in the United States prior to the Civil War.

I'm chagrined to admit that I'm not really sure where in Europe any of my ancestors came from. I posed no questions to my grandparents and few to my parents, nor have I ever done any real digging. When my mother spoke about her parents' families, it sounded like they came from Russia, but it might have been Poland, and nothing was linked to a single city or area. As for my father's family, I always assumed they hailed from Germany, based on the surname "Freund" (which means "friend" in German); but they may well have been from some bordering land with a partially German population.

My maternal grandparents gathered their family together for Friday night dinners with some regularity, and I remember hearing readings in Hebrew, but the evenings didn't seem especially religious. I can't recall any theological references at all emanating from my father's family.

I did, however, have a personal religious immersion beginning in my early youth, but it wasn't to Judaism. At some point after their wedding in 1929 and before my birth in 1934, first my mother and then my father converted to Christian Science. Beginning in toddlerhood and continuing every week until I went away to college, I attended Sunday School at 13th Church of Christ, Scientist, on 83rd Street between West End Avenue and Riverside Drive. As a teen, I often accompanied my parents to the Church's Wednesday night testimonial service. I don't recall seeing the inside of a temple until I began attending the Bar Mitzvahs of my many 13-year-old Jewish friends.

I never did find out why my mother made her conversion. It may well have been induced by the successful treatment of a health problem through non-medical means in the Christian Science tradition; but I never pressed her on it, and she didn't raise the subject. Once she converted, however, I am sure she quickly exhibited her special brand of zeal for this new discovery, and I can understand why my father soon joined her – although in fairness to him, he never gave any indication of questioning his decision, and appeared devoted to the faith.

Without getting into the particulars of Christian Science, its most recognizable aspect is the shunning of doctors and medicine – handling matters of health on a spiritual level. While that may seem radical in this medically-driven age, church members point to many instances where such prayerful healings have taken place, even when the medical establishment didn't think it was possible.

Although I became increasingly quizzical about Christian Science, I did not rebel from it while living at home. I can remember catching colds as a kid, which seemed to keep me out of school for longer periods than other children so afflicted; but I wasn't unhappy at home on weekdays, listening to radio soap operas and reading books about sports heroes.

In those days, schools were open on Jewish holidays, with Jewish kids excused from attending classes. I can still picture myself as a teenager at Horace Mann (which had a heavily Jewish population), being one of the few students around on those days.

Truth be told, although I dutifully followed my parent's lead and regularly joined them at church, I was unable to wrap myself around the teachings of Christian Science. To me, it seemed too extreme, too dogmatic, too violative of the physical realities I was witnessing daily.

So, when I went away to college, I ceased my affiliation with the faith despite the disapproval of my parents. I've been known to say that this was because at Princeton I learned to drink and smoke – both of which are banned for Christian Scientists – and indeed, that may well have played a role in my apostasy; but the fact was I no longer subscribed to the core tenets of the faith.

My religious affiliations since college have been sporadic. My first wife, Barbro, came from a Lutheran background in Sweden, and our marriage was presided over by a Lutheran minister. While married to Barbro I attended West End Collegiate Church with her on occasion, usually during holidays, and our sons were enrolled in its Sunday and nursery schools. It was at Collegiate that I began a life-long friendship with Ken Gorsuch, the church's outstanding pastor. When my father passed away,

I didn't trust myself to read the emotional eulogy I'd written, so Ken delivered it for me at Dad's funeral. He also presided over the marriage of my son, Erik. Now that Ken and I are both retired, we've been meeting regularly in recent years to discuss both weighty and non-weighty matters.

When I married Barbara Fox in 1985, the service was conducted by a judge. I never embraced her Judaism, although I do attend temple with her on certain high holy days and join in Seder readings at our dinner table. I sometimes attend a nearby Unitarian/Universalist Church on holiday occasions – especially to hear the excellent music – but I haven't advanced any further in that direction.

From time to time I'm bothered by my lack of a sustainable faith, but I haven't found anything that strongly appeals to me. I'm not an atheist, although I might be called an agnostic, which is defined as someone who doesn't deny the existence of God or heaven but holds that one cannot know for certain whether they exist. I confess, however, to remaining hopeful that one of these days I'll experience a religious epiphany and introduce genuine faith into my life.

I need to include one postscript to this subject. My mother never ceased in her efforts to bring me back into the Christian Science fold. Over the years we had numerous discussions on the subject, some of which got a trifle heated. But one day, after she turned 100 and had pretty much given up on me, she tried a different tack. "Well, Jim, you had good training for a number of years in Christian Science. What did you get out of it that served you well in later life?"

It was a fair question, to which I replied that I'd give it some thought and respond on our next visit. After pondering the matter, here's what came to me. Although I could not accept the invincible attitude Christian Scientists have that belief in God can solve all health problems, the optimism underlying their approach left a definite residue. I've always been a glass-half-full kind of guy, and much of this attitude may well have stemmed from observing the church's positive thinking. As for Mom, although still preferring me to re-convert, she seemed at least partially contented by my response.

Dad, Mom, and Jimmy – 1934

My maternal grandparents,
Esther and Julius Coleman
* * *
With my cousin Judy,
then and now, a dear friend

My paternal grandparents,
Mollie and Emanuel Freund
* * *
Heading from infancy
into childhood

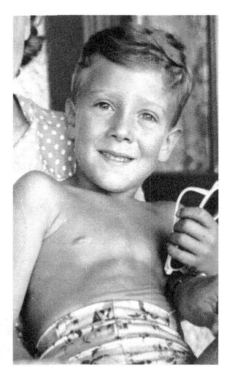

With Mom, with Dad, and with my buddies (and the ball) at summer camp in the mid-'40s.

3. MY MOTHER AND FATHER
MARCY AND SYLVAN FREUND

I was blessed with wonderful parents, to whom I wish to pay tribute.

After brief capsules of their early years, momentous meeting, and entry into marriage, I've divided the balance of this chapter into three periods:

- From my birth in 1934 until my graduation from high school in 1952, during which time I lived at home, where they were the central figures in my life;

- From when I went away to college in 1952 until my father's passing in 1974, during which time I no longer lived in my parents' home and our relations became more complex; and

- From 1974 until my mother's passing in 2013 at age 105, during which time she was on her own, with increasing support from me (as well as a number of others).

Their Years Prior to 1934

Sylvan Freund was born on October 16, 1906. His parents, Emanuel and Mollie Freund, were both born in America into families that had emigrated from Europe. Sylvan and his sister Ruth grew up in and around New York City and nearby Long Island.

I regret that I don't have much to say about his adolescent years. Sadly, I never asked him what went on in his early life, and he didn't volunteer any information that I can recollect.

Dad must have been a smart kid because at age 15 he matriculated at the University of Pennsylvania. I've been told (although not by him) that at first things didn't go smoothly due to his youth, and he took a year off. Ultimately, however, college worked out well – he made many friends, several of whom remained close in subsequent years; he engaged in fraternity hi-jinks, the memories of which I recall him trotting out on occasion; and he graduated in 1927 with a degree in business from Wharton.

Marcella Freund ("Marcy" to me, my kids and her numerous friends) was born in 1907 in New York City. In a 105th birthday tribute to her that aired on Fox Five's *Good Morning* TV show, anchor Dave Price, in saluting this "remarkable woman," termed her "a living piece of New York City history" and enumerated some of the events happening here in 1907: for example, regular taxicab service began, the first Ziegfeld Follies was presented, and the Plaza Hotel opened to the public.

Her father and mother, Julius and Esther Coleman, had come to America from Europe, and made good lives for themselves here. Mom loved them very much and remained a devoted daughter through the years. In addition, Marcy had two brothers, Harry and Milton, and a sister, Deborah.

Mom's memories of a happy Manhattan childhood remained vivid in her later years. For instance, she could still recall that when the Armistice ending World War I was announced in November 1918, she and her brother Milton took pots and pans from the kitchen out on the fire escape, beating them loudly to celebrate the victory. She spoke of scenes taking place in the living room of their neighbor, the George Gershwin family; and she remembered her childhood performance in a monkey costume behind the young Milton Berle, while he sang "Aba Daba Honeymoon" in a local revue.

As I noted in Chapter 1, I've long been fascinated by what I call "sheer happenstance" – how the voluntary decisions we make and the chance occurrences that happen as we travel through life propel us in directions which lead to relationships and outcomes that only happened because of those choices and random occurrences. Yet they can make all the difference in shaping our future years.

When Mom was 101, I showed her a draft of a piece I'd written on that subject, using various examples from my own life. After reading it, Mom said, "I like this, but you left out an important chance meeting."

"Which one?" I asked.

"How I met your father."

I certainly couldn't argue with her – that was indeed a fateful day for yours truly, well deserving of a spot in my personal pantheon. So I asked Mom to revisit the scene, which she promptly proceeded to do, minute by minute – her memory of that day being as lucid as if it had just happened, rather than having occurred almost 85 years previously.

It was Easter Sunday 1925, and Mom (then Marcella Coleman) was spending the day with her girlfriend, Connie Freund. (The last name was strictly a coincidence – no relationship.) The girls were in Connie's home, an apartment on 77th street off Central Park West, expecting a date with two promising young fellows. As it happened, though, the guys called to say they had to return to Yale; so Connie and Mom were relegated to passing a dull afternoon looking at movie magazines.

The phone rang. The caller was a friend of Connie's named Murray. "What are you doing today?" he asked her.

"Nothing," she replied, "but I'll be taking the train back to college in Boston later this afternoon."

Murray wasn't easily dissuaded. "Why don't I just come over for a little while and play the piano for you. And by the way, I have a guy with me . . . ."

The guy was my father, Sylvan Freund, who at the time was a Penn undergraduate. Murray did not attend Penn, but he had entertained on the piano at Dad's fraternity, which was where they met. Murray, a New Yorker, had urged Dad (whose home was then in Far Rockaway) to come into the city, where Murray promised to introduce him to some girls. Presumably, Connie was Murray's first choice for fixing up Sylvan. (I wonder whether it was because of their identical last names.)

Connie mentioned that she was with a girl friend. Murray noted that his friend was driving his father's Packard, so they could take her to the station later. Connie acquiesced, inviting them to come over for a few hours.

The boys arrived, and that was it. Dad only had eyes for Mom. She, in turn, was attracted to him – although, she admitted to me, it may have been partially attributable to his Packard.

They took Connie to the station, dropped Murray off at the subway, and were finally alone in the car. Dad said, "Why don't we go to Tip Toe Inn and get something to eat?" Mom agreed. On the way, though, Dad took a detour to visit Grant's Tomb on Riverside Drive. And that's when he uttered the magic words: "Can you hold New Year's Eve for me?"

Mom replied, "Are you crazy – it's nine months away. I might not even know you then."

Dad's response: "You'll not only know me – you'll probably marry me."

And all this took place before they even got to Tip Toe Inn! When Dad returned to Penn that night, he wrote Mom a letter from the train, stating, "I meant every word I said." And he did.

That's how I ultimately made it into this life. But I can't help wondering . . . . What if the Yale guys had shown up? What if Mom decided she wanted to spend Easter on Fifth Avenue in an extravagant hat? What if Murray hadn't met Dad at the piano in the fraternity house? What if Murray hadn't brought Dad into the city to meet girls? What if Dad had been attracted to Connie? What if he hadn't been driving the Packard? What if he wasn't so incredibly romantic on an empty stomach? The answer to each of these queries is – you wouldn't be reading this now!

They were married in New York on November 17, 1929, just a month after Black Friday decimated the Stock Exchange.

Their only child was born four-plus years later.

From 1934 until 1952

Mom and Dad enjoyed a very fine marriage. He was devoted, faithful, and protective towards her; she loved him dearly and was a constant support. They were seldom at odds with each other, and the only times I can remember Dad losing his temper with me was when I dared to raise my voice to Mom. The two of them created a warm and human family environment for a boy to grow up in.

Focusing on Dad first, I'll start with memories from my earliest years. As I mentioned in Chapter 2, from my toddler stage on, the Freunds owned a movie camera which Dad (mostly) and Mom (occasionally) used to record family life, vacations, and special occasions. Enough managed to break through the jerky cinematography to confirm that my happy childhood was in large part a result of having very caring parents.

I reviewed these images a few years ago and could see the joyous relationship between father and son.

- There's that memorable beach scene – the two year-old trying to race into big ocean waves, Dad grabbing me around the tummy with his strong right arm and hoisting me back to land, the kid immediately trying the same thing over again, but with the same result.

- Shots of me climbing all over Dad and hugging him – on the beach, under the Christmas tree (next to the Lionel toy trains), and elsewhere.
- The two of us on swings alongside each other – cut to Dad standing behind and tickling me (to my delight) as I swung by.
- Dad pulling me on a sled, helping me build a snowman – and then we're laughing as we hurl snowballs at each other.
- Ice-skating together at a rink, holding hands – and then the kid falls and he lifts me back up.
- Scenes of mock boxing and wrestling
- Visiting zoos populated with flamingos and alligators.
- Standing together at the Tomb of the Unknown Soldier in Arlington.
- The two of us at the US Open, played on the grassy tennis courts of Forest Hills in those days.
- An abundance of scenes from parents' day at my various summer camps.

There were many special times between us not preserved on film which I recall vividly. I can remember many a fall Saturday – Dad and I taking the morning train from New York City to Philadelphia, then walking over to Franklin Field to watch his alma mater, Penn, play one of its football rivals. The next morning, Sunday, we'd be out early on a field in Riverside Park (near our apartment at Riverside Drive and 102nd street), where he would instruct me in the arcane mechanics of drop-kicking a football to split the uprights for a field goal.

As in many families where the father was immersed in his business, Mom played the leading role in my upbringing. We spent a lot of time together – I was definitely her project, and she threw herself into taking scrupulous care of her only child.

Marcy was forceful and definite in what she expected from me, and I chafed at some of the "rules". So we clashed at times as I grew older and more assertive. But I seldom prevailed in those tiffs, Mom never issued any sort of apology, and my temporary resentments were something I learned to get over.

One of Mom's keen interests was my education. As noted in Chapter 2, she played a crucial role in seeing that I gained admittance to Hunter College Elementary School and later to Horace Mann. I so appreciate the initiative she showed in getting me placed in those excellent institutions.

As I also discussed in Chapter 2, prior to my birth Mom converted her religion from Judaism to Christian Science, and my father followed her lead a few years later. Mom's faith was an every-day-of-the-week matter, and it became a major factor in my young life, including the Sunday School class I attended weekly.

Marcy Freund was a superior hostess and I recall the many lively evenings when my parents entertained at home. The food and social interplay had to be superior because no alcohol was served. The big party held on Christmas Day (coinciding with her birthday) included lots of family, kids, presents, food and music – memorable events seven decades ago.

Dad loved to travel, to explore. Many of my fondest early memories are of sitting next to him in our car, taking a new back road that he wanted to try out, discovering an out-of-the-way point of interest. He had a special thing for convertibles; I remember him once returning from a southern vacation driving a new one that he and Mom had just bought while down in Dixie.

They came to visit me each summer at camp around the time of my birthday. There were enjoyable family trips to places like Florida, Savannah, Washington, Boston, Montreal, etc. The one I remember best occurred during World War II when Dad attended a business convention in Texas and took Mom and me along. Our schedule called for us to make an afternoon change of trains in St. Louis. Dad had planned it so that there was just enough time for the two of us to attend a Cardinals baseball game at Sportsman Park.

During World War II, Dad was too old to be drafted so he donned a white helmet and served as an air raid warden on the block where we lived – making sure all blinds were drawn tight to prevent German and Japanese pilots from seeing any bedroom lights that would assist their bombing raids on Manhattan.

Dad told me he was one of the initial hundred people to buy a Polaroid camera when they first came out after the war. The prints were sepia-toned, and even after you smeared them with fixer cream, they faded in a few months – but he saw the possibilities. His confidence, however, did not extend to investing in the stock. For the rest of his life, he told me, every time he snapped an instant picture, he felt a genuine pang of regret.

As my teenage years arrived, we spent less time together, but Dad and I remained close. I remember Saturday mornings when the two of us ate breakfast while Mom slept. His favorite dish was French Toast, which he taught me how to make – it's still just about the only thing I can do by myself in a kitchen.

We took joyous trips together as a family, sometimes bringing along one of my friends; Dad came to watch games of mine (football, basketball, baseball) at Horace Mann; he taught me to drive; and for the most part, our relations remained warm.

I do have a memory, though, of playing tennis with him one day as a teenager. I was unskilled at the game, but in those days very competitive in sports and hard on myself for "stupid errors." Dad must have felt sorry for me after several adolescent outbursts, so he let me win a game by hitting several balls way out of the court – rather obviously, I thought. As the last ball hit the fence, I *knew* he'd taken a dive. I was irate, "Play the damn point over!" I insisted. That wasn't the way I wanted to win. (Later on, the remnants of that experience rattled around in my unconscious as I went through my own similar fathering experience with my sons, Erik and Tom.)

Mom took great pride in my high school achievements and never stinted in her praise. As I became more mobile in high school and stayed out late on dates with girls, Mom would wait up to make sure I was safely in the apartment before dozing off.

Her last official act during this first period of my life came when, much to my amazement, she consented to my driving around the U.S. for two months with my buddy Paul during the summer after I graduated from high school (a trip detailed in Chapter 5). This loosening of her grip on me proved to be symbolic of the major readjustment about to occur in our lives.

* * *

I should say a few words about my father's business career.

After college, Dad joined the display business that his father, Emanuel Freund, and a partner had formed.

The company was called Decorative Plant Corp., and its retail displays adorned department store windows and interiors. They also did many special projects such as exhibits for both of New York's World's Fairs and the artificial tree that unfurled onstage during the New York City Ballet's annual *Nutcracker* performance. One of their huge, ornate trees made both the front page of the *Daily News* and the cover of *Business Week*.

Decorative Plant pioneered the first outdoor display on Fifth Avenue – a pipe organ and choral group mounted on the façade of Saks. It prompted a letter from Cardinal Spellman, presiding at St. Patrick's Cathedral next door, praising them for bringing the spirit of Christmas to Fifth Avenue. Bridging two centuries, they were responsible for the yuletide choir of angels which is still on display each year at the Rockefeller Center promenade.

As a businessman, Dad had a strong sense of responsibility to those who worked for him. For example, although in great discomfort the day he was finally taken to the hospital, he insisted on going to the office in order to clear his desk and personally distribute Christmas bonus checks to employees.

I won't attempt to enumerate all of Dad's business accomplishments, but here's a eulogy tribute he received from the managing director of their trade association, National Association of Display Industries (NADI):

> "Sylvan Freund was one of display's truly great figures. He was loved for his compassion and humanity. He was admired for his creativity and for his innovations in our trade. His name was a byword for honor and integrity.

> "For over 30 years, he was a major influence in the display industry association, serving as president of the NADI for four years, as chairman of various committees, and later as a life-time Board member.

> "He was always an energetic and resourceful participant in the wide range of industry and association projects. He brought a statesmanlike approach to everything he did.

> "In 1965, he was given the industry's coveted Annual Display Award for his score of achievements over a long span of years.

"His leadership and greatness of character will always serve as an example to all of us who follow him."

Dad himself was inordinately modest – perhaps the most endearing of his traits. He simply refused to blow his own horn. There was a complete lack of pretension about him. When I visited his place of business just before his death – at a time when he'd been running the company for several decades – I noticed that the nameplate on the door of his office still bore the name of my grandfather, who had passed away eight years earlier.

* * *

Dad had a great zest for life – including food, to the frequent distress of my mother, in her mostly fruitless efforts to pare his waistline. He was fascinated with facts – names, places, dates. Like many men of his generation, he was rarely philosophical or introspective, but happiest when immersed in the details of daily living.

He enjoyed sports, and my attraction to athletics was definitely stimulated by his example. For many years he was a serious golfer despite the fact that he could never seem to cure the slice on his drive, to his great frustration. The summer before he passed away, he entered a senior tennis tournament on Long Island, and it took a tie-breaker to knock him out of the running. He also took his spectator sports seriously. During the time he was in the hospital in his last days, he followed the NFL playoff games with intense interest, looking forward to watching the Super Bowl (which he didn't quite make).

The dominant impression I have of my father is of a man of strength. That's the way I always thought of him. In part, this consisted of physical strength. He seemed to be able to lift anything. He worked longer hours than anyone else. He could drive a car hundreds of miles without a break. He was rarely sick or fatigued until near the end. He was robust and powerful and uncomplaining – endurance personified. I can picture him so clearly, diving again and again into the ocean waves, letting the spray beat against his body.

In greater part, Dad's strength was that of character. He was very principled. I never knew this man of integrity to take advantage of any person or situation, or to contemplate an act that was mean or petty. But he was no chameleon; when his mind was made up about something, that was it – there was no changing course. His word was his bond and a handshake meant everything to Sylvan Freund.

Just as he was strong, he was also a gentle man. Or, as so many people told me over the years, a gentleman – a man without enemies. He had a temper; when he was under pressure, it would flare from time to time – but then it would quickly subside. I'm sure that those who worked for him could cite chapter and verse. In his personal relations, he radiated warmth and consideration of others, flowing spontaneously from a disposition that was not offensive. I will never forget one of the last things he said to me in the hospital at the end: 'You know, Jim, I really ought to get a private room. I'm probably keeping these other fellows awake.'

As noted, my father was an active member of the Christian Science church. Although he was a religious man, he never wore his religion on his sleeve. It was an inner matter, through which he seemed to find abundant peace and well-springs of resilience. He read *The Bible* and Mary Baker Eddy's *Science and Health* each morning; he attended church every Sunday morning and Wednesday evenings, and was active in all its affairs. I know his faith was with him at all times, especially at the end.

A colleague of mine once showed me a letter that my father had written to him upon hearing that he'd suffered a serious accident. Although Dad never met this individual (their prior contacts having been by phone), his letter provided my associate with great comfort – and perhaps also served to sum up Dad's own view of life. Let me quote just one representative sentence:

> 'These things are quite a blow when they happen –
> but when they do, we are able to overcome so much,
> and usually are much stronger mentally as a result . . . ."

From 1952 to 1974

After graduating from high school in 1952 and taking that cross-country trip over the summer, I matriculated at Princeton. From then on, my parents were no longer the centerpiece of my life. I won't speculate as to how this affected them, but to be honest, I didn't feel a great sense of loss. Rather it represented a freeing up. My parents – and especially my mother – no longer controlled my agenda, although they did support me during the college years (except for tuition, books, and a small monthly sum paid for by the Navy).

I don't mean to imply that we were estranged during those college years. We spoke at least weekly; they came down to Princeton for such occasions as a freshman football game, an NROTC parade, and graduation; I usually came home for the holidays and sometimes for weekends; and our mutual feelings remained warm. They were very welcoming of the friends I often brought with me, and would even temporarily vacate the apartment when a party was taking place. But our relations were certainly different than when I was living at home.

There is, however, a wonderful movie clip from the time when Mom and Dad came to pick me up in Norfolk after my first NROTC summer cruise. I'm wearing dress khakis on a hot day and lugging a big duffel bag on my shoulder. Dad lifts the bag up with ease and drops it into the back seat of his convertible, then helps me off with my jacket. . . .

I spent the three years after college on a Navy icebreaker journeying from the Arctic to the Antarctic (an experience detailed at length in Chapter 7). Except for the few times I managed to score enough leave to come to New York, I saw very little of my parents during this period; and our communications by phone and mail were relatively infrequent.

After a great '59 summer travelling in Europe, I packed off to Harvard Law School, where I spent most of the next three years. We did have occasional visits in New York and Boston, but Dad was enmeshed in business and I in my studies, so our personal involvement was minimized.

In the summer of 1960 (between my first and second years of law school), I decided to give my father a hand working for his business. During those several months, I lived in my parents' apartment and saw a lot of them. I also recall eating lunches at Schraft's with my grandfather, Manny Freund, who was still an active executive. We shared a mutual love of sports, discovered other interests in common, and enjoyed each other's company.

I had already made the decision not to join the family business as a third-generation partner, and I must say that the summer work experience there validated my decision. Dad's business faced tough times financially. Almost everything was custom-made (so it lacked economies of scale), the competition was fierce, and the customers (mainly big department stores) bargained hard over pricing. The business was usually in debt, was invariably short of cash, and had to resort to borrowing from high-interest factors.

I didn't take to any aspect of the business, although I received grooming at various tasks. I dimly recall a business trip I took to Canada, peddling Decorative Plant's goods to various department stores in the provinces of Ontario and Quebec. I can picture my parents seeing me off on the train to Montreal, introducing me to the intricacies of my "roomette" for the overnight trip. But I disliked being a salesman and clearly wasn't good at it – although it did serve to relieve my busy father from having to make the trip that summer.

* * *

My father died 46 years ago. As I look back on my relations with him, I can see they were at their warmest in my first eighteen years (until I went away to college in 1952), and then again in the years from 1966 (when my first son was born) until Dad's untimely passing in 1974. What concerns me, though, is my sense that our relationship during those fourteen in-between years was somewhat cooler. It's not that we were ever estranged or even had a serious dispute that I can recall. What bothers me today is that I didn't make the effort to connect with him in a more meaningful way during this period. Of late, I've been trying to figure out why.

Part of it, of course, had to do with our physical separation during most of those years. From 1952 on, I was away from home for the next decade – in college, the Navy, and law school – so there wasn't much time for us to spend together. When I did come to New York, I was busy catching up with my friends, while he was consumed by the overriding task of keeping the business afloat.

Still, I fear that other factors were also at play. For instance, I have a nagging feeling that I was just too big for my britches during much of that period. With the wonderful education I had received at Horace Mann, Princeton and Harvard Law School, followed by the professional status of being a lawyer, I sometimes became impatient with others who didn't seem to process concepts as quickly as I did. To my everlasting regret, this may have included my father.

Another reason that played a factor – one that I struggle to admit – was an inchoate feeling, left over from my teenage years, that Dad had let me down. During this adolescent period, my mother and I were engaged in a sometimes stormy relationship. I often chafed at her strictures and demands, which I considered unreasonable, and it wasn't easy to reason with her on such matters. But when I'd turn and plead with my more reasonable father for support, none was forthcoming. "Do what your mother says," was his uniform response. Today, I can appreciate the wisdom of his hands-off disposition – I suspect that he just didn't want to go head-to-head with his high-powered wife. But back then, given my teenage mindset, it may well have caused resentment on my part at his lack of support.

For some reason, Dad found it difficult to articulate his feelings or bestow compliments on a face-to-face basis. I never fully understood this facet of his personality, and there were times when I admit to being disappointed at the absence of verbal reaction from him. For instance, I can't ever remember him commenting on my piano playing, or even requesting a favorite song. Also, there wasn't a lot of the hugging and such I've enjoyed with my own sons. I suppose the emotions were all there with Dad, but (as perhaps was typical of his generation) they percolated under the surface.

It's clear to me now that I should have tried to be more helpful to him as he struggled with his business. I'm not sure I would have had any good advice to offer – business strategy has never been my strong suit – but if I had made myself available, he might have used me as a sounding board, or at least a shoulder to lean on. The most frightening aspect of this admission of guilt is that it's possible I thought less of my hard-working father *because of* the fiscal squeeze he found himself in.

Even during those years, however, Dad influenced me in ways that I've come to appreciate. For instance, when I was in the Navy, there was a girl I was close to in Seattle – a flight attendant from a small town in rural Minnesota. My officer friends were fond of her and pressed me to propose engagement before I left the service. I sensed it wouldn't work out but was reluctant to cut the tie. My mother's negative comments about this young lady only seemed to make me more determined to hang on to her. Then my father came to visit us in Seattle – I can't recall the reason, but it probably related to his business. He was warm and courteous toward the girl and never said a negative thing about her to me. Yet somehow I could sense that he thought she and I wouldn't be right for each other living in NYC for the rest of our lives. Dad and I never talked about it, but I definitely received a wise subliminal message from him.

Another time Dad came through for me was when I was about to marry my first wife, Barbro, who came from a small town in Sweden. No one from her family could make the trip to NYC, and she had no family or close friends in the States. Dad could tell that she was downcast about this, so he stepped up and played a superb parental role to ease her discomfort – including walking her down the aisle in true fatherly fashion.

It's sad for me to realize I have no recordings of his voice. (The home movies in pre-digital days were all silent.) Another regret is that I never sat down with him to probe what his life had been like as a young man, nor even to discuss the issues of the day. In sum, I realize now that I did not reach out as I should have – that I wasn't there for him when he needed (but seemed unable to ask for) support from me.

I learned to appreciate him again when I saw how splendidly he interacted with my sons. But then time ran out for Dad, much too soon. The sad irony is that we became close again just as he was approaching his final days.

* * *

Whatever shortcomings there were in our father-son relationship, Dad was clearly an estimable family man. As a husband, he was a model to us all – absolutely devoted, faithful, loving and protective towards Mom. The two of them created an extremely warm and human environment for a boy to grow up in – and I learned well what the concept of family was all about. He loved his home, and one of his great joys was entertaining his relatives and friends, mixing up his latest batch of non-alcoholic punch for the holidays. Fortunately preserved on film is a scene where Dad and Mom danced beautifully together at the 50th anniversary party of his parents – a memory that really resonates with me.

As a father-in-law, he helped to make my first wife, Barbro, feel so at home here that it greatly eased her loneliness for her own family in Sweden. As a son, he was ever respectful and deferential to his parents, in a way that you rarely see nowadays. As a brother, he was loving and attentive, a strong shoulder to lean upon for my aunt Ruth. As a brother-in-law, nephew, uncle and cousin he invariably exhibited a strong sense of family ties. His niece Joni told me, "I cherish the memories of time spent with uncle Sylvan. I was hoping he would walk me down the aisle at my wedding, but unfortunately he passed away two months earlier."

It was as a grandfather, however, that I observed him most closely in his last eight years. It was in this role that he was truly superb. He had an instinctive way with children that we marveled at – enormous patience and a gift of communicating with them in a way they could readily grasp. Erik and Tom responded with such intensity that when Sylvan was around I was lucky if the boys even noticed their father.

Erik, who was eight when Sylvan passed away, says, "I can remember Sylvan's voice and his charm. He was so big but very gentle too." They played casino and then watched television together, comedies and football games. "He helped me learn to write," Erik reported; "We had a game where I would have to write down his messages and read them to Marcy." And Erik recalls going to Sylvan's office, being amazed at the size of his desk, "and he put me on his lap and we wrote a list to Santa."

Tom, who was only five at Sylvan's passing, also has a number of pleasant memories but one above all. "I was being rambunctious and started to jab the fork into their wood dining table. Marcy got very mad and told me it was a valuable antique. I was shocked and thought it was the end of the world; I felt so bad that I ran into the living room. God bless Sylvan, who came in two minutes later – he had seen how upset I was. He calmed me down, held me, and said, 'It's okay, don't worry, Tom, we know you didn't mean it, and it's *not* the end of the world'."

I have a favorite mental picture of him, totally immersed in a game of cards with the boys, having shaken off all the cares of life, and knowing pure joy. And I'm touched by the last picture I took of him with the boys – up in the stands at Columbia for the Penn game, shortly before he entered Mt. Sinai Hospital.

The hospital would not permit his grandsons in to see him, so they made an audio tape which I played for him. I also found a window on his hospital floor where he could view the boys waving to him from the street below.

I was just coming into my own as a lawyer at the time. My first book, *Anatomy of a Merger*, was due to be published not long after he died. I wanted Dad to know that things would be all right. The last words I spoke to him, just before he passed away, were, "Don't worry about Mom – I'll take good care of her." That's a pledge I feel I fulfilled.

It was very sad at the end. As noted previously, I wrote a warm eulogy for him but felt unable to deliver it – my good friend and pastor, Ken Gorsuch, read it at the funeral. For Erik, this was his first experience losing someone close to him, and he has told me it really hurt. Erik also remembers crying with me at the funeral – "Another first," he said, "as I don't think I had ever seen you cry."

Every year after his death, I took Mom up to Kensico Cemetery in Westchester to visit him on his birthday, and I've continued to make the trip since her passing. It's usually a beautiful autumn day, with the trees in full color and the sun glinting off a little lake. I reminisce a bit, tell him how the boys are doing, and usually read him his favorite psalm – 121 – which closes with these words that were of great comfort to him during life:

"The Lord shall preserve thee from all evil; he shall preserve thy soul.
"The Lord shall preserve thy going out and thy coming in
from this time forth and even for evermore."

From 1974 to 2013

The third period of my relations with Mom lasted for 40 years and dominates my memory. Until Dad died, the question was always how closely my mother would be bound up in *my* life. Now, however, I found myself bound up in *her* life. I needed to develop an enhanced sense of responsibility toward her.

With her husband gone, the business which had dominated their lives for so long was sold. Marcy Freund had to carve out a new life for herself and to overcome the loneliness of having no one in the bed next to her. She had to take charge of aspects of her life – particularly financial ones – that my father had always handled. I'm not sure my mother ever wrote a check before Dad passed away. With some help from me and others that I engaged, she persevered.

For 25 years, she participated in continuing education courses for retired professionals – first at The New School downtown, to which she traveled by bus each day throughout the winter and where she gave witty, informative talks on such notables as Woody Allen and George S. Kaufman. Later on at Marymount College near her apartment, she participated in art and theatre programs.

Mom travelled a lot. Some of it was with our family, such as a trip we took to Sweden not long after Dad passed away. Some years later, she and I took an enjoyable cruise around eastern Canada together. Other excursions she made on her own or with a friend, to places such as Egypt (where she rode a camel), Russia, Alaska and the Caribbean.

Marcy was a skillful artist. Her genre was oil painting, both landscapes and portraits. Her work was displayed at The New School and once in a special exhibit at the Metropolitan Museum – and every visitor to Marcy's home received a guided tour of her efforts. My artist friend, Carole Eisner, who bonded with Mom on many occasions, felt that painting was the "abiding love of Marcy's life – that "she was very blessed with this talent and fortunate to be able to pursue her art for many years."

There was nothing devious about Mom. The sentiments she pronounced were honest expressions of her views; you always knew where she stood. She valued that trait in others – a favorite compliment Mom bestowed on someone she liked was, "That woman has no guile."

She wasn't mean-spirited, but in her continual desire to make things better, the words she said could sometimes come across as hurtful to the listener. If I later called her attention to this, she would shrug and quote her own mother's adage, "What's on my lung is on my tongue."

By the way, this truth-telling wasn't only directed at those she didn't care for. Take me, for example. She was always my biggest fan, boasting about me to everyone within earshot. I recall her once raving on video about a photograph I'd entered in a photo contest in Connecticut. In her later years, one of my piano albums was playing on her machine every day when I came over.

Now fast forward to one day in her 105th year. I was attempting to make her feel good by listing the many traits I thought we shared. I talked about how we both like to give advice, we both have a sense of humor, we're both optimists, and then I said, "And we're both good story-tellers. I've always admired you, Mom, for your ability in this area. You start at the right place, you keep to the point and don't introduce too much extraneous material, and you know how to hit the punch line."

To which she replied, "Well, frankly, Jim, I've never cared too much for *your* stories."

Then there was the time she attended one of my senior citizen singalongs (touched on in Chapter 20), and the group presented me with a handsome sleeveless sweater as a Christmas present. I immediately put it on, turned to my mother, and said in a voice that all could hear, "Hey, Mom, how do you like the way this lovely gift of a sweater looks on me?" To which her full-throated reply was, "Pull it down."

She didn't pester me with calls – perhaps because almost every night I would phone her, usually just before I went to sleep around midnight. She was always up, watching "The Late Show" or other television fare, and we would chat (except that, if she had been viewing something interesting on the tube just then, she would ask me to call back in ten minutes.) Even at times today, as I'm getting ready to turn in for the night, I still reflexively think I shouldn't forget to make that call to her.

I married Barbara Fox in 1985, and Mom was a real presence in our lives thereafter. She spent many weekends at our home in Connecticut, and we would often celebrate Thanksgiving with the Fox and Hilton families in Wilton – Mom cooking a ham (her specialty) to go along with the turkey.

* * *

Of all her activities, what gave Mom the most pleasure was interacting with her two grandsons. They had marvelous relationships with her, and she proved to be a wise counselor to them as they passed from adolescence to maturity.

Here's an illustration of how Mom felt about the boys – in this case, Erik, although it could easily have been Tom. When Erik graduated from high school, it was a memorable family occasion. I ran around snapping dozens of photos. To my chagrin, something went wrong with the camera or the film or the developing process – the net result of which was that the bulk of the film was never exposed.

When I found out, I was heartsick – a once-in-a-lifetime moment, and I'd blown it. I behaved like an infant, ranting and raving at the manufacturer, at the processor, at myself. What particularly concerned me, though, was what my mother's reaction would be – she was so proud of her grandson, she had taken an active part in the festivities, and she was featured with him in many of the missing snapshots. I put off telling her for as long as I could, but finally decided one day to face the music.

After all those years, I thought I knew my mother pretty well, but her response took me quite by surprise.

"I know you feel awful, Jim," she said, "but don't feel bad on my account. I don't need any photographs. Every moment of that day – the way Erik looked, the procession, the setting, how I felt – is etched in my memory; and I know that as long as I live, it will never fade."

A major theme for Marcy was the continuity of close relationships. As the boys went off to California, Colorado and other places, she worked hard to get the three of us together; and when Mom was able to accomplish this, she was at her happiest – urging us to "stay embraced" throughout our lives. When we weren't together geographically, her signature phrase – one that all in the family (including her great-granddaughters) picked up on – was, "There is no separation".

My sons really cared for Marcy in many different respects. Erik put one aspect of it this way, in a letter to her on her 105th birthday: "As I grew up, you were always there for me and encouraged me to stand tall and feel good about myself. These lessons in self-confidence have stayed with me and I use them almost every day." In his eulogy at her funeral, he added: "Marcy mentioned many times to me that I was so valuable to my various employers that I should *demand* a raise so that I could take better care of my family!"

Tom spoke at the funeral about another facet of Marcy's personality that always impressed him. "She liked everything just right. It was her thing; she would say that's good, it's good. My daughter Delilah says that too now, and I think they're connected. And that went for everything. Oftentimes my hair (or my brother's) wasn't right, or our clothes or those of our girlfriends or wives didn't measure up to her standards, and she would simply say, 'I'm an artist, I can't help myself, I know what it should look like.' She did this because she wanted everyone to be at their best."

Erik hit on another aspect. "Marcy was an optimist. She seemed to always be able to view events and happenings in a light that felt good. I can remember telling her stories of how things in my life weren't right; but rather than complain, she always seemed to be able to turn the story around, so that I could feel joy about the positive aspects of my life and not focus so much on some of the less desirable parts."

And Erik added, "Marcy used to say to me from the very beginning: '*Try it . . . you'll like it.*' This started when I was young and refused to try new foods, but I think the concept holds true throughout life; and as I have grown, I've tried to open my mind up to new ideas, experiences and different ways of looking at the world."

Both boys were impressed by Marcy's spirituality. Tom put it this way. "She was always 'doing work' for us – whether we were travelling, had a big test or an upcoming concert. She always said, 'I'll know the truth,' which meant that we were in God's hands . . . . when I would go to her for help, even though she didn't understand the details of my problem, she had a way of 'putting it in God's hands'."

Erik said, "Marcy often spoke to me about God and taught me to believe that there was a higher power that oversaw everyone and everything and would guide us through our lives. She explained to me, starting at a very young age, that if I was open to God's signs and followed them, that there was no obstacle too great to overcome."

As I mentioned earlier, my mother remained a committed Christian Scientist all her adult life. As contrasted with many of us for whom religion is a more occasional experience, for Mom her faith was always an every-day-of-the-week matter. She read all the books, did the lessons, sang the hymns, studied with prominent teachers, and went to church twice weekly. My mother attributed her good health and longevity in large part to her faith.

She spoke often of her one-on-one relationship with God, telling me of their frequent dialogues, which often occurred late at night. She believed fervently in – and would often quote to me by heart – these words from Proverbs: "Trust in the Lord with all thine heart; and lean not unto thine own understanding. In all thy ways acknowledge Him, and He shall direct thy paths."

* * *

In 1992, when Mom was 85, I dedicated to her my book, *Advise and Invent,* and wrote a belated tribute to the woman who had meant so much to me over the years. Here, in part, is what I said:

"It's fitting that a book being dedicated to her is about giving advice. In this regard, she was a hell of a role model. My mother gave, and still gives, yards and yards of advice – to her son, to her grandsons, and to anyone else who happens by. Maybe because I wasn't paying for it, I didn't always appreciate the counsel – but the tradition of counseling managed to sink very deep roots.

"It has taken me a long time to realize how much I owe to my mother, but the moment has now come to acknowledge the debt. Three lessons I've learned stand out in particular:

- "For Mom, there has always been a right way to do something, and that's the way it should be done. Often, we didn't agree on what the right way was, but I now understand that the specific subject matter was much less important than the underlying principle. Marcy Freund turned thumbs down on poor performance and has refused to settle for conduct that didn't come up to her standards. When I grasped that this brand of integrity was equally applicable to one's own performance, I was on my way.

- "My mother is, and always has been, an incredibly positive thinker. This sometimes rubbed me the wrong way, as when it clashed with my own penchant for figuring out what can possibly go wrong; but one aspect of her brand of optimism has stuck with me in spades – the notion that one person alone (namely, you) can make a difference. You need a dose of this dauntlessness to take on the tough tasks in life, and Mom saw to it that I was well-prepped.

- "My mother is remarkably consistent. On a bad day, I might have substituted the adjective "relentless" – but the lesson imparted (seasoned with a pinch of flexibility) has stood me in good stead. We work hard to establish our character and professional persona, and we should be vigilant in spotting deviations that send confusing signals to those who have come to rely on us. With Marcy Freund, the signals have never been confusing."

At a wonderful party she gave at her home in 1993 when she was 86, for a number of my friends from high school and college to whom she felt very attached (she liked to call them, "my boys"), Mom capped off the evening with a heartfelt speech to us that closed with the lines, "I'm proud of you boys, and forever more, stay friends."

Good friends of mine – including John Doyle, Bill Silver, Ann Leyden, Nancy Martin and Claudine Bacher – made periodic pilgrimages to Marcy's apartment in her latter years to engage in lively discussions with her. Mom liked to reminisce about her youthful days in visits with Claudine, who vividly recalls one of Marcy's favorite childhood stories, featuring New York social doyenne Mrs. Vincent Astor riding along the avenue in her elaborate horse-drawn carriage from which she threw pieces of candy to Marcy and the other children. With Nancy, Mom took on more of a counseling role ("Marcy was pretty direct, but her words helped me gain perspective with issues I had, and I appreciated and often think of her advice.")

The first year after I retired, when Mom was 90, we put on a performance at Marymount College based on the wonderful Maurice Chevalier-Hermione Gingold rendition of the *I Remember it Well* duet from

the movie "Gigi." It's about the aging man who forgets the myriad details of their youthful affair (which she recalls flawlessly), until he finally asks her, "Am I getting old?" – to which Mom replied, in a tone I'll never forget, "Oh no, not you / How strong you were / how young and gay / a prince of love in ev'ry way" – and now, reassured, I could respond, "Ah yes, I remember it well."

In her 90's, for another class at Marymount, Mom did a solo performance (with my piano accompaniment playing on a cassette) of Stephen Sondheim's *I'm Still Here* from "Follies." I'll always remember the meaningful way she delivered those final lines, which expressed so aptly her own personal feelings: "I got through all of last year / and I'm here / Lord knows at least I was there / and I'm here / Look who's here! / I'm still here."

And she was. On the occasion of her 95th birthday, she completed an oil painting, which we displayed (along with many of her prior works) at the National Arts Club exhibition upon publication of my photo book, *Slices of the Big Apple.* In later years, when she didn't feel physically capable of painting to her high standards, she used her still supple hands to knit – a red poncho she wore, colorful scarves for her son and grandsons, stylish woolen hats for her great-granddaughters – all exhibiting fine craftsmanship.

* * *

When my contemporaries and I were all turning 65, I gave an after-dinner speech to my college classmates at a dinner at the Princeton Club, to which event I invited Mom. The theme of the speech was coping with advancing age; and after I finished my prepared remarks, I opened it up to comments from the audience. One after another guy stood up to complain about something – a loss of hearing, aching joints, poor eyesight for night driving, etc. Then I saw Mom waving her arm to participate. "Forget it, Mom," I said, "this is for the guys." "No, no," they chanted, "let her speak." So, reluctantly, I gave Mom the nod. She rose to her feet, surveyed the room, and began a series of remarks belittling our complaints with this opening line: "To me, you're all children!"

That became one of her pet phrases as she grew older. When she was over 100, I brought a woman from my senior singalong group up to my mother's apartment. The woman proudly announced that she had just turned 90. Mom looked at her with a slightly bored expression and said, "You're just a child."

I found it interesting that for so many years Mom was fiercely protective of her age, and would grow furious if she thought I had let anyone know how old she was. If someone asked Marcy about her age, she would reply with relish, "I'm as old as my little pinky," waggling her fifth finger at the inquirer.

Once I took her to the hospital for some tests, but had to make a call while she was being checked in. Upon returning, I looked at the nurse's computer screen and noticed she had inserted a birthdate for Mom of 1917. Assuming it was a clerical mistake, I corrected it, and then went over to tell Mom. "They got the birthdate wrong and put '1917' instead of '1907' " – to which she replied with vigor, "They don't have to know how old I am..." – at which point, I realized this was no clerical error.

And then, as she neared the century mark, her age slowly turned into a badge of honor. One day I was receiving a community award for leading the senior citizen singalong at Goddard Riverside, and had invited Mom to the ceremony. In my acceptance remarks, I paid tribute to her as the woman who had started me on the piano and made me practice as a boy, concluding with, "And I know she'll kill me for saying it, but Mom, who's sitting right over there, will be turning 100 this Christmas." At that point, the entire room of several hundred people stood up and applauded her with great vigor. When I returned to our table, a little worried about how Mom would react to my disclosure of her age, she smiled sweetly and said, "Did *you* ever get a standing ovation?"

From then on, I would hear her asking people, "Do you know how old I am?" She would often say to younger folk, "It's nothing to be 100, and I'm sure you'll get there too" – but I think she was very proud of it, and my guess is she privately doubted that many others would match her record.

Shortly before her passing, I saw an article in a Harvard magazine that named the ten oldest living graduates of the countless thousands of Harvard and Radcliffe alumni. Only one was older than Mom – and who knows what condition he was in. No matter how she played down her longevity, she was unique.

* * *

When Mom turned 100 in 2007, we had a big party at the Princeton Club to celebrate the major occasion. Here are some excerpts from my talk at the time, which not only summed up how she was then, but for additional years to come.

"It's not just that she's arrived at this chronological milestone – it's that she has gotten there with so many of her faculties in good shape. Let me count the ways:

"Mom's senses – eyes, ears, taste buds, sniffing ability – are all intact.

"She still cares about her appearance, and (as you can see tonight) gets herself up in fine taste for occasions like this.

"She expresses herself clearly and at times, quite forcibly.

"She has retained her excellent sense of humor.

"Mom is secure in her faith and comforted by it. If she is apprehensive about the future (and I doubt she is), she never shows it to those around her.

"She remembers events and people from many years back with remarkable clarity while bemoaning the inescapable fact that so many of her relatives and friends have predeceased her.

"Mom still cares deeply about things – both in her own world and with regard to what's going on in the world at large (which she keeps current on). And although her outdoor excursions have become less numerous, she still fills me in on the weather and various forces of nature – and not just in New York. If there's a forest fire or earthquake tremor anywhere in Tom's home state of California, you can bet Mom's right on top of it. And when Erik lived in Colorado, I used to get a daily winter briefing on snow conditions in the Rockies.

"She stays up into the wee hours every evening. Most days I call her at midnight, and she has to turn down the TV volume to talk to me.

"She feels frustrated by her inability to get around as well as she used to, and the need to rely on others for locomotion. What she really wants to do – and has expressed to me on numerous occasions – is drive one of those motorized scooters around the New York City streets, and she gets mad at me for vetoing the idea.

"Mom holds views on a number of matters, and these tend not to be in the center. Something or someone is terrific, or it or he is terrible. Age has not transmuted these black and whites into more docile shades of gray.

"Down though the years, I would sometimes ask Mom how she felt about aging, and whether she had any advice for the rest of us on the subject. One day, some years back, Mom gave me a quote from General Douglas MacArthur that she had found, and said it neatly summed up how she felt on the subject of growing old. Here it is:

'People grow old only by deserting their ideals. Years may wrinkle the skin, but to give up interest wrinkles the soul…. You are as young as your faith, as old as your doubt, as young as your self-confidence, as old as your fear, as young as your hope, as old as your despair. In the central place of every heart there is a recording chamber; so long as it receives messages of beauty, hope, cheer and courage, so long are you young. When… your heart is covered with the snows of pessimism and the ice of cynicism, then and only then are you grown old – and then indeed, as the ballad says, you just fade away'."

On her 100th birthday, Mom had not faded away one bit.

Here's an excerpt from what Mom then said to the assemblage on that occasion: "Yes, I've been around for 100 years, and really, it's not that remarkable. I have never felt that numbers were accountable for my stability, my capability or my longevity. God is what really matters – not numbers. I really have been blessed . . . and as the saying goes, I'm still here."

Tom and Erik each have wonderful daughters, Delilah and Paige. Mom really took to being a great-grandmother to them, although she didn't let anyone call her "Grandma" – it was always "Marcy." (And she didn't want them calling me "Grandpa" either, so she coined the name they've always used, "Jimpa".) When Delilah and Paige were infants, she cuddled each of them in her arms and sang her favorite lullaby (the one she had sung to me as a baby, and then to each of my sons): "Lula, lula, lula, lula, bye-bye / In your mommy's arms be creepin' / And soon you'll be a-sleepin', lula / lula, lula, lula, lula, bye." She encouraged Delilah's artistic and dramatic efforts, reveled in Paige's dancing and exercise routines – and the girls had a rare chance to absorb some great-grandmotherly wisdom.

When I was turning 75 and Mom was 101, she became enamored of Bert Bacharach and Hal David's song, *What the World Needs Now is Love*. During my big birthday party at our weekend home in Connecticut, she sang it solo and then got everyone to join in – insisting that the message was "so appropriate for our times that it should be heard everywhere": "What the world needs now / is love, sweet love / It's the only thing / that there's just too little of / What the world needs now / is love, sweet love / No, not just for some / but for everyone." I daresay that no one who was in attendance will ever forget that moment.

No matter how she might have been feeling in the preceding days, Mom invariably rose to the occasion when she knew a party was coming up. She would take pains to get ready for it cosmetically, citing her usual couplet: "A little powder / a little paint / makes you look like / what you ain't." She retained her fine sense of style and would pick out attractive outfits. She was always the first to arrive at the party and the last to depart.

Her appetite remained strong until near the end. She would express yearnings for steak or lobster or crab legs, and we'd bring them over. Often I'd pick up a dozen oysters and some clams at Citarella, and the two of us would have a feast together in her dining room.

In her latter years, Mom received marvelous support, assistance and love from four wonderful caregivers – Remy, Angella, Jane, and Jane's daughter Ari – and Mom developed a warm relationship with each one of them. I owe them limitless gratitude. I'm also very appreciative for the splendid efforts on Mom's behalf over many years by our housekeeper, Gloria; by my former secretary, Ann Leyden, who spent long hours compiling Mom's specific wishes for when she'd no longer be with us; and by my associate, Raymond, who handled all her mail and administered her financial affairs so capably for her final decade.

* * *

After the excitement of Mom's 100th birthday, I realized she needed a new goal to shoot for. 101 was obvious but insufficiently ambitious, and other possibilities didn't resonate. And so the aggressive quest to attain 105 came into focus. I read her the line in the lyric of that inspirational song for seniors, *Young at Heart,* that goes:

"And if you should survive to a hundred and five,
Look at all you'll derive out of being alive . . . ."

I told her that the lyricist was probably using 105 to reflect an absurd span of years that no one could even consider attaining, and I said, "Let's fool everybody and have you actually do it." She liked the concept and memorized the line; and as the years went by, we'd often recite it to each other. When the big day finally came, all those assembled for the occasion, led by the splendid baritone voice of my friend Dick Fabrizio, sang the words to Mom with gusto; and a broad grin broke out on her face, as she reflected with real satisfaction on her accomplishment.

The relentlessness I previously alluded to remained part of Marcy's package as a centenarian. When she asked you to do something, she would ask again the next time you showed up, and then again – and any hope you harbored of her forgetting about it was slim indeed. The woman stayed focused.

I remember once when Tom and I were with Mom (who was in her 100's), and the talk turned to Tom's musical career, in which she always took a special interest. This evening, though, she was giving Tom a hard time about the need for him to hire a manager. "Marcy, I have a manager . . ." said Tom, but that didn't slow her down a bit – she kept going on about what he should be doing in this area; and I could see that Tom was getting uncomfortable. I decided to ride to the rescue with a recent development.

"Mom," I said, "I've got good news for you! I just resolved one of those mediations I've been wrestling with for weeks." She had been taking a real interest in my professional activities, and I knew she'd be pleased. "Oh," she said, "that's wonderful! You know, when I talk to God each night, this is something I always pray for – that Jim will be able to resolve these disputes he mediates" – at which point she paused a beat, and then steered back on track " – and that Tom will get a manager!"

As the years went by, her spirituality continued to increase. I recall one day in her final year when she spoke to me repeatedly about God and how he was taking such good care of her. After several minutes of this, I became a trifle vexed and, having in mind all I was doing to support her, said: "Hey, Mom, God's great, sure, but how about *me*, your son? Don't I take good care of you also?"

Mom didn't pause two seconds to reply: "You're able to take care of *me*, because God takes care of *you*." Touché.

When Mom was about to turn 105, I obtained gracious letters to her from President Obama, who wrote that she should "take pride in all you have accomplished"; from Governor Cuomo, who called her "an extraordinary individual"; and from Mayor Bloomberg, who said she was "an inspirational role model for us all." (She also received fine letters from the two Presidents Bush upon turning 100.)

When the first letter came in from the Governor, a few days before her 105th birthday, I took it over to her apartment, and did a little gushing.

"Look, Mom, at this wonderful letter from the Governor of New York State. He talks about your "special milestone"; he applauds your contributions to family, community and state; he says your longevity inspires everyone you know; he sends his warmest regards. How about that, Mom – and from Governor Andrew Cuomo."

She looked up at me, a wistful expression on her face, and said, "I wish I liked the man more . . . ."

We gave Mom a terrific party for her 105th birthday. At the end of the shindig, I interviewed her for a video we were making of the occasion. "How did you like the party?" I asked. She replied, "I thought it was the best party I ever went to. I feel much richer tonight than I did before." Then I pressed her on how it felt to be 105 – did she have any secrets about her longevity? I cracked up at her initial response: "Well," she said, "it takes a lot of living . . . ." But then she quickly gave credit where she believed it was due: "Everything I ever wanted I asked God about."

Until she passed away in 2013, Mom lived in the same apartment at 242 East 72nd Street that she had moved our family to in 1947 – six and a half decades earlier. Even in the later years when she needed round-the-clock care, the idea of continuing to live in her own home was very special to her.

I remember one day during Mom's 90s when I took her with me to Manhattan's poshest assisted-living enclave, where I was about to entertain the residents. Before my show started, the lady in charge took Mom and me on a tour of the facilities. Mom was in one of her gushy moods, calling out a string of upbeat comments from her wheelchair: "Oh look, Jim, they have a large pool" . . . "And there are daily art classes, how about that" . . . "Such lovely living spaces" . . . and so on. The lady in charge, envisioning Mom as about to become their newest resident, was beaming; and when we finished the tour, she asked Mom: "Well, Mrs. Freund, what do you think of our residence?" Mom's reply was loud and clear. "It's terrific – I'm going to tell all my friends about it!"

I visited with her just about every other day, and our conversations invariably ranged over a wide variety of subjects. And each day upon my departure, as I began walking out her bedroom door – no matter how tired or uncomfortable she may have felt that day – I heard her intone those familiar words, loud and clear, "Stand up straight! Head up! Shoulders back!"

During my frequent sessions with Mom, I would often read aloud her favorite passages from the Bible, as well as the words of hymns from the Christian Science Hymnal. One of her favorite passages, that she always directed specifically at me, was from Isaiah:

> "For unto us a child is born, unto us a son is given: and the government shall be upon his shoulder: and his name shall be called wonderful, counselor –"

At which point she would interrupt me to point out that "counselor" was really just another name for "lawyer."

Other favorite biblical passages appeared to be her own preparation for what was to come. For instance, there were these lines from John:

> "In my Father's house are many mansions: if it were not so, I would have told you. I go to prepare a place for you. And if I go and prepare a place for you, I will come again, and receive you unto myself; that where I am, there ye may be also."

And these lines from hymn 148:

> "Green pastures are before me / which yet I have not seen / Bright skies will soon be o'er me / where darkest clouds have been / my hope I cannot measure / my path in life is free / my Father has my treasure / and he will walk with me."

And finally, hymn 64, "From Sense to Soul", whose final six words she loved to repeat back to me after I'd read them – an image that gave voice to her sense of what lay ahead:

> "The way leads upward and its goal draws nearer / thought soars enraptured, fetterless and free / The vision infinite to me grows clearer / I touch the fringes of eternity."

As for me, I'll close this section with the image I choose to hang onto – a comforting vision in an extended metaphor. It's something I heard years ago at a friend's funeral and then at Barbro's memorial service. The author is Henry Van Dyke and it's called "Gone From My Sight." Here's how it goes:

I am standing upon the seashore
A ship, at my side, spreads her white sails to the morning breeze
and starts for the blue ocean.
She is an object of beauty and strength.
I stand and watch her until, at length,
she hangs like a speck of white cloud
just where the sea and sky come to mingle with each other.
Then someone at my side says, "There, she is gone."
Gone where?
Gone from my sight. That is all.
She is just as large in mast, hull and spar
as she was when she left my side,
And she is just as able to bear her load of living freight
to her destined port.
Her diminished size is in me – not in her.
And, just at the moment when someone says,
"There, she is gone,"
there are other eyes watching her coming,
and other voices ready to take up the glad shout,
"Here she comes!"

I loved you, Mom – and I'm sure those "other eyes" and "other voices" do too.

Dad and Mom at various stages of their young lives.

Dad and Mom – the romance in full bloom.

Dad and Mom on their honeymoon in Atlantic City – November 1929

Growing up as one of a caring threesome.

Department store interior decked out by Dad's firm, Decorative Plant Corp.

They mounted the first outdoor display on Fifth Avenue, on the facade of Saks.

The Decorative Plant managerial and sales team

1965 Winner of Annual Display Award for lifetime achievement

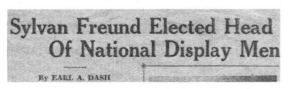

Dad and Mom on their honeymoon in Atlantic City – November 1929

Growing up as one of a caring threesome.

Department store interior decked out by Dad's firm, Decorative Plant Corp.

They mounted the first outdoor display on Fifth Avenue, on the facade of Saks.

The Decorative Plant managerial and sales team

1965 Winner of Annual Display Award for lifetime achievement

Sylvan Freund Elected Head Of National Display Men

By EARL A. DASH

On the ice   *Behind the wheel*   *Proud grandparents*

Some snaps of Mom and Dad on vacation

Dad's favorite arms-full moments

Mom entertaining at home, lecturing in class, displaying her artwork, traveling in Egypt, preaching "no separation" to her grandsons, and hosting a party for the gang she called "my boys."

As is evident above, Mom aged quite gracefully

Wearing the poncho Mom knitted as she neared 100

The day we performed "I Remember it Well" at Marymount College

With daughter-in-law Barbara

Great-grandmother of Paige and Delilah

Mom at 100, anchoring 4 generations

Mom at her 105th birthday party

4. HORACE MANN (1947-1952)

In my adult life, upon receiving an evaluation as to how well I'd been doing in my profession or at some other pursuit, I've taken to uttering a favorite rejoinder, namely: "Hey, I peaked in high school! – haven't done anything equivalent since." To which the listener usually responds with a dubious chuckle.

It's not just a quip, though. I belted it out of the park in high school, so to speak; and at least arguably, the subsequent years have not produced any comparable unqualified success.

In particular, my performance in high school stands in marked contrast to my relative lack of achievement during the decade-and-a-half following my 1952 graduation – right up to joining the Skadden Arps law firm in 1966, when I finally figured out what was needed to succeed as an adult. The source of my success in high school was the ability to thrive in a variety of capacities – athletics, scholarship, leadership, and (I'm told) popularity. This premise went into a virtual deepfreeze for those next 14 years. But in the late '60s, I finally embraced versatility as my personal marching orders for the next six decades.

That 14-year deepfreeze period was comprised of college – a sparkling experience at Princeton (discussed in Chapter 6), but not particularly distinguished – and three less lustrous pursuits in the Navy, at law school, and with my first law firm. I'll be discussing each of these endeavors later, but during those years I never came close to matching my high school performance.

* * *

Horace Mann School ("HM"), which I entered in the eighth grade, was an all-male private school in the Riverdale section of the Bronx. There was no school bus, so I had to take a laborious route each morning from where we then lived on 72nd Street between Second and Third Avenues. I'd start out on the 72nd Street crosstown bus which, after reaching Fifth Avenue, went south to 57th Street, before continuing west to Eighth Avenue. Here I entered the subway, riding the IND express up to 155th Street, where I switched over to the IRT, staying on until its last stop at 242nd Street and Broadway. The final leg of the journey was to hike up a steep hill to HM's 246th Street location. It's a trip I'd be reluctant to undertake today.

There was, however, one advantage to that long subway ride – namely, lots of girls, most of them heading up to the nearby Fieldston School. This presented a prime social opportunity for us female-starved testosterone-charged all-male Horace Mann teenagers.

The HM campus offered an attractive change of scene for city dwellers. It had the look of a pint-sized college, with 100 yards of athletic field situated between the main academic building and the gym – a welcome escape from bustling Manhattan streets into countrified grass and trees.

Not only was the HM student population all-male but little else about it would pass for diversity nowadays. In our class, we had a single Asian (captain of the tennis team and son of a UN delegate), no African-Americans, and perhaps a few Latinos (although not identified as such). I estimate that 85 to 90 percent of the students in our class of about 100 were Jewish, with a light sprinkling of other faiths. As a dutiful Christian Scientist, as I pointed out to Chapter 2, I got to know the minority pretty well on Jewish holidays when HM stayed resolutely open with precious few in attendance.

We wore jackets and ties and were generally well-behaved. I did not smoke or drink except for nursing an occasional beer through the entire evening as the minimum price of admission to hear jazz at Birdland, Bop City, The Embers, or the Hickory House.

We had excellent teachers, and the educational quality was high. My favorite subjects were English and History. I wasn't interested in science; in fact, I recall my faith-centric mother dissuading me from taking an optional course in Biology. Although I didn't care much for languages, my French teacher, John Oliver, was a particular favorite. The educator that I admired most (and to whom we dedicated our senior yearbook) was William J. Nagle, an old school, much-revered Latin scholar who taught perhaps the school's toughest course. Gordon ("Moose") Miller ably coached the H.M. baseball and basketball teams, but the coach I felt closest to was Charlie Avedisian, a former starting guard for the New York Giants and an unforgettable taskmaster on the football field.

I did well academically but was too involved with three sports to spend much time in other extra-curricular activities (which nearly every college applicant nowadays seems able to boast of). I was elected class president one year and held various other student administrative positions. I enjoyed my gig as Co-Feature Editor of the H.M. student newspaper, *The Record*, where I co-wrote a periodic column under the title "Cool Corner" – more about this in a bit.

I'm embarrassed to say that during my high school years – and continuing right through four years of college and three years of law school – I don't recall undertaking a single activity that served the public interest. Although it doesn't excuse my neglect, the fact was that not too many private school students were performing meritorious deeds in those days.

I was surprised to discover a long article I had co-written in December 1950 for *The Record* – a detailed tribute to Hampton Institute of Hampton, VA (identified in the article's sub-head as a "Negro College"). Our stated rationale for this choice of subject matter was that Horace Mann had "maintained a scholarship there for countless years," plus which the "famed Hampton singers" had delivered a concert at HM every year until World War II. The tone of the article might today be considered patronizing, and the way we concluded it does seem a bit supercilious: "Now that you are all familiar with the various functions at Hampton, maybe you'll appreciate what a glorious tradition we have had here for so many years."

We didn't complain much about the absence of females at HM, and it did have the effect of avoiding undue distractions to our studies. Most of us were able to meet girls on the subway or elsewhere, so we didn't lack for weekend feminine companionship.

In addition to forming many acquaintances, I made some lasting friendships at Horace Mann. (An expanded list of my cohorts can be found in the Appendix.) Many of the relationships still endure. In addition to regular five-year reunions, a number of us still get together quarterly for lunch in Manhattan. Of the dozen or so of my best friends, two-thirds are still alive; I see a half-dozen of them on a more-or-less regular basis. Five (now, sadly, four) of us have for many years enjoyed an annual country luncheon reunion at a scenic Connecticut inn overlooking Lake Waramaug.

* * *

A few words about music. I played the piano during those years, but not very well. My friend John Flaxman was recognized as the premier pianist in the class. He was also a dexterous drummer, and we would sometimes entertain at dances or parties – Jim on piano, Johnny on drums (and then, he and I playing piano duets, with Johnny ultimately taking over the keys). I idolized Stan Getz in those days, and at one point bought myself a well-used tenor sax; but as much as I puffed out my cheeks around my fledgling embouchure, I couldn't get anywhere near that cool Getz sound – so I eventually returned the horn to its threadbare case and donated it to charity.

During my Junior and Senior years, as I mentioned, classmate Larry Shadur and I were Co-Feature Editors of the newspaper, and we wrote a column (originally titled *Popular Music World*) that appeared periodically. We focused on musical matters, including the possibilities available in NYC clubs, on radio or TV, and on 78rpm records available to those willing to pick through multiple bins in musty Greenwich Village shops. Jazz was our chosen genre, and we devoted columns to our favorite big bands, small groups, and vocalists (plus some we didn't care for too much). One highlight was attending and reviewing the 1950 Jazz at the Philharmonic concert at Carnegie Hall, featuring Ella Fitzgerald, Oscar Peterson ("We had never before had the pleasure of seeing him, and he certainly impressed us as one of the finest keyboard artists we have ever listened to."), Charlie Parker, Lester Young, Coleman Hawkins and Buddy Rich.

Later we changed the column name to *Cool Corner*, declaring that we would not be limited to music but rather "devoted to anything and everything that we term 'cool' – although admitting that 'cool' was "a very strange word, because it is such a precise description of the almost indescribable." Joe Louis was our "cool" boxer, but then we wrote about his failed comeback, contrasting it with Winston Churchill's success – "the one, a thrilling victor; the other a sadder and wiser loser." Still, most of the columns drifted back to music – to Louis Armstrong, Duke Ellington, Billie Holiday and others. We also reported on a few interviews we conducted, including those of Alan Dean (the "British Frank Sinatra") and HM graduate Johnny Green (composer of *Body and Soul*).

We attended two concerts featuring George Shearing and Billy Eckstine at Carnegie Hall. After the earlier one, we wrote: "When 'Mr. B' strode out on the stage, the place really went nuts. Some chick in back of us let out an impassioned wail, and the nice looking unescorted girl to JF's right slumped ecstatically into his lap. Freund: 'I could tell at once this Eckstine was all right.' " We later went out and bought white dress shirts with those high-curling collars that Mr. B popularized.

At the second Eckstine-Shearing concert, we managed to get backstage in order to interview the principals. To our dismay, they were surrounded by friends and business associates; and as people began to leave, we gave up on Shearing. "But we were determined to nail B. We did, as he passed on the way out. 'Mr. Eckstine, we just wanted to tell you how great we thought you were today.' He replied graciously (in that full rich baritone), 'Well, thanks a lot. I sure appreciate it. Good luck'." And here's how we ended that column: "Don't nobody never say that we haven't interviewed no one!"

My co-columnist Larry Shadur had a fine singing voice – ultimately going on to perform in international operatic roles – and I enjoyed accompanying him on piano as he imitated vocalists of the day.

One day we decided to try out for a spot on Ted Mack's "Amateur Hour," a popular TV program at the time. I can still visualize the audition hall – a two-story-high room, bare except for a piano, bench, and mic, with the producer faintly visible behind an enclosed glass panel up high at one end. Larry hit paydirt with a prime rendition of Billy Eckstine's big baritone vocal on *Everything I Have is Yours*. As he concluded on that memorable full-throated high note, we were feeling full of beans – confident of being selected for the show.

An amplified voice came down from the producer on high: "Thank you, Mr. Shadur; we'll get in touch if there are any openings . . . . Now please bring on the next contestant." As Larry and I were departing, the next contestant turned out to be an old grizzled man who gimped his way over to the mic, sat down on the bench, pulled two tableware spoons out of his pocket, and began clicking them together to the pre-recorded tune of something like *Ain't She Sweet*.

We listened in youthful disdain to this living relic of vaudeville days. But when he finished, the disembodied voice from on high became animated – taking down the geezer's contact information, and giving him instructions on where and when to appear. Clearly, the superannuated spoon-man had beaten us out. It was our early introduction to the meaning of the word "crestfallen". . . .

* * *

Athletics played a major role in my life at HM – three years of varsity football and baseball, two of basketball, eight letters in all. These were terrific bonding experiences, and a number of my friends were on one or more of the teams.

The most dramatic occurrence of my athletic career came junior year in the middle of the football season when the team experienced an epidemic of polio, resulting in the death of teammate Bob Buzzell, and leaving two other players partially disabled. It was a very scary time; we were in quarantine for weeks, worrying whether it would infect someone else. Although the school wasn't closed, three of our next scheduled football games were called off.

My baseball career was not overwhelming. I could hit well on occasion but not with consistency. I was an infielder until destiny intervened. One of the polio-disabled football teammates was the catcher on the baseball team. When the baseball season rolled around, our coach Moose Miller —also an assistant coach on the football team — said to me, "Hey, Freund, you're a tough football player – I'm making you our catcher." There was no recourse.

So I donned the catcher's heavy paraphernalia — we termed it, as I recall, "the tools of ignorance" – and endured bruises galore for two seasons. It wasn't my natural position, but *The Record* was able to report that "Jim Freund deserved a lot of credit for adeptly handling a position which was entirely new to him." Actually, I began to enjoy being in on the action pitch-by-pitch and managed to become moderately competent at the task. My real problem was a continuing inability to hit a curve . . . .

I was a starting guard on the HM basketball team for two years, but here too I had an unfortunate weakness — less-than-stellar shooting accuracy. What would you expect anyway from a guy who clung to a two-handed set shot and persisted in shooting fouls underhanded? I was better at moving the ball around, hustling, playing defense, and especially rebounding. (Coach Miller was quoted as saying that "Jim Freund, shorter than most of the starting squad, was invaluable to the team because of his steady rebounding.") We had a good team senior year and took great pride in winning the Ivy Prep League title.

I did have one unexpected flash of accuracy junior year in a big win over our arch-rival, Trinity. Here's how the enthusiastic reporter from *The Record* wrote about it: "Jim Freund, whose great outside shooting in the first half forced Trinity to spread her defense . . . scored what is probably the most amazing shot ever made by a H.M. player when he sank a fifty foot set shot as the buzzer sounded ending the first half . . . ."

My best sport was football. I started out as the only sophomore on the '49 varsity team – a reserve wingback. The team was just so-so, and the one venture outside our league, against powerhouse Scarsdale High School, proved to be a disaster. I still recall a memorable run I made in that game – dodging back and forth, eluding tacklers, and finally making it back to the line of scrimmage.

At the outset of junior year the starting left end was injured, and Coach Avedisian switched me to that unfamiliar position. Again, *The Record* was supportive: "Jim deserves a lot of credit for the ease in which he has accustomed himself to the new position." This was the year of our polio epidemic, and I've blocked out most memories of that difficult time. But in the one game we played at the season's end prevailing over Concordia Prep, I caught a long pass for a touchdown, and ran 60 yards for a score on an end-around.

When senior year began, I still found myself playing left end, although I knew my forte was as a running back. HM didn't produce much offense in losing its first two games. And then, early the next week, came an exhilarating moment that remains etched in my memory.

I was at home that night when the phone rang. (I can still picture answering the call on the unit with a rotary dial that we kept in the foyer closet, and which my mother continued to use until she passed away 65 years later.) I heard the unmistakable gruff voice of Coach Avedisian, saying he had decided to switch me to halfback for the upcoming Friday game. "Do you think you can learn the plays in time, Jim?" My answer was a ringing, "You betcha, Coach."

That Friday, we played host to St. Paul's school of Garden City, and also to a battalion of girls from Brearley School who had come to H.M. *en masse* that day to participate in the festivities. Here's how *The Record* handled the story:

> "It seems the only things that Horace Mann needed to blossom out into a gridiron winner was the Brearley girls to back them, and the shift of Jim Freund to the backfield . . . . Jim Freund, who always is a standout, burst out into a mythological 'superstar'. . . Scoring four times and making tackles all over the field, Freund was completely unstoppable."

I was treated as a hero. Two moments still stand out. One took place after the game when the legendary Latin teacher Mr. Nagle (in his standard dark three-piece suit) came into the locker room and over to the bench where I sat taking off my shoulder pads, to congratulate me on our win and tell me what a great game I had played. The other was later on that day, entering the assembly hall to the sound of loud cheers – including those of the Brearley battalion of girls.

Although nothing matched the St. Paul's day, I did well in the remaining games – with the friendly reporter for *The Record* still giving me high marks. "Jim Freund who played so brilliantly two weeks ago against

St. Paul's, once again was the outstanding player on the field. Although hampered by a leg injury, Jim starred on both offense and defense, galloping 70 yards for H.M.'s only tally" against Poly Prep. And here's what he wrote when we played Adelphi: "In the last three seconds of the game London threw to Freund who grabbed the ball from three defenders for the score as the small crowd on hand went wild. Freund ran the extra point as the game ended in a 13-13 tie."

My memory is that the team captaincy was rotated game-to-game, but in the team's official picture I'm holding the football in the middle of the first row. I made the New York All-City Private School first team that year – mainly, I'm sure, on the basis of my one big day against St. Paul's.

An article in *The Record* quoted Coach Avedisian's letter to the head football coach at Amherst College (which I had contemplated attending):

> "Even though our season at Horace Mann was a bit on the mediocre side, we did manage to produce one bona-fide football star in the person of James Freund. Speed, deadly tackling, and aggressive spirit made this boy the top player in these parts. I recommend him without fear of error or contradiction. Being a class leader and an honor student enables Jim to seek entrance into a fine college like Amherst. Freund is a fine all-around athlete, but the sport he likes best and performs in excellently is football."

* * *

When the awards were given out at graduation, I was a multiple winner. Three of us were inducted into the Varsity Club; *The Record* selected me as Athlete of the Year; I was one of four inducted into the Archon Society, H.M.'s highest honor for civic accomplishments in non-athletic extra-curricular activities, and one of a dozen in the *Cum Laude* Society for scholarship and citizenship. I received the Stroock Award for character and scholarship, and the Buzzell Memorial Award (honoring the player we lost to polio) in football. Two of us won honors in English, and also in French (in which I must have been good at conjugation, because my accent was dreadful.)

My classmates, asked to pick the three top individuals in each category, named me in the following half-dozen spots: most likely to succeed, most collegiate, most respected, best athlete, most popular, and most versatile.

As I reflect on it today, it was that last category – versatility – that probably served me best. It's what made me stand out – the combination of achievements in the three major sports, good marks, and character and leadership qualities.

I took out my dusty copy of our class yearbook recently. Even discounting for the often overheated prose of such memorabilia, what I found was notable. From the opening reference to me ("The idol of every lower schooler, Jim began his Frank Merriwell record at HM . . . .") to the laudatory inscriptions from dozens of my classmates, the overall effect lifted my octogenarian spirits.

Best of all were two inscriptions by faculty members: one (with a hint of Mr. Chips) from the school's most respected teacher, Mr. Nagle (who was retiring after 41 years teaching): "To a truly incomparable boy, scholar, gentleman and leader, with unbounded pride and affection"; and the other from my peerless coach, Charlie Avedisian: "The best of luck to the finest all-around athlete, student and gentleman I ever worked with."

I think you can see now why I claim to have peaked in high school – it couldn't (and didn't!) get any better than that . . . .

Horace Mann School – the main building, athletic field and gym, and some of my assembled classmates (Class of 1952).

The three teams my senior year

*On
the
playing
field*

*The photo
(above) was
taken the night
in 1952 that our
basketball team
won the Ivy Prep
League title.*

*The photo (left)
was taken in
Niagara Falls,
near the end of my
post-graduation
cross-country trip
with Paul
Margulies, when
we met up with
Mom and Dad.*

5. THE SUMMER OF '52

I probably should have spent the summer of 1952 doing some manual labor or other activity that would have gotten me in good shape for the Princeton freshman football team I'd be part of that Fall. But a summer adventure beckoned that I just could not turn down.

It was a two-month cross-country auto excursion with one of my best buddies from Horace Mann, Paul Margulies. Although it lacked any positive features in terms of physical conditioning (for which I paid dearly that Fall), the trip ranks as one of my favorite lifetime experiences.

I'm devoting generous space to this adventure from 68 years ago because it was so eye-opening to me in many respects – new vistas glimpsed, life lessons learned, clues unearthed as to the adult I was to become. For most of the trip, I actually kept (and recently discovered) a handwritten diary of each day's activities and my reflections on them – something I'd never done previously nor ever undertook thereafter. The diary provides real insights into how my mind was working at age 18, how I expressed myself, and what was important to me back then.

I titled my diary "Our Trip to the Great Unknown," which was just how we felt about it. Neither Paul nor I had previously ventured across the continent – it was something completely new to us.

Here's a quickie itinerary so you can visualize our journey. We headed west from NYC through Pennsylvania, Ohio, Missouri, Kansas, Colorado, New Mexico, Utah, Nevada, and to Los Angeles. From there we drove north to Yosemite, San Francisco and southeast Oregon, then swung east through Salt Lake City, Yellowstone, and South Dakota. We hit some Midwestern cities including Chicago and Detroit, then Niagara Falls and New England, and ended up visiting a friend in Montreal.

A terrific trip – and yet, it might well never have occurred, since it required permission from (and funding by) my parents. As an only child, my adolescence had been marked by my mother's incontrovertible edicts and protective custody. So I deemed the odds of her approving the trip as slim. (My father, as I have mentioned, usually tended to go along with whatever she decided on such matters.)

Looking back on it now, I must acknowledge that there were plenty of valid reasons for her to turn me down, namely:

- Although I'd taken some trips with my parents and had attended summer camp in New England, I'd never been anywhere on my own before – and the sheltered life I'd lived to date was hardly adequate preparation for being "out there" up to 3,000 miles from home.

- I was definitely not an experienced driver, having lived my whole life in the city with no need to get behind the wheel. All I had was a so-called "Learner's Permit," subject to various restrictions, and it wouldn't blossom into a full-blown license until I turned 18, which was to take place a full month after we set out.

- There were no cellphones or emails in those days, and we had no fixed itinerary. Unless I initiated contact with my parents, they would have no idea of my location and what I was up to. My past history on this score was not reassuring; both at summer camp and on other occasions, I'd never proved to be a reliable correspondent, either by mail or phone.

- Although we would be traveling in budget style, the trip was still going to cost what must have seemed like a lot to my parents, who were far from affluent.

So, I ask myself now, how could she have said okay to my pleading to go? (The act of pleading had not managed to work well for me on a number of prior occasions.) Did my father – who loved to drive and explore new territories – intervene on my behalf? If so, neither of them gave me any sign of this. Was it a reward for having done well at Horace Mann and being accepted at Princeton? Could she have been influenced by all the priceless Americana I would view and experience? Did she think it would develop in me a sense of responsibility, or an ability to manage my finances through prudent budgeting of the traveler's checks they would be providing me?

My own guess is that it was primarily because Paul had not only gotten permission to go and received funding from his parents, but they were prepared to furnish us with a car – a convertible, no less. It might have been embarrassing for my parents not to show similar confidence regarding their own son. Perhaps it was just a combination of all the above – I honestly don't know. When I finally raised the subject with my mother 75 years later, she herself found it hard to believe she had acquiesced.

But she did – and, as far as I'm concerned, it was one of the best things my parents ever did for their son. It brought me out of that New York private school cocoon and into the real world.

Paul – who sadly passed away a few years ago – was a terrific guy, a wonderful companion; I don't recall either of us growing irritated with the other, as sometimes occurs in such close quarters over an extended period. But he happened to be extremely casual about such matters as what town we'd be visiting next, where we'd sleep or eat, what we needed to see, and how many miles it was to the nearest gas station. Paul was also capable of falling asleep anywhere – most notably, catching some shuteye in the passenger's seat while I drove. So at times I found myself having to get nervous for both of us. But in retrospect, this worked out to my advantage – forcing me to take responsibility for these matters and honing my judgment as to various workaday affairs that I rarely needed to deal with back home.

So now, return with me to the magical summer of '52 – with verbatim quotes from my diary rendered in *italics* – as we drive our sporty convertible along legendary roads like Route 66, amused by such sequential roadside signs as:

Proper distance

To him was bunk

They pulled him out

Of some guy's trunk

BURMA SHAVE.

In perusing my diary, the first recurrent theme that strikes me is our preoccupation with the heat. The nation was baking that summer as we drove across its scorching midlands. Nowadays, we have become so used to our creature comforts that we hardly recall a time when refreshing temperatures weren't constantly available. But our car had no air-conditioning, and most of the low-cost motels we stayed in lacked cooling devices. For instance:

The proprietor of the motel [in Harrisburg, PA] said that there was a nice breeze that came in from the west most nights. Last night it died. I've never been so hot in my life (so far). It was impossible to sleep . . . . We both woke up around five-thirty after tossing all night . . . .

One option often available to us was to forsake steaming motels and sleep out in the open. But that didn't always work either.

We went back to our campground [in Columbus, Ohio], stretched out the sleeping bag, and were bitten alive . . . . The mosquitos sounded like small fighter planes – you could imagine yourself on an island during the war . . . .

What might have been (but wasn't) the worst experience occurred while we were sleeping in the Yosemite camping grounds. *During the night I heard Paul say, "Jim, Jim!" I woke up sort of half-way, and he said, "There's a bear right next to you." I knew there were bears in the woods but this kind of stunned me. Half out of fright and half from annoyance I turned my back on the creature (if there was one) and went back to sleep. Paul swears there was one there about a foot from my head. As for me, I don't think about it much . . . .*

We had another way to deal with the heat, although not always triumphantly.

It was hot again, and we had the top down so it was hotter. We got to Columbus around noontime, and immediately inquired as to the nearest pool. We were directed to it, and it looked great. There was a doll of a lady lifeguard, and we dove happily in. But the water was tepid, and it wasn't much good. Neither was the lady lifeguard up close . . . .

My diary deals with the meals we ate on a daily basis. Although we were on a thrifty budget, I seemed to genuinely enjoy the available food – at one point noting (after a good meal in Santa Cruz), *You can really eat very well in the west – don't let anyone tell you different . . .* And in Los Angeles, I commented: *The drive-in restaurant is a real institution out here, with one practically every block. All pretty good too. We ate there a lot while in L.A.*

Sometimes I actually waxed ecstatic, such as in this entry from Denver: *We parked and ate at a swell place, the Blue Parrot. Good, fairly inexpensive food. I had fried brook trout, a staple out here, but a great delicacy to my eastern pallet. It tasted wonderful, best fish I've ever eaten.* And in L.A., family friends treated us to more expensive meals, viz: *We went to Lawry's Home of the Prime Rib. They only serve roast beef and the chef brings a well done, medium and rare one around to your table. Best I ever had.*

The gustatory treat of the trip was the night in L.A. when we were taken to *Don The Beachcomber* restaurant by a prominent Hollywood agent who was married to my mother's cousin. *It was the best meal I ever had – all those exotic Cantonese dishes. I'm not much for chow mein, but when those barbecued ribs and pressed duck and shrimps and unbelievable vegetation came out, I really flipped.*

(I can't resist including a wry footnote to that experience. The agent and his wife were dropping a lot of celebrity names, including that of Howard Hughes who, they said, *had flown them down to Las Vegas for a weekend of gambling in his private Constellation which he pilots himself.* I confess to having been skeptical about this boast, but after our meal, to my amazement, the headwaiter wouldn't let the agent pay the bill, saying, *"Mr. Hughes is treating tonight."* . . . . It didn't cross my mind at the time, but now I can't help wondering whether the agent might have underwritten that seeming largesse himself, with a big tip for the headwaiter's cooperation, in order to impress these Big Apple visitors . . . .)

In terms of lodgings, our preference was to save money by camping out – mosquitos and all – but it wasn't always possible. One night, we searched for a place to camp in the hills outside Denver, but *everything was barb-wired.* We got so tired that around three a.m. we succumbed and took a motel room at Idaho Springs. The next day we discovered that five minutes from the motel was a beautiful place to camp, which triggered the following irritated reaction: *So we blew 4 bucks.* Most of the motels we stayed in weren't expensive; for example, we secured lodgings for an extended stay in Los Angeles at a motel *covered with various floral ornaments and exceptionally reasonable at 30 clams for the week.*

Motel life wasn't always great. One night, for example, we went back to our motel room, *washed our own clothes! and went to sleep.* (The exclamation point was mine from back then – washing clothes never being my strong point.) And although many motel rooms we stayed in boasted two beds, the cheaper ones had only one double bed for us to share. The result: *Paul doesn't bother me at all, but I'm kind of a restless sleeper and as I roll over and move around I hit him many times during the night. It's pretty tough on him . . .*

In addition to heat, food and lodging, another recurring diary theme involves the women that we spotted, ran into, met, and sometimes dated. It's all so innocent – nothing of note ever seems to take place. Here's a typical extract from Echo Lake, Colorado:

We ate, making friends with all the waitresses and other assorted girls that were around . . . . [Then we went up Mt. Evans.] *Very exciting, hairpin turns all the way, sensational views, huge drifts of snow – to a lodge on top with some more swell gals. We sort of make friends with everyone we have contact with.*

Some of the girls were terrific, like the multiple collegiate co-eds we befriended in Yellowstone, whose antics over several days took up pages of the diary. Others received less space but seemed memorable nonetheless. At a fruit stand in L.A., we began talking to *a cute blond on the stool next to me . . . She told me she's a singer, had sung for Kenton, and when she knew we dug it, she really let out – rattling off names, imitating singers, her life history, all in her real jivey lingo:" Man, it was a regular hassle"* – *"Four key changes in a row – I died" etc. etc. It was a terrific half hour.*

(Here's the note about the songstress that I appended in my diary: *I mention it now not for others who can't appreciate it, but for me to look back upon. She was really terrific, probably the most fabulous character I've ever met. But like all characters you can't put down her expressions and actions on paper. Suffice to say, this will remind me of her . . . .* Unfortunately, though, I'm now forced to report to my much younger self that I have trouble picturing this worthwhile lass today . . . .

Other interactions didn't turn out so well, and my overly critical eye wasn't about to let such occasions pass. For instance, at the Grand Canyon, *We met some nice gals from Milwaukee. One was very good-looking, one small and cute, one had a nice personality, and the fourth was tall and angular, homely and senseless and she talked with a schlurp – She took a liking to Paul . . . .* Does anyone reading this know what a "schlurp" is? And in Salt Lake City on July 26, celebrating my 18th birthday, we *looked for some action around town but it was pretty dead. Met two girls, one of whom didn't open her mouth for 30 minutes. We went back home and to bed – some birthday.*

Of course the diary is full of observations about the sights we encountered. Here's one that describes a scene I'll never forget.

After the flat topography of Kansas, we were looking forward to Colorado, whose scenery we'd heard was beautiful . . . . We expected right at the border for the majestic Rockies to replace the uninteresting plains . . . . We must have driven 200 miles into Colorado that day and we didn't see a hill. It was practically the same thing as Kansas – as Paul puts it, "miles and miles of miles and miles."

As we approached Denver, there was still no sign of the Rockies. Then we went down a side street that ended up at a golf course and took a look across the links. *It was the most thrilling sight I have ever seen. Rising majestically against the sun which had almost set and which had given off a rich orange streaked with yellow tint to the beautifully formed clouds and sky, were these huge almost black mountains, thousands of feet above us. It took our breath away . . . .*

We hit the Aztec Ruins National Monument, the Painted Desert, the Petrified Forest, the Great Meteor Crater – and then there was Grand Canyon. *You come to the edge of it for your first look and it's unbelievable – you think it's being done with mirrors – There may be more beautiful places in the world (although I don't see how there could be) but there certainly are no grander, more magnificent, huge, imposing, majestic – well, I'm stuck for adjectives.*

Then – as a precursor to my present passion for photography – here's how I closed my treatment of Grand Canyon (after much description of how it looked and statistics as to its magnificence): *You can only describe the Canyon by pictures.* But, sad to say, I had no still camera with me. I did have a primitive movie camera, but film was expensive; so when I deigned to take a clip, the results were spasmodic and forgettable. I just wish I could make this same trip today with my advanced digital camera . . . .

Our first glimpse of the Pacific engendered a blasé response: *Looks just like the Atlantic. Funny, isn't it. Come 4,000 miles to see the same thing we've got home.* Later, however, *we went up to the top of the palisades* [in Santa Monica] *and got a much nicer view from between some beautiful palm trees.* But when we went in for a dip, the most I could muster up was *it's pretty nice – colder than the Atlantic – same kind of waves.*

A bigger disappointment was *the corner of Hollywood and Vine, which is really nothing, less exciting than 86th and Broadway . . . .* Yosemite proved to be a mixed bag. Upon arrival, *it really got beautiful. Huge trees and winding roads, mirror lakes and gushing streams. Things you read about.* But I couldn't help complaining about one aspect: *I would have liked Yosemite best of all the places we went if it weren't for the overabundance of people – It lost something, became less natural, more commercial.*

We took in San Francisco, then drove north, stopping briefly at the town of Eureka. *Paul was dying all day to be able to say, "Eureka, I've found it."* Along the Pacific Coast, *there were a million logging trucks on the road with immense logs on them, being hauled to one of the hundreds of mills we saw along the way.* The road was narrow, and I was worried that one of them would hit us. *We were 50 feet from the ocean and we couldn't see it, the fog was so thick – and then we started inland and it broke so fast that it was unbelievable – the sky was bluer than I've ever seen it.*

After a bad night in sleeping bags at Crater Lake in Oregon, we arose early and *drove up to the lake for another look. It was the top sight of the trip. The sun was just lighting one-half of the crater and the water was just like a mirror reflecting the darkened cliffs so well that you couldn't tell where the shoreline was. The sky was beautiful, the sun bright.*

We were impressed with the interior of the Tabernacle in Salt Lake City. *The acoustics in this building are so perfect that a fellow whispered and dropped three pins in the front of the room and you could hear it perfectly in the rear.* But there was no beach at the Great Salt Lake. *Besides it cost a buck to get in and get dressed and that bummed us.* Anyway, *after rocks and filthy water and bugs near shore, it got better further out. Then we gave it the big test – we lay back in the water and bang! Up popped our feet . . . It was amazing – so buoyant that it was absolutely impossible to sink.*

Here are some things I learned about myself at 18 from reading the diary. For instance, I liked to term things "the best" and "great" – absolutes that in later life became a casualty of the two-sides-to-every-argument relativity I was imbued with in law school. (But then, the second time around, I married a devoted practitioner of best-and-worst superlatives.)

Apparently I wasn't adverse to a little deception when I considered it harmless. We needed ID's for when we were carded in places that served alcohol. Paul had a Panamanian license, and I had a Canadian one, each of which listed our ages as 21. (I had been using the Canadian card in New York, where the age limit was only 18; in order for it to work nationwide, I had to erase the "18" and insert "21" – a procedure performed so sloppily that it was unlikely to pass muster with anyone who bothered to take a close look.) Our cards was almost always accepted, although we were sometimes asked by a nosy bartenders: "How did you two non-Americans get together?" Our reply was, "Oh, we met at the motel swimming pool," delivered without a trace of shame.

I was delighted to learn from the diary that even back then I was at my happiest when playing the piano for an enthusiastic audience who sang along with me. I sat down at the keys on an impromptu basis in a number of venues. Here's a diary description from one of the best nights:

I started playing the piano and soon got a real crowd over. We sang for about 2 hours, around 20 people. They were real hep, too. I didn't have to play the current crap. All the standards I knew, they did too, and some I didn't . . . . You can't imagine how happy I was – really in heaven. Playing what I wanted to with people who appreciated it (or at least pretended they did).

It became even better when I had company. One night, after a lodge dance, I sat down to play, and a drummer from the dance band joined me. *He was great – a real good musician. We jammed for about 15 minutes. Got a big crowd. Tremendous kicks . . . they made us stop finally – we were waking up the guests.*

And I loved hearing the greats. The highlight for me in San Francisco was listening to the Dave Brubeck Trio playing in a small jazz spot – and *we spoke to Paul Desmond, the grandest altoist around . . . . It was a wonderful evening for me – got me right back in the groove.*

Well, if those musical moments were among the highlights, listen to my diary as it recounts one of the real low points – a memorable comeuppance for the dynamic duo.

Right across from where we ate there was a carnival – lights, colors, etc. – a real hick traveling show. So the two big New York sharpies walk in to try their luck on these poor country folk – sophisticated, blasé, seen it all, from the main stem . . . . A guy tried to rope us in to a concession where you hit a nail and win big money. But it was pretty easy to see the nail was put in crooked, and we walked away – very proud of ourselves.

Then we got called over to "the game." There are a hundred balls, bouncing around in a machine, each with a different number. Each number means a certain number of points . . . . I started to play and he let me win, although I didn't get the money – he held it. Finally I hit ten points and won twenty bucks – I had started with 50 cents – Man, did I feel great. The guy behind the counter was going, "Man, I never saw such luck." A bystander (who I later saw behind the counter) kept encouraging me and marveling at my success . . . .

Then, they got Paul playing (I gave him some of my money), and he too was winning – to the point where he only needed a half-point to win about $150. But, of course, he couldn't pick up that last half-point, and the ante to play kept going up, finally to $20 which we didn't have, *so we dropped all our dough . . . about $25 plus the $20 that I had won. It was a never-to-be-forgotten lesson . . . .*

All was not lost, though; we had enough left *to see Shanghai Lil and her wild revue – a real hick cooch show. Very, very entertaining – better than any burlesque show I've ever seen.*

I'll close with two indelible memories from the trip involving automobiles – so indelible they didn't need to be written down (and weren't).

I'm driving our car out west somewhere on a three-lane highway – one lane going our way, one the opposite, and a middle lane that could be used by either side to pass slower vehicles. Paul is asleep. I'm stuck for awhile behind a slow car, so in frustration I decide to pass, even though we're approaching a hill. I swing into the middle lane and pull up even with the car I'm passing as we reach the top of the hill.

Suddenly a car comes into view over the crest of the hill heading right at me in the middle lane. I can't bear right to get back into my own lane; I'll crash if I keep going straight. So I take the only course remaining – I steer to *the left*, crossing over into the other guy's regular lane, passing his car on his passenger's side. It would have been curtains if the car he had been passing was right up there, but fortunately that vehicle had been overtaken a ways back. So after passing the guy in the center on the wrong side, I was able to swing back into the middle lane, speed up, and then ultimately return to my own lane.

It was nerve-wracking. As soon as possible, I pulled off the road to catch my breath and to realize – even as today I flash back periodically to the very moment – that this could have been the end of our young lives. After all, we were in a convertible with no seatbelts or airbags. As for Paul, amazingly he didn't wake up. I can't remember if I ever told him the full story. I certainly never told my parents. But I'm revealing it now.

The other auto story isn't as dramatic but involves personal shame – the memory of which is hard to shake. It happened in Montreal, where our Horace Mann classmate, Norm Namerow, lived.

One night Norm hosted a party to which he invited a number of lively local French-Canadian girls. I hesitate to categorize them, but let's just say they were a lot more sophisticated than us guys (other than Norm). But we did our best to look like we knew what the hell we were doing. At the evening's end, Norm asked me to drive two of them back to their homes, and he loaned me his car to make the trip.

The problem was that it was a shift car, and I'd never driven one. All my meager driving experience had been with – what did we call them? – hydromatic or fluid drives that had no clutch and didn't require the shifting of gears. But I was too ashamed to plead incompetence to Norm or to the girls, so I gave it a try.

It turned out to be one of my most embarrassing hours. I tried mightily to shift gears and manipulate the clutch – but all that I managed to accomplish was to stall the car at least a dozen times en route. And meanwhile, the girls were sitting in the back seat, laughing uproariously at my ineptitude, and commenting in French on my questionable manhood – *mon dieu*, I can't go on . . . .

At any rate, it had been a great trip. There were highlights and then there were some not-so-highlights – but that's just the point. It served as ideal preparation for what to expect in adult life.

The trip provided me with a geographic compass, which served me well in college as I came in contact with contemporaries from all over the nation. It taught me lessons in taking responsibility that were useful during my years in the Navy. It was also a great exercise in male bonding. Meanwhile, along the way, I brushed up on driving a car, meeting new girls, sleeping in a bag on the ground, managing on a slim budget, and more.

A couple of well-spent months, I'd say.

6. PRINCETON (1952-1956)

One of the most enjoyable periods of my life was the four years spent from September 1952 to June 1956 as an undergraduate at Princeton University.

I'm in awe of the continuing excellence of the University – not least as the result of the 1969 admission (and now central significance) of women. Its academic pursuits are world-class, its student body superb and well-diversified, its administration extremely competent. And the communal spirit that bonds generations of Princetonians together is mind-boggling.

But this section of my memoir is devoted to the years I spent there six decades ago. I've attempted to pierce the gauzy glow of the intervening years in order to recapture what it was like for me back then – and to assess what role the Princeton experience may have played in shaping my adult values and attributes.

Here, to be frank, is what I found. On the one hand, I forged a number of lasting personal relationships. I honed my writing skills. I was exposed to the broad range of information that a liberal arts education provides. I had some eye-opening learning experiences, both positive and negative, from which I derived important lessons that have proved helpful in later life.

On the other hand, I can't recall much that qualifies as lasting character development. Rather, what sticks in my mind most clearly are the undergraduate hi-jinks I engaged in over those four years – attributable in large part to my being effectively unleashed fifty miles from any home-based repression.

I had a terrific time at Princeton from start to finish, but I didn't emerge as a finished product, nor was I particularly well-prepared for the years ahead. I see myself back then as being in a sort of time-warp cocoon – enjoying life to the hilt, blissfully unaware of (and rarely interested in) what was going on in the outside world, and clueless about what I'd be doing the rest of my life.

It's worth noting that we were known as the "silent generation." Except for one incident (related later), I don't remember being stirred by anything going on at the time in Washington or elsewhere on the planet. I would never have considered marching in a parade to promote a cause or carrying a banner that trumpeted any strongly-felt views. I don't recall engaging in bull sessions with my buddies about the issues of the day. We were certainly aware of the Cold War, but the Korean conflict had by then simmered down to a cease-fire, and the Cuban missile crisis was years away from developing.

Since my graduation, I've stayed very close to Princeton. I had the honor of serving as a University Trustee, elected by the entire alumni body. I've been quite active in the affairs of my Class of 1956 – first as its secretary responsible for periodic classmate updates in the Princeton Alumni Weekly, then as class president during the five years leading up to our major 25th reunion in 1981. I received a Distinguished Classmate award; and I believe I'm the only '56er who has touched all four bases: alumni class president and secretary, Distinguished Classmate, and University Trustee. I've also played the piano for dozens of reunions, not only for my class but also for five adjacent classes, plus 1948, 1949, and what Princeton calls the "Old Guard." And I have served as one of the leaders of the alumni foundation our class created, ReachOut56-81-06, heading up its annual award of public service fellowships (funded by class members) to standout graduating seniors, as related in Chapter 19.

But all of these activities occurred *after* I graduated. My intention here is to tell the tale, as I remember it, of my life as an *undergraduate*, warts and all. Please join me as I revisit my own personal yesteryear.

* * *

I ended up at Princeton only because I'd won a Holloway scholarship through the Navy's NROTC program – a government initiative I discuss in Chapter 7. My first-choice college, Amherst, did not have an NROTC unit, so the appeal of having my next four years publicly funded led me elsewhere.

With Amherst eliminated, my choice boiled down to Harvard or Princeton. In this contest, Harvard had a lot going for it.

- In my circle of acquaintances, Harvard was considered the premier university in the country.
- My closest friend at Horace Mann had been accepted at Harvard and was strongly urging me to room with him.
- I spent a terrific weekend there with my buddy and others who were already collegians. They enthused about what Harvard had to offer.

As for Princeton, I didn't know any undergraduates well; and the weekend I spent on campus with the unexciting son of one of my father's Penn classmates was deadly dull – nothing to encourage a choice of Princeton.

So why did I end up at Old Nassau? It's a little embarrassing to admit, but I think a lot of the impetus came from how entranced I was by the way the college looked. I was a city boy, and that splendid leafy Princeton campus, adjacent to the attractive small town housing it, was exhilarating. (By comparison, Harvard's presence in downtown Cambridge didn't give off the same vibe at all.) Fancying myself a prospective college gridder, I was also taken in by the tremendous success of the Princeton football teams of '50 and '51, led by Dick Kazmaier who won the Heisman Trophy. In addition, two good friends from Horace Mann, Dick Kluger and Larry Goodman, were headed to Princeton, and rooming with them seemed a propitious way to embark on this adventure.

So I made my choice – Princeton.

* * *

I might as well begin the Princeton experience on the sour note of my "athletic adjustment." As I noted in writing about Horace Mann, my prior experience before college has been marked by a high level of athletic achievement – football hero, basketball starter on our league champion team, catcher for the baseball squad, one of three members inducted into the prestigious Varsity Club, and selected as Athlete of the Year by the school newspaper. Sports had been a big part of my life, and I reveled in my self-image as a first-rate student and school leader who also happened to be a top athlete. Now, as a college freshman, I was about to embark on the next chapter.

I arrived at Princeton in September 1952 for pre-season freshman football practice a week before classes started. Having spent the entire summer on my cross-country trip, I wasn't in prime shape. Practice had not even begun when I ran into a guy who was there for the same reason. He had the largest neck I'd ever seen, atop a classic square-cut football frame. (It was Jack Thompson, who became Princeton's excellent starting center.) I knew at a glance that my collegiate football career wasn't going to be a walk in the park.

Once practice started, it didn't take me long to realize that this was a far cry from Horace Mann. I made the team, but strictly as a substitute. I rationalized this by noting that my experience as a T-formation running back in high school didn't prepare me for any of the positions in Princeton's classic single wing formation. The tailback had to be able to pass as well as run, and I wasn't much of a passer; the blocking back and wingback were supposed to be fearsome blockers, not my strong suit; the fullback was the guy who plunged through all those large defensive lineman in the middle of the line. That's where I was slotted in, at fullback, a rough road for a guy who weighed about 165 pounds. The starting fullback was Dick Martin – heavier, solidly built, a prototype fullback, who also excelled as a linebacker on defense, since we played both offense and defense in those days.

I got into a few freshman games that fall, usually in the fourth quarter when we'd successfully wrapped things up. I recall just one instance where I expected to be called on for more significant duty. On the previous play, Dick had carried the ball and been hit by a half-dozen defenders. When they climbed off him, he was lying prone on the turf, inert. I hoped he was all right, of course, but could see that he needed a substitute. Pulling on my helmet, I headed over to where the coach stood, ready to rumble.

Then, in one of the most miraculous recoveries since Truman beat Dewey, Dick popped up off the ground, shook himself a few times and joined the huddle. The man was indestructible, and I remained forever sidelined.

I will say, though, that the disappointment I felt at being such a little fish in a big pond was offset in part by the realization that this turned out to be a wonderful way to meet lots of good guys quickly. Many of them became friends throughout college and during the alumni decades to come.

After football season, I played intramural basketball. One of the football coaches who refereed our games liked my hustle and willingness to mix it up under the boards. He invited me to attend the varsity football training camp in Blairstown before school started in the fall.

That spring I played freshman baseball, but I didn't shine as a catcher, and my continuing inability to hit a curve relegated me again to a substitute role with little chance to play. Once more, I got to know a number of classmates, so the experience wasn't a total loss.

The summer after freshman year I went on a long cruise to fulfill my NROTC requirement. Again, I did nothing in the way of physical exercise to prepare me for varsity football camp when I returned. The camp began days before my arrival, but once there I was thrown right into the tough regimen. I was so out-of-shape that I still recall the first evening after practice, when my buddies had to help me climb up the three short steps to the mess hall – my body was so stiff.

What happened next remains uncomfortably fresh in my memory today. A combination of bodily agony, a realization that my chances of achieving college football success were slim, the appeal of a girl I was anxious to see in New York after a summer of separation, and a regrettable lack of willpower to endure what promised to be a painful experience all contributed to my seeking out our legendary coach (Charlie Caldwell) to tell him I was dropping out of the football program. I don't recall my exact words to Caldwell, but privately I no doubt rationalized my decision six different ways.

Still, in my later reckoning, I've come to realize this was a bad decision, a perpetual source of personal chagrin. I should have stuck it out. It's clear to me now that up to that point in my life, things had come too easily for me – not only in sports but elsewhere too – and I was simply not yet equipped to handle adversity.

That was really it for me in terms of organized sports at Princeton – I just wrote athletics out of my life. A mainstay of my self-image from prior years had evaporated overnight. Looking back now, the experience can perhaps be deemed an eventual character-builder – but truth be told, it still rankles.

* * *

Turning to academics, there's no doubt that Princeton back in the '50s was, as it remains today, a superior undergraduate teaching university. Other than my obligatory Naval Science subjects (referred to in Chapter 7), the content of the courses and the level of instruction was high.

Princeton offered some wonderful teachers, such as Professor Huber, who brought real drama to the study of Shakespeare during my freshman year. My favorite courses that year dealt with European History, taught by Professors Harbison (in the fall) and Craig (in the spring) – enlightening lectures by eminent professors to large roomfuls of students, which were supplemented by small precepts of under ten students, in which junior instructors led the discussions.

Still. I don't believe I dug deeply enough into any subject to extract the actual depth of what was being offered. Horace Mann had done a good job of getting me ready for college classes, so I had no trouble keeping up. But I don't recall participating actively in the precepts or working anywhere near my capacity.

As an example, my freshman year math class was taught by a renowned professor with a thick European accent. I can honestly say that I never really grasped what calculus was all about – I simply memorized enough stuff to end up with a good mark.

So much of what passed for intelligence on the tests we took was in fact just our skill at memorizing materials in our readings and lecture notes. (By contrast, law school exams several years later presented a different and tougher sort of problem, as I will discuss in Chapter 10.) The information didn't stick in memory very long; that's why many of us crammed for exams one or two nights just before the test – to be able to regurgitate stuff that might be difficult to recall a few days later.

I should put in a good word here for Princeton's honor system. Except in Naval Science courses, no instructor policed your exam-taking. We attested to our not having cheated, and the University trusted our word. It worked well, and we were imbued with a sense of honor that had a lasting influence, extending beyond college and permeating areas other than academics.

Back in those days, your marks in each course were posted publicly on long lists hung up in Alexander Hall. This made for nerve-racking moments, as you envisioned the entire world being alerted to your mediocre grade in Economics or French. It worked the other way too – after ascertaining my own marks, I usually spent a few minutes checking how friends made out.

In my sophomore year, I decided to become a History major, which edged out my second choice of English. History seemed to me the least confining of all possible majors, providing access to a number of subjects – politics, economics, literature, and so on. I had to write two papers junior year; one was on the Munich conference of 1938, but I can't recall the subject of the other. Nor do I remember much about the various classes I attended, except for one that took place either junior or senior year.

The course was an elective in the Politics department, taught by Hugh Wilson – a firebrand professor with a reputation for telling it like it was. (He also hosted a nighttime precept at his home, complete with six-packs of beer that he supplied.) One particular session produced the most electric classroom experience of my college years.

Those were the Joe McCarthy years when the Wisconsin senator, capitalizing on the country's anti-communist fears, was riding high and terrorizing all branches of the U.S. government. Hugh Wilson had been a strong dissident voice against the senator. In the crowded lecture hall that day, Wilson began by stating that several members of McCarthy's staff were present in the back of the room, "taking notes" as to what he was about to say, to be used against him. We all swiveled around in our seats to catch sights of those spies. Nevertheless, Wilson said, he'd give the same lecture that he would if they weren't there – and he launched into a devastating putdown of everything McCarthy stood for. At the end of the lecture, the entire room (except, I assume, the McCarthy spies) burst into a remarkable round of sustained applause.

As someone not political in those days – rarely current on the news and lacking strong feelings on topics of national interest – Wilson's "McCarthy" class constituted a real wake-up call. I was never quite as uncaring thereafter.*

For my senior thesis, the subject I was most interested in was how the U.S. evolved from isolationism to internationalism in the '30s, but I needed a hook on which to focus such a big topic. I learned that Harold Ickes, Roosevelt's Secretary of the Interior, was someone who recognized the Hitler threat early and was influential in changing the posture of the New Deal on this subject. It just so happened that Ickes' diaries and papers had recently been deposited in the Library of Congress. So I went to Washington to peruse them – one of the first persons to do so. They were quite instructive (and contained many gems, such as a congratulatory personal telegram from Churchill). The experience gave me a good feel for historical research. My resulting thesis received a high grade, helping me to graduate *magna cum laude.*

---

* When I was in the Navy and decided to apply to law school, I needed a reference letter from a Princeton professor. I hadn't been close to any of my history professors, and the man I most admired was Wilson. I didn't know whether he would remember me from those beer precepts at his home, but I wrote him to ask if he'd give me a reference. To my delight, he undertook the task without hesitation and wrote a fine letter – helping me gain admission to every law school I applied to.

* * *

Here's a differential slant on the academics. We were entitled to share a two-man carrel (a small office) in the depths of Firestone Library to work on our senior theses. It was quiet and conducive to deep thinking about the views we were about to transcribe on paper. At least that was the Library's intention. But after too many hours in these carrels, our energies ran in a different direction – so we used the library corridors as raceways to compete against each other with tiny model cars.

After an hour or two in the library (interspersed with forays to the corridor racetrack), some of us craved a libation. Our favorite spot on Nassau Street was called The Annex. But it closed around 11 p.m. (the curfew time for bars in Princeton township). Too early for us – we were just getting started. So we hitchhiked a few miles out to the town of Kingston, where we downed dime beers and vied at shuffleboard and darts at the K.I. (Kingston Inn) or another place we called "The Bar." When they finally closed – was it at 2 a.m.? – we still had to get back to campus, and few cars were on the road for hitchhiking. So these evenings often ended up in a long semi-inebriated hike back to the dorms.

For me, one of the best aspects of Princeton was the variety of new friends I made. I met them different ways – in dormitories, through sports freshman year, in classes, at social gatherings, and later in the eating clubs. For instance, I got to know Jack Fritts because the two-letter match that began our surnames meant we were seated alongside each other in every required class freshman year. Meeting Jack Veatch, who became a close friend (and my ultimate carrel-mate), was the result of a chance encounter (me bumming a cigarette from him) outside the library on a dark night.

Back then, our Princeton class was not "diverse" in the modern sense – no girls, few Latinos or Asians, one African-American. Still, for a guy like me who came from an undiversified environment growing up, it was an unbelievable broadening experience. For instance, three new buddies of mine who roomed together freshman year were all from Little Rock; and on the basis of their last names – Ted Bellingrath, Fritz Hollenberg and Bick Satterfield – I was convinced that everyone in Arkansas had a three-syllable handle.

Sophomore year was very pleasurable. Most of us lived in a dormitory called Holder Hall, with a large but cozy courtyard for getting together. I roomed with Dick Kluger, John Doyle and Lew Gatch. I didn't really know John and Lew, but Dick and John had become friends working for the *Daily Princetonian*, and John had roomed with Lew the prior year. It worked out well. There were other good mates in our entryway, including Royce Flippin and Tom Meeker. From across the courtyard came the guy who turned out to be my closest friend, both at Princeton and for life, Fred Bacher.

I gained access to a suite on Nassau St. that consisted of a living room and a half-dozen small rooms with pianos. Ostensibly it was to be used for practice on the keys, but I must confess this became a weekend party room for those of us with imported dates, who had to clear out of the dorm rooms once the sun went down.

We chafed at the rule prohibiting cars on campus – particularly since most of the girls that interested us were at distant New York and New England colleges This resulted in a lot of hitchhiking, wasted time, and circuitous routes. But in retrospect, it may have been the difference between life and death. My buddies and I drank way too much in those days, and cars weren't equipped with seatbelts, airbags or other safety features.

Hitchhiking anywhere was tough even when we were solo or a twosome, but it became really hard with larger groups – no one wanted to stop for a bunch of us. So a real windfall (except as regards Tom) occurred when Tom Meeker broke his leg in football, had to wear a gigantic exposed full leg cast, and needed crutches to get around. We would select a roadside spot where the rest of us could hide behind bushes while Tom, using his crutch, tried to flag down a ride. Cars would stop to give this poor unfortunate lad a lift, whereupon we'd all spring out of the bushes to take advantage of the opportunity.

The big decision sophomore year involved joining one of the eating clubs, Princeton's version of fraternities, through a process called "Bicker". In those days, if you wanted to eat on campus during junior or senior years, you needed to affiliate with a club, since the university provided no dining alternatives. But the clubs were selective in their choice of members, so guys couldn't always join the one they liked best. For a few unfortunate fellows, there was no landing spot – at least until a drive for 100% fulfillment at the end of the Bicker process forced some clubs to accept those who were "homeless." It was distressing.

I was headed for Cannon Club, my favorite, where I had received positive vibes from the members and where friends like Fred Bacher and Jack Veatch were signing up. But I also had a number of buddies, including Royce Flippin, Mort Chute and Tom Meeker, who were going to Cap & Gown – a fine club and higher on the unwritten scale of social acceptability than Cannon.

I can remember Flippin telling me that he and the others wanted me to join Cap & Gown. Although that club had shown minimal interest in me during the selection process, Flip (who was the star of the football team) and the others apparently possessed sufficient influence to persuade the Cap officers to accept their good friend, Jim Freund. It was tempting, I'll admit, but in the end I told Flip not to pursue it. I wanted to be in a club that wanted me – not one forced to take me due to pressure exerted by others.

It was a good decision on my part. I delighted in Cannon and made many good friends within its walls over the next two-plus years. They were a great bunch of guys who didn't take themselves too seriously, yet ended up as doctors, lawyers, business execs, a judge, a U.S. senator, a New Jersey attorney general, and so on. The food was decent, the drinks ample, the surroundings passable, and there was a working piano.

Junior year was spent in a Blair Hall foursome – Bacher and I in one little room, Flippin and Meeker in the other, plus a joint living room. Our friends, John Doyle, Lew Gatch, Joe Walsh and Marco Grassi, occupied other accommodations in the same entry.

Fred and I put hooks on the wall for outer garments, and between our beds was a permanent pile of soiled clothes. When we took off something we'd been wearing, it went on the top of the pile. When we needed something "fresh" a week or two later, it was drawn from the bottom.

Royce Flippin received a great deal of attention for his football exploits that fall, even generating a healthy sprinkling of fan letters. When he injured his wrist, Fred and I helped out by writing replies for him to his fandom. The big game that year would be taking place in New Haven, where we'd go to watch Flip and his teammates take on Yale. But Fred took sick during the preceding week; I have a picture of him fixed in my mind – sitting woefully in an old rocking chair that we'd picked up, blanket draped over his knees. Still, he was determined to come. But when we got to East Orange to pick up his car, Fred's mother took one look at his condition and packed her son off to bed. We had to proceed without him – but it was a good trip, culminated by a Flippin-sparked victory in Yale Bowl.

I played piano at parties, often at Cannon Club, and also on the campus radio station, WPRU. The keyboard proved to be an effective way to meet girls. For instance, my friends and I would visit a dormitory at one of the women's colleges such as Vassar. We probably didn't know any of the girls in that dorm, so we couldn't announce our arrival, and we weren't allowed above the main floor. But a piano often adorned the reception room.

I'd start playing, and soon the girls would drift down from their rooms, gathering around to sing. I had thought this would work out well for me, but what usually happened was that my buddies quickly paired up with the attractive ones, and what I was left with – seated next to me on the piano bench – had little to offer but a sonorous soprano voice.

* * *

One positive experience I enjoyed at Princeton was the opportunity to write. A lot of it took place in the academic area, notably with respect to a senior thesis and two junior papers. I re-read my thesis a few years ago and was pleased to discover that the writing seemed pretty good. I think that background in college paved the way for the two serious books (*Anatomy of a Merger* and *Lawyering*) I authored in the '70s.

My other major writing took place in the pages of the school newspaper, the *Daily Princetonian* (or the "Prince"), where I was an Assistant Managing Editor. I also wrote some pieces for *The Tiger*, the college's humor magazine. Much of my output for the Prince appeared in a weekly column entitled "Jazz, etc." which I authored from February 1955 until January 1956. I like to think of these efforts (plus my "Cool Corner" column in the Horace Mann Record) as the building blocks for the multiple columns I wrote for *Legal Times* in the early '80s (later collected in three books and a spoken CD album).

One of my main interests was writing about music. I reviewed concerts at the local McCarter Theatre by such notables as Louis Armstrong. I reviewed albums by both of Princeton's *a capella* male singing groups – the Nassoons and the Tigertones. I was very high on Stan Rubin and his Tigertown Five, considering them the best college Dixieland band I'd ever heard. Although I did offer some criticism ("The biggest single abortion in the pop music racket is the 'Hit Parade' . . ."), I also praised performers I liked and still do, such as George Shearing, Stan Getz, Paul Desmond and Frank Sinatra,

One of my favorites was the Sauter-Finegan band, a melding of two fine arrangers for the Benny Goodman and Tommy Dorsey orchestras. "Extremely versatile," I wrote, with "a score of outstanding instrumentalists", and added that "they not only appeal to the listener; they are indeed highly danceable." What I didn't say was that I was the member of our Junior Prom Committee in charge of arranging for the music – and I selected the Sauter-Finegan band! They played up a storm for us, but it wasn't exactly dance music to squeeze your sweetie to – for which I did take a little heat from my colleagues.

I was proud of being a denizen of New York City and held nothing back from the naysayers hailing from other locales. So a recurring subject for me was informing Princetonians about what was going on in NYC over Thanksgiving or on other weekends for their occasional visits. In addition to my own stuff, I co-wrote on these subjects with my roommate John Doyle, and with two eventual Pulitzer Prize winners, Dick Kluger[*] and Bob Caro.

The other favorite subject to write about for the mostly-male readers was the female situation. My prime article was a long piece detailing an extended visit to Mt. Holyoke College in Massachusetts ("an ideal example of the modern, well-rounded, stimulating women's college"). Fred Bacher was the designated photographer for the piece; and although the old speedgraphic camera he'd hustled up for the trip held no film, it proved a great way to meet girls.

As a senior, I wrote a long piece in *The Tiger*, directed to freshmen, on how to handle the necessary safaris to find dates. *The Tiger* subtitled it, "A Famous Habitue of Eastern Girls' Colleges Tells You What to Expect – and How to Go About It."

I had something to say about the girls and the scenes at twenty colleges: Vassar, Smith, Mt. Holyoke, Sarah Lawrence, Bennett, Briarcliff, Bryn Mawr, Penn, Finch, Centenary, Trenton State Teachers, Douglass, Connecticut College, Manhattanville, Ladycliff, Marymount, Skidmore, Wellesley, Radcliffe and Bennington.

---

[*] I also co-authored a piece with Dick on cigarettes. Many years later, he received his Pulitzer for the book *Ashes to Ashes* on that very subject.

Another reporter referred to me in print as the "Ivy League Weekender editor and girls'-school-snow-job expert, Jim Freund," giving advice on "proper ploy tactics." * That's probably why in the Senior Poll I placed first as "Biggest Playboy" and third (behind my roommates Gatch and Bacher) as "Biggest Ambassador on the Eastern Seaboard." (More mysterious was the category – immediately following "Most Likely to Succeed," in which I didn't place – of "Most Likely To," where I came in second.)

My buddy Jack Veatch and I wrote a lengthy piece on the virtues (and shortcomings) of Princeton's venerable single wing offense. I wrote two short stories for *The Tiger*. One of them (re-read recently) was so bad that John Doyle's negative review was actually kind (". . . unfortunately [it] is burdened by a central intelligence in the form of an egotistical narrator with upper-class money and lower-class manners."). John and I remain close friends, and he's often tough on my current prose – a superb editor on whom I frequently rely.

In my final "Jazz, etc" column, I summed up its assets (e.g., "The many complimentary letters we have received from misanthropes, derelicts and the Yalie Daily") and liabilities (e.g. "The certainty that not one opinion has changed, not one action taken, not one tradition even barely shaken by anything gurgled in this space"). "Nevertheless," I concluded, "it has been fun" – and indeed it was.

* * *

What I remember most vividly about Princeton was that during junior and senior years, my buddies and I worked hard at cultivating a sort of "bad boy" image – trying to be "cool," and engaging in a lot of hi-jinks. It was as if we were determined to get all this stuff out of our system in a relatively safe place, before we had to face up to that sober, serious world "out there." In contrast to numerous forgotten happenings of those days, the anecdotes of our adventures have survived in my memory bank, revived

---

* One of my columns included some lyrical advice on what to look for in a girl that you might invite down to Princeton for Houseparties weekend: "Not short or tall, thin or obese / Just make sure she doesn't cease / If two quick drinks will make her pass / you better find another lass / A figure pert, a visage gay / and not an awful lot to say / Bermuda shorts and hair cut short / and make sure she's the friendly sort / Two eyes of blue, two lips divine / a puggish nose, you're doing fine / Tiny feet and a medium seat / she mustn't eat, she mustn't cheat / She should relate some racy jokes / her front can't prove to be a hoax / And gentle reader, if she's free / tell her to get a friend for me."

over the years in confabs with friends at reunions and other gatherings. In their own odd way, these are the things that made Princeton special to me, and thus they dominate this last section of my collegiate memories.

The fuel that often fired us up was alcohol – dime beers, scotch, gin, vodka. I don't recall us drinking much wine, and there was never even a whiff of pot or other drugs – so our principal source of illegality was that in most localities we were underage. We drank often and sometimes to excess, which loosened our scruples and incentivized our pranks.

Do the youths of today still engage in drinking games as we did back then? The two I remember best were "Wales, Tails" and "Thumper". A group of us would sit in a circle, directing queries back and forth at breakneck speed (and incessantly banging on the table in Thumper), with the loser required to chug his beer. This wasn't just a "guy" thing – several of our pluckier dates often joined us in these sessions.

Much of the action during senior year revolved around our quarters in Walker Hall – generally referred to as "The Rockefeller Suite." This was a much-prized choice of rooms which for years had been hogged by senior members of Charter Club, who had devised a system to beat the roomdraw lottery. But for some reason their system failed that year, and we were lucky enough in the lottery to latch on to the Suite.

The seniors from Charter were sore about this outcome, but reluctantly had to admit defeat. Soon after classes began, however, they came to the Suite to inform us of its "long-time tradition" – that the new occupants pay the outgoing group $1,000 for the used (and quite threadbare) furniture strewn around the Suite. We, of course, refused to do any such thing; they became angry, threatening to return late one night and trash our living room; we replied that we'd be lying in wait – and although we did post sentries for a few evenings, no further conflict ensued.

That wasn't the only time we flashed our tightwad nature. When Princeton beat Penn at Franklin Field thanks to a late touchdown run by sophomore tailback Tom Morris, we joined the wrecking crew on the field and came away with a four foot section of the wooden goalpost, which we displayed with pride over the Suite's fireplace. A few days later, Tom Morris (whom none of us knew) appeared at our door, saying (with the appropriate deference sophomores accord to seniors), "I hear you guys have a piece of the goalpost from the Penn game. I was really proud of scoring the winning touchdown – I wonder if you could break off a splinter of it for me." "Absolutely," we replied. "You can have a splinter, for – let's see – how about 25 bucks."

Poor Tom looked crestfallen – he obviously didn't have that kind of loose change. It still pains me to recall that we remained intransigent . . . . When I later became good friends with Tom in law school, I apologized effusively over the incident – for which he (sort of) forgave me.

The Suite was comprised of a large living room, bar area, and two bedrooms – one occupied by Fred Bacher, Bob Watson and yours truly, and the other by classmates John Doyle and Lew Gatch, plus junior Bill Tangney (included in our group so that the Suite would "stay in the family" to beat the next year's roomdraw). The living room and bar area had a rough-and-ready appearance that suited us perfectly.

The little-known secret that made the Suite special was contained above a trapdoor in the ceiling of a raised area just beyond the bar. When the trapdoor opened, a rope ladder dropped down to enable us to climb to an unlighted room containing several beds (I seem to remember them as double-decker). It was the ideal place for amenable women companions to hide after daylight hours (since to be caught by a proctor with a woman in the dorm after 7 p.m. in violation of the so-called parietal rules was a sure path to probation). As a bonus, there was another hatch above the secret room that led out to the open roof, where we partied on many a sunny spring day.

* * *

My roommate and almost constant companion those upper-class years was Fred Bacher. We were always tuned in to the same wavelength. For example, Fred and I were wont to proclaim (in flagrantly embellished terms) that of all the different dates we'd invited down to Princeton for home football games junior year, not one of them was speaking to us by Sunday! (If anyone from "#MeToo" is reading this, let me point out that I doubt we ever did anything that crossed over the line into sexual harassment; the bad feelings we admittedly generated were most often caused by too much attention to booze and not enough to our dates.)

Fred's mother and stepfather kept a yacht in Florida, which they allowed a group of us to claim for our holidays and spring breaks. We lived like kings, with a captain and crew to attend to all the boating stuff – good meals, plentiful booze, and a seemingly endless supply of women. We would leave the boat each morning to recruit girls on the beach for a yachting adventure, haul up anchor and head up the intercoastal waterway on a curfew-less excursion.

One of our most memorable land adventures occurred up the road from Princeton in New Brunswick. It was just prior to the opening week of the school year (so cars on campus were still legal), and a group of us – Fred Bacher and I in one car, three friends in the other – had gone to an open house at Douglass College. The gathering was uneventful, and we headed back in our cars to Princeton. Needing a bathroom break, we stopped in a New Brunswick residential area and urinated on the lawn of a darkened house.

Whoops! – out of nowhere a police car appeared. We quickly cut off the flow, and when asked by the cops what we were doing, replied "just stretching our legs". The cops, suspicious at having Princetonians invade New Brunswick turf, gave us some lip and angrily ordered our group to "get the hell out of here."

Fred and I went back to his car, an open convertible, while the other three piled into the second vehicle. I can't recall how drunk Fred and I might have been, but we were definitely aggrieved by the nasty attitude of the local police. And so, as we drove off, we shouted in unison an obscene oath unmistakably earmarked to the constabulatory.

I'll never forget the sound of the police car siren as they took off after us. The cops pulled over both our cars and then led our caravan to the courthouse/jail. Once there, the authorities took away our ties and belts (so we wouldn't hang ourselves) and threw us all into cells to pass the night before our appearance in court the next morning. We did negotiate for one of us – not Fred or me! – to be released, so he could round up money back on campus to pay our inevitable fines.

After a restless night in the bare little cells, we were summoned to the courtroom to stand before the bench. Fred and I stood to the far left – there was a clearly discernible gap between us and our three friends, who were undoubtedly furious over the mess we had created but politely declined to hurl accusations of blame our way.

I recall the judge querying each of the three about their college records and receiving a panoply of daunting achievements. "Well," said the judge to them, "You three have some outstanding credentials." Then, turning toward Fred and me, he said, "Should I infer that you two do *not* have comparable records?"

We gulped, expressed our contrition, and received a stern lecture from the judge, plus a fine we were able to cover through the contributions solicited overnight from friends back in Princeton. The judge's final words, clearly aimed at Fred and me, were along these lines: "Leave town and don't come back. If we catch you in New Brunswick again, I'm going to lock you up and throw away the key!" *

We left the courthouse. As Fred and I approached his car, we glanced at each other – our mutual expressions signifying an intent to scream out another dual curse on New Brunswick law enforcement. But the cooler segments of our heads quickly prevailed, and we got the hell out of town.

That was a good warm-up for a trip Fred and I took in his car up to Canada. It was a terrific journey – Montreal, the Laurentians, Quebec, and points between – but I'll just focus on one incident.

We picked up two local girls in Montreal and were riding around with them, trying to decide where to go and what to do. Then one of us had a bright idea. We had recently seen a Cold War spy movie in which an innocent woman was walking along a German street, when all of a sudden a car careened up on the sidewalk near her. The back door opened, hands reached out to yank the woman in, and the car roared off – a classic kidnap. Fred and I decided to act out the same scene.

We persuaded one of the girls to be "the victim," walking slowly along a sidewalk in a quiet part of town. Fred was driving, I was the snatcher in the back seat. He eased the car up onto the sidewalk and drew abreast of the girl. I opened the back door and reached out for her. But for some reason she decided to react in realistic fashion – struggling against being forced into the car. It took me the length of the whole block to get her inside and the door shut – so far down the sidewalk that Fred had to exit it at the next cross street. And there, waiting in a parked car, was a policeman.

---

* I stayed out of New Brunswick thereafter, except for one time recently when I was rendezvousing there with my two sons for an Atlantic City junket. Erik, who knew the college story, reminded me: "Hey Dad, I thought you weren't supposed to ever come back to New Brunswick." Notwithstanding the passage of six decades, I still slunk down low in the back seat until we hit the outskirts of town. By the way, I've lately heard tell of a recent court decision which held that cursing at cops is protected language under the First Amendment.

We tried to explain to him that this was just a prank, acting out a certain scene from a movie, but he wasn't buying it. The girls were released, but Fred and I were hauled in to the police station, where we were subjected to very hostile grilling by cops whose native language was French-Canadian.

It just so happened that this very week there was a slasher on the loose in Montreal, terrifying the city. He would get behind women boarding a bus and slash the back of their legs with a razor. The police – frustrated at their inability to solve these crimes amid growing criticism from the press and citizenry – speculated that Fred was the slasher (and I, presumably, the slasher's accomplice).

Since we were scheduled to be brought before the court the next morning, they decided to keep us imprisoned that night to avoid any further threat of slashing. It was clear to us that, as contrasted with the relatively benign New Brunswick jail we'd recently occupied, this big city lock-up was not a desirable place for a couple of apple-cheeked Princetonians to spend the night. But given the ambiguous situation and the language barrier, we were unable to convince the cops to set us free.

Then I had a brainstorm. My HM buddy Norm Namerow lived in Montreal, spoke serviceable French-Canadian, and had very practical adult instincts about such matters. We received permission to make one phone call, and fortunately were able to reach Norm. He came down to the station, spoke the language to the gendarmes, and must have done something else (Sweet-talk? Bribe? Take responsibility for us? – I can't recall) that persuaded them to let us out for the night.

The next morning we appeared in court, along with many others who'd been flagged for violations the previous day (although none for snatching a woman off the sidewalk into a car). Ominously, the local newspaper had reported that the slasher was still on the loose. After a few other defendants were sentenced by a stern-looking judge, the bailiff called out in a thick French accent, "Monsieur Baché." Fred Bacher (pronounced "Baker") didn't move. The bailiff repeated the call. "Hey," I nudged him, "that's probably you."

Fred walked up the aisle to the bench. He quickly ascertained that the charge against him had been reduced from slashing or kidnapping to just driving on the sidewalk. And the policeman who arrested us wasn't in court, so none of the specifics of our crime were brought before the judge.

Asked how he pleaded, Fred produced an instant masterstroke: "Guilty, with explanation." He went on to explain, in eminently logical terms, how he'd been trying to get out of a tight parking space, but the wheels had slipped on the icy pavement, and part of the car had somehow ended up on the sidewalk just as the policeman happened to come by . . . .

It worked – Fred received a stern warning but no fine. As he came back down the courtroom aisle, he recalls observing a lot of chortling from skeptical onlookers. But we were free men – and although outside the building we briefly contemplated another farewell shout at local law enforcement, we made a quick inventory of our financial status (barely enough money to buy gas for the trip home) and remained mute.

* * *

We enlarged our duo one night junior year. I was enrolled in a Politics course that included a field trip to Washington. That evening, after we had visited the pillars of government, I joined my friend Jack Kraus, a friend of his and that friend's friend, Bob Watson, for an evening out in D.C. I took an immediate liking to the friend's friend, who then cemented my positive feelings toward him by displaying a unique command of the forces of gravity. This involved an intricate stain-avoiding maneuver on the side of a low grassy knoll – what you might call prone hillside urination.

Fred Bacher had invited me and several other classmates down to spend the upcoming vacation on his stepfather's yacht in Florida. I remember returning to Princeton from Washington and telling Fred, "Hey, I met this great guy named Bob Watson." I then described his knoll feat, closing with, "He'd be a great guy to have along on the boat." Fred's prompt response was, "Invite him" – and thus was born a three-way friendship that has lasted and prospered for 65 years.

It's understating the matter to say that Fred, Wats and I were a little scruffy when we roomed together senior year. For example, each of us lacked a cleaning service. Most undergraduates received clean sheets for their beds every week; we had only the original sheets we started out with. But this didn't bother us – in fact, we turned it into a contest, doggedly competing to see who could retain the same unwashed sheets on the bed the longest. Although, truth be told, Wats and I considered Fred the favorite to prevail (his resolution in all things was mind-boggling), none of us budged as days turned into weeks, and weeks into months.

The three of us were in the room one day when Fred's girlfriend (and future wife) Claudine appeared in the doorway, took one look at Fred's bed, and in a decisive moment – underlined by her shout of "This is a disgrace!" – ripped the sheets off Fred's bed and dumped them into a garbage can.

The three of us were stunned – but I must confess that Wats and I were secretly pleased. It was clear that Fred would have to replace the sheets and forfeit his chance of winning the contest. But credit Fred with quickly regaining his footing. Rather than replace the sheets and lose the contest, he did the only thing that kept him a contender for the "longest no-change of sheets" honor – he proceeded to sleep thereafter on the bare moth-eaten mattress! Disgruntled by this turn of events, Watson and Freund were soon forced to concede victory to Bacher.

Remember that Penn weekend when we claimed a piece of the goalpost? After the game Saturday afternoon, we went to a Penn fraternity party where, as you might imagine, we were not especially welcome. As we left, one of the fratboys followed us out to the sidewalk and began taunting Watson, repeatedly flicking Bob's necktie with his finger. The insulting maneuver enraged Bob, who knocked the taunter out with a single blow to the chin. As the guy collapsed to the sidewalk, his head accidentally hit the curb. Several of his buddies crowded anxiously around his body, which appeared dead to the world. One of us cried, "Let's get the hell out of here," and we jumped in our car for the 50-mile drive back to Princeton.

Frankly, we were terrified that the curb might have caused permanent damage to the taunter. We woke early Sunday morning to get ahold of a Philadelphia paper, apprehensive that a recent student death might have been reported. None had, which enabled us to breath a little easier, although we knew we still weren't out of the woods.

Later that Sunday morning a classmate came up to our digs on the top floor to report a Bloody Mary party in progress on a lower level – "and you guys are invited." So Bob, Fred and I swung into action, descending the stairs to join the festivities.

Thirty seconds later, a scream erupted from one of the guests. He leapt to his feet, pointing a finger at Watson and yelling, "It's him! – he's the guy who decked me last night. I'm getting the hell out of here!" and he ran for the door. It was the same guy we had left for dead on the street in Philadelphia 15 hours ago! The coincidence was astounding, but we were relieved to see him still alive. And, of course, we stuck around for the Bloody Marys.

* * *

One of our close friends was Jack Veatch, a terrific guy who sadly passed away last year. His special forte was spinning wonderful tales of what transpired during our adventures. Jack was constantly broke, but we used to subsidize his expenses in order to bring him along on excursions – thereby not only insuring a lot of laughs along the way, but also the certainty that tales of our hijinks would receive Chaucerian explication among receptive groupings during the following week.

This was on my mind when I got an assignment to write a big article for the *Daily Princetonian* on the cream of eastern women's colleges. The plan was for me to interview girls on their campuses, while Fred posed as a photographer. But we needed Jack Veatch to join us for this trip – not only for the great fun he'd provide day by day, but later to tell uproarious embellished tales about the trip to our other buddies. Unfortunately, though, Jack declined to join us for this jaunt, claiming other obligations, imminent tests, no cash, etc.

We weren't about to take no for an answer. Fred's convertible car was on campus (authorized for the assignment), and we pulled it up outside Jack's dorm in the early morning, top down. We climbed the stairs to his second floor room, and – with Fred at his feet and me at his arms – yanked him out of bed, carried him down the stairs, and dumped him into the open car. We then drove out toward Route 1 with Jack protesting loudly in just his skivvies. He finally gave in, persuaded us to take him back to the room to pick up a shirt, pants, shoes and a toothbrush, and joined the team for one of the most uproarious weeks of our lives.

There was another episode involving Jack Veatch which contains a visual image that, after six decades, is still vivid in my mind. Jack had been dating a girl named Debby from Vassar but had not yet cemented the relationship. I also had my eye on her, a fact which Jack was aware of but we didn't discuss. One weekday morning when Fred's car was nearby, I called Debby, made an afternoon date with her for a picnic ("and bring along a girl for Fred"), and Bacher and I decamped for Vassar.

A short while later, I'm told, Jack came into Cannon Club and inquired as to my whereabouts. "Oh," said one of the guys, "he and Fred took off for Vassar." Jack frowned, and then suddenly a metaphorical light bulb switched on over his head. "Why, that sonofabitch Freund is heading up there after Debby!" Jack quickly enlisted another of our friends, Don MacElwee, who housed a convertible nearby. "Let's take off for Vassar, Mac – you can catch up to those guys."

Fred and I arrived at Vassar and proceeded down a long street, at the end of which was Debby's dorm. The two girls came down with blankets, thermos and food. As they were about to get into Fred's car, we heard a great roar from up the road. A quick look revealed – here's that lasting image – Don's open convertible barreling down the road toward us, with Jack standing up in his seat, shaking his fist angrily. "Uh, uh," I said to Fred. Jack arrived fuming, claimed his girl (thermos and all), while Fred and I slunk away to check out other prospects.

Another time Fred and I joined Don in his car going up to Vassar for the weekend. When Sunday came, Don said he had to get back to Princeton for a Monday test. Fred and I didn't want to leave and tried hard to persuade Don to stay, but he wasn't budging. We got in his car but continued abusing him for being a kill-joy. Half-way across the bridge leaving Poughkeepsie, Don stopped the car, glared at us, and said, "If you guys want to stay so much, then get the hell out." Which we did – right in the middle of the bridge, with no extra clothes, no money, no place to stay.

We wandered around that night, got into some trouble with the cops, finally ended up breaking into a room at the Vassar theatre where they keep the costumes and props for shows. I remember sleeping with a lion's head for a pillow . . . .

* * *

I'll close this section with one of my favorite stories, which also concludes with another visual image I find indelible. Wats had briefly dated a girl named Irene whom I considered quite lovely. When he moved on to other companions, I asked if he'd mind me asking Irene out. This was fine with him, so I invited her down for the final home football game of our senior year.

We were playing Dartmouth, and a win would give us the Ivy League title. Unfortunately, the game was played in a heavy snowstorm; and all my friends, including Lew Gatch and his date, decided to leave at halftime and return to the Suite for drinks. Irene, chilled to the bone in the stands, opted to go with them. I stayed in the harsh conditions of the stadium to root for the Tigers. Sure enough, after another hour or so, we won – the League title was ours.

When I got back to the Suite – agog over our victory – I looked for Irene, who wasn't immediately visible. Finally I spotted her in a dark corner of the room, nestling with my roommate Lew, whose own date was wandering around, unattended and miffed. I made a feeble effort to reclaim Irene but my absence had been long enough for Lew to flash his bird-dog charms, against which a blizzard-prone football fanatic didn't stand a chance. So I did the only decent thing left – I paired up with Lew's date who, although less fetching than Irene, turned out to be a good companion for the balance of the weekend.

When we exited the Suite, the various couples split up. I took Lew's date back to my club, Cannon, for food and drinks. We were getting along pretty well by then, and I hoped to pursue a little intimacy. But where to go?

Through the haze of too many drinks, I remembered that Wats and Gatch, both of whom belonged to Quadrangle Club next door to Cannon, had told me of a secret, dark, deserted room, deep in the bowels of their club, which contained a number of well-used couches suitable for our purposes. It seemed an opportune time to try out the locale, and I coaxed my new date into the adventure.

We crept down a back stairway in Quadrangle and, after groping around in the basement, located the room I had heard about. The door was unlocked. We entered into pitch-black space and stumbled forward until finally bumping into one of the couches. We sank down heavily, and I began to contemplate some serious action.

Then, from a distance across the inky room, I noticed the faint glow of a lighted cigarette, an image fit for a Hitchcock movie. Suddenly I knew . . . . "Lew, is that you?" I asked. "Yes," came the stiff reply, in a voice that I couldn't help interpreting as Lew silently admonishing his roommate along these lines: "This is my room, buddy; I told you about it; and even though I'm now with your girl, I think you should get the hell out of here." I probably could have stayed, but I had to give Lew credit for besting me twice in a single evening!

* * *

And that's the way it was for me at Princeton . . . . But where, you may ask, is the portion where Jim enumerates how he used those precious years to prepare for the decades to come? My honest answer is that during college I paid almost no attention to what I would be doing the rest of my life. After all, I told myself, "you've got three years to serve in the Navy –

x

you'll figure it out then – and maybe you'll even want to stay in the Navy!" So I ignored the issue of post-college preparation – feeling no down-the-road pressure, avoiding graduate school tests, not interviewing for any jobs. I had no idea what my future might look like, didn't bother thinking about it, and really enjoyed myself.

Still, these years were not wasted by any means. In addition to all the lifetime friends I made,* Princeton broadened my perspective, exposed me to a first-rate liberal education and served as a platform to hone my writing skills. I also experienced insightful moments that helped shape my future character and outlook, such as the debacle of the Alumni Weekly incident described in Chapter 1.

But that's enough about college. With the reality of graduation and the approach of my 21st birthday, it was time for me to venture out into the real world, which began with my three-year tour in the U.S. Navy.

---

* An expanded list of Princetonians I befriended, both during college and later as alumni, can be found in the Appendix.

Princeton University – Nassau Hall, the gate, and those tigers.

Our freshman class (I'm in there somewhere) and freshman football team (#33)

PRINCETON'S FRESHMAN FOOTBALL SQUAD

"The Gun" members of Cannon Club our senior year (I'm in the 5th row, far right).

Our graduating class, resplendent in their beer jackets, (I'm in there somewhere).

Graduatiom Day in 1956, with my parents, grandparents, and friends (Jack Veatch, Toby Wise, Fritz and Connie Hollenberg); and the day before in Ensign's uniform with Mom and Air Force 2nd Lt. Bob Watson.

The class of '56 at our 25th Reunion in 1981
(I'm in the 3rd row far left), spurred on by cheerleader Mac Francis,
and with my sons, a temporarily injured Erik (see text) and Tom.

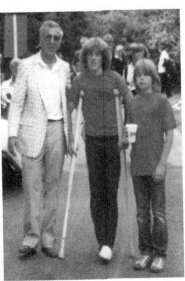

My boys at Cannon Club; with Barbara at Reunions; my good friends Dick and Phyllis Kluger; and Bacher, Veatch, Watson, Doyle and Freund, five-plus decades after graduation.

Below is the pitch I used when I ran for alumni trustee in 1981 and was elected by the alumni body.

I attend Alumni Day (below right) almost every year.

Our class has mini-reunions most years – this one (right) a few years ago in Richmond.

My trio (bottom right) entertaining at one of our class reunions.

James C. Freund '56

In addition to *Anatomy*, Freund has published a guide to attorneys on the practice of law, *Lawyering* (1979), as well as various articles on securities and corporate law. He has participated as chairman or speaker in numerous legal and business seminars, and this fall served as a special consultant to the Securities and Exchange Commission, proposing changes in SEC policy on negotiated corporate acquisitions.

The father of two boys, ages 15 and 12, Freund lives in New York City. He plays tennis and skis with his sons, but his principal relaxation is playing jazz and popular piano. He is a trustee and alumnus of the Horace Mann School.

A current member of the National Annual Giving Committee, Freund has served previously on the Executive Committee of the Alumni Council and from 1973 to 1976 on the Committee to Nominate Alumni Trustees which he chaired his final year. He was Secretary of the Class of 1956 from 1971 to 1976. For the past five years, he has been President of the Class of 1956, which is celebrating its 25th Reunion this June. "I keep asking myself: Where did all those years go? But the 25th represents a wonderful coming together, a unique opportunity to relive the past and refresh the present."

With regard to his nomination for trustee, Freund notes that his particular area of law is "geared to problem-solving, to communicating clearly, to negotiating—not just to get a leg up but to resolve apparent discord—and to the exercise of judgment. I like to think that these skills are transferable to the context of a board of trustees. The university is managed by a dedicated and innovative administration, but the Board's function remains central: to shape basic policy, by achieving a consensus of sound opinion; and to act as a check, through asking the probing questions, monitoring cost effectiveness, and offering constructive criticism where warranted. That's what Princeton trained us for in the first place—as so often, we come full circle—and the best old place of all deserves no less."

"It is one of the rare legal texts that can be read as a novel," a reviewer said of James C. Freund's *Anatomy of a Merger* when it appeared in 1975. Now in its fifth printing, *Anatomy* distills Freund's experience as a partner specializing in corporate mergers and acquisitions in the New York law firm of Skadden, Arps, Slate, Meagher and Flom. Focusing on the bargaining dynamics between seller and purchaser, the work leads legal practitioners through the tactics and techniques of negotiation.

Freund honed his writing skills on the *Daily Princetonian* and *Tiger* magazine. A history major, he earned letters in freshman football and baseball and worked on the Memorial Fund and Junior Prom Committees. After graduation, he served for three years in the U.S. Navy before entering Harvard Law School. He received his J.D. in 1962 and spent several years with another New York law firm before joining Skadden Arps in 1966.

Freund sees a close connection between his daily work at Skadden Arps and his undergraduate education. "Princeton challenged us to think for ourselves," he said recently, "to develop inquisitive minds, to reject superficial answers to tough questions. Unfortunately, this good academic training was often dissipated in an outside world which emphasizes conformity and the pressures of hierarchical life.

"I was lucky enough to escape this fate," he continues. "I'm no apologist for lawyers—a profession to which sham and mediocrity are no strangers. But the kind of fast-paced, think-on-your-feet, get-the-deal-done legal practice at Skadden Arps has taught me anew the value of close and independent scrutiny."

7. THE NAVY (1956-1959)

Maybe it's because nowadays I get a warm frisson hearing *Anchors Aweigh* being played, but whatever the reason, the time has come for me to re-evaluate my service in the United States Navy – an interlude that I've consistently ranked close to the nadir of my lifetime experiences.

Sure, the tedium of daily life, the restraints on free movement, my vexation with an unsavory superior, still rankle. But as I reconnected with the distant past, aided by some late '50s prose and photos, memories of my Navy days came flooding back. And what I found was that the special incidents from those three years – some scary, others funny, a few unique – remain more sharply etched in my mind than those from other pursuits, both before or after. The lessons I absorbed – albeit not always consciously at the time – served me well in the years ahead. And the Navy was the birthplace of my eventual choice of career. Sadly, though, my good friends from those days are no longer around to share my recollections – so I'll share them with you.

* * *

First, some background. It's the winter of 1951-1952, my senior year in high school, and I'm in the middle of the college application process. I'd done well at Horace Mann School, and pretty much had my pick of institutions.

As noted in Chapter 6, the college that appealed to me most was Amherst. Its bucolic setting in the rolling hills of Massachusetts promised to be a delightful shift from my citified upbringing; the enrollment was small enough that I wouldn't feel lost; its neighbors were the eminent all-girl colleges Mount Holyoke and Smith (not an insignificant factor for a guy hailing from an all-male high school); and my football coach, who knew Amherst's football coach, had sent him a fulsome letter of recommendation for his prize halfback.

In late 1951, the Korean War was on everyone's mind. With the military draft in full swing, the fear spread that the Army might draft those without deferments right out of college. The idea of fighting in a land war against Communist Chinese hordes near the Yalu River didn't appeal to me; whatever patriotic fires might still have burned within from my World War

114

II adolescence were banked for this savage and unpopular military engagement.*

The classic college deferment tactic was enrolling in the ROTC. It meant a period of mandatory service as an officer after graduation, but that wasn't so daunting because otherwise we were almost certain to be drafted after college. The remaining question was which branch of service to join.

In terms of the Korean War, there was no comparison for a non-heroic guy like me – the Navy won hands down. Far from freezing your butt off in the frigid hills north of the 38th parallel with the Army or Marines, or joining the Air Force and braving MIG's and murderous anti-aircraft fire while going after the bridges of Toko-Ri, the popular view was that sailors ate heartily at clean mess tables and slept in warm bunks before lobbing a few unopposed shells in the direction of Inchon harbor.

The Navy also had a special NROTC scholarship program called the Holloway Plan. If you were fortunate enough to be selected, the Navy covered your entire college tuition, bought your books, and paid you $50 per month toward living expenses – all of which, at the time, seemed a meaningful stipend. My family wasn't wealthy, and the expense of sending me to a good college was going to be a stretch for them. Although neither my father nor mother ever pushed me in that direction, I felt that getting an NROTC scholarship would be my thank-you to them for their 18 prior years of solid backing.

I applied for the Holloway Plan and was accepted, subject to a physical exam scheduled for the following week. This led, however, to a personal crisis which is still fresh in my memory.

The Horace Mann basketball team was in a tight race for the league title, and I was a starting guard – not a star, but part of the successful team fabric. The date for the physical exam coincided with the day we played Adelphi, one of our toughest foes. I don't think our coach went so far as telling me to forget about the Navy physical, but he certainly made me aware of his displeasure over my prospective absence.

---

* I should note that the male line in my family has managed, through the accident of birthdates, to avoid bearing arms in any global conflict. My grandfather was too old for World War I; my father was too young for WWI and too old for WWII; I was too young for Korea and too old for Vietnam; and my sons were too young for Vietnam and too old for Iraq and Afghanistan.

I had to make a tough decision. I seriously considered not showing up for the physical, but I didn't want to lose the scholarship. So, in my usual style, I tried to cram everything in – praying I could complete the physical in time for me to make it to the game, which was being played at Adelphi's home court in an outer borough.

But the exam dragged on interminably; and by the time I arrived at the Adelphi gym, the game was already underway, with Horace Mann behind by seven points. As I burst into the arena in my street clothes, some of our fans recognized me and cheered my arrival. It was a heady moment for yours truly – Freund to the rescue! I located the locker room, changed quickly, and took a seat on the bench.

The timing was ideal, I thought, to insert me into the game – providing an emotional lift for our beleaguered team. But the coach – perhaps out of pique, maybe to teach a life lesson to his young charges – refused to acknowledge my presence. Even with some fans chanting, "Put Freund in!" he sat there impassively, continuing to use substitutes at my position for the rest of the game. We ended up losing. Even though we ultimately managed to win the league championship, it was a bleak day in my young life – a mixture of anger at the coach and guilt for showing up late.

I did pass the physical and was accepted into the Holloway program. That was good news, but with one hitch. To take advantage of it, you had to attend a college with a Naval ROTC program. Amherst – situated far from deep blue water – had none. So, although my heart was still in the Berkshires, my head said, "Take the scholarship and settle for a second choice." And that's how I came to choose Princeton (as further explained in Chapter 6), which turned into a lifelong love affair for me, as to which there was but one notable exception – the NROTC.

* * *

I have often been heard to complain about the fact that 20 percent of my education at this prestigious Ivy League institution consisted of courses on gunnery, marine engines, seamanship and the like. And even courses that might have been informative – like World Naval History – were taught by officers with minimal pedagogic skills.

I can still picture the officer who taught that particular course, standing at a lectern, reading from his syllabus, and asking the class – a puzzled look on his face – "Did the Greeks have a Navy?" Since there was no immediate response – we were all comatose – he answered the query himself, in a suddenly loud, definitive and enthusiastic tone, as if he were discovering this fact along with us: "Yes, the Greeks had a Navy!"

But in reviewing a first draft of this section, John Doyle, one of my college roommates and a superb editor of prose, opened my eyes to reconsidering the scorn I had long heaped on my NROTC college experience. He pointed out, among other things, that I must have realized I'd be required to take these courses under the scholarship. He was right, of course, and the difficulties of integrating two such disparate programs was simply one consequence of accepting the benefits of the Navy's helpful grant.

I must say, though, that it grated on us when the commissioned officers teaching the NROTC courses did not abide by Princeton's venerable honor system. At exam time in every other course, the professor would hand out the test to students and then disappear from the classroom until time was up, at which point he returned to collect the booklets. We took pride in the trust the University displayed toward us and never even considered cheating. But in Naval Science courses, the officers paced resolutely up and down the aisle throughout the duration of the exam, eyes peeled for possible violations.

In addition to cursing the early morning hours of the NROTC classes (often 7:40 am), I really deplored the drilling. For some reason, I just couldn't master the rhythm and cadence in marching and other training exercises. My unwashed, unpressed uniform did nothing to ameliorate the negative impression I made on the officers. In my fourth year – when every senior was given some position of authority in the NROTC hierarchy – I received the lowest possible command rung, squad leader. Then, within a matter of weeks that amply demonstrated my drilling incompetence, I was ignominiously demoted and returned into the ranks, replaced by a more martial junior classman. Oh, the shame of it . . . .

Each summer during college, the Holloway midshipmen were obliged to serve with the regular Navy in its various activities. For the first and third summers, we took two-month shipboard cruises, while the second summer was split – three weeks at Little Creek, Virginia for Marine training and three weeks in Corpus Christi, Texas at a Naval Air station.

On those cruises – my first on a light cruiser, USS Worcester;[*] the second on a battleship, USS Wisconsin – shipboard life was unpalatable. We were the lowest of the low – even the rawest seaman apprentice could give us orders. So we swabbed the decks and performed other dreary tasks. I think I developed my long-time vulnerability to claustrophobia from being shut up in a congested engine room for a sustained period.

There was one silver lining to the cruises for which I give the Navy credit. They introduced me to Europe, which I'd never previously visited. We made port in Norway, Denmark, and Scotland.

I remember taking ill as we approached Edinburgh. Rather than turning myself into sickbay and risk being prevented from leaving the ship, I was determined to take advantage of the liberty provided. Although suffering from chills and light-headedness, I boarded a train by myself to London, a city I wanted to see above all others. I wandered around there for a sickly day or two, then headed back to Edinburgh for a quickie Scots tour before finally seeking treatment on board.

My favorite stop was Copenhagen – a buoyant city featuring Tivoli Gardens, the colorful waterfront, friendly people, and beautiful girls. But at the outset of our visit, my buddies and I ran into an unexpected obstacle in our hot pursuit of female companionship.

We were required to wear into town our white sailor suits and those round sailor caps – except that for us midshipmen, there was a black rim around the white caps. As we attempted to pick up girls the first day, we were met with negative reactions from several likely candidates. It took a few inquiries to discover the reason – the ship's regular seamen had been spreading a rumor that the sailors with the black rims had the clap!

One of my most enduring memories of Copenhagen is now almost too scary to recall. After we managed to controvert the clap rumor, my new buddy from UCLA (Charlie Fried) and I got involved with two lovely Danish girls. We had a super time for several joyous days that included consuming a lot of aquavit. On our last night, as the curfew hour neared to return to the ship (which was scheduled to set sail after midnight),

---

[*] How's this for a coincidence – it turns out that Ed Schiff, one of my good friends in recent decades, was serving as an officer on the Worcester that same summer.

I adamantly refused to get out of my girl's bed. "I don't want to go back on that damn ship!" I shouted at Charlie, as he tried without success to coax my drunken self into leaving.

Well, thankfully he persevered and was able to load me into a taxi. We reached the ship just before they pulled up the gangway. I hate to think of what would have befallen me if I'd gone AWOL that night – I'd probably still be in Portsmouth Naval Prison today!

As for that second summer, my dominant memory of Corpus Christi, Texas was flying very low over the Gulf of Mexico in the back seat of a two-man trainer, wearing one of those tight-fitting leather helmets from World War II, pushing back the plastic cowling to let the wind hit my face, and praying I wouldn't be called upon to do anything that might adversely affect the plane's minimal altitude.

The Marine training at Little Creek, VA was really tough – stuff like crawling on our bellies across a muddy field, while what appeared to be live ammo was being fired just above our heads, plus a lot of running, climbing, jumping, and carrying heavy packs in extremely hot weather.

The worst moment for me came when, laden down with heavy backpacks, we were jammed into a small landing craft, as part of a simulated assault on an enemy-held island. Our boat's engine proved faulty, so we were forced to return to the troop ship, which (with the troops now off) sat very high out of the water. The crew lowered a flexible Jacob's Ladder down from the stern to our boat, and we were directed to climb up its narrow rungs to the deck of the ship.

I was unused to such heroics. Weighed down by the heavy pack, I froze during the climb and just couldn't seem to make it. I contemplated letting myself fall into the water to be rescued, but I was afraid I might land on the hard metal of the boat itself. I begged a crewman up on the ship's stern to give me a hand, but he refused. I finally mustered my last ounce of energy to make it all the way up, collapsing in exhaustion on the deck.

It's now over six decades ago, and I still can't get that panicky memory out of my head . . . .

* * *

I have a theory (but no hard evidence) about how I got assigned to the ship on which I would be spending the next three years after my Princeton idyll.

119

Other than in NROTC, I had done well in college. But my marks in Naval Science subjects like artillery were mediocre; my uniform was scroungy enough to cost me periodic demerits; no one confused me with John Paul Jones onboard ship during the summer cruises; and I couldn't march worth a damn.

During senior year, the Navy solicited our views as to what type of sea duty we preferred for the three years of service that lay ahead. A battleship? A destroyer? Truth be told, I didn't want to be on any ship at all. Was there any kind of vessel I could tolerate? My eyes scanned the list of possibilities. And then I had an inspiration: how about a hospital ship, complete with female nurses! I checked the applicable box.

In case they were unable to accommodate your specific choice of vessel, the Navy also asked you to indicate the category of ships it fell into, to insure at least partial fulfillment of your desires. A battleship, for example, was a "Large Combatant"; a destroyer a "Small Combatant." A hospital ship was an "Auxiliary," so that was the category I checked.

I've often fantasized about the scene at the Navy's Bureau of Personnel in Washington when they received my papers. I can just hear the guy reviewing my application chirping to his colleague, "Hey, Harry, listen to this. One of those lightweight Princeton boys, with the lowest Naval aptitude in the entire class, and a disheveled uniform to boot, is asking for a hospital ship – to get near the nurses, I'll bet! . . . . Let's see what other kind of auxiliary we can put this bozo on – one where females aren't even close to being available. . . ."

I will never forget the day we received our orders to active duty. Every NROTC senior on campus was excited about his assignment. "Hey, it's the battleship Wisconsin for me!" "Look, I'm on a can in the Med!" My orders, however, left me puzzled. I was assigned to a ship called the USS Staten Island AGB-5. I had no idea what an AGB was – except I knew instinctively that it was not a hospital ship. Based on the name of the vessel, it could have been a local ferry – although I duly noted that its home port wasn't in New York City but across the continent in Seattle.

No one could figure out what kind of ship I'd been assigned to, so a group of us sought out the crusty veteran Chief Petty Officer who'd been in the Navy forever and had seen just about everything. "What is it, Chief?" I asked – "What's an AGB? What kind of ship am I on?" A look of absolute glee appeared on the Chief's face as he contemplated the orders received by his least-favorite midshipman. "Get this, boys," he said to our group, his rotund body bouncing in merriment. "Lady-killer Freund here has been assigned to a goddamn icebreaker! I bet he won't be getting much ass at the South Pole!"

And that's how I ended up for three years on the USS Staten Island AGB-5.

* * *

Back in those days, Navy icebreakers were called upon to do just what the name implies – break through the pack ice to reach a blocked destination. In our case, the goals were usually to deliver supplies and such to one of the American bases in the Arctic and Antarctic, often shepherding in a much larger cargo ship that wasn't able to transit the ice by itself. For reasons I'm not privy to, there are no Navy icebreakers on duty today.

Our ship resembled a squashed destroyer – shorter in length, wider in width. It had virtually no keel, which made it susceptible to pronounced oscillations even in not-so-rough water. We liked to say, "It rolls in wet grass." And when the sea did get rough, we often experienced alarming, seasick-causing gyrations.

The ship broke the ice by amping its diesel engines to full throttle and riding up onto the floes, breaking a pathway through the ice by the sheer weight and thrust of the icebreaker's bow. The ship also had a small flight deck accommodating two helicopters, which were used to fly ahead and scout optimum routes for us to follow through the ice. It had a complement of 250-plus officers and enlisted men.

The Staten Island had been launched during World War II and promptly turned over to the Russians for their use in Siberian and other far-north waters. It was returned by the Russians in the late '40s, apparently in terrible shape; some sailors who were in the original post-Russian crew still served on the ship in 1956 when I came aboard.

Our home port was Seattle, berthed at Pier 91 on Puget Sound. Seattle was a pleasant enough place but nowhere near the sophisticated urban metropolis it has become today. There was an excess of rain and the fog could be daunting. I remember once driving my car with the door ajar, so I could peer out to locate the white centerline of the road.

Most of the time we were at sea on five lengthy cruises – two to the Arctic, two to the Antarctic, and one towing four overage destroyers out to Eniwetok Atoll for use in the nuclear testing that took place there in the late '50s.

I was an Ensign for half my three-year term and a Lieutenant (junior grade) for the balance. I served as communications officer, navigator, and the officer in charge of the Operations Division, plus handling a number of collateral duties. When we were at sea, I stood four-hour watches twice a day as officer of the deck, in temporary command of the ship's movement and well-being.

I made some good friends among my fellow officers – many of whom came from states that weren't near New York and had attended colleges I knew little about, thereby broadening my geographic horizons. Three of those friendships – with Jim Messing, Noel Peacock and Jack Taylor – endured beyond our time together on the ship, although sadly all three shipmates have now passed on.

Serving as an officer on the ship was my first opportunity to manage other people, particularly during my final posting as head of the 50-odd sailors in the Operations Division. I found myself working with warrant officers and chief petty officers who were older and much more knowledgeable about naval matters than I, with kids just out of high school, and with others who were more senior but not necessarily wiser. As I look back now, this was a valuable experience for me to have, even if it didn't register at the time.

On a practical basis, I learned about such subjects as seamanship, navigation, radar, sonar, and telecommunications. This was also my first real introduction to photography, as one of my collateral duties was Photography Officer. The first class petty officer who was the ship's photographer provided some useful instruction in picture-taking and darkroom procedures, and I often hung around the photo lab – especially when I wasn't anxious to be located by the Captain or Executive Officer.

On Arctic cruises, which lasted several months during the summer, we traveled up and around northern Alaska to resupply the DEW-line outposts that stretched across Alaska from Point Barrow into Canada. These bases were a Cold War tripline to give early warning of a Soviet aircraft or missile attack on the U.S. We never got off the ship on these missions, except once for a half-day visit to Nome – not exactly a sparkling treat.

We departed Seattle for the first of my Arctic cruises within weeks after I arrived at the ship. I hoped it would be a fascinating experience, but it fell short of that. I do recall seeing a few polar bears, seals, and possibly a walrus on ice floes as we muscled through the icepack; but the scenery consisted mostly of ice or tundra, the sun rarely made an appearance, and stars were non-existent. The whole operation never got my senses stirring.

A new Captain of the ship had just taken over the helm. (Let's call him by his nickname among the crew, "Jumbo.") The more experienced officers spent a lot of time trying to figure Jumbo out, but I was too far down the executive ladder to have much direct contact with him. I did sense from our minimal encounters that he held me in low regard – "one of those pampered Ivy League kids they sometimes send us," he was probably thinking. I reciprocated by being on the lookout for Captain Queeg-like tendencies in him – shades of *The Caine Mutiny*, a favored fiction of the day.

Upon our return from Alaska, we had a few months in Seattle to prepare for the longer journey to the Antarctic. I invited one of my college girlfriends, Louise, to join me for this period ashore. We settled into a comfortable one-month rental apartment in town. But I wasn't prepared for how this would be viewed by the wives of the ship's married officers.

There was a lot of socializing among the officers and their wives/girlfriends when the ship was in Seattle, but the ostracism Louise and I encountered six decades ago caught me by surprise. (An exception to this were the Messings – Jim, having completed his Navy tour and taken a job at Boeing, and his lovely wife Ellen with whom I'm still friendly today.) Most of the wives were so aghast at our breach of mid-'50's decorum – two unmarried adults shacking up – that they refused to socialize with us; and their husbands just shrugged and went along with them.

* * *

The highlights (and low points) of my naval experience were two Antarctic voyages of five to six months each. They featured alluring scenery, some sunny days (albeit cold as hell) and no nights, a lot of penguins, and several interesting cities we visited on the way down and back. Most of my enduring Navy memories stem from these two cruises.

We were part of something called Operation Deep Freeze. Its goal was to complete building sturdy bases around the Antarctic continent that would be used by scientists during the International Geophysical Year

1957-58 and subsequent periods. Our presence down there came in the Antarctic summer (North America's winter), but the bases would be manned throughout the cold and dark Antarctic winter, when there was minimal contact with the outside world.

For the first cruise in 1956-57, we were part of a 3,500-man contingent in twelve ships, plus air support. The Staten Island's particular mission was to enable a base to be built from scratch in the Antarctic's most treacherous and remote oceanic area, the Weddell Sea. That's where Ernest Shackleton suffered his disastrous adventure many years earlier – his ship broken up in the grip of the ice, the great man leading his crew on a memorable escape journey on foot, as related in *Endurance*. It was known as the "hellhole of the Antarctic," and information about it was scanty. Our task was to lead into that hellhole the USS Wyandot – a cargo ship that had crammed into her holds 5,600 tons of the material and equipment to build and stock the base.

On the way down, after a brief stop in San Diego to pick up our helicopters and their crews and gear, we visited Panama and Valparaiso, Chile – enjoyable stops, although not providing me with any strong memories.

We then traversed the famed inland waterway to reach one of the world's southernmost outposts, the Chilean town of Punta Arenas at the tip of South America. After a brief stopover there, we took off for the Antarctic.

Most of that latter voyage was through heavy ice-cold seas whipped into a frenzy by severe wind gusts. Our no-keel design wasn't made for such conditions, and life became decidedly uncomfortable. At meals, we had to strap ourselves into seats at the wardroom table, snagging bites of food from gyrating individual trays. I can recall playing a pump organ in the crew's mess hall for a church service one Sunday morning with the ship rocking like crazy; fittingly, each stanza of the chosen hymn seeking God's protection ended with the words, "For those in peril on the sea."

But my moment of real terror occurred after we'd maneuvered through a heavy concentration of icebergs and were in relatively calm waters just outside the extremity of the sprawling ice pack.

Atmospheric conditions were clear that day, and the pilots of our two helicopters decided to test the equipment. The junior pilot (let's call him Bob) asked me if I'd like a ride – something I had never experienced. I said "Sure," and the next thing I knew we were airborne and flying over the ocean at a considerable distance from the ship, with no ice in sight.

That's when it happened. A strange loud noise came from the equipment, and a few seconds later, Bob mouthed the most chilling sounds I'd ever heard emanate from human lips: "Uh, oh . . .". I looked over his way and saw a man in a clear state of panic – wide-eyed, punching gauges, twirling knobs. The helicopter began to lose altitude.

I was wearing a life preserver but knew damn well that the human body would last about two minutes in those ice-cold seas. All I could do was silently wail, "Why the hell did I accept Bob's invite?!"

To my great distress, Bob seemed thwarted in his attempts to even diagnose the problem, let alone correct it. I, of course, could be of no help.

Finally Bob had the good sense to make radio contact with the senior pilot (let's call him "Joe") in the other helicopter. Bob bewailed his predicament in a frightened, excitable voice, using technical terms I couldn't understand. I don't remember ever enduring more terrifying moments.

Then Joe's voice came into our cockpit, cool and composed, asking a few pertinent questions, then instructing Bob on what steps he should take. Bob complied and, almost miraculously, the helicopter stopped losing altitude and resumed flying as usual. Whew!

P.S. I didn't ask Bob what had gone wrong, and he clearly didn't want to talk about it with me. Although the crisis didn't last long (yet seemed to be an eternity), it was very scary . . . .

Lesson learned: I never again ventured up in a Navy helicopter. Broader life lesson: be wary of volunteering for activities that have a possible risky downside.

It was probably just as well that this was my airborne swan song because later in the voyage one of our helicopters crashed on the flight deck while taking off. Although no one was injured, the wrecked craft (minus some salvageable parts) was pushed over the side to a final resting place on the ice, dubbed by the crew, "Helicopter Hill."

Before we departed Seattle, I bought one of the first Wurlitzer electronic pianos ever produced, which was put to good use on Christmas Eve. At the time, we were beset in thick ice. The hull of the cargo ship had been smashed, causing water damage and lost fuel, and several tips had broken off her propeller blades. To raise spirits, we carried my piano up to the flight deck, where a good segment of the crew had assembled; and I played familiar carols for them to sing. It was so cold that between carols I had to plunge my hands into the parka pockets to keep them limber enough to play the next one. A night to remember . . . .

Here's the text of a radiogram message I recently found, that I sent my parents the next day: "Shepherds saw star Santa sleighed south and ship snow sobriety seldom smother seasonal spirit Merry Christmas."

* * *

Until this recent re-evaluation of my naval service, I usually backdated the villain's role played by the first Captain to our earliest contacts. But though I've racked my memory, I haven't come up with any specifics to plead mistreatment during my initial half-year under Jumbo.

As a matter of fact, my first encounter of note with the Captain didn't occur until several weeks after the caroling session; and although it was one of the worst moments in my naval career, this clash with Jumbo was totally my own fault.

It was early in January, and the two ships had again become beset. We were frozen in the ice about a thousand yards apart, with the intense ice pressure preventing the Staten Island from getting any closer to the cargo ship. But we needed to do so, because the ice was gashing in the Wyandot's hull – damage that might well be ameliorated if we could get alongside.

That stalemate went on for days, and things grew increasingly tense. This was, after all, Shackleton territory. There was no way to rescue us if we couldn't make it out on our own, especially once the Antarctic winter began.

The duty officers still stood regular four-hour watches on the bridge every day and night, but with the ship stuck in the ice, there was little to do. One evening when I had the watch, I avoided the frigid temperatures on the open bridges outside the wheelhouse and plunked myself down indoors in the "Captain's chair," immersed in trying to memorize a favorite poem, Matthew Arnold's *Dover Beach*.

As usual, a movie was being shown in the wardroom that evening. When it ended, the Captain, as was his habit, came up to the bridge for a brief visit before retiring to his cabin for the night. Anticipating his arrival, I mouthed a final ". . . on a darkling plain," stashed the poetry book, stood up from his chair, and saluted as Jumbo entered the wheelhouse. After mumbling a few words, he went out onto the open wing of the ship's bridge to survey our static situation.

"Freund!" came his sudden shout, "Get the hell out here!" I did, took a look around, and couldn't believe my eyes. The pack ice that had held the ship so tightly in its grip for a week – so tight that it actually lifted the ship out of the water several feet – had abruptly eased off. Blue water was visible alongside the ship, and the outline of a narrow channel appeared between us and the Wyandot.

"When did this happen?!" Jumbo roared at me. I was speechless – I hadn't gone outside to take a look for at least an hour.

The Captain then turned his attention from me to the ship. He was all business – ordering the engines made ready to get underway, setting an operational watch of the crew, signaling the Wyandot that we were on our way, etc. But alas, it was to no avail. As swiftly as the ice pressure had eased, it quickly returned; and before we could even get underway, we were once again locked in tight.

Although it was never clear whether or not, had I sounded an earlier alarm, we would have been able to reach the Wyandot before the ice pressure resumed, the Captain was furious at me for my dereliction of duty – and rightly so. My relations with Jumbo now went from mediocre to much worse. To him, I was just a preppy Princetonian, not fit to serve our country.

The sole redeeming feature of this sorry episode is the *lesson I learned*: Never assume a damn thing! Don't take anything for granted – including, but not limited to, the consistency of pack ice pressure. You can never tell what's around the corner. Just when you think you're so damn smart – so full of yourself and the facile assumptions you make, the shrewd inferences you draw – life throws you a helluva curve ball. This became a byword for me in both my legal career and personal life, serving me well and often through the years.

Finally, after eleven days frozen in place near the Wyandot, the ice pressure mysteriously eased. It had something to do with tides or currents, but the mystery was never resolved. We gained enough leeway to reach the

Wyandot and lead her out of the pack. The ice remained heavy – so tough to get through that we broke a blade on one of our propellers – but we finally located a section of the ice shelf extending from the coast that would permit offloading.

The Staten Island now acted like a bulldozer, using its prow to trim the ice shelf and knocking away rough edges so as to fashion an unloading pier. Then all of us on both ships worked around the clock to get the base built and up-and-running. Ellsworth Station came into being in just 12 days, after which we set off for home. It was quite an achievement – even my cynical self back then had to admit that we'd accomplished something worthwhile.

Incomprehensible as it now seems, I might not have been aboard the Staten Island for the trip back. A few days before we departed the Weddell Sea, word was passed that they needed an officer from one of the ships to volunteer to "winter over" at the base. As distasteful as the idea was of spending a whole winter at 50-plus degrees below zero in an isolated hut, I seriously considered volunteering. That's how bad life with the Captain had become for me after my screw-up on the evening watch. I'm sure Jumbo would have been only too happy to grant me permission to volunteer . . . . At any rate, sanity finally won out – maybe I was following the be-wary-of-volunteering lesson I'd absorbed from the helicopter incident – and not without some regret, I turned down the proposal.

Our first stop on the way home was again Punta Arenas. There was no opportunity to go ashore, but a British naval ship in the harbor sent a message inviting the Staten Island officers to lunch. I was one of those who took them up on the overture.

Unlike the sparse trappings of U.S. Navy ships, the wardroom area of the British vessel had the look of a well-appointed living room on a passenger vessel, including a plush carpet covering the deck. Another big difference was that on British naval ships, unlike those in the abstemious U.S. Navy, they served hard liquor.

I hadn't tasted anything alcoholic for months – since our stop in Chile on the way down. The scotch that was offered came neat – no rocks, soda or water. I gulped the first one down. Then another. And then – shortly after knocking down my third – I threw up all over the plush carpet!

The Brits were solicitous, but I'm sure they got a big chuckle out of it. For me, though, it was quite embarrassing – although not as bad as when I was brought back to the Staten Island in a close-to-comatose state, and virtually carried aboard the ship, to the delight of a full crew of sailor onlookers.

Lesson learned: stick to a two-drink limit where plush carpeting is involved.

After departing Punta Arenas, we stopped at Talcahuano, Chile, where a shipyard repaired our broken propeller. Talcahuano was the port for the small city of Concepcion, and many of us ventured downtown nightly during our stay. The only places of entertainment to visit were the whorehouses, and I have a distinct memory of playing the piano at Concepcion's finest– shades of Scott Joplin!

* * *

We later visited Callao, Peru (the port for Lima), and I had the chance to do some enjoyable sightseeing. Then came the long trip back to Seattle. Somewhere near the equator I shaved off the beard I'd acquired in the Antarctic – the heat emanating from our polar-insulated quarters made that shaggy adornment itchy and unbearable.

The voyage home was dull except for one unforgettable occurrence. Each year, the Navy holds several simultaneous fleet-wide exams that serve as a pre-requisite for sailors to advance to the next higher rating. The 1957 date for this occurred while we were at sea, but we had received the necessary testing materials and were all set to administer the exam.

I was on our ship's testing committee which was headed up by my friend, a veteran officer I'll call Phil. When I heard that the exams were scheduled to be given the next day, I contacted Phil and volunteered to help him supervise the exercise.

"No need," he said, "I'll handle it."

"Don't be silly," I replied. "I'm happy to pitch in."

"Jim," he said, his tone ominous, "you don't want to be involved in this."

His comment was mysterious, so I decided to show up the next day anyway to help monitor the tests. Phil shook his head sadly when I appeared, but didn't order me to leave.

The exams took place in the mess hall. Those being tested were seated at the long rectangular tables that filled the room. Standing around the perimeter of the mess hall were a number of chiefs and first class petty officers, representing each of the operational departments on the ship.

Once the tests began, every minute or so one of the exam-takers would signal by hand for a certain chief or first class to come over to his seat. The testee would then point to the question being asked, the chief or first class would supply the correct answer, and the testee would so mark it on the answer sheet.

I couldn't believe my eyes. I went over to Phil who, when he saw me approach, wouldn't meet my gaze.

"What in hell's going on here, Phil?" I asked, clearly agitated.

"Captain's orders," Phil replied. "As Jumbo put it to me, 'In recognition of the fine job the men did on the cruise, I want each of them to do as well as possible on the exam'."

That evening, I sat with Phil in his stateroom, contemplating our fate. We had heard that at least one sailor who wasn't taking this year's test had found out what happened, was reportedly furious, and threatened to call his Congressman.

"This is awful," I murmured. "We could get into terrible trouble."

"They could lock us up and throw away the key," said Phil.

No more was said about this incident until about a month after our return to Seattle. Then one day an official-looking letter came to the Staten Island from the Bureau of Personnel. I was the ship's administrative officer, so it landed first in my hands. I was certain it would announce that an official inquiry had been ordered into what happened on that test date, preliminary to convening a court martial to try the officers responsible.

With trepidation, I slowly opened the envelope. Here, paraphrased, is what the letter said: "Congratulations! The officers and crew of the Staten Island are to be highly commended. On the recent fleet-wide exams, those tested on your ship achieved the highest cumulative score of any ship in the Navy. Please see that this commendation is placed in the record of those responsible for this result."

When I sent the letter up to Jumbo, he wrote back: "Make sure this goes in the Captain's record."

The *lesson learned* here, which poked holes in my youthful naiveté, was that although virtue may be its own reward, vice occasionally pays off. I've tried hard to abstain from following this advice, but it has made me aware that some folks you run into do subscribe to that nasty message – so you're wise to be prepared for such encounters.

There was one incident on the last leg of the voyage that, although trivial, sticks in my mind. When we stopped in San Diego to offload our one remaining helicopter. I was the officer on the quarterdeck, overseeing people boarding or leaving the ship. Standing on the dockside was a young Naval officer, wearing a full-dress white uniform with a ceremonial sword dangling from his belt. I thought, what the hell is this? Then it hit me; we'd gotten word that a new assistant supply officer would be joining our ship's company, a recent graduate of the Naval Academy.

You have to understand that up to then we had zero Annapolis graduates in our ranks. All the officers came from NROTC or OCS or had been promoted from the enlisted ranks. And after almost six months at sea, we were a scruffy bunch indeed.

The elegantly bedecked Ensign requested permission to come aboard, introduced himself, and then took out what appeared to be a business card, handing it to me and saying something like: "Please deliver my compliments to the Captain, and let me know when I may have the pleasure of introducing myself to him."

This was evidently something he'd learned at the Naval Academy. I had never heard of this kind of ceremony, and at that moment the Captain was busy supervising the offloading operation. So I fetched a messenger to take the Ensign to his quarters and told him we'd be in touch shortly after departure.

After we set sail for Seattle, the Pacific Ocean offered up some pretty rough seas – although nothing like what we had encountered between Chile and the Antarctic.   I went down to the Ensign's quarters later that day and found him lying glassy-eyed in his bunk. A nearby bucket contained his most recent meal.

For the next several days, almost until we reached Seattle, he never emerged from his quarters, which reeked from what he continued to throw up daily. On each visit, as I left, he asked me in a weak voice to please convey his regrets to the Captain. I doubt he ever got to meet Jumbo before we finally reached port.

The Ensign turned out to be a nice guy, but I'm ashamed to say that the rest of us adversity-hardened non-Annapolis shipboard veterans felt sheer joy at the idea of this former midshipman being stricken with an interminable case of seasickness in these relatively benign seas. Oh, how cruel we were . . . .

* * *

After several months in port, we embarked once more on an Arctic cruise that occupied the summer of '57. The Captain, in a grant of partial absolution from my Weddell Sea screw-up, designated me as the ship's navigator, a position of some importance. I enjoyed the responsibility and considered myself fairly competent at the job. My main memory of the voyage coalesces around three days near the end of our time up north.

Just as the other ships in the Arctic were ordered to return to the lower forty-eight, we received a different directive from Naval authorities. We were informed that a team from a leading oceanographic institute would be boarding the Staten Island shortly to spend up to a week taking sonar depth soundings of the waters north of Point Barrow.

Since all of us were anxious to get back to Seattle, this extension was upsetting – and no one was more irate about it than the Captain. But it was a fleet order and thus unchallengeable.

A key role in ensuring the success of this assignment would be played by the ship's navigator, namely me. For the depth soundings to have any significance, each had to be recorded at the exact location on the navigational chart where it was taken. Unfortunately, though, for an icebreaker in the Arctic back in 1957, this presented real difficulties.

Few of the plotting aids that seamen rely on nowadays to fix their position were available to us that summer. The sky was never clear enough for a sextant to help position us by readings of the sun or stars. For technical reasons, the newly-installed Loran system was of little help. We were too far from shore to get any assist from our rudimentary radar. Even the basic dead reckoning system used by ships when nothing else was available – based on the ship's speed and the course followed – was questionable, because the frequent ice floes we encountered required us to make temporary shifts of course and adjustments of speed to deal with those obstacles.

The oceanographic team was responsible for dictating the various courses it wanted us to follow during this exercise. The navigator was required to furnish them a written report of the ship's location at three designated times each day. Before we began taking the soundings, I informed the Captain of the difficulty I anticipated in fixing our location – a disclosure that Jumbo took in without comment.

So there I was in my cramped charthouse, trying to fix the first noon position I needed to report, when the Captain materialized. I don't recall him ever having stopped by there before.

"Well, Mr. Freund," he said, "where are we?"

"I hate to be vague, Captain," I replied, "but I'm really wrestling with this." We had been maneuvering around and through ice all morning, and thus lacked precise criteria from which to judge our exact location.

"Well," the Captain interrupted, "I'll tell you where we are" – and his index finger stabbed the chart at an otherwise unidentified spot. "We're right here!"

"That may be, Captain," I protested, "but I'm just not sure. . . ."

"Did you hear me, Mr. Freund," Jumbo snapped – and then, banging his fist down on the spot he'd previously identified, announced in a loud, resolute voice, "I said we are HERE!"

"Aye, aye, sir," I replied, marking the spot with my pencil. This became the position I delivered to the oceanographic folks ten minutes later, without excuses or qualification.

This same scene played out at regular intervals over the next two days – the Captain entering the charthouse prior to the issuance of my report and telling me precisely where we were. I had no idea where we actually were located, and I'm sure he didn't either. But I could see what the circumstances called for. Jumbo wanted to get this assignment over with quickly and return to Seattle, and I wasn't about to stand in his way.

I don't recall the oceanographic people openly questioning my reports, although I sensed their skepticism. Then, on the third day, they tried a new tactic. We were directed to follow certain designated courses during the afternoon that caused the ship to cross over a spot it had traversed in a different direction that morning.

A few minutes after the crossover, the head of the oceanographic group confronted me angrily in the charthouse. "Freund," he said, "you don't know where the hell you're at!" He placed a chart on the table that showed the ship's courses over the period, with the various depth soundings noted at regular intervals. In the space where the ship's later path crossed over the earlier one, the depth intervals leading up to and following the crossing spot on the afternoon's east-west path were (let's say) 48 fathoms, 49, 50, 50, 51, while on the morning's north-south course they were 23, 24, 25, 25, 26 – a basic impossibility. I didn't even attempt to respond.

The next thing I knew was that, much to Jumbo's delight, we were on our way back to Seattle. The oceanographic group had concluded that nothing reliable was ever going to be forthcoming from this Staten Island navigator!

The moral of the story: you can fool some of the people all of the time, and all of the people some of the time, but you can't (etc.) . . . .

There's a postscript to this incident. We were never told the reason why the oceanographic folks were doing the charting, but not long afterwards, the nuclear submarine USS Nautilus made its heralded first crossing of the Northwest Passage. I just hope they weren't relying on our soundings.

* * *

A gap of a little over a year occurred between that voyage and my second Antarctic cruise. During that time, my steady date in Seattle was a Northwest Airlines flight attendant named Alice, who was fun to be with . She lived in a house out near the airport with several of her colleagues; I introduced them to my shipmates, and the house quickly became a welcome home-away-from-home for my buddies and me. I moved my electronic piano out there, which contributed to some enjoyable evenings. We even experimented with concocting our own home brew in the basement, inaugurating it at a big party – not very good stuff taste-wise, but oh, what a sense of accomplishment . . . .

A choice recollection from those days is when Alice managed to obtain several consecutive days off from flying, I took a short leave, and we drove the old used car I'd bought down to San Francisco. Neither of us had ever been there, and we enjoyed the visit thoroughly.

What I'll never forget was the scene that played out when we arrived at our el cheapo hotel room. I said to Alice, "Let's take stock of how much money we have between us." (Neither of us had anything like a credit or debit card.) We each took out all the bills and change in our pockets, wallets, her handbag, etc. and put the lot in the middle of the bed. It was pretty paltry. Out of this, we transferred to a table the amount the hotel would cost and what was needed for gas and food to get back to Seattle. The meager sum left on the bed was all that we had to spend on food and entertainment in San Francisco.

Still, the two of us made do – eating at cheap diners, searching for tourist freebies wherever available. It was a worthwhile and enjoyable experience.

Each of us had comparable deadlines to get back to Seattle. We stayed in San Francisco as long as we could, leaving just enough time to drive straight through to Seattle. The roads in those days were not as good as they are today, my car was an old wreck, and – worst of all – Alice didn't drive! So it was all on me. I would stop every few hours, ask her to wake me in 20 minutes, and then catch a few winks by the side of the road. It was exhausting, but we made it back with less than an hour to spare.

As I previously mentioned, the Staten Island's major service assignment during this period was to tow four over-age decommissioned destroyers across the Pacific to Eniwetok Atoll, where they would be used in the nuclear testing program. I was sent down for a few days to Long Beach, CA, where the destroyers were tied up – supposedly to inspect them for seaworthiness. Having no idea what I was looking for, I went through some plausible motions during the days – peering at the hulls, paying quickie visits to the inoperable engine rooms, and so on – and hit the local bars at night.

The voyage to the atoll was grueling. Due to the combined bulk of the four ships we were towing, we had to travel at sluggish speeds of three or four knots. I was still the navigator at this point; and unlike conditions in the Arctic, I was able to take reliable sextant readings to fix our position. But the position changed so little from, say, eight in the morning until noon, that the marks I made on the large scale Pacific Ocean chart were typically within a hair's-breadth of each other.

It was really hot, our route being not far from the equator. Icebreakers of the '50s, which were insulated for the cold weather, had little ventilation and no air-conditioning. I couldn't sleep in my bunk and had to come up on deck at night, strapping myself to some low-hanging superstructure before hitting the hardwood.

The only notable event on the trip occurred when a sailor who worked on the mess deck went nuts, tried to stab one of the cooks with a big kitchen knife, and then – thwarted by others – ran to the ship's rail to jump overboard. He was caught just in time and locked up in the ship's brig for the balance of the trip. Upon arrival in Eniwetok, we turned him over to U.S. Navy authorities.

Something really bizarre – a touch of comic, but with plenty of potential for misfortune – occurred after we were back in Seattle. The Captain's best friend on the Staten Island was the officer (Pete) who served as Chief Engineer, a crucial posting on the ship. For some valid personal reason, Pete wanted to leave the ship, and Jumbo wished to accommodate him. But the Bureau of Personnel wouldn't allow a Chief Engineer to leave a ship unless there was a replacement for him. On the Staten Island, none was available.

About then, I received a summons to report to the Captain. I had no idea what was in store, but given my prior experience with Jumbo, approached his cabin with trepidation – which turned out to be quite justified.

"Freund," said the Captain, "Pete is leaving the ship, and I'm appointing you as the ship's new Chief Engineer."

My first thought was that Jumbo was joking, although he wasn't known for having a sense of humor. "You're kidding, of course, Captain. Me as Chief Engineer? I know nothing about things mechanical or electrical, engines, pipes or wires . . . ." My voice trailed off as I took in his steely expression.

"I'm not kidding," he said. "You're it . . . . Now get the hell out of here!"

And thus began one of the diciest periods in my Naval career. I had no idea what I was doing – a total misfit in the role, and everyone in the crew knew it. At one point, I latched on to a paperback pamphlet they earmarked for the lowest grade of new engineman recruit, just to impart some basic knowledge of the field into my head ("This here is a diesel engine . . ."); but even at that rudimentary level, I found my mind going blank.

During this time, we took the ship out of Seattle on a short training mission. Here's a snapshot of the way things went. I'm sitting in the wardroom drinking a cup of coffee. The chief machinist, a knowledgeable warrant officer, comes in and says, "We've had a problem with [something or other] on Engine #2, and we need to take it off-line for further checking. You ought to tell the Captain."

So I go up to the bridge, salute, and tell the Captain we have a problem with Engine #2 and need to take it off-line. He says, "What's the problem?" I salute again and say, "I'll find out." I run back to find the chief machinist, who describes the problem, which I don't understand but manage to memorize (something about a certain valve, or was it a gasket?). I go back to the Captain and repeat it. Then he asks how long the engine will be off-line, and I have to go through the same drill again with the chief machinist.

There's no telling how long this charade might have gone on, but for a lucky break. Dave Reedy, an officer who had been the Chief Engineer on a destroyer for several years, got tired of the duty and put in for a transfer to any other ship where he would be able to serve in a different capacity. The Navy sent him to the Staten Island. The day he arrived, the Captain – who by now had come to realize the absolute folly of me serving in this office – made Dave the Chief Engineer, much to the latter's chagrin. "But, but, but . . ." he sputtered, to no avail. He got the job, and I was returned to a posting where mechanical aptitude wasn't essential.

* * *

During this period before my second Antarctic cruise, an incident occurred that, six decades later, still produces an occasional nightmare.

Our ship was heading west through the Straits of Juan de Fuca toward the Pacific Ocean. I was the officer of the deck; Ron a junior ensign, was assisting me.

An assortment of small craft were running in these waters, although they usually kept their distance from us. But one vessel's captain had a different idea. He was operating a large ferry a few miles away on our port bow, proceeding north – perpendicular to our westerly course.

I told Ron to keep an eye on the ferry, which meant he needed to track its bearing from us. If the numerical bearing steadily decreased, that meant the ferry would pass astern of us. If the bearing increased, it meant the ferry would pass ahead of us. And if the bearing stayed the same, it meant the two of us were on a collision course . . . .

And so we were. "Bearing remains the same," Ron sung out at thirty-second intervals. As the icebreaker and the ferry closed in on each other, I grasped the crisis at hand.

For military and non-military vessels alike, maneuvering at sea is governed by the so-called "Rules of the Road." The rule applicable to this particular situation states that the ship (here, the icebreaker) that has the other ship (here, the ferry) on its port bow is the "favored" vessel and is required to maintain its course and speed. The other ship, the "burdened" vessel, must change course or speed to avoid the favored vessel. This meant that under these circumstances I was to do nothing but continue to proceed on the same course and at the same speed as I was operating on. The ferry was required to take the necessary evasive action. But despite the rule, the ferry wasn't taking such action and gave no sign that it would do so.

"Bearing remains the same," Ron intoned mechanically. I couldn't help wondering whether he was conscious of how serious this was – two vessels heading at top speed toward each other, risking an unavoidable collision. And where, you may ask, was our Captain for expert assistance? He had informed me a half-hour earlier that he'd be taking a badly-needed nap in his stateroom and should not be awakened except in an emergency.

Was this an emergency? I thought so, as the ferry bore down on us without slackening speed or altering direction. Did the ferry captain even know the Rules of the Road, I wondered – did he realize he was supposed to yield?

I could see the disturbed look on the face of our helmsman at the steering wheel, who did realize what was happening. He was the guy to whom I would have to give any order to alter course so as avoid the ferry. But acting in disobedience to the Rules carried real risk. If I turned to my port, and the ferry – with its captain finally awakening to the problem and realizing he was required to do something – turned to his starboard, we would probably collide.

Another option was to give a command to the engine room to stop all engines – or even more severe, "All back full." But even this would be a violation of the Rules, with the same risk of confusing the ferry captain. And since the ship would then jerk noticeably and make a loud noise, it would wake up the Captain – something I wanted to avoid at all costs.

These were the kinds of thoughts that were streaming through my head during the last few minutes of the looming encounter . . . .

In the end, I did nothing – perhaps not so much because it was the right decision to make (which it was), but more because I froze into a kind of fatalistic immobility.

I won't keep you in suspense. The ferry passed just ahead of us, with its fantail so close I could see the startled expressions on the faces of the people standing there – a matter of mere yards away.

I can't remember how I handled this with Ron and the helmsman afterwards – was I cool and collected (just another day at the office), or did I figuratively wipe the sweat off my brow after a close call? I think I must have just walked out onto the wing of the bridge, where I could be alone with the reality that we'd just narrowly avoided a disaster.

As I thought about it later, I was sure the ferry captain knew the Rules. This was probably a game he liked to play with the Navy ships that occasionally cruised in these waters -- ships being handled by novices like me. He, on the other hand, plied these same waters every day of his life; he had total command of his craft; and he managed his speed expertly to just miss us – not by a mile, but rather a seeming millimeter – with the goal of giving heart palpitations to the Navy's latest incompetent young officer.

* * *

Jumbo finally left the ship for another assignment. I was delighted that the Staten Island now had a new Captain (we'll call him Patrick) who would be in charge on our second Antarctic cruise. I hoped my relations with Patrick would prove to be better than with Jumbo.

To stimulate good relations, I invited the new Captain to join us when my friends and I decided to have a big party at Alice's house prior to leaving port. I was aware that Patrick's wife hadn't come to Seattle inasmuch as he'd be at sea for the next six months. I thought he might be lonely – perhaps concerned about the big task he was about to undertake – and would enjoy a change of pace. Patrick was delighted to be invited and promptly accepted.

By coincidence, a classmate of mine from Princeton happened to be passing through the area, and I invited Dick to join us also.

The party was terrific. I took on the task of introducing the Captain to everyone he didn't know (including Dick, whom I identified as "my good friend from college"). The introductions included an attractive flight attendant friend of Alice (let's call her "Nancy"), who was there without a date.

A half hour later, I saw the Captain canoodling with Nancy in a corner of the room, looking very happy. I was pleased; obviously I'd already gone a long way toward getting Patrick to appreciate me – if not for my nautical skills, then at least for my matchmaking ability.

After that, I lost track of things while playing the piano and joining in a ceremony to introduce our home brew. When this ended, I looked around for my friend Dick, who seemed to have disappeared. I asked if anyone had seen him and was told by a fellow officer, "Oh, Dick left ten minutes ago with Nancy." Just then, I caught sight of Patrick, visibly angry, putting on his jacket and stalking out of the house.

Well, I figured, to make it with the new Captain, I guess I'll have to fall back on my nautical abilities after all . . . .

The ship was now preparing to embark on a six-month cruise to the Antarctic, one of the world's coldest and most isolated outposts. No liberty, no booze, no women – it was a trip to tax the fortitude of Job.

I was the duty officer one day, standing on the quarterdeck. All of a sudden, I saw on the gangway the same crazy sailor who'd tried to stab a cook and jump off the ship – the one we had to lock up and put ashore in Eniwetok.

"Permission to come aboard," he barked, saluting smartly.

"What the hell are *you* doing here?" I sputtered.

"Reporting for duty, sir."

Needless to say, I barred him physically from entering the ship, and immediately called the Captain. We got in touch with the authorities, told them of their terrible mistake in ordering this nut back to our ship for the arduous Antarctic trip, and managed to get his orders changed.*

* * *

For my second Antarctic trip, as part of Deep Freeze IV, the Staten Island produced its own commemorative cruise book. Yours truly wrote the text – serviceable, if a trifle over-the-top. From time to time, I'll be quoting from the book (text shown in italics). Here's an excerpt from the book's introduction, under a big photo of the ship breaking ice:

> *The quiet sense of destiny that underscores life on the sea was very much in evidence that bright October morning in 1958, as USS STATEN ISLAND (AGB-5) made her final preparations for getting underway. Amid the kisses and sobs, the last-minute instructions concerning the family car and the whispered words of good-bye, was the curious sensation that many thousand miles away, under a milky curtain of ice and snow, the ship had a strange rendezvous to keep – in a land that some had seen but no one really knew. And, intermingling with the regrets at departure and the anticipation of adventures ahead, was the disquieting knowledge that the icebreaker would confront its fate alone.*

---

* I used that incident in an article I wrote many years later called, "An Ode to Embellishment." After having related the story to an acquaintance just as I wrote it here, the thought had occurred to me that perhaps I wasn't really standing on the quarterdeck when the crazy sailor arrived back at the ship. Maybe I was just embellishing the story. My memory was even dim as to whether the sailor actually returned to the ship. We may just have received an advance copy of his official orders and complained to the authorities. Still, my article endorsed the possible embellishment in this case (while tut-tutting about it in other instances) – it enhanced the tale, allowing me to express the incredulity I felt at the time, and it didn't falsify the point of the story, namely the Navy's bureaucratic snafu. [See also my reference in Chapter 1 to Oliver Sack's piece entitled *Speak, Memory*, regarding the potential invalidity of many seemingly impregnable memories.]

As it turned out, the trip from Seattle to New Zealand (with only a brief stop in San Diego to embark our helicopter unit) was the most comfortable we ever experienced.

Nary a coffee urn was overturned nor a recent recruit tossed from his rack; no flying missiles in the wardroom nor independent garbage cans on the mess deck marred our journey.

We had several scientists aboard conducting various projects – such as the study of cosmic rays emitted by the sun at 18 different latitudes between Seattle and Antarctica – for which I foresaw great things:

It will be some time before the ultimate result of their research is known, but this and similar studies being conducted elsewhere will eventually play a considerable role in man's conquest of outer space.

There were also physicians doing research into the virus connected with the common cold, and scientists conducting an intensive oceanographic program.

Crossing the equator on a US Navy ship is a big deal. Those who have crossed before (called "Shellbacks") terrorize the first-timers ("Pollywogs") regardless of rank, making them endure all kinds of sloppy and funny initiation rites. You have to be there to grasp the absurdity of it all. But it does serve to bond the crew together.

Our major stopover in New Zealand was at the small city of New Plymouth. We were the first American ship to ever pay the town a visit, and the locals rolled out the red carpet. Maoris danced on dockside; sailors were entertained in private homes and plied with food and drink; and the whole ship's company paraded (with me out of step once again) through the main street of town to cheering onlookers. We visited the scenic splendor of Mt. Egmont, and I was smitten by a charming lass – a three-day relationship ultimately doomed by my never having a subsequent opportunity to return to New Plymouth.

After stopping briefly for fuel and fresh provisions, we headed south. Two days out from New Zealand's south island, as I later recounted, *"We ran into mountainous seas and high winds which tossed us about with reckless abandon."* Rolls of up to 55 degrees were experienced. Eating and sleeping became major efforts.

As we neared Antarctica, one night in particular sticks in my mind. The weather was horrible – a driving rain, freezing temperatures, rough seas, almost zero visibility. I was the Officer of the Deck, in charge of the ship as the Staten Island fought through all this mess, pitching and rolling violently. A junior officer was glued to the radar, searching for any signs of obstacles to our progress, and we posted a seaman lookout in the open area above the bridge.

I was peering out the window of the wheelhouse through that cold driving rain when all of a sudden, without any warning, I saw a huge shape loom up close to the bow of the ship. Neither the radar operator nor the lookout had provided any warning of anything being out there, although we were aware that the region might contain icebergs . . . .

And that's just what it was! – a huge iceberg that the radar had failed to detect, the lookout had neglected to notice – and we were heading right for it!

(If those first terrifying seconds had made it into the cruise book, which I ensured they didn't, I would probably have termed that initial sighting a Titanic moment – envisioning the huge ocean liner being sent to its watery grave by a berg smaller than this one; and I certainly would have mentioned that these waters were so cold no one could last in them more than a few minutes.)

This time however – as contrasted with my timidity in that ferry incident reported earlier – I acted instantly and with decisiveness. "Right full rudder! Starboard engine back full!" The ship responded, began to come about slowly to the right, and the turn was finally completed – with us only a short distance from a disastrous collision.

After we had changed course to go around the iceberg, I finally caught my breath and wondered why I hadn't been warned of this danger earlier. The radar was an early model that wasn't good at picking up smooth icy objects, but how about the lookout? So I used the intercom to call up the seaman.

After unloading a few choice expletives on him, I closed with: "Goddamit, what the hell are you doing up there?" And the voice came back over the bridge loudspeaker, in a tone marked by an icy shiver, "I'm . . . freezin' . . . to . . . death." We all cracked up – we needed a good laugh – picturing him huddled beneath some canvas, facing away from the bow, trying to keep warm, and probably still unaware that we'd encountered an iceberg.

Lesson learned: when you're in charge of something important, be wary of dependence on others – especially when they're cold and wet.

By the next day, the storm had eased. As we neared the icepack, we saw the sun glistening on another iceberg, which I could (and did) write about:

We passed this silent sentinel of the Antarctic with awe and slight apprehension, and turned to our duties with new vigor.

Then we hit the icepack, at first plowing easily through small belts of scattered brash, and then contacting the main bulk of the pack. It was the first time that the new Captain had ever encountered ice; and, except for two of us, all the other officers who had been on our first voyage to Antarctica had been replaced by individuals with no polar experience. The other veteran was sick this day, so when we reached the first real obstacle in the ice field, the Captain called me to the bridge.

"Okay, Mister," Patrick asked with a modicum of seeming respect for my prior Antarctic experience, "what do I do now?" I supervised some minor unskilled maneuver, and we slithered away from the smallish ice floe that had been blocking our path. A little later, we encountered more serious ice and again he sent for me. I tried a different technique, slightly more complicated, and after a few minutes we were again free.

This went on a few more times, and then we came to some thick blue ice. I ran through my repertoire, but the ship didn't budge.

"Well?" the Captain inquired.

"That's it," I answered.

His face flushed as he stammered incredulously: "Is that your whole bag of tricks?"

"That's right," I replied, smiled weakly. and headed for the wardroom.

Needless to say, Patrick didn't call me to the bridge again. I'm informed that, shortly upon returning from the voyage, he decided to write his own book about piloting ships in the ice!

We spent the next several months actively engaged in the Antarctic. Here are a few highlights.

- The sun never set. Everyone's hours were disoriented; for instance, the mess deck was busy at 3:00 am.

- The ship rode smoothly in the ice (except for an occasional jolt as a tough floe was shouldered aside), in contrast to the pitching and rolling experienced in the Pacific Ocean coming down from New Zealand.

- When we had to halt to await better conditions, groups went penguin hunting, bringing some birds on board. I posed happily for a picture holding one of them; five seconds later, the little bugger crapped all over me.

- At one point when we stopped for a longer period, an ice football game was arranged by crewmembers.

- The huge icebreaker USS Glacier broke two blades off her screws (and bent the other four), was virtually helpless, and had to proceed back to New Zealand for dry-docking. This resulted in Staten Island having to do both her own job and the Glacier's. Forgive me, but I just can't resist quoting the apocalyptic terms in which I described this back then:

It was a grim moment, for the fate of the entire operation depended on whether she [the Staten Island] could accomplish the task of breaking the channel into McMurdo for the cargo ships and tankers – all by herself. The best-laid plans of mice and men could not have prefigured this development; never before had the channel been carved out solely by a wind-class icebreaker.

But a new and resolute spirit was emerging among the old hands and first-timers aboard STATEN ISLAND as she picked her way down the narrow leads and broke through the thick ridges en route to the Naval Air Facility. If it was possible, and there was reason to believe it was, we were sure we could accomplish it; after all, we had emerged undamaged from the worst the Antarctic had to offer.

Slowly our channel began to take shape, about a mile's worth per day . . . and our [McMurdo Sound] objective started to come into focus. Working steadily around the clock, with no rest for the tireless diesels, the icebreaker that was too small for the job was getting it done.

- We tasted tinned biscuits preserved in Scott's 1910 hut at Cape Evans, and later we "rescued" (and dined on) steaks buried in the ice from Admiral Byrd's Little America V (established in the '40s) on the Ross Sea ice shelf.

- One of our missions took us to Cape Hallett, the "garden spot" of the Antarctic, where we visited a large penguin rookery. Listen to me, marveling over the experience:

Of all the magnificent and other-worldly vistas to be viewed in the Antarctic, there is a little doubt that Cape Hallett is the most breathtaking. It is ringed by jagged mountains and picturesque bergs; glaciers and icefalls abound; and with every passing hour the Antarctic sun changes the shadows and glinting colors in a glorious panorama.

- Going over to Wilkes Station on the Indian Ocean side of the continent, we encountered beautiful sunsets, now being far enough north to experience night. Once there, we officially turned over the American encampment to Australia in a simple ceremony, but one in which I saw larger import:

The Antarctic is a fertile breeding ground for international amity. Let there be no doubt of that, and this was one more example of cooperation between nations in a scientific venture that vitally concerns all.

* * *

Finally we headed back north. It was a long tough tour, but all this would soon be redeemed – because we were about to spend a week in Melbourne, Australia. I can still picture one of these late evening sessions on the way there, with a grizzled chief petty officer – who had spent some time in Australia during World War II – holding forth on what was in store for us.

"Oh, you're gonna love that place. The people are so friendly, the women are beautiful and available, the goddamn beer is fantastic . . . ."

I had arranged with one of the less adventuresome officers to assume my duties, so that I could take the entire week off "on the beach." It was shaping up to be one of the highlights of my life.

We arrived in Melbourne, berthed the ship, and were poised on the quarterdeck to go ashore when an urgent message was received. "Return to McMurdo Sound." There was a rumor about a Japanese ship being stuck in the ice or whatever, but it didn't matter – the sickening point was that our ship would have to leave the next morning for the Antarctic. We were devastated, although I tried to put a better face on it in the cruise book:

> It was a hard blow to take after so long in the ice, and with Melbourne beckoning and Seattle not far away; but once more the icebreaker responded to the call . . . .

But not before we had one night in Melbourne – one night to make up for the week they were robbing us of. My buddies and I took a big suite at a hotel, located some of those beautiful Aussie women, stocked up on booze (we might also have had some food, but I don't recall any), and threw a helluva party.

My enduring memory of that night was being so drunk that at one point I claimed loudly to be indestructible – whereupon I proceeded to open a window all the way, climb out onto the ledge, and try to sidle along the ledge toward the next window of the suite. Fortunately, cooler heads prevailed – I was pulled back into the room and dumped on a couch.

Lesson learned: When blotto, stay away from open windows.

Meanwhile, the ship's crew, irate over the change of plans, marauded all over the city – breaking things, accosting women, getting into fights with locals. I was later designated by the Captain to write letters of apology for the crew's conduct to a plentiful number of local institutions and establishments – definitely not the Staten Island's finest hour.

I can't remember much about that detestable trip back south, except to recall that we had to move fast because in a few weeks this part of the Antarctic would begin to seal itself off for another winter. I don't even remember seeing a marooned Japanese ship.

When it ended, we weren't able to return to Melbourne but instead hit New Zealand again. This time it was Christchurch and the beautiful cosmopolitan city of Wellington, which made up in part for the disappointment over Melbourne.

On our way back home, we made a visit to tiny Niue Island, a New Zealand dependency in the South Pacific which had been struck by a brutal hurricane that depleted its food supply. The island had no airstrip, so we were called upon to transport supplies of tinned corned beef and mutton to the island.

We finally got back to Seattle in mid-April. I can't resist quoting myself on the dock scene and how we felt:

> *Wives and sweethearts lined the pier, and a Navy band broke into the familiar strains. Reporters and cameramen swarmed aboard as the brow went over; the return of the icebreaker was big news. Men saw small children they had never seen before, brought into the world during the five and one-half months we had been away. It was a reunion en masse, and it felt very good.*

> *And as the general pandemonium subsided, we were able to draw up a final balance sheet on our accomplishments. It was indeed a favorable one. Many thousands of miles away, we had encountered our special enemies – ice, bitter weather, uncertain seas – and we had emerged victorious. We were still strong and very much in commission. We had completed all missions assigned in the face of very special difficulties. We had, indeed kept our rendezvous with Antarctica.*

* * *

What disappoints me, as I look back at those years from today's vantage point, is how I managed to waste so much time. During most of the ensuing years – and even through retirement – I've treasured spare hours to accomplish things I considered meaningful. Back then, not so much. There was a lot of dead time on the ship that could have been productively employed, but I utterly failed to utilize it.

For instance I did like to write, and I could tell from the outset that I'd be exposed to fruitful story ideas aboard ship. (Maybe a little something along the lines of *The Caine Mutiny* . . .) Even if I didn't write the book or articles while onboard, at least I could have taken notes to serve later on as my primary source material for works of either fiction or non-fiction.

For a few weeks at the beginning of the three year hitch, I did jot down my fresh impressions. But then I just stopped, neither writing nor collecting information, acting as if the whole experience just wasn't worth it. I was wrong.

Another thing I initially vowed to do was to read – to devour good books that I fancied but hadn't perused in college. My starting point was Dostoyevsky's *The Brothers Karamazov*, which I cracked open the first month on the ship. By the end of the three years, I hadn't ventured beyond page 50. Likewise with other classics, many of which weren't even opened.

What did I do with my spare time? I really don't know. I played gin rummy, flipped through magazines, fooled around on my electric piano, dozed off – it's painful to think about how I let three whole years get away from me.

* * *

Two lifetime events of real significance did happen to me in the Navy. The first of these was the way in which the Navy shaped my subsequent professional life.

For some people, the choice of career is almost foreordained – a youngster going into his or her parent's business, for instance, or someone who has long yearned to be a doctor. But for me growing up, the issue was subject to benign neglect.

My eventual career choice turned out splendidly. Looking back on it today, practicing law might have seemed a natural evolution – the several requisites for success as an attorney playing generally to my strengths. But in no way was this career foreordained. Moreover, who could possibly have predicted that the USS Staten Island would be responsible for my eventual choice of profession? But it was – and here's how it came about.

Back in college, when my friends were worrying about what they wanted to do in life, I refused to think about it. There wasn't anything I craved. I was never tempted to go into my father's (and grandfather's) business which, although operated with pride and due care and capable of turning out estimable products, was quite demanding and only marginally profitable. I found it almost painful to observe my father's adept and unstinting efforts leading to little financial success.

149

Business in general held no allure for me. (I remember having a subscription to Time magazine and avidly devouring its contents each week – except for the "Business" section, which I passed up with regularity.) I liked to write, but never saw it as my life's work. Teaching held some interest, but the meager pay scale was unenticing.[*]

I don't recall ever seriously considering law as a career. Back then, lawyers weren't nearly as much in the news or all over the TV screen as they are today. It seemed a rather refined profession, operating quietly behind the scenes. Our family knew few lawyers, so I wasn't subjected to any avuncular encouragement.

As a result, while many college classmates were taking the law school aptitude test or applying to graduate school or being interviewed by prospective business employers, I stood off to the side. My rationalization was that inasmuch as I had to serve three years in the Navy, that would be when I'd decide what I wanted to do with my life. I don't recall even speculating about my future; when asked, I took to replying, "Maybe I'll want to stay in the Navy."

That, by the way, accounted for the only such decision I made during my first months on the ship – that I would *not* make the Navy my career! But I still seemed no closer to choosing anything else until, quite unexpectedly, I found my calling.

When an enlisted man on a ship goes "over the hill" or commits some other dereliction of duty, the captain convenes a special court martial to try him, find the seaman guilty, and sentence him. The consequences can be serious, ranging up to six months in prison, loss of pay and a bad conduct discharge. The accused is entitled to be represented by an officer acting as defense counsel, but the officer doesn't have to be a lawyer so long as the prosecutor isn't an attorney. On a large ship, I might never have gotten involved in the process, but our icebreaker had just a small complement of officers. Moreover, because icebreaker duty was so tedious, we had more than our share of seamen going astray.

---

[*] I heard a good tale recently, as reported by Chief Justice John Roberts (contained in David Rubenstein's book, *The American Story*). At a time when Roberts was a college student looking forward to an academic career in history, he mentioned to a cab driver that he was a history major at Harvard. The cabdriver replied, "I was a history major at Harvard." This was the moment, Justice Roberts related, when he decided to go to law school.

As a very junior officer on the ship, my first assignment was to sit as one of the five judges on a special court martial, along with four hardened warrant officers. I approached this with an open mind but soon discovered that my fellow judges had little patience for the process and a low regard for the accused. I'll never forget observing one of the judges, while listening to testimony about a seaman's AWOL, doodling a hangman's noose.

Shortly after, though, I was assigned as defense counsel for an accused sailor, and that's when I found my calling. Serving as defense counsel was a job that none of the other officers wanted, so it was continually available to me. To handle the job, you only had to read one book – the Manual for Courts Martial, which I devoured. Although my clients were convicted with regularity (after all, they were clearly guilty), I fought hard to keep their sentences to a moderate (non-noose) level.

Although I was inclined to disparage almost everything else that came my way in the Navy, I found the court martial work absorbing – and for the first time in my life, I knew what I wanted to become. I sent in my application to law school from the Antarctic and took the LSAT test when we returned to Seattle. Harvard accepted me – I probably had the advantage of its geographic diversity quota, beating out a couple of overachieving penguins!

That's how my career at the bar began. But I must go back to the Staten Island for one more reminiscence. Most of the cases I handled on the ship were cut-and-dried, but there was a single trial worth mentioning.

I was assigned to defend a guy we'll call Kyle, an arrogant young seaman who was disliked by officers and enlisted men alike. He had been accused of taking a swing at a respected petty officer (whom we'll call Porter). Kyle's story was that he threw the punch in self-defense after being attacked by Porter. No witnesses to the incident had come forward.

As we discussed the case in my stateroom, Kyle suddenly turned to me, speaking with deep emotion: "Mr. Freund, you gotta get me off! I hate the goddamn Navy. I've only got three months left to serve before I get my discharge. But if I'm convicted, they can stick me in the brig for up to six months and then they add another six months to the time I have to serve. I swear, Mr. Freund, I won't make it through another year."

"Well, Kyle," I replied, "I'll do what I can, but it's a tough case for you – your word against that of Porter, a well-regarded petty officer, who claims you assaulted him without provocation."

"He's lying," said Kyle. "He hates me from something that happened between us way back when, and this is just his way of evening up the score." He looked pleadingly to me. "Look, Mr. Freund, I've got to beat this rap. I've saved up some real money I won at gambling, and it's all yours if you can get me off."

I smiled. "Listen, Kyle, that's one of the benefits of being in the Navy – you don't have to pay your defense counsel! I'll try my best and you save your money for when you get out of the service, which I hope will be earlier rather than later." But I had little confidence that Kyle would be acquitted.

Three days after meeting Kyle, there was a knock on the door of my stateroom. A seaman we'll call Seward entered. "They told me you're defending Kyle, Mr. Freund."

"That's right."

"I just wanted you to know that I saw the whole thing between Kyle and Porter, from up on the 40-mm turret where I was oiling the guns."

"You saw it? I didn't realize there were any witnesses . . . . Well, Seward, tell me what happened."

"They started yelling at each other, and then all of a sudden Porter took a swing at Kyle, missed him, then threw another punch that Kyle blocked, and then Kyle belted him on the chin."

I remember the excitement I felt at that moment. Seward's eyewitness account of the incident, describing Kyle's blow as having been struck in self-defense, represented total exoneration for my client. I tried the case, highlighting Seward's testimony. In what might have been the first acquittal ever obtained on the icebreaker, the court dismissed the charges against Kyle. I was jubilant, Kyle even more so.

A week after Kyle's acquittal, I woke up one morning with a start. Suddenly it all came into focus – Kyle's desperation to beat the rap, his mention of having saved up some cash, Seward materializing after a previously unsuccessful search for witnesses – my God, I realized, Kyle used those funds to pay Seward to lie on the witness stand! It was all quite obvious – but I was wet behind the ears and had been so delighted with Seward's testimony that the thought never occurred to me until the trial was over.

I remember wrestling at the time with the issue of whether to do anything about my belated surmise. If I'd realized during the trial that I was sponsoring false testimony, I would have taken immediate steps to rectify it. But now the trial was all over. Could I overturn what had already happened? And besides, I rationalized, there was no proof of what Kyle and Seward had cooked up – only my own after-the-fact suspicion.

So inertia ruled the day. I didn't nose around to see what I could find out, or have any further contacts with either Kyle or Seward, or approach the president of the court or the ship's executive officer to relate my conjecture. I had to live with the knowledge of my inaction through the law school years that followed and on into practice – and, truth be told, almost 60 year since, I still feel a sense of discomfort over the case.

* * *

That completes the tale of my stint in the Navy. It was clearly not my favorite experience. The interminable cruises, the turbulent waves, the long hours of tedium, the arrogance of those in authority – I couldn't wait for the three years to end.

But now, in revisiting my service six decades later, I realize I've been short-changing the experience. I retain vivid memories of some unforgettable moments. I learned some valuable lessons. It furnished an estimable transition between those rollicking college years and the relative sobriety of my subsequent life. And it backed me in to my ultimate profession.

There's one other aspect of this that I've always been reluctant to point out – but I'll endorse the words of my Princeton NROTC classmate, Ross Webber, who characterized it so well:

"Like most of our contemporaries, I have come to value more my time on active duty as it has receded into the past. Perhaps this reflects a sense that we did sacrifice something for our country even if its value was not ever clear to us. Today, so few young men and women have such an opportunity (or want it, apparently)."

* * *

Oh yes, I mentioned earlier (before my launch into the lawyering discussion) that there were *two* events of real significance that happened to me during my time in the Navy. The second one, which occurred about a month before the end of my active duty, was meeting Barbro Hellström from Sweden, who 30 months later became my first wife – a narrative recounted in Chapter 9.

Commissioned as a Navy Ensign, alongside Marine Corp 2nd Lieutenants
Royce Flippin and Mort Chute

Assigned to the U.S.
Navy icebreaker
U.S.S. Staten Island
AGB-5

On my first
Arctic cruise
in the summer
of '56, we
sighted this
denizen of the
ice cap.

My first Antarctic cruise in 1956-7.

Playing carols for the crew on the Staten Island's freezing flight deck Christmas Eve.

Our ship trimmed the Weddell Sea ice shelf to fashion an unloading pier, which led to swift construction of the Ellsworth Station.

Home on leave in mid-1957 – donning my uniform for my parents,
grandparents, and a planned appearance before an elementary school class.

The Shellback-Pollywog rite crossing the Equator

In port in the southern hemisphere

Breaking the ice pack to lead the supply ship into the base

*One of the penguin rookeries – plus a personal encounter
with a cuddly bird that didn't end happily (see text).*

One last assignment through the ice

On our way home, we stopped at Niue
to restock the hurricane-ravaged South Sea island

The homecoming scene in Seattle

My Navy career, as caricatured by the wonderful illustrator Joe Azar, who created the cover of this book and whose other work for me can be viewed in the Appendix.

8. THE SUMMER OF '59

In between a pair of three-year experiences I did not enjoy – serving in the Navy and attending law school – there was a most welcome interlude during the summer of '59: a whirlwind journey around Europe.

Following a quick taste of the Continent on the NROTC summer cruises and entranced by such books as Hemingway's *The Sun Also Rises*, I was anxious to get back to Europe. My golden opportunity arose during the summer after my Navy tour ended in late May, up until my arrival at Harvard in early September. I canvassed my buddies, but no one was available to join me on the trip – except Bob Watson for the special portion described below – so I decided to go solo.

I'm really glad that I did, and the experience was both educational and great fun. But I would have relished having a cheerful companion or two along to reduce that sometimes uneasy feeling of being alone in unfamiliar settings and facing a language barrier (English being a much less universal tongue back then).

I traveled primarily by train, toting only one mid-sized bag. (That fact alone is so at odds with my current addiction to multiple pieces of luggage . . . . Is it possible that I actually washed things in my hotel room sink and hung them over the bathtub to dry? . . .) I made no reservations in advance. When the train arrived at each destination, I would inquire at the station's info booth about the best cheap hotel nearby, and then stroll over to it, toting my bag.

My funds available for this trip, which consisted of whatever I'd managed to save from my meager Navy salary, were minimal. There were no credit cards back then, so I used American Express traveler's checks – visiting the AMEX office in each city to convert into local currency, pick up any mail, and occasionally meet other American tourists. I was equipped with the hot new guidebook that year, *Europe on $5 a Day*, which pointed me in a useful direction for meals and such, although my daily outlay never quite got down to that level.

I was intent on dashing around to fit everything in, not missing anything of note but rarely lingering anywhere more than a day or two – concerned that I might never make it back there again. I took in lots of good sights, cultural and otherwise, but what's hard to believe – given my current delight in photography – is that I wasn't carrying a camera. (What an international montage I might have put together . . . .)

I flew from Seattle to New York, then took off to London and Paris, and from there boarded trains for Belgium and Holland – a great start to the summer.

Next was Wiesbaden, Germany, where my college roommate, Bob Watson, was stationed. With two of Bob's Air Force buddies, we piled into an Opel, heading across France to Spain – in particular, to Pamplona for the annual running of the bulls. This turned out to be a real highlight of my European trip. While specific memories of other places have mostly faded, the Pamplona junket remains unforgettable, to wit:

- Stopping to buy shriveled "authentic" bota bags before hitting town – but oh, how lousy the wine tasted that we squirted from them.

- Arriving at night, getting drunk at an outdoor café, buying a balloon salesman's entire stock for resale at higher prices – but while out hawking them, having the balloons punctured by local youths who didn't welcome American tourists competing in their market.

- Sleeping in a field, mosquitos galore, waking up with sheep all around, washing our faces at the town pump.

- Spotting Hemingway holding court outdoors at a restaurant on the town square.

- Drinking cheap red wine in a bar while gobbling up the offered tapas, assuming they were included in the wine tab; then "running the check," being corralled outside and hauled back in to pay up.

- Joining the joyous daily march to the *corrida*, music playing, wine being shared (except for the many locals who shunned the vile-tasting liquid from our bota bags).

- Being entranced by the first bullfights I'd ever witnessed.

- Staying up all night so as to not miss the "running of the bulls" the next morning.

- Running the bulls, terrified, just making it to the center of the arena in time, then jumping into the stands when an animal got too close (while one of Bob's cohorts tried to steer-wrestle a bull, to the boos of the crowd).

We then joined a group of Italians/Belgians that Princeton classmate John Gewalt had assembled, traveling to Barcelona and the Spanish Riviera. Then over to the French Riviera (failing in our attempt to catch any sightings of Brigitte Bardot in San Tropez), where I parted company with the Watson group, who returned to Wiesbaden.

Next, hitching a ride down to Rome with a rich American guy driving a red Mercedes convertible. Then, curses! – a big frustration in the Eternal City. I'd met an attractive American girl and rented a motor scooter for us to sightsee and perhaps travel to distant metropolises. But the scooter had gears I couldn't handle. It just kept stalling – shades of Montreal! – until the girl, in hot pursuit of a more competent vehicular companion, ditched me.

Florence was next, but I got sick there and stayed in bed in my hotel room for several days. Then on to Switzerland and finally Berlin. I recall a night club there with a phone on each table and a large plaque showing the number, so you could dial up a pretty girl at an adjacent table for a dance – but my efforts were unavailing.

Then came the second highlight of the trip. I had met and fallen hard for Barbro Hellström of Sweden during my last month on the ship in Seattle (events I'll describe in Chapter 9.) We'd arranged to meet in Germany, where we rented a Volkswagen Bug and drove north through Denmark to Sweden. After a short stay in Stockholm, we headed up to her northern home town of Östersund, where I hit it off well with her extended family.

To make my flight home in time, I had to leave town before Barbro. The airport in Stockholm was my immediate destination. In checking the map, I saw a direct route from Östersund that looked to be much faster than the lengthier coastal circuit we'd travelled on the way up. Although the locals warned me – "I don't think you want to take that route" – I nevertheless persevered.

Ten miles out on the unpaved road, a big rock bounced up, smashing the VW's windshield to shreds. I wasn't hurt, but had to drive back to Östersund with my side window open so that I could stick my head out – both to see the road and to avoid the glass fragments that kept breaking off

164

the smashed front pane. It was a chilling experience, but I finally made it, got the windshield replaced, and resumed the trip – this time taking the paved road on the roundabout route to Stockholm.

At the beginning of my trip in Paris, I'd gone for supper at a little bistro recommended by *Europe on $5 a Day*. It was terrific – uncrowded, tasty food, very reasonable prices. When I got back to Paris for my flight home, I revisited the bistro. Evidently, though, every American tourist had read the same guidebook. Now there was a line to get in, the food quality had markedly decreased, and the prices had increased so much that the place was undoubtedly deleted from later editions of the book. Such is the price of fame.

And that, in a nutshell, is a quick recap of my very enjoyable summer of '59.

The two highlights of my European trip during the summer of '59: running the bulls at Pamplona, and traveling with my new girlfriend, Barbro Hellström, to meet her family, including sister Siv and her husband Bengt, in Östersund, Sweden.

9. MY FIRST WIFE, BARBRO HELLSTRÖM

My first wife, Barbro Hellström, and I met in 1959, married in 1961, and were together until 1980. These were very significant years for me, which featured the births of our two sons, Erik (in 1966) and Tom (in 1968), their childhoods and adolescence. Barbro played a major role in my life throughout the period. Although our marriage did not have a happy ending, I retain many positive memories from those two decades, which I want to record in this memoir.

I'll begin with the unlikely circumstances of how we happened to meet. It represents a classic example of what I call *sheer happenstance*. As you can tell from other chapters of this book, I've long been fascinated by how the voluntary decisions we make, or seemingly random events that occur, propel us in directions which lead to unexpected outcomes and relationships that can make all the difference in terms of our future years.

Barbro came from a modest-sized town in northern Sweden named Östersund. In her late teens, she left home for the United States, initially as an *au pair*. But her driving ambition was to become a flight attendant (then called a "stewardess") for Pan Am, the number one glamour airline of its day, with its world-wide routes and extended crew layovers in exotic locales. Barbro was unable to land this prize on her first try (although she did manage it a few years later), so she joined United Airlines. After a period of stewardess training, she was assigned to United's small base in Seattle – arriving in town less than a month before our meeting.

As for me, I was then in the final days of my Navy service. A few weeks after Barbro's arrival, my ship returned to its Seattle home port from a five month-long Antarctic cruise. In about six weeks, I would be discharged from the service and heading back east to attend law school that fall (after a summer in Europe).

A week or so after our arrival in Seattle, one of my shipmates, Chris (who himself was scheduled to leave the ship shortly for transfer to another city), happened to be at the local Naval Officers Club (which I don't ever recall visiting myself). By chance, he met a United stewardess there, and they got talking. One thing led to another, and they arranged for Chris to bring some of his shipboard buddies over to her place the following night to meet a group of her fellow stewardesses.

The next morning, Chris invited me to the impromptu party. I wanted to attend but couldn't manage it because of a date I had that evening with Alice, my girlfriend at the time, who was a Northwest Airlines stewardess. Late that afternoon, however, Alice called to tell me she had suddenly been assigned to take a flight out that night. So, after driving Miss Northwest to the airport, I dropped by Chris's United party and was dazzled by the lovely Barbro and her irresistible Swedish accent. Thirty months later, after ample back and forth, we made it to the altar.

I prize the multiple coincidences in that tale – the pinpoint timing between Barbro's arrival in Seattle and my imminent departure, the unlikely Officers Club rendezvous, the fortuitous Northwest evening flight – to say nothing of the twists and turns that catapulted Barbro to Seattle from distant Östersund, and the convoluted tale of how I ended up on an icebreaker based in Seattle [described in Chapter 7).

At the time we met, Barbro was 21 and quite fetching. She exuded a European charm, was intelligent, spoke fluent English, and tempered her serious side with an engaging laugh. She was pretty, well-proportioned, and had a twinkle in her eye. I had never met anyone like her.

We spent an exhilarating month together in Seattle on days she wasn't flying, with the Northwest stewardess abruptly relegated to the sidelines. Then my Navy tour ended, and I set out on my mostly solo European trip that I'd planned for the summer (detailed in Chapter 8).

As I mentioned earlier, the capstone of the trip came toward its end when Barbro and I met up in northern Germany (was it Hamburg or Lubeck?) rented a car, visited Denmark, and headed north through Sweden to her family home in Östersund. Although no one spoke much English, I got along well with her family – especially her terrific sister Siv and brother-in-law Bengt. It was a delightful week that helped cement our relationship.

I'll never forget our concern – remember, this was six decades ago – over how the hotels and inns at which we bedded down would react to an unmarried couple sharing a room. I recall buying her a cheap gold-colored band that could pass as a wedding ring, which she flashed at the innkeeper as we checked in the first evening in Denmark and surrendered our passports. When we came down to dinner, posted in large white chalk on the blackboard identifying room occupants, was "JAMES FREUND/BARBRO HELLSTROM" – an unmarried couple if there ever was one! But nobody except us seemed to care.

Back in the U.S., I headed up to Cambridge. and Harvard Law School, while Barbro remained in Seattle. It was an unsatisfactory state of affairs for lovebirds, and I pressed her to be transferred to United's base in Boston. Lo and behold, she managed to pull it off. Barbro shared a downtown apartment with Dottie, another United stewardess whom we liked very much – but the best times were when Dottie was out on a flight and Barbro wasn't.

By Christmastime of 1960, we decided to become engaged. I bought a ring, and my parents sent out invitations to an engagement party. The week before the party, Barbro paid a visit back to Sweden. That's when she received a letter from Pan Am – the airline of her dreams – finally accepting her long-standing application to join them as a stewardess.

And that's when I received a "Dear John" telegram from Barbro – "Sorry, must try Pan Am." Our engagement was off, the party cancelled. (I was, however, able to return the ring, through the good offices of the jeweler's granddaughter, my friend Claudine Bacher.) I was quite depressed – it was probably the low point of my life up to then. My parents tried to cheer me up with a holiday trip to the Poconos, but I wasn't good company.

During the balance of my second year at law school, Barbro flew for Pan Am from New York City, and I didn't see or speak to her. Some of her clothes and possessions had ended up in my garret closet, and I had a recurring vision of some hulking Nordic guy appearing one day to demand them back on her behalf. But no such gentleman showed up – and then one morning, Barbro herself unexpectedly knocked on my door. No apologies or anything, but it didn't matter – I welcomed her back and our separation was scarcely mentioned.

* * *

In retrospect, what happened in the next phase of our relationship did not represent my finest hour. I wasn't willing to take a chance of Barbro experiencing another change of heart. (I had a vision of multiple movie-star-handsome pilots, copilots and flight engineers cornering Barbro into compromising situations in New Delhi hotels during extended layovers.) And so I began pressuring her for an immediate marriage.

My marriage fever was woefully short-sighted. Barbro had finally achieved what she'd long hoped for – flying all over the world to interesting places, with time to sightsee, sample the local cuisine, meet new folks. But

Pan Am had an ironclad rule that stewardesses couldn't be married – so all this would have to end upon our nuptials. I knew this and still continued to press her. Barbro – perhaps feeling (although never admitting) some guilt at having squelched our engagement – ultimately acceded to my wish and ended her career at Pan Am. Though she never said so explicitly, I believe she never forgave me for the needless urgency of my wedlock pressure.

We were married in New York City on December 30, 1961, halfway through my final year at Harvard Law School. Barbro, a Lutheran by birth and upbringing, chose St. Peters Church (54th and Lexington Avenue) for the ceremony. Nowadays this congregation is housed in a sleek modern building in the shade of Citicorp Center, but back then it was an elegant aged edifice. boasting handsome wooden trimmings around the altar and other distinctive adornments.

No one from Sweden came over for the wedding. This didn't represent a boycott. Back then people didn't readily cross the Atlantic for brief stays. And I imagine the prospective outlay of substantial kroners discouraged her folks of modest means.

Still, I'm sure this must have been sad for Barbro. In lieu of her adored sister Siv acting as matron of honor, she asked Ellen Donovan, the wife of my best law school friend, Bob Smith – a lovely woman, but hardly a confidante of Barbro's. She was walked down the aisle and "given away" by *my* father who, to my delight, handled the assignment splendidly.

My best man (Bob Watson) and ushers (Fred Bacher, John Doyle, Jack Veatch and Bob Smith) were all close school buddies, and we enjoyed a lively bachelor party the night before. Although memories of the wedding itself have faded, I retain a vivid image of being closeted with the minister and Wats in a private room before the ceremony. At this seminal moment, instead of reflecting on the joys and responsibilities of marriage, the minister and Bob were engaged in a vigorous discussion of Wall Street matters, with Bob (then a stockbroker) strongly recommending certain promising investments.

The wedding reception was held at the Freund apartment (242 East 72nd Street). It was a good party, although I can't seem to remember whether my teetotalling parents served alcoholic beverages.

I do recall, however, the presence of one of my best friends from law school – Tex Wilson (more about him in Chapter 10). He may well have been the first black person to enter that apartment (other than housekeepers) since we moved there after the end of World War II. It wasn't that my parents and I were bigoted; it's just that, as was not unusual in those days, there had not been any individuals of color (other than Tex) in the circles in which we traveled.

Classes would be back in session right after the impending New Year's celebration, so we had time for just the briefest of honeymoons. We chose Atlantic City, and a travel agent (my father's cousin) made the booking. Barbro and I changed clothes when the reception ended, boarding a Greyhound bus that evening for the trip down to the Jersey shore.

It was late at night when we arrived at our destination – the hotel Haddon Hall, one of the more estimable establishments in the pre-gaming atmosphere of the town (ultimately incorporated into the first of the casino hotels, Resorts International, where it still stands today).

"Ah, yes," said the smiling desk clerk, "Mr. and Mrs. Freund, the newlyweds – we've been expecting you. And I'm sure you'll be delighted to know that you will be occupying our special bridal suite."

Barbro's face glowed, but I hadn't expected anything like this – and my response reflected a very practical consideration: "What's the nightly fare for the bridal suite?" I can't remember the exact number he then quoted, but it had three digits – an enormous sum for me in those days. Lacking a credit card, I simply didn't have enough to pay for our three-day stay, even if we fasted and eschewed all resort activities.

"Thanks for the thought," I said to the clerk, "but that's out of our league. We'll just take an ordinary room." I could tell that Barbro was deflated by my counter, but I was sure she'd come around to realize that we couldn't commit beyond our slim means.

"Oh, I'm afraid that's impossible, Mr. Freund," said the clerk. "After all, this is New Year's holiday, and every one of our other rooms is fully occupied. We've reserved the bridal suite for you, and we don't have any alternative to offer."

I was shocked. My anger at our travel agent for not warning us of this was mixed with chagrin over my failure to inquire about it earlier. I simply didn't know what to do.

The clerk was sympathetic to my plight. "If you can't afford the suite, Mr. Freund, I can call the Howard Johnson's Motor Inn which isn't too far away and see if they have a room for you and your bride."

I have to confess that this sounded to me like a reasonable solution for our problem, and I was about to give him the go-ahead when I glanced over at my new wife. Barbro's dejected expression, with a few tears slaloming down her cheek, melted my heart. Clearly, she hadn't contemplated spending our first ordained night together in a Howard Johnson's motel room.

Well, I managed to come through in the clutch. My wallet had enough money for the first night, although not for the rest of our stay (or for any honeymoon meals or entertainment); and since I was reluctant to spoil the glow of our nuptials, we took the suite. I figured that if I couldn't raise the needed funds the next day, Barbro would be willing to view the situation in a new light, and we'd check into the motel.

I must have gotten some help from my father on the 31st (leaving him to castigate his cousin for her extravagance), because we stayed the full time in the suite, managed to eat pretty well, and enjoyed some activities like riding horses on the beach.

Still, I didn't initially cover myself with glory. The spacious suite contained a large TV set, ideal for viewing the NFL Championship football game that I very much wanted to see. It was not a good choice for me to make on our first day as a married couple. (Not only that, but the Green Bay Packers destroyed my prized New York Giants, 37-0.) I behaved better for the rest of the honeymoon, but I'm not sure Barbro ever got over my pigskin callousness.

For the next five months of law school, Barbro and I lived in Boston in a "railroad flat." It was a one-room apartment on the top floor of a rental townhouse in Kenmore Square, adjacent to the tracks. Trains rumbled by at all hours, causing the glass skylight above our bed to rattle loudly through the night. (Just after we left for New York, our building and others along that strip were torn down and combined with the tracks roadbed to form the spacious lanes of the new Mass Pike.) Still, it was all ours, and a mostly happy place.

Barbro's job as a legal secretary in a law office near the Boston Common must have paid the rent and covered our meals, since I had no income at all. I hope that I showed some gratitude, although the recurring scene that sticks in my mind doesn't bear this out. Boston was very cold that winter, and Barbro had to put on extra layers of clothing for her long morning walk across the Common to her office. I, on the other hand, had managed to avoid scheduling any early morning classes. I can still picture myself, lying in the relative luxury of our bed, calling out to her bundled-up self as she left for work – "Hey, honey, ask your boss for a raise . . . ." Ugh!

Here's my favorite example of how tight a budget we lived on. I recall going to the butcher shop and asking the counterman, "What's the cheapest cut of meat you have?" He looked over all his offerings and replied, "Lamb liver." The thought of it still repels me – and the taste was appalling – but that's what we bought. (I also recall, but with greater pleasure, the 99-cent odd-shaped bottle of Chilean Riesling that we splurged for on occasions when we felt like celebrating.)

My classes at Harvard finally ended, Barbro left her job, and we moved to New York. Our prize possession that year had been a tiny Vespa car (which I'll elaborate on in Chapter 10). I'm sure we must have sent some of our things by freight, but what I remember was stuffing the Vespa's tiny back seat (there was no trunk) with so much stuff that it pressed us forward up to inches away from the front windshield throughout the 30 mph journey.

* * *

My parents had found us a two-room apartment at 175 West 79th Street (corner of Amsterdam) at a monthly rental of $114 (the number sticks in my mind). Barbro got a good job as a legal secretary. After studying for the bar exam, I became an associate at Davies, Hardy & Schenck starting at $7,200 per year. (My experiences at that law firm are covered in Chapter 11.) We weren't penniless during these first few NYC years, and it was a happy time, which included some stimulating trips – such as the one we took to Canada in the summer of '65 when Barbro was pregnant with Erik.

Erik was born in January 1966, the same month that I switched from Davies, Hardy to Skadden Arps [covered in Chapter 13.] I'm embarrassed to admit that a few days after Erik's birth, I took off for a solo New England ski trip. I felt this was needed to clear my head before plunging into the activist atmosphere of Skadden Arps. It couldn't have pleased Barbro; but her mother had come over from Sweden for the event, and between her Lydia and my thrilled mom, Barbro had all she could handle.

A few years later, Tom was born in August 1968. Barbro was fully engaged with our two sons, while I was going full speed at Skadden Arps. Most of our time together was spent with the kids, who were a delight to be around. Each year we had a different *au per* from Sweden living with us. They were of great help with the boys and we treated them as an integral part of the family.

Our summers were dominated by Fire Island. For two years we shared a house with the Klugers (Dick and Phyllis) and the Foggs (Fin and Diane), first in Fair Harbor and then in Seaview. We rented our own place for several years in Ocean Beach before buying a house there (at 333 Surf Road) in the early '70s. It wasn't fancy but proved truly serviceable. (The house went to me a decade later in our divorce; I then gifted it to the boys when they became adults; and eventually they sold it after hurricane Sandy did substantial damage, much of which wasn't covered by insurance.)

Barbro and the boys would go out to Fire Island when school ended in June and stay through Labor Day, rarely returning to NYC during the summer. I worked weekdays (except for one week of vacation), but headed out as early as possible on Friday – fighting through the weekend traffic to catch the ferry. The trek back to the city began on the early boat Monday morning. Barbro loved it out there, and it was nirvana for the boys – no cars to worry about, lots of freedom not available in the city, good friends, and plenty of sporting activities, including water-skiing in Great South Bay behind several modest motorboats we owned over the years.

One real highlight of our time on Fire Island was a big all-weekend party we threw (with the Bachers) for our long-term friends the year Fred and I turned 40 (1974). There was a memorable birthday dinner at a big restaurant in town and cookouts at our home, plus a plethora of notable events that we still laugh about 45 years later (ask me sometime about the colorful details).

We took some fine trips with our kids during those years – back to Sweden, to the Caribbean, to ski areas and such; and Barbro and I also traveled with the Bachers to Bermuda, Aruba, and Monaco/French Riviera.

Not only Barbro herself, but our whole family was proud of Barbro's adult academic accomplishments. Majoring in Art, she received both Bachelor and Master's Degrees from Columbia – all while running our household and mothering the boys.

We attended, and Barbro became a member of, the West End Collegiate Church, with the boys enrolled in Sunday School and participating in annual Christmas pageants. We became friendly with the splendid minister and associate minister – Ken Gorsuch and his wife Judy – and Ken and I still get together frequently.

* * *

I've always considered Barbro as having been a wonderful mother to Erik and Tom, and the boys certainly felt the same way as they recounted to me in several recent conversations. They loved her dearly. They spoke of the intimacy – hugging, kissing, and also verbal ("I love you"). "She was very caring," said Erik – "she nurtured me. You were good for baseball, Dad, but if I needed a bandaid or to get a splinter out, it was Mom I turned to." And Tom echoed the thought – "It was very warm, I felt safe, there was a lot of love in the house – and she gave equal time to each of us."

The boys were impressed – as was I – with Barbro's bilingual talent. They were proud of the fact that though grew up in a different country, she had mastered English so well. Tom recalls her reading to him in his early years, and how she savored the English language. When the family went to Sweden, they marveled at how Barbro handled things. As Erik put it: "She was proud of showing us her country. And she was our link; we would have felt weird without her there, but she made us feel welcome."

Although she didn't teach the boys to speak much Swedish (other than a few practical words and phrases they were fond of using), she did imbue them with her homeland's customs, especially those surrounding the holidays. For instance, presents were always exchanged on Christmas Eve, not the 25th. Each of them has special memory of the pre-Christmas Santa Lucia rite, when Barbro and the current *au pair* would attach lit candles to their headgear and serve me breakfast in bed.

Barbro wasn't a disciplinarian, but as Tom recalls, "She did speak up when we were too frisky. And she did care about our table manners." They were impressed with Mom's work toward bachelor's and master's degrees at Columbia. (Tom even remembers her having commented on a class she took with Margaret Mead.)

Tom told me of the great pleasure he felt when she approved of something he did. For instance, he remembers one such incident occurring in our apartment when he was about six. He said to his mother, "This room could use a little more white." The next day, she bought a white shag rug for it and told Tom, "You were right."

The boys recall how much Barbro loved being out on Fire Island with them – playing tennis, entertaining friends, and having parties for Tom's birthday each August. (Once, when he was very young, we gave him an early birthday party in June in order to convince him that he was old enough to pass the Youth Group's cut-off minimum age, if questioned.) Erik was also the subject of a joyous birthday party in the city each January.

Tom spoke of the strong positive feelings his friends had for his mother. (Many of my friends also felt the same way about her.) One of them told Tom that observing his excellent relations with Barbro proved to be the key to improving her relations with her own mother.

Barbro prepared a wonderful smorgasbord on special occasions. I can remember the boys passing over the initial dishes of seafood to get right to the smoked meats and meatballs. On regular nights, Barbro cooked lasagna and various ham, chicken, and egg dishes. She was ahead of the curve as a devotee of health foods.

The boys recall how competent Barbro was on skis – bringing back warm memories of our many ski vacations. I can still picture Barbro tenderly helping pre-school Tom put on his tight boots, while I waited impatiently for the family to get going. When it was cold, Barbro mixed coffee and hot chocolate together to create a tasty mocha drink.

They remember their mother as being very thrifty – foregoing taxicabs and other costly expenses. She kept a clean house, but largely by herself without help.

Barbro was very supportive of Tom's musical career. And Tom remembers her singing hymns in church, "with a sweet singing voice." I also can recall her sitting with me at the piano, singing along on the Swedish folk songs I liked to play.

* * *

In 1975, after years of living in a modest apartment on West End Avenue, Barbro decided it was time for us to move. She found a terrific 10-room apartment for sale, located in one of Manhattan's finest buildings, the Beresford (81st and Central Park West.) Because of the financial woes New York City was suffering at that time, the price tag on this beauty was only $100,000.

I was moving up in an expanding Skadden at that time but unsure as to what the future held. So even though the apartment was selling at a clear bargain price, I recall contacting Peter Mullen, our Executive Partner, to ask his opinion on whether I'd be able to afford it. He was confident that I would. Then I asked my friend, Joe Grotto, a Princeton classmate who had succeeded in real estate, for his view as to the merits of the purchase. I also consulted with Kit Watson, Bob's wife, to get her expert view on the decorating aspects. Both were quite enthusiastic. So I decided to move forward on the deal.

At that time, Barbro had taken one of her trips back to Sweden, and I received a troubled letter from her questioning whether we should go ahead with the purchase – she was worried that it would impose too serious a financial obligation on us. So she had given me an opening to back out – but by then I was convinced it was a good investment and went ahead anyway.

It proved to be a fine move from an investment point of view, but paradoxically it didn't turn out positive for us as a couple. (Perhaps I was receiving an omen of this the night before the move, when I sprained my back packing our possessions and had to lie in bed the next day while the movers and Barbro handled the whole thing.) Whatever the reason, our marriage didn't prosper in the fine setting of the Beresford. Here we were in the lap of luxury; and yet, what should have been our best time was the worst, ultimately leading to our mutual decision to separate in mid-1980.

I have various theories as to why things didn't work out between us, but I think it's best to keep those intimacies private. I'll just say that we each shared partial responsibility for the bonds ultimately dissolving. On my part, I can see now that I was not as attentive to Barbro as I should have been. I was working long days at the office, plus trying to write my *Lawyering* book in the remaining hours. When I did get home, I tended to focus my energies on the boys. Still, none of this constituted a justifiable excuse for my inattention.

I had few contacts with Barbro (who changed her last name to "Helm") in our post-divorce years. She moved to Greenwich, and Tom spent his last two years of high school with her there. According to the boys, she had a good life in Connecticut with friends and playing tennis regularly. And she always had room for the boys in later years when they would come back from where they were then living – even, Erik said, "when I arrived with a girl friend and a dog."

Barbro visited the boys out west and attended (as did I) each of their college graduations. She was a much-loved grandmother to Delilah and Paige. Tom can picture her reading Harry Potter to Delilah and recalls the connection they had through love of art; Erik recollects Barbro and Paige doing a craft together on one of her visits to their New Jersey home.

In later years, my relations with Barbro became more amicable, and we enjoyed periodic lunches together at her favorite restaurants in Greenwich. Things finally got to the stage where I felt we could reminisce about our past good times – something I was really looking forward to – when she passed away suddenly in 2012.

Barbro and I had some rough stretches – especially toward the tail-end of our marriage and in the early years thereafter – but I've tried to put that aside and to remember some enjoyable times we shared together. And what I'm proudest of, in retrospect, was our joint heartfelt efforts regarding our terrific kids, Erik and Tom – efforts in which we were almost always on the same page.

Photos of Barbro Freund
(née Hellström)
(later Helm)

The bride and groom, the comely bride, with attendants Ellen Donovan and Bob Watson,
and with my parents and grandparents.

The bridegroom with attendants Bacher, Veatch, Doyle and Watson.
The five of us together again about 60 years later.

Five photos of us (plus two ponies) from our brief honeymoon in Atlantic City. We revisited A.C. a decade later with the boys and our au pair Elizabeth (below).

Mother and child –

– plus proud grand-parents

Tom's christening at St. Peter's church, 1968.

Barbro with the boys and
our first au pair, Anneli;
Erik with Barbro and me;
the boys with Barbro's
father, niece and nephew;
celebrating the
pre-Christmas
Santa Lucia
rite with au pair Birgit;
celebrating Christmas
with the boys, my father,
and au pair Ylva.

These two photos illustrate the close kinship between Barbro and the boys. In the photos below she is with her mother (left) and sister and brother-in-law (right).

We made a number of trips with Fred and Claudine Bacher – some of our most enjoyable moments.

The group picture below, which includes the Watsons, Bachers, Riordans and Silbeys, captured another welcome occasion.

The whole gang at my memorable 40th birthday party weekend in 1974, anchored by our OceanBeach house. On other weekends we hosted guests, such as Ken Gorsuch's family.

Barbro graduating from Columbia.

10. HARVARD LAW SCHOOL (1959 – 1962)

Since I later achieved some success as a lawyer, one might assume that I must have relished law school. But that assumption would be wrong – I didn't enjoy it at all. One might also assume, since the institution happened to be Harvard Law School (HLS), that I got a lot out of the experience. For many years, however, my response would have been equally negative. But in reconsidering my past experiences for the memoir, I've given this a fresh look and now have a more nuanced view of my HLS days.

I'll get to the positive factors a little later. First, though, I feel obliged to focus on why I disliked law school so intently back then. You want to know how intently? So much so that I actually found myself at times pining for m prior life in the Navy! After graduation, not only did I decline to contribute annually to the Harvard Law School fund, but for years I even declined to repay my student loan.

My animus to Harvard Law School can probably be traced to a combination of factors.

First, unlike most of my law school classmates who came there directly from college (or one year later, if they'd served the then typical six-month tour of Army duty), I was a full three years away from the scholastic pressure of academia. The atmosphere on the icebreaker had been decidedly non-cerebral, and I found it hard to shake that off – slow to regain the rapt attention needed in class and to develop constructive study habits.

I also attribute part of my angst back then to impatience. There I was, receiving news about Horace Mann and Princeton classmates who were already out there prospering in the business world. By contrast, I was strapped financially and enmeshed in the seemingly never-ending task of getting a law degree – and even that would only represent the starting point in my quest for a comfortable life.

It wasn't just the three-year gap that accounted for my academic discomfort. The plain fact was that I found law school tougher than college. Part of this was due to the courses I was required to take. Although some of them (such as Contracts) did interest me, many others (like Civil Procedure) didn't, and I found it hard to wrestle with their nuances. Also, while some of the professors were excellent (e.g., Lon Fuller for Contracts), I found some others – legal scholars though they may have been – wanting as

188

teachers. In one case, the combination of a subject I didn't take to and a professor I had no use for put such a negative slant on real property that I shunned realty transactions throughout my legal career.

Little empathy existed between teachers and students at HLS back then – at least any I was privy to. The Dean was a hard-nosed guy who projected a very tough, friendless image for the school.

The Socratic method used in almost all my law school courses at the time may have been pedagogically sound, but it didn't inspire much affection for the underlying subject matter. I found the trudge through the cases to be tedious, and listening to other students attempt to address the professor's questions soon became tiresome.

For anyone familiar with the books or cinema versions of *One L* and *Paper Chase*, these were accurate reflections of the pressure we felt to be prepared on the current study assignment, so as to be able to reply with some conviction when called upon in class by the professor. I rarely felt any confidence on that score; and I'll now confess that there were many days on which I abandoned my assigned seat (where the professor, consulting his seating chart, might have called on me by name) for a cowardly anonymous perch in the rear of the classroom.

As contrasted with college where most courses were half-year, many of the law school courses ran for a full year – and the only mark that counted was how well you did on the final exam in May, eight months from when the course began the previous September. So you needed to study and lock in legal principles a long time before having to prove you knew your stuff, which frankly seemed agonizing.

As I reflect on this now, I realize there's another reason that I found law school tougher than college. As an undergraduate, the key was to memorize a lot of stuff fed to you in the course and then regurgitate it on the exam – something I was good at (*magna cum laude*-wise). In law school, though, you first had to grasp the applicable legal principle (from the morass found in the cases we'd read and the often ambiguous lessons absorbed in class), and then apply it correctly to the hypothetical situation described on the exam (which differed from the ones in the cases) – something I struggled with in law school (although still managing to graduate *cum laude*) and only became comfortable with in practice.

I can still remember the Civil Procedure session on the first day of the first year. One student had evidently gotten hold of the initial reading assignment before school started and began pontificating in class about all the stuff he'd already absorbed, to the utter distress of the rest of us.

Nor did things change with time. Here's an instance from the third year. I always wrote my exams by hand, but since my handwriting wasn't good, I began to wonder whether the professors might be penalizing me for forcing them to decipher illegible answers. So, I decided to type my exam for one course, in a separate room for typists only. (For youngsters reading this, it was many years later before personal computers came into being.)

Most exams were such that you needed to spend the first 20 minutes or so reading over the entire problem before you could decide how to attack it. On this day, however, within two minutes of the exam being handed out, one guy started typing. The loud racket of his typewriter reverberated around the room. It scared the hell out of me, and I did poorly on that exam. Needless to say, I reverted back to my illegible handwriting for subsequent tests.

It wasn't just the courses that contributed to the bleakness of Harvard Law School. What got me off to a bad start was living in a dorm the first year. The small unadorned room that each of us inhabited may have been barely adequate, but it was the atmosphere of the place I found to be chilling. I can't remember developing a single friendship in my dorm. The adjacent school cafeteria was also appalling – I usually passed it up for a nearby place outside the school that served fast, cheap, edible food.

My worst recurring memory of the dorm was returning there at midnight after an evening out on a date or with friends, walking down that long interior hallway to my room – and hearing the typewriters clicking away in every room I passed! Such serious guys . . . .

After about 25 years, I mellowed in my view of law school– even paid off my student debt – and have been attending reunions every five years since. But I still get a funny feeling in the pit of my stomach when I return to Cambridge – the same one I felt back then every spring as exam time approached. And at times I still experience that recurring nightmare – an exam coming up tomorrow for a course in which I'd failed to attend a single session.

Those bad dreams do remind me of one of my buddies who rarely went to class. Then, the night before the exam, he'd pore over some course notes prepared by others and end up with pretty good grades. Except for one time, when he actually attended the last session of a course he was enrolled in but had never previously been to, simply to find out the room number where the exam would take place. When he inquired about that, the professor asked him. "Who are you? – I've never seen you here before" – to which he candidly responded by admitting he hadn't attended any classes. This proved to be too much for Harvard, and they kicked him out of school for a year.

* * *

Let me now turn from the negatives to a few positives which have gradually claimed a place in my appraisal of the experience.

I'll start with the unsurprising observation that you need a law school degree to practice law – and this was my license to practice. You also need to pass the state bar exam, which I managed to do on my first try. (Harvard has to share that credit with the bar review course I took and the force-fed cramming I endured over many weeks prior to the exam.)

I also have to acknowledge the positive impact a Harvard Law School degree has in professional circles and with the general public. It undoubtedly stood me in good stead in future years, and (as you'll see in Chapter 13) it played an indirect but crucial role in my ending up at the law firm that made my dreams come true.

Amidst my negativity about the courses I took was one bright spot. Back in those days, many of the numerous required courses proved to be tedious. I didn't do much better on elective courses. (One of the few absorbing ones I took wasn't even at the law school – it was on foreign policy, taught in another part of the university by a young Henry Kissinger.) What best exemplifies my lack of initiative was when I decided to pass up a well-regarded securities regulation course taught by a prominent scholar simply because it met early on Saturday morning.

Finally though, in my third year, I found a well-taught course that I enjoyed immensely and which inspired me in the direction of my eventual practice. David Herwitz, a memorable teacher, introduced us to problem-solving, negotiation and handling transactions. It's hard to believe now, but back then I think he was just about the only professor doing something practical like that in the whole school. I was delighted not to have to wrestle with all the case law learning (which was primarily aimed at those who would become litigators), and to come face-to-face with what would turn out to be my life's work – doing deals.

Many other students who took the Herwitz course over the years were also grateful to him. About 40 years later, when David was retiring from the Law School, Delaware jurist Jack Jacobs and I threw a surprise party for this modest man at my New York home (to which David's wife lured him on a false pretext). That evening, a few dozen of his admirers (whom we culled from his class lists) told David in person how important he'd been to all of us.

Given my more benign current attitude towards HLS, I should mention two significant long-term takeaways for me from all those classes I scorned. First, the recognition that there was almost always more than one way to come out on any issue; and second, the force-fed learning of how to reason analytically, without which I doubt I'd have been able later to exercise good judgment in both professional and personal situations.

Here's a third plus. I previously touched on the agony of having to study eight months ahead of a test. Well, I ultimately came to realize that this served to underscore the significance of appreciating deferred gratification – a lesson which proved invaluable during the much longer periods it took to complete the books I wrote in later life.

* * *

Putting aside negatives and positives, let me reflect a bit on what I did during those three years.

There were two private clubs available to law students. I chose Chancery, the more raucous of the pair. They served meals and had a bar and party room in the basement, with an aged piano bereft of ivory on most of the keys. There was also a tiny room wedged in the garret of the old building.

I was basically broke, so I worked out a deal with Chancery for my second and third years to let me use the little garret space as my bedroom and to provide me with free meals, in exchange for my taking charge of the club's bar activities (which at times included bartending) and playing some late night piano, especially on weekends and party evenings. The accommodations weren't plush, and the food scarcely gourmet, but it was a definite step up from the dorm and cafeteria.

192

I stayed in that little room from June of 1960 through December 1961. Then, after marrying Barbro between Christmas and New Year's, I moved to our railroad flat in Boston (described in Chapter 9) for the balance of my third year.

A Navy buddy of mine, Jim Messing, and his lovely wife Ellen (still a good friend today) were living in the area; and Jim, along with a partner, became a franchisee of the Vespa company in Italy. Vespa's main product was a motor scooter, but at this time they were experimenting with a small car. I'm talking really tiny – it made the VW Bug and Fiat appear sedan-like by comparison.

I needed a means of transportation, and (after a bad experience with a used car in Seattle) wanted a spanking new vehicle. By far the cheapest new car around was a Vespa, clocking in at a four-digit figure that began with a "1". Still, I didn't have even that much dough, so I bought a Vespa on credit – although the credit was Barbro's, who was holding down a real job as an airline stewardess. She had to sign as my guarantor, without which even my buddy Jim wouldn't sell the car to me. I always appreciated Barbro's willingness here to step up to the plate for me even before we were married.

The Vespa had a two cylinder, two-cycle engine that produced minimal horsepower. While pumping gas, you had to manually stir oil in with it. The car's performance, although agonizingly slow, was passable on flat roads (and a little better on those that tended downwards), but it just couldn't handle a steep hill if someone was sitting in the passenger seat. I still remember the evening when my buddy Bob Smith and I were visiting our Princeton friend, Don MacElwee, who lived in a Boston suburb. We encountered a hill along the way, and the Vespa was overtaxed by our combined weight – so Bob had to exit the car and jog alongside until we reached a level stretch of road.

The Vespa, though, was great to park in town – taking up less space than even one of those Smart cars nowadays. There was, however, one recurring risk. On more than one occasion, I'd come down in the morning and find the Vespa sitting in the middle of the sidewalk (or worse) – it was just too tempting for a few drunk guys to hoist the little fella onto their shoulders and plunk it down somewhere else.

I didn't have the wide circle of friends at Harvard as I'd had at Princeton. This may have been more attributable to my own sour attitude then their availability. Some good friends whom I've nurtured in later years through reunions and otherwise – such as the delightful Louis Braswell from Mobile, Alabama, and Harvey Feuerstein of New York – I didn't get to know as well as I should have in law school. Still, a couple of guys from those HLS years do stand out.

My big buddy at law school was Bob Smith. He was a clubmate from Princeton, a year behind me there. We weren't close back then, each of us being more intent on spending time with his own circle of classmate friends. After Princeton, Bob served two years in the Marines, so we ended up in the same class at law school – and fortunately were placed in the same section, which meant we shared all classes together for our first year and most of the second. We discovered each other the first week of school and were inseparable thereafter – at least until each of us got married during the third year.

Smitty and I fell into a routine that first year. After the final morning class, we'd head over to a small joint on Mass. Avenue, gulp down a quick lunch, then move on to the basement of the women's dormitory (yes, there were a handful of girls in law school back then), where a rarely used ping pong table resided. We would then take out all our frustrations in a fierce, sweaty hour-long rivalry. Bob usually won – although not before I had to duck his racket flying across the room to punctuate a missed shot. This, by the way, was about the only exercise I remember getting while in law school.

After competing we'd retreat somewhere to study together, although that could be almost as hectic as the ping pong. Smitty had a brilliant sense of humor, and I was no slouch, so we'd bat things back and forth , with sly digs and such, at a furious pace. I can picture us second year, studying in that tiny garret room of mine at Chancery, where I'd put up a dart board behind the door. At intervals, as we completed a tough section of study, we'd take turns hurling the darts at the board with a ferocity born of acute frustration.

When I took over responsibility for the bar (a commercial enterprise) at Chancery, Bob (also a member) and I plotted how to go about rejuvenating its lagging revenues. I suggested a large well-publicized party opening night, at which free beer would be served. The party was a huge success, lots of people showed up, and I was ecstatic – certain that this presaged great things ahead. Bob's reaction was more reserved – let's see who comes next week when they have to pay, he said. And he was so right – only a handful showed up. We had a good laugh, as we absorbed this important lesson that came in handy the rest of our lives.

Bob was an usher at my wedding, and his first wife Ellen was Barbro's matron of honor. Then, after studying together for the New York bar, we went to the same law firm, Davies, Hardy and Schenck (discussed in Chapter 11). Later, Smitty moved to Atlanta and ultimately became the managing partner of a good-sized firm there, which ultimately was absorbed by the Jones, Day firm. Unfortunately we haven't seen each other much in recent years.

One of our best friends at Harvard was Tom Morris, who'd been two years behind me at Princeton. You may remember Tom from the tale I told about the football goalpost in Chapter 6 – the one in which my roommates and I were such troglodytes. When we met again at Harvard, I confessed my guilt to Tom, who remembered the trauma but was good enough to forgive my youthful indiscretion. We developed a warm relationship – and, as it turned out, not only on the law school campus.

Tom, as a college football star, had become the coach of the tackle football team fielded by one of the Harvard residential houses. They played the teams of the other houses in a vigorous intramural league, with the league winner taking on the top team of the Yale residential colleges at the end of the season.

When an opening to coach one of the other Harvard houses developed during our second year, Tom – knowing I'd played freshman football at Princeton – recommended me, and I got the job. We practiced once or twice a week, then played a game. My team wasn't too successful, but we were competitive. As a welcome break from the tension of law school, I enjoyed it thoroughly.

Still, here's the football scene I remember best. One Sunday I'd watched a New York Giants game on television and got excited about a play they'd used, which I thought would be well-suited for my team. So, at our Monday practice, I introduced it into the playbook – diagramming it from memory. Since the team's quarterback couldn't attend practice that day, I filled in as quarterback as we ran through the play.

Except for me in my street clothes, the players were all in full football uniforms. I took the snap from the center, whirled to fake one handoff and then slip the ball to the second guy, when all of a sudden, I was blindsided – smacked in the head by the helmet of one of the halfbacks. (Either I'd mis-diagrammed the play or the halfback wasn't following instructions – I never did find out which.)

The collision with the helmet fractured my nose, leaving it dangling way to the side. My HM friend, Ed Aronson (who acted as my assistant coach while at Harvard Business School), rushed me to a local hospital where they snapped it back in place, but my nose has never looked quite the same since. Ed called my parents with this message: "You might want to come up and see Jim – but don't be surprised, he doesn't look like you remember him."

I don't usually focus on matters involving the Almighty, but I've long held the view that what happened to me that day at Harvard was the Lord's payback for the goalpost indignity I'd subjected Tom Morris to at Princeton . . . .

Through my HLS buddy Jackie Haas, I met Tex Wilson who became my first African-American friend. Prior to meeting him, I simply had not come into contact with any blacks – not at Horace Mann nor Princeton, not in the Navy, not anywhere. Tex, who stood well above six feet, was a wonderful guy – smart, funny, the works. He had a booming baritone voice and sang with real zest. Most weeks we had at least one late night session around the rickety piano in the Chancery basement. *Old Man River* was his tune of choice – reaching way down for those low notes, and then hitting the high ones at the end to display his awesome range.

For reasons I don't remember, I decided to stay in Cambridge during the summer between my first and second year, moving into that little garret room at Chancery. Tex also stayed in town that summer, and we spent many evenings together at the club, drinking beer, watching TV, and schmoozing. It was 1960, the fascinating year of the Kennedy vs. Nixon election campaign.

Both of us needed money and took odd jobs where available. We saw an ad one day that said painters were needed on a certain local construction job. I'll never forget the scene – Tex and I arriving at the site in my tiny Vespa, our doors opening to reveal to the assembled construction workers the short white guy emerging from the driver's side and the tall black guy from the passenger side – not a combo people were used to seeing back then. The onlookers may have been aghast, but we got the job – although it only lasted for a day. After that, Tex went on to land a prime all-summer job, driving a Mr. Softee truck around town.

We stayed friendly after he graduated – he came to my wedding (as I've said), we got together for sing sessions in NYC and DC. Then one day, Tex took a nasty fall down a flight of stairs in his home and went into a coma. I remember visiting him in the hospital, turning on my cassette player for him – I'd recorded *Old Man River* on the piano – to see if I could generate some reaction. I couldn't, and soon thereafter he died at an early age. I had I lost a special friend.

My next job that summer in Cambridge was the worst – an encyclopedia salesman. We had to make cold calls on the phone, and then, if any interest was shown, arrange to go out that night to visit the prospect. Only a few calls clicked – and then I felt bad at the home, trying to talk these people into buying something they would probably never use and could not really afford. I finally quit, with just one sale to my name.

Then I found something more in my line of work. I'd gone over to the law school placement office to see if any opportunities had surfaced, and this time one had. I'd be working for an attorney in downtown Boston named Francis Juggins.

Juggins was a real old-time lawyer – a single practitioner, semi-retired, with just a single case that needed some help on the brief. I'd go to his downtown office in the morning, work a little on the brief, and eat a quick lunch. Then each day I'd be called into Mr. J's office. It wasn't to discuss the brief, though – he just wanted someone he could talk to.

He was a fascinating story-teller, with a lot of material from "the old days." Recognizable characters often flitted in and out of a story – such as Jack Kennedy's mother, Rose – and several of the stories were repeated day after day. Then, every afternoon after talking without any interruption for a half-hour, the voice would suddenly cease and I could tell that he'd fallen asleep. I'd wait a few minutes, just to be sure, and then tiptoe out of his office into mine, where I spent the rest of the afternoon reading a magazine or novel while he slept. We did finish the brief (although I never learned how the case came out); and I made just enough money to cover my meals and entertainment.

The next summer between my second and third years, which was spent working for my father, has been described in Chapter 3.

* * *

When it came time during the Fall of the third year to interview for permanent jobs, I developed a plan to provide me with a variety of opportunities. I would seriously consider one large firm, one medium-sized firm, and one small firm, all in New York City; I'd also look at one firm based outside NYC, one corporate counsel slot, and one government job.

Firms were not exactly falling over themselves to snap me up – especially once they determined that I was not related to Paul Freund, a high-profile Harvard Law professor often mentioned for the Supreme Court. So, when a good mid-sized firm in Cleveland showed some real interest, I quickly plugged them in as my choice for outside-NYC.

The firm flew me out to Cleveland at their expense, and a partner picked me up at the airport. We drove back to town through the estimable Shaker Heights suburb, and I remember him saying, "Here's where you'll live."

At the firm – a good one with very intelligent lawyers and an interesting practice – I was treated grandly. I met many of the partners, each of whom made a fuss over me. Several of them took me out to an excellent dinner at a private club, following which they drove me back to my downtown hotel at about 9:30.

Hey, I found myself thinking, this just might be the right firm for me. . . . They're skilled, they do good stuff, they care about yours truly. . . .

Back in the hotel room, I took off my three-piece interview suit and changed into some informal clothes. After a long day of acting as a professional, it was now time to hit a few bars, hear some music and such.

I took the elevator down, strode through the lobby, and came out on this prime downtown street, alive to the possibilities. And then – just nothing. The town was completely dead; Cleveland had gone to sleep by ten pm.

I turned around, went back up to my room, flipped on the TV, and realized I could never move to the Midwest. (I recall thinking that I wouldn't even be able to get a good pastrami sandwich there . . . .)

But if the firm had kept me at dinner for a few more hours, I might be out there today, cheering for the Browns and Indians . . . .

The corporation and government jobs didn't work out, so it was New York for me. I got an offer from one large firm – not of the highest rank, but well-known and boasting a large Princeton contingent. What I didn't like about the firm was my sense that I was only being tapped because of my Princeton connection – I guess I wanted to be yearned because of me.

The small firm that went after me turned out to be Roy Cohn's firm. This happened because I knew one of the associates there, and he got the firm to make me an offer. I didn't meet Cohn, but he was controversial enough for me to seek advice from a lawyer friend of my parents. The friend waggled his head from side to side: "Don't go there," he said, and I didn't. Whew!

The medium-sized firm that both my buddy Bob Smith and I were attracted to was Davies Hardy & Schenck. They had a good group of young lawyers who wined and dined us when we visited, made us feel wanted – and the two of us liked the idea of staying together.

So that's where we went . . . . but things didn't quite work out as we anticipated.

11. DAVIES, HARDY & SCHENCK (1962 – 1965)

My first 40 months as a lawyer, from the fall of 1962 through all of 1965, I spent as an associate at the law firm of Davies, Hardy & Schenck ("DH&S").

This is the third of those three activities between Princeton and Skadden Arps – totaling about 10 years in the aggregate – that I've characterized as the dismal decade of my adult life. But this DH&S chapter differs in one key respect from its predecessors. I actively disliked the two prior experiences – serving in the Navy and attending law school – and although I've tried in this memoir to acknowledge some of their constructive elements, they remain in my mind as predominantly downbeat.

In contrast, the DH&S years were by and large enjoyable – spent in a pleasant enough environment, neither arduous nor intimidating, and in the company of a lot of good people, especially my buddy Smitty. So my negativity here was of a different shade – emanating from the sense I had, right from the start, that my voluntary decision to join the firm had been a mistake. I simply wasn't learning anything of consequence or progressing as a professional in a meaningful way; the trifling prospects for improvement there were unlikely to change; and I could tell that extricating myself from this self-sprung trap would not be easy to do.

But I'm getting ahead of the story. First, let me provide some backdrop about those three-plus years.

* * *

DH&S was a firm of around 40 lawyers at a time when almost all the so-called large firms had under 100. Its lineage traced back to the late 19th century. The offices were in the relatively new (but not first-class) building at Two Broadway, adjacent to Bowling Green at the southern tip of Manhattan. Its practice areas included litigation, corporate, real estate, tax, estates/trusts, and labor/employment. The partners were competent and ethical, the associates a talented lot from a variety of major law schools.

So what was the problem? It was simply that the firm lacked a workload of sufficient business – especially in the corporate department that I'd joined – to provide constructive activity for the associates. As for the reason, well, right from the start I became aware of an event – occurring before I got to DH&S but well-known to all there – that was a major cause of this sorry circumstance.

Davies Hardy had been faring pretty well into the mid-20th century, primarily on the basis of having two excellent corporate clients – IBM and Woolworth. (The firm never really capitalized on its representation of Irving Trust and the Episcopal Church.) Then in the '50s the U.S. government brought a major anti-trust case against IBM. Unfortunately, DH&S had no lawyers who specialized in anti-trust. Although there were a number of highly competent anti-trust lawyers in smaller firms whom DH&S could have brought aboard to handle the case, DH&S chose a different path. They turned the case over to Cravath, Swaine & Moore, the behemoth of NYC law firms. In short order, Cravath infiltrated all aspects of the DH&S/IBM relationship (anti-trust, after all, cuts across most corporate disciplines); and before long, Cravath had run off with IBM as a full-time client.

With IBM gone, Woolworth wasn't a substantial enough source of business to energize DH&S. None of the DH&S corporate partners were effective business-getters, so very few new clients came in the door. One sign of their lackluster mentality with regard to generating new business was that DH&S lawyers were not permitted to carry business cards, which must have seemed to the firm's venerable powers-that-be too commercially grubby.

Another painful tale going around when I arrived at the firm focused on one of the hottest young brokage/investment banking firms in the '60s, which by that time was being represented by another law firm. The story was that these securities hopefuls had originally come to DH&S in order to get themselves organized to do business. But because DH&S had no background in this area, it over-lawyered the simple process egregiously and then handed the start-up firm a big legal bill – thereby dooming the relationship before any momentum could be generated.

Didn't I have any warning of all this? No, back then there were no publications (like *American Lawyer* and *National Law Journal*) that later specialized in providing info on how various firms were doing. I hadn't been a summer associate at the firm, which might have offered some clues. I was regrettably innocent enough of business realities not to have asked any pertinent questions in the interview process. In short, I had little idea about this lack of operational pizazz until I was already signed, sealed and delivered.

* * *

I spent much of my time at DH&S – from the early days when new associates were given a desk in the library to my more elevated status occupying a cubbyhole office in a lesser section of the floor – on the lookout for something of significance to do, but finding few possibilities.

Inspired by a nascent interest in securities law and that stimulating third year class at law school with David Herwitz, I had opted for corporate practice. But during the whole time I was at DH&S, I recall being involved in just one or two uninspiring acquisitions and a single mundane public offering. What I did do were some very tedious chores for Woolworth – activity related to multi-state taxes, or examining (while huddled in a small airless conference room) hundreds of leases of a multi-location retail group to check the wording of the assignment clauses for a potential acquisition.

Here's a prime indicator of how bad things were. Another associate and I were asked to draft an indenture covering some bonds or debentures being issued. This was the most boilerplate legal draftsmanship imaginable, but neither of us had any experience with indentures. So rather than simply copy one from the many publicly available, we decided to flesh out the assignment by building a new indenture from scratch. We went over each stale provision with a fine tooth comb, running up numerous hours, simply to have something to do when we came to the office in the morning.

I emphasize "in the morning," as contrasted with "in the night". It was well-known that Julian Davies, the senior partner, did not like to see anyone still at work after six pm and was reported to have had the heat turned down early each winter evening.

Regarding Mr. Davies, fellow associate Joe Hilton (with whom I'd attended Horace Mann a decade before) recently reminded me of another idiosyncrasy of the senior partner. Davies required every lawyer who worked with him to bring a hat to the office, and he insisted that they never go out on appointments without one. Joe recalls a painful day when Julian asked him to "put on your hat and join me for a meeting with Irving Trust" – but Joe had no hat to wear and was forced to endure Davies' withering stare bareheadedly.

Smitty and I once composed a song about Davies, Hardy (sung to the tune of "In China they never serve chili") which we performed at a firm party. Fellow associate Bernie Althoff still recalls the words of the repetitive chorus as: "Aye, aye, aye, aye / On Wall Street they never call Julie / So here comes another day / that's just like the other day / Dull work and the wages are coolie."

Speaking of wages, we certainly weren't overpaid for our lack of effort, although our starting salary of $7,200 per annum was the same that associates of every sizeable firm in New York City received. Then, each year, it would go up by $1,000 – although lacking any bonus feature, as some other firms had instituted.

I remember the time the Cravath firm broke that spell and increased associate salaries to a higher level. Some firms followed suit, but not DH&S. So Smitty and I approached our favorite partner, Bob West, to ask why we weren't being similarly treated. His very matter-of-fact answer – "Because you don't work as hard as those guys do" – said it all, and we had no rejoinder.

So how did we pass the time? Well, for one thing, we took long enjoyable group lunches at various restaurants of note in the financial district – often accompanying the hearty food with beer or, on occasion, something stronger.

Tom Adams, a fellow associate I remained friendly with in later years until his recent passing, liked to tell this story. When he first came to the firm, he was taken out to lunch by a senior litigation partner. The partner told the waiter, "We'll have two martinis." The waiter asked, "Gin or vodka?" The partner replied, "Gin". After the waiter left, the partner instructed Tom as follows: "When you drink a lunchtime martini on a working day, Tom, be sure it's a gin martini – not a vodka one. That way, if you screw up on something in the afternoon, the partners will know the reason was because you'd been drinking – not because you're incompetent."

Since we could stretch those lunch hours out indefinitely, I took to engaging in other activities. I remember once when my friend, Tex Wilson, joined Smitty and me at a golf driving range in Brooklyn to hit some balls.

And then there was the incident on the ferry. . . . Fred Bacher worked down in the Wall Street area, and we would sometimes play chess at lunchtime. One day I figured out that we could conduct our game on the Staten Island Ferry – getting a little salt air and finishing the game on the round trip, in time to get back to the office.

It so happened that on a certain day when we'd planned to lunch on the briny, a DH&S senior partner had given me an envelope of important documents which, rather than entrust to a messenger, he wanted me to personally deliver to an important Woolworth executive in the Woolworth Building. I didn't want to break my date with Fred, so I took the envelope along with us on the ferry, to be delivered after we got back.

What happened – oh, this is still painful to recall! – was that I became so involved in our chess match that I forgot about the envelope (which I'd placed on an adjacent bench while we played), and I walked off the ferry without it. By the time I remembered the envelope and tried to reboard the ferry, it was back at sea. Panic seized me. I called the ferry office to see if they could locate the envelope, but to no avail. Frantic by now, I made my way back to 2 Broadway, where an urgent message to see the senior partner "immediately" awaited me.

It turned out that someone had indeed found the package. He called up the Woolworth executive to whom it was addressed, said that he found it "on the Staten Island ferry," made some blackmail-like remarks before offering to return it "for an appropriate reward" – oh God, I can't go on....

Well, Woolworth did eventually receive the envelope, no meaningful corporate secrets were publicly disclosed, and our main client wasn't out too much reward money – but my reputation, both at the firm and at Woolworth, never did fully recover.

There was one special activity we engaged in to pass the time – so special that in 1965 I wrote an article about it for the Sunday magazine section of the New York Herald Tribune entitled *Let the Umpire Beware* (my first post-college published piece). Here's how the article began.

> *From May through August each year, the self-styled Law Firm Softball League operates to provide young men from a score of New York's most prestigious firms a temporary balm from cerebral demands. Every weekday evening during the sticky summer months, elite refugees from the halls of ivy do battle on the dirt playing fields bordering the city's melting pot.*

The article, although not without factual basis, abounded in mockery of lawyers and legalisms. Here's a scene, for instance, from a meeting the teams held to revise the league's rule book:

> *Some instructive legislative history can be gleaned from a comparison of the annual amendments. An attempt to be too specific, for example, might require future generalizing modification. Thus, the 1963 rule outlawing fast pitching prohibited:*

(a) windmill windups;
(b) pitches that rise as they near the plate, and
(c) pitches that would commonly be considered fast (e.g., the fast pitches of the three league pitchers known last year as being "fast ball" pitchers.)

The correlative 1964 rule, which also proscribed pitches that "would commonly be considered fast," was forced to omit the parenthetical clause because the three young men in question, their high hard ones muted during the 1963 season, had presumable departed, disgruntled, for private industry.

The bulk of the article involved the inevitable disputes arising on the field over such matters as what degree of darkness terminates the game prematurely, the use of non-legal "ringers" on a team, and how worthwhile is a city permit to claim the diamond when it's currently occupied by "seven angry men of underprivileged background." I enjoyed writing the article, and it received a lot of attention at the time.

* * *

So, what (if any) long-term good came from the Davies Hardy experience?

I picked up some familiarity with legal instruments that resulted in ultimate benefit. For instance, that extended indenture boondoggle I mentioned earlier did make me more aware of how business/financial documents work, a major point of reference in my later writings on acquisitions.

I'm sure I must have garnered some useful practical knowledge from the capable corporate department partners I worked with.

The minimal hours of billable work permitted me to take some continuing education courses of value, especially in the field of securities.

I learned this important fact about myself – that I didn't like being under-utilized. It may have taken just this extended post-Navy exposure to tedium to awaken my innate desire to get fully involved in and skilled at my chosen profession.

Most notably, the opportunity to re-unite at the firm with fellow associate Joe Hilton paved the way for our telltale meeting on the street two decades later that eventually sparked my most delightful change of life – but more about that in Chapter 18.

* * *

Although the nagging feeling that I wasn't getting the kind of experience needed to excel in the profession increased monthly – as did my fear of being doomed to mediocrity – I still wasn't doing anything about it. I probably could have found something useful to do that would have furthered the firm's interests, but I lacked the zest to make the effort.

I've given some fresh thought as to what produced this lethargy in me and have come up with several different theories. Most likely, it was a mélange of them all.

First, the absence of pressure that accompanied life at DH&S wasn't such a bad thing at the time, following as it did the constant stress I'd felt at law school. Frankly, the short hours suited me just fine during that first portion of my marriage to Barbro, good years indeed.

Second was the atmosphere at the firm. I discussed this recently with my friend, Dick Scribner, a fellow Princetonian at DH&S who went through the same process I did before emerging from the firm's cocoon about a year after me.

"You know, Jim," Dick said, "a lot of what kept us there was due to the guys who were associates. *[Guys, I should insert, because there was only one woman in the whole firm.]* We were all buddies, pals – the atmosphere was like one of our Princeton eating clubs, hanging out with the guys. I had some good relationships at places I worked later on, but I thought of those people as colleagues rather than friends. My memories of DH&S are mostly warm ones about the people." I concur with Dick's observation.

Another reason for delay was that it wasn't so simple in the '60s for associates to switch law firms. All the significant firms had policies in place not to accept lateral entries, so the only places you could hope to land at were smaller, less well-known firms – which didn't strike me as the kind of step up I was looking for.

I'm not sure what finally got me to shake off my torpor and search in earnest for another job. Maybe it was because Smitty left DH&S to move to Atlanta, and other friends also departed or were contemplating it. I could foresee that those enjoyable gatherings we'd been having might be coming to an end. Perhaps it was because Barbro was pregnant, our first child was due to be born in January 1966, and I wanted to be resettled by that time.

In any event, I finally swung into action during the second half of 1965, taking steps that ultimately resulted in one of those serendipitous happenings (*sheer happenstance*) that influence the rest of one's days. It's a tale I'll relate in Chapter 13.

12. MY SONS, ERIK & TOM

Two momentous events in my life occurred simultaneously in January 1966. One of them– the beginning of my career at Skadden – I'll cover in the next chapter. The other was the birth of my first child, Erik.

Therein lies a tale I can't resist passing along. It's now the first weekend of the New Year, and Barbro's due date for the emergence of "the baby" is drawing near. We don't know what the gender will turn out to be (although truth be told, I'm rooting for a boy). Her obstetrician (let's call him Dr. K) is out of town, but we're told not to be concerned because his capable partner (Dr. S) is available.

Sure enough, Barbro's water breaks. We're aware that time is short. After notifying the hospital and Dr. S's office, we proceed to the hospital where Dr. S will be meeting us. But when we get there, we're told that Dr. S has not arrived.

I handle this news in the same impassive, controlled fashion I treat all such crises – namely, I start yelling, cursing, waving my arms and creating a real scene.

A senior nurse approaches to calm me down, saying something like, "Don't be anxious, Mr. Freund – I'm sure Dr. S. will be here momentarily. And even if he's delayed, the Chief Resident is in the building – a man well-skilled in obstetrics and able to handle the delivery."

I feel a little relieved, although still on edge. A few minutes later, I notice walking down the hall a guy in scrubs whom I recognize immediately as one of my former drinking buddies from Cannon Club at Princeton. In fact, the last time I remember seeing him the two of us were down on the floor near the Club's bar, chugging beers. I'd lost touch with him in the decade since we graduated.

"Dick," I cry out – "What are you doing here?"

"Hey, Jim – I'm the Chief Resident . . . ."

I won't keep you in suspense. Dr. S. never does show up; Dick Hnat (completely sober and quite skilled) handles matters flawlessly; and I break down, weeping with joy in Dick's arms, when he enters the waiting room and certifies that my wife is in good shape and we have a healthy son.

I can't claim to have thought much about being a father before it occurred, but bonding with first-born Erik and then with his brother Tom (who joined us in August 1968) became and remains one of the enduring joys of my life. Still, as gratifying as each of these five-plus decades of fatherhood has been, I often find myself drawn back into those memorable early years, when I watched the infants burgeon into smart, witty, engaging kids. Back then, I made notes of their most memorable pre-school utterances, which I can't resist sharing here.

One day Tom (not yet three) was writing out all the words he knew how to spell – "cat", "dog", etc. Viewing the list, I spotted a surprising word – "noon" – and remarked on it. "Wait," said Tom, "that's 'no' and 'on' – they got too close."

Erik placed three dominos on the bed and asked me what it looks like. "I don't know," I said. "Well, try," said Erik. "Okay, it looks like a house." "Think again." "It looks like a rhinoceros." "Think again," said Erik. "Okay," I said wearily, " it looks like an Indian on a horse with a bow and arrow." "No," said Erik. . . . "But if they were put down this way . . ." whereupon he rearranged the three pieces . . . "*then* it would look like an Indian on a horse with a bow and arrow."

One day when Tom was 2½ years old, he hit Mommy (not very hard). She pretended to cry, "Boo hoo," to make Tom regret his action. Tom murmured some soothing sounds, but when this failed to still the outcry, he tried the technique that had often worked so well on him – asking her solicitously, "Candy, Mommy?".

A year later, Tom spotted Barbro wearing a sexy black nightgown, which was split up to the thigh on one side. "Hey, Mommy," he said, pointing to the slit, "Let me show you where you're going to be cold!"

Erik: "Buy me a Volkswagen bus."
Mommy: "I'd like to but we don't have that kind of money."
Erik: "Well then, buy that kind of money."

At bedtime, I was asking Tom the usual questions about his nursery school. Suddenly, he turned and asked me: "Where do you go to school?" I replied that "I used to go to Princeton, but not anymore." Tom said: "I will go to Princeton, too" but then paused to add – "Not now, though, 'cause I'm in my pajamas."

When Erik was three, I said to him, "Won't it be nice, Erik, when Thomas can walk and talk and you'll have someone to play with?" Erik agreed, though with this caveat: "But I'm going to have to teach him to jump because that's not an easy trick to do."

Karen, one of our *au pair* girls, shared a wishbone with Tom one night and cautioned him that if he told anyone what he'd wished for, it would not come true. Next morning at six am, Tom woke Karen in her room. "Do you know what I wished, Karen? I wanted a baby. But I've been thinking, and I don't have any clothes or things for a baby – so that's why I have to tell you."

My parents had given me a new overcoat as an early Christmas present. The next day I gave Erik (not yet three) 35 cents and asked him to buy me a present. "Okay," said Erik, "Maybe I'll get you a coat – or something like that." There was a pause before he continued: "Or maybe a piece of gum." I guess I looked startled at the come-down from the coat, because he quickly added, "Or maybe two pieces."

One night I took Erik (but not Tom) to a track meet, but only after I told Tom that from time to time I would do something with only one of them (such as when I just had two tickets), but it didn't mean I loved the other any the less, etc. Tom seemed to understand and made no fuss. The next day, when Barbro and I were about to leave the house, Tom handed me a drawing he'd done, saying: "Here's something so you'll remember me . . . ."

Erik loved presents and I gave him lots of them. But he didn't like me to go to work, and would often say "Daddy, don't go to work," or "Why do you have to go to work?" My stylized answer was: "I have to go to work to make money to buy you presents." One day, though, he couldn't stand that any more, and replied: "Don't make more money, I have enough presents."

We used to play a game where I would make up a hypothetical situation in which the boys might find themselves and ask them what they would do. Here's what I posed one day to Tom: "You're in a zoo, and a funny-looking man with a beard comes up to you and says: 'Where are the lions?' You tell him. One minute later you hear a shot. You go to investigate and find that a lion has been killed. A policeman comes up and asks: 'What's going on here?'. . . . Okay, Tom, What do you do?" Without hesitation, Tom answered: "I say: 'I didn't do anything!' "

Erik and I were talking on the phone – it was one of those nights in which I would not be coming home from the office until later than his bedtime – and after a while I said: "Okay Erik, see you in the morning. So long." There was a pause and then he said: "I can talk to you longer if you'd like to."

But things didn't always go smoothly. One day, I took Erik to the Princeton Club and we had a good time, playing squash and exercising. That night, Erik was acting badly and I said in a stern voice, "You're not the same boy I took to the Princeton Club today and had such a good time with and who behaved so well," etc. A little later, he got worse – so I picked him up, smacked his behind and dumped him in bed. As I was leaving the room, I head him scream through his tears, "You're not the same *man* that took me to the Princeton Club!"

One day, out at Fire Island, we set up a basket. Unfortunately, the big basketballs were too heavy for Tom – and the light one floated in the wind – so I said, "Let's go down to the store and buy Tom a ball." Fortunately they had the right one – an in-between size. We took it home, and Tom promptly sank a basket. Then he turned to me, worshipfully, and said: "You know just what to do."

One of Erik's best remarks of all came when I asked him, "What is a Mommy good for?" He replied "For Erik."

I think my favorite moment with Erik came one morning when I was shaving and Erik was watching. "What do you want to be when you grow up, Erik? The President, like Nixon?" . . . . "No," said Erik, "a man – like you."

* * *

I remember happy days galore with my sons, but I can also recall some sad ones – notably, the day their beloved grandfather Sylvan passed away.

The boys grew up on Manhattan's Upper West Side, with all it had to offer (including a few minor muggings that they survived). Each year we had a new Swedish *au pair* living with us, easing the stress on Barbro. The boys attended nursery school and Sunday School at nearby West End Collegiate Church, and participated in its Christmas pageant each year, usually as shepherds or magi.

Every summer, as I mentioned, Barbro and the boys left town to spend several months at our house on Fire Island, in the community of Ocean Beach. Here, they were free of our residual concerns for their safety – no cars, no muggers – and they thrived on their bikes and scooters, running errands "into town," circling back and forth to the beach.

I couldn't wait to join them every Friday evening – trying to beat the traffic out of the city, racing to catch the ferry from Bayshore. Then, after a fulfilling weekend, I'd awaken at dawn Monday to catch the early ferry that kicked off my return to NYC. The commute was tough, but I always considered my half-hour spent on the open deck of the ferry crossing Great South Bay to be vacation time.

I picture us frolicking on the beach at various activities – a favorite had me at quarterback tossing shaky spirals with a rubberized football as they ran split end routes along the shoreline. The back deck of our house became a makeshift paddleball court, while inside could be found a dartboard and huge backgammon board that were often in use. The boys belonged to the local Youth Group where they kept busy with sports and other camp-type activities during the weekdays. They interacted so very well with each other – inventing games, listening to music, spending long hours together – the closeness between them was palpable.

Most years we had both a motorboat and sailboat. I recall our Hobe Cat sailboat that I captained with minimal competence, frequently relying on my sons to paddle hard in order for us to "come about." We rode the motorboat all over Great South Bay, often with the boys waterskiing – an activity at which they became quite skillful.

Both boys ended up at the all-male Collegiate School, which was close to where we lived on West End Avenue. It was difficult for me to spend much time with them during the week (other than in the early mornings) due to the pressures of lawyering and writing books, but we had fine weekends together. On many of these I introduced them to the joys of playing tennis, one of our favorite continuing activities.

Speaking of tennis and the matches we played during their teen years, although the temptation was sometimes strong, I never took a dive to deliberately let them beat me. I felt they ought to earn their victories, which shouldn't be handed to them through purposeful miscues on their father's part (which, as I mentioned in Chapter 3, had irritated me, with my own father).* So, when they finally started to prevail, not only could they exult, but I felt great about it too – marking a very special moment in my father-son relationships.

I have already commented on our many delightful family trips during vacation periods – ski outings to both eastern and western mountains, trips to Sweden to visit Barbro's family, wonderful long Thanksgiving weekends (along with the Foggs) in the Catskills at the home of my partner Barry Garfinkel and his family, and to other places.

One of our prime activities in those years – especially when car trips were involved – was listening to taped recordings of our favorite comedians: Mel Brooks (especially as the 2000 Year Old Man with Carl Reiner), Woody Allen, and Mike Nichols and Elaine May. The boys had super-retentive memories for this kind of schtick; and each of us was able to come up with appropriate excerpts while waiting on ski lines and elsewhere. It wasn't only the punch lines (Mel Brooks: "I have over 1,500 children and not one of them ever comes to visit!") but those priceless straight lines that lead up to them – the whole dialogue or monologue invariably producing raucous three-way laughter, even on the tenth hearing.

Back in those days, I wrote both the music and words of a song I called *My Boys*, which spelled out how I felt about them. Here's part of the lyric:

> "My boys don't read much / books don't seem to count at all / (Play ball!) / My boys don't need much / help in finding good friends who call / They specialize in hanging out / I'm learning what they're all about / have no doubt / They play in rhythm / I'm happy with 'em / It's so fine to father two such boys."

In retrospect, I think that at least until Barbro and I separated in May 1980 (when Erik was 14 and Tom nearing 12), I managed to function pretty well as a father. Notwithstanding the pressures of work that limited the quantity of time I could spend with them, I tried to focus on the quality of our moments together. And the feedback I've gotten from them in more recent years, as they reflect back on that time, has been reassuring. Tom: "I remember your laugh and the feeling you gave me with love and being proud of your kid." Erik: "I remember how much I wanted to spend time

---

* This situation is at the core of the essay, "The Tenth Reunion," contained in my book *Advise and Invent* (see Chapter 16).

with you – it was always so exciting . . . . and I remember how much we laughed together . . . ."

* * *

Sadly, however, the intimacy the boys and I enjoyed become a lot more difficult to maintain after the marital separation, with me no longer living in their apartment. I've come to recognize in the years since that this wasn't solely due to the decreased amount of hours I spent with them. What I failed to realize at the time was that I should have been more sensitive to the difficult situation the divorce had created for the boys – more helpful in terms of what they were going through.

Here's an oversimplified version of a typical encounter between us back then. I'd pick them up for the weekend and say, "Well, how's everything going? Are you guys okay?" Their answer was always the same, "We're doing fine – no problems." Only in retrospect did I realize they had developed a stiff-upper-lip approach to the situation – something that may well be typical of many adolescent boys going through a family split-up. They might have perceived me as shallow in posing the "how are things" question, so they decided to forego candor in order to tell me what they knew I wanted to hear.

And what was my response? "Okay, then – let's play ball!" or whatever else we were going to do. I didn't dig in to try to learn what was really happening, to assess their actual state of mind, and to find out whether they had problems that I might have been helpful in dealing with.

In fact there were some problems, and they had some decisions to make – matters I didn't get too involved in because they hadn't raised them with me and I was reluctant to probe for trouble. As a result, there were times when, as Tom later put it to me, "Frankly, you were M.I.A." – wrapped up in work and my new marriage, and in his view, "not checking in" with him during certain important junctures. "You could have gotten involved in making me feel comfortable and discussing with me my feelings and concerns . . . . but you weren't around and you weren't doing that."

In addition, there was something else I never realized. When Barbro and I jointly decided to separate, we called the boys in for a four-way session on our king-size bed. We broke the sad news, assuring them that this wasn't in any way their fault – and then proceeded to paint a relatively rosy picture of what life for the kids of a divorced couple was going to be like ("You'll sleep in your same beds . . . You'll have twice as many vacations . . . .").

We thought we'd handled this delicate moment pretty well, but thirteen years later, at Tom's college graduation, the boys corralled Barbro and me to tell us in private that the *worst* thing we had done was to *lie* to them – to paint a rosy picture of what would prove to be for them an uncomfortable time. It came as a real body blow to both Barbro and me.

Since then, when friends with young kids divorce, I've made it my business to alert the husbands to two necessities: first, to be realistic (not rosy) with their children as to what lies ahead; and second, to probe beneath those "Everything's fine" assurances they may well get from kids like mine, and make a sincere effort to find out if anything is happening that a father can be helpful with.

* * *

Notwithstanding all that, the boys and I still managed to have some good times during those challenging years. I recall some delightful trips to ski out west, to the big island of Hawaii, to the Caribbean (especially to Jamaica where we stayed up all night at a star-filled concert headlined by the Grateful Dead), plus a few other notable excursions.

Erik switched school in the 10th grade to my alma mater Horace Mann – which featured a campus, a football team, and girls that Collegiate didn't offer – and Tom followed suit a year later. Erik became a backfield starter on the varsity football team (I made it to a number of his games), while Tom was an up-and-coming running back on his class's team. The boys remained exceptionally close to each other throughout the difficult years following their parents' separation.

Erik had taken up the drums and was developing well musically. When Tom made known his intention to start on an instrument – his first choice also being the drums – Erik vetoed that particular idea ("one drummer per family"). So Tom was relegated to the guitar where he turned out to excel, which led to his future professional career.

I'll never forget one special incident during these years. In the spring of 1981, Erik suffered a scary accident to his foot that had him on crutches for a number of weeks. I was president of our Princeton Class of '56, which was celebrating its 25th reunion at the end of May. The highlight of every Princeton reunion is the P-Rade, in which all the alumni classes join the graduating class for a lengthy trek from Nassau Hall to a distant campus outpost, with large crowds of onlookers lining the entire path. Historically, the 25th Reunion class led the way, right behind the Princeton band and university president. So there I was in the first rank; and there was Erik next to me on crutches, somehow managing to make it the full length of the parade, to rounds of rousing cheers from the onlookers – and an abundance of family pride felt by his father.

Erik graduated from high school in the spring of 1984, and in September matriculated at his first (and only) choice college, the University of Colorado. I helped him get settled out there, uttered some sage words about not letting skiing get in the way of his studies, and returned east.

The ensuing decade proved to be a complex one for Erik, which I won't dwell on here (except to salute the highlight trip the two of us took to Las Vegas for his 21st birthday in 1987). But it ended up well, with him receiving his degree from the University of Colorado and then plunging into the corporate world, landing several jobs out west and then later on in New Jersey.

As for Tom, he left Horace Mann to spend a year at Music & Art (as his musical career was beginning in earnest), after which he moved with Barbro to Greenwich, CT. There he attended Greenwich High School and played in its excellent student jazz orchestra which won many scholastic competitions. His first choice of college was Berkeley School of Music in Boston, which provided him with some solid musical groundwork. After one year there, he attended several different schools on a part-time basis, ending up with two solid years at (and graduation from) Pitzer College, one of the Claremont Colleges in southern California.

At Pitzer, Tom met, played alongside in a rock band, and recorded with the talented Ben Harper (the two remain close to this day). After graduation, Tom furthered his own musical career, leading to many gigs and a fine debut album *North American Long Weekend*. With the exception of a few years in New York (which included a 21st birthday getaway to Atlantic City with his dad), Tom opted for a home base in the Los Angeles area.

Tom has had an exciting music career as a singer-songwriter.[*] In addition to recording a number of albums of his own notable songs, he has played gigs all over the United States, Europe, Japan, and other locales.

---

[*] *All Music Guide* said: "Tom Freund is indeed one of the great singer-songwriters. He constructs a unique world, defines it, and then burns it to the ground. Truly unique and absolutely brilliant." And British pub-rock legend Graham Parker hailed Tom as one of "the best singer-songwriters operating today."

Barbara and I are avid fans and enjoy catching his performances in New York, New Jersey and Connecticut.

For the past decade, Erik has worked as a Meeting Planner and Sales Trainer in the medical device field and more recently in Accounts Receivable for the large importer Conair Corporation. His present focus is to work with Marketing and other internal departments to put processes in place to reduce compliance-related chargebacks from retail customers such as Amazon and Target.

In their early adult years, both boys had significant relationships with a number of women. These ultimately culminated for Tom with his marriage to Francie Wong in 2003 in Hawaii, and for Erik with his marriage to Wendy Waters in 2003 in Morristown, NJ. Sadly, each of their marriages ended in divorce. But joyously each produced a sparkling daughter – Delilah (for Tom) who is now 16, and Paige (for Erik) who is 14. Both Erik and Tom maintain effective relationships with their ex-wives, so that choices are made in the best interests of their children.

The girls are fantastic – intelligent, great fun to be around, good-looking, coping well with their parents' divorce, and loving their dads – with a little left over for Jimpa (the name Marcy anointed me with for the girls to use). They are doing quite well in school, working wonders on computers and cellphones, and giving me a tough struggle at the backgammon table. I only wish they lived around the block, since my time with them is limited.

The boys are wonderful fathers who spend much time with their daughters on a weekly basis, and take them on ski trips and other excursions over holidays. Each girl also has an adoring NYC grandfather, who has been smitten with them for the past decade-and-a-half.

Since my sons spend so much more time with their daughters than Jimpa does, I asked them to pass along some of their impressions about the girls.

Tom: "Delilah is the best thing I ever made. She gives me great excitement to hang out with her, do sports, eat, watch our favorite shared TV shows, ask her about what to wear that evening . . . ."

Erik: "Paige is an intelligent, responsible, mature, creative, funny, compassionate, athletic and hard-working teenager."

Tom: "Delilah is so diligent in her schoolwork, a ready study for all sorts of courses . . . including – I don't know where this came from – biology and trigonometry! It's great to see her future interests lie in the medical field and also environmental – in other words, the future of the planet."

Erik: "Paige has very strong feelings about equality for all people and maintaining the environment. She works at creating relationships that allow her to communicate effectively and share ideas."

Tom: "On Delilah's after hours school days or during the summer she has volunteered at Cedar Sinai to do lab work and medical experiments, putting in hundreds of hours so far. She got me to turn off the faucet while I brush my teeth and to get rid of single use plastic products in the house."

Erik: "Paige can understand complex concepts and problem-solve. She is open minded and optimistic. She enjoys music, fashion, reading and writing."

Tom: "Mostly Delilah makes me laugh and I make her laugh, I think I know where they got the term "charge" from. She is my charge and she charges me up. And I've noticed this with people around her, friends and adults, she charges the room, and I am happy to say responds with vigor and sharpness, but always acts her age as well (in the good way) – she can still be a kid."

I echo all of those thoughts.

* * *

I'm pleased with the adult relationships I've developed with the boys (if you can call men over 50 by that name). We have serious discussions; on occasion they seek my advice on problems they're facing, both personal and career-wise; and I still make myself helpful on their major financial issues. (I must say, though, that it's frustrating for a father who used to be able to solve all their childhood problems, to be confronted with the inability to make some of their adult problems go away.)

The best times have been when the three of us get together for an infrequent trip to a ski area or gambling casino – what a ball we have. I also enjoy periodic days or weekends with each of them separately, sometimes with their daughters. One of my favorite moments is when I stand next to the boys at the crap table, each of us betting his own way, cheering each other on when things go well, and commiserating on the downside.

Music is still important to us. The best times are when the three of us can jam as a group, such as at Princeton reunions. Tom and I play a lot of guitar/harmonica or piano/bass duets when we're together, especially late at night – and at times he will even ask me up on stage to perform with him at local NYC and CT gigs.

Erik remarked on one of the most important things I can impart to them now, as each goes through some negative moments in their lives: "I always admire your ability to stay positive when life gets tough, I see you have joy in your endeavors and in connecting with people." I hope I'll always be around to remind them of the many affirmative aspects of their lives, which sometimes get hidden when troublesome things are going on.

For my recent 85th birthday, each of them wrote me a meaningful letter, containing words dear to my heart. There was Tom's reference to "our discussions, which I can't do with anyone else quite like I can with you and which give me great solace." And Erik's acknowledgment: "You have taught me so many important things about life. You have always been so supportive of me even when I made choices that weren't in line with your better judgment." And Tom again: "I love being with you and I love having you and your support in my life."

Although we share certain traits, each of the boys is different from me and from each other in a variety of ways. Some of the qualities we do share, to name just a few, are good senses of humor, athleticism, memory of past events, and, I believe, strong moral fiber.

In addition to being excellent fathers, the boys are also fine sons to their dad, as they were to their mother, and they enjoy good relations with step-mom Barbara. They're also close brothers, always feeling connected, and with a lot of helpful communication going on between them even though a continent apart.

Erik is very detail-oriented – an exemplary planner, great on handling advance reservations and such. Tom and I tend to wing it more in this area.

Tom is very imaginative, as can be seen in the lyrics of the multiple songs he has composed. They contain interesting connections and observations, and he's not afraid to leave a little ambiguity as to what the takeaway should be – unlike his dad, who prefers to nail down the message. Tom is also "out there" – a real performer who loves to be on stage and is very good at it. Erik is more restrained, but in recent years I've noticed how much he enjoys meeting new people and taking on fresh initiatives.

Erik has good judgment – he can agonize for a while, but he makes good analytical decisions. Tom is less analytical, tends to go more with his gut, but usually with good results. Erik is more methodical, Tom more of a risk-taker.

I'm proud of what I've instilled in the boys, but I also celebrate the ways in which we differ, as well as the contrasts between them. All in all, we've forged very good relationships, which I'm certain will endure into the years ahead.

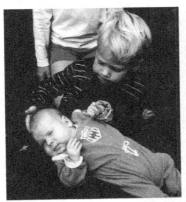

Some early shots of Erik & Tom, 2 1/2 years apart in age, and (after a cryptic start in the middle left shot) best buddies all the way.

My father's greatest joy came when he was actively engaged with Erik & Tom – and the feeling was definitely mutual.

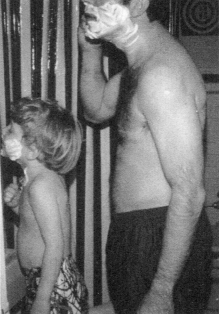

Some of my best moments with the boys occurred early in the morning – before my work and their school – and often took place (as here) near the bathroom sink.

This is my favorite family foursome photo from about 1970

The boys took to football very early

(Below) With the Sussmann family (L to R) Judy, Marjorie, Ruth, Barbro, Michael, Herb, Marcy, Joanie, Sylvan and (front row) Tom, Michelle, and Erik. (I'm busy taking the picture.)

*The boys were sports-oriented –
here with Barbro and me on skis,
and guarding Fin Fogg on the
football field.*

We went on some great trips together – among the most notable, skiing in Zermatt (that's the Matterhorn in the background) and a Mediteranian cruise that ended up in Venice. The musical shot (below right) was taken when we formed an impromptu Bahamian trio on the streets of Nassau.

These were wonderful years for the boys – and certainly for me too – as you can see in these pix.

I took the photo below of the boys (one of my favorites) on a trip we made along the rocky ocean coast of Massachusetts.

I took the photo above in honor of their grandmother Marcy, posed in front of the Christian Science "Mother Church" in Boston.

The boys and their dad, years ago on the beach –

more recently at our home in Easton, CT –

and one fine day at the Town Tennis Club in NYC.

My boys – together at our CT house, Erik solo, Tom turning 50 on Fire Island (note the sign language), and both of them at the book party for my novel.

Tom, the singer-songwriter: (top) at the start, a mid-point, and recently (on California beach); (above) in concert at the prestigious State Theatre in New Brunswick, NJ; (below) outside one of Tom's gigs, jamming with Phil Lesh (of Grateful Dead fame), and in his "hometown" of Ocean Beach, Fire Island.

A NYC hotel scene from a dozen years ago

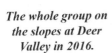

The whole group on the slopes at Deer Valley in 2016.

Here we are on that same family ski trip, at the fireplace (minus Barbara who was the photographer).

Tom and Delilah, early and more recently;
Erik and Paige a few years ago; Paige and me
a little while back, and at the football stadium
under the "modern" Princeton tiger.

A montage of family trios (plus one quartet)

Delilah and Paige: from the tub to the chairlift; from acrobatics to a hug; from the shore of Great South Bay to shut-the-box competition.

*A montage of the girls –
balancing, scaling walls,
bonding with canines, and
snapping pictures on their own.*

13. SKADDEN ARPS (1966 – 1996) (#1) – FINDING MY FOOTING

The centerpiece of my professional life was the 31 years (January 1966 to December 1996) that I spent from age 31 to 62 at the law firm of Skadden Arps, Slate, Meagher & Flom LLP. Those years comprise three decades of prodigious accomplishments by the firm, as well as an exciting journey for me.

When I arrived, the number of Skadden lawyers – all housed in one undersized Manhattan office – was in the teens; the firm wasn't widely known; and it had yet to achieve major success in terms of attracting clients and earning money. By the time I left, it was the home to well over a thousand lawyers in 25 offices around the world, was well-known in both the legal world and business community, had attracted a host of important clients, and was quite successful financially.

When I came to Skadden, I'd hardly distinguished myself during the previous decade spent in the Navy, law school, and my first law firm; I was virtually unknown in legal circles; I had no clients and my personal financial condition was insubstantial. When I retired three decades later, I'd carved out a successful legal career representing numerous major clients, authored respected books, and chaired significant seminars. I was well-regarded in the legal community and related fields, and had achieved sufficient affluence to afford early retirement.

Skadden's amazing voyage would have taken place with or without me. The timing of my arrival was personally serendipitous, but many factors were responsible for the firm's tremendous spurt in the '70s and '80s. I sincerely doubt that I'd have done anywhere near as well unaffiliated with Skadden.

I will offer some reflections on Skadden Arps generally, so that the reader can appreciate the circumstances in which I found myself. But since this is a personal memoir, I'll focus mainly on how I went about striving to thrive in the Skadden environment and the efforts I made to distinguish myself among so many first-class lawyers.

My lawyering skills, which hadn't been previously ascertainable, came to the fore at Skadden. I was called upon to deal with challenging situations, develop good judgment, handle difficult clients, teach other lawyers and law students, speak in public, write books and articles, relate to my partners, supervise associates, and cope with adversaries. I like to think that the Jim Freund who emerged during the Skadden years wasn't a completely new guy, but rather someone who had been concealed in the shadows during the preceding decade.

I encountered a lot of ups and also a few downs during my time at Skadden. At least up until the last several years before retiring, I had to deal with a consistently heavy workload, a good deal of tension, and an ongoing compulsion to excel. (A singular irony is that through all those turbulent years my blood pressure remained normal; but shortly after relaxing in retirement, I developed a moderate case of high blood pressure. Go figure . . . .)

Because these years were so significant in my life, I'm going to explore in some depth the matters I worked on, my writings and seminars, the cast of characters with whom I interacted, my state of mind at various junctures, and the decision to retire early. I've divided the subject into five distinct segments, with a separate chapter for each:

- Skadden Arps #1 – Finding My Footing
  How I came to the firm, what things was like back then, becoming a partner, the firm's ascendancy, the direction I took, the *Anatomy of a Merger* book and its annual M&A seminar spinoff, my primary influences at the firm (Joe Flom and Peter Mullen), and the subject of negotiating.

- Skadden Arps #2 – Deals Galore
  The second half of the '70s, my *Lawyering* book, a mild depression and its cure, the big decade of deals (the '80s), making acquisitions and defending against takeovers.

- Skadden Arps #3 – The TWA Takeover
  An in-depth analysis of my most significant legal assignment – defending TWA against Carl Icahn's takeover bid.

- Skadden Arps #4 – The Challenging '90s
  The troubling years coming down from the M&A high of the '80s, pep talks to associates, a few more deals, my book *Smart Negotiating*, a final report to the partners, and tributes to my Skadden colleagues.

- Skadden Arps #5 – <u>The Decision To Retire Early</u>
  Musing on my decision to retire early, including the complete text of the contemporary article I wrote on the subject for the ABA periodical *Business Law Today*.

* * *

My coming to Skadden Arps was another one of those recurring instances of *sheer happenstance* I've experienced.

In 1965, after three years at Davies Hardy & Schenck, I finally swung into motion to leave for greener pastures. But back in those days finding a new job wasn't so easy. The sizeable firms concentrated on hiring directly from law school and rarely took on associates laterally from other firms. As for joining a small firm, I regarded this initially as a step down.

One small firm of good repute exhibited an interest in me, at a time when no other prospects were in sight. This firm took the process of associate selection very seriously – insisting that I spend up to an hour with each and every one of their lawyers, both partners and associates. Although the firm obviously prided itself on the commitment it displayed, this seemed to me an interminable process. I realized they wanted me and thought seriously about joining them. But a variant on Groucho Marx's fabled dictum kept flashing into my head – I just didn't yearn to be an associate at any firm that cared so intensely about the low-level decision to hire me – so I rejected their offer. (I still amuse myself by thinking that if I'd gone with them, I might have spent a significant portion of my working life interviewing other youthful applicants.)

Although *sheer happenstance* often involves taking a positive action that sets things in motion, I've also come to realize that much in life can depend on decisions made *not* to do something – the path you decide to forsake. My determination not to go with the firm that interviewed excessively represented that kind of critical juncture for me. If I had accepted their offer, my future professional life would likely have been all right, but it wouldn't have generated nearly the excitement and growth I experienced at Skadden.

Sometimes, an occurrence that clears the way for *sheer happenstance* to strike isn't a matter of your own choice but is made for you. I also had one of those.

Two good friends of mine – George Riordan and Bob McCabe – were rising stars as investment bankers at Lehman Bros. They learned of a vacancy in the Lehman legal department and, being aware I was pursuing new employment, arranged a job interview for me with Lehman's general counsel.

My past three years with Davies Hardy had not been a positive experience. Finding a better law firm opportunity already seemed problematical. I liked the idea of joining a top-ranked investment banking firm, as well as working with my friends. I recall thinking that if an offer were to be forthcoming from Lehman, I should probably accept it. That would have changed the whole trajectory of my life; and while such a livelihood was far from paltry, I doubt it would have led to a career of distinction. As it happens, though, I didn't have to face up to that potential decision, since Lehman never made me an offer.

So I slogged onward, trying without success to find a more attractive situation. Then someone told me about Ken Everett. He was a Harvard Law School-educated partner at a modest NYC firm who had become the self-styled unofficial matchmaker between HLS-trained associates hunting for new positions and NYC firms looking for lawyers with HLS degrees.

I'll never forget the day I found myself sitting in Ken's office, watching him dip into the contents of a large file drawer at the bottom of his old-fashioned desk. Although he didn't know me, he was trying hard to come up with something helpful. After a few false starts, he struck pure gold.

"Hey, Jim, here's one you ought to try. It's a real good small firm that's very much on the make. You would be coming in as the senior corporate associate, replacing a guy who just left to go inside with a firm client."

As he pronounced the firm name which I'd never previously heard, the confluences of each unfamiliar syllable – "Skadden… Arps… Slate… Meagher… Flom" – sounded like a guy falling down a flight of stairs: "Skadden-boom/Arps-oops/Slate-thud," etc.

"Who are those guys?" I asked with a good deal of skepticism. "Just go meet them," Ken insisted. "Talk to this guy Flom. You'll see." And so, almost reluctantly, I made an appointment to be interviewed.

* * *

Back then, the offices of Skadden Arps – perched over the Fifth Avenue headquarters of an upscale haberdasher – were just a notch above miniscule. There was no reception area as such, while the receptionist also functioned as the telephone operator and typed a little on the side. The library was tiny, about the size of a partner's office; additional law books were on shelves in the halls and along the wall in the single conference room – often requiring lawyers to interrupt client meetings to locate a particular volume. Other than secretaries, its entire support staff consisted of one aging bookkeeper (whom I learned later had a lot of trouble with figures).

The firm was formed in 1948 by Les Arps, John Slate and Marshall Skadden. The threesome had been associates at the predecessor of the Dewey Ballantine firm, but weren't made partners; Slate had moved to the legal staff of Pan American Airways; and since they'd all topped out where they were, they decided to start over on their own.

Joe Flom, fresh from Harvard Law School, was their first and only associate that year. Here's how Joe described[*] the initial naming decision made by the firm:

> "They opened their doors on April Fools' Day in 1948. First, they had to decide on a name. Les was very involved in launching the Firm. In the normal course of things, it would have been called Arps, Skadden and Slate. But that would have been a problem on the second sheets of the stationery, which just had the initials. So Skadden and Slate flipped a coin. Skadden won, and his name went first."

I showed up in 1966. The firm, which had opened its doors 18 years earlier, had been adding lawyers at the rate of less than one per year.

At my interview session, I met Joe Flom briefly – just long enough to realize he wasn't cut from ordinary cloth. I spent more time with the other man I'd be working for, Peter Mullen – later to be named the firm's managing partner. I took an instant liking to him as just the kind of person I'd enjoy reporting to. A pair of upbeat litigators – Barry Garfinkel, who became one of my closest friends at the firm, and Bob Ensher, who died much too early – put a big rush on this previously underachieving associate. Without knowing much at all about me, they wanted Jim Freund to come to Skadden Arps.

---

[*] His remarks can be found in *The Skadden Story,* a self-published autobiography of the firm (2014), on p.3.

Forget the modest quarters and slim staff – to me the firm was like a breath of fresh air. You felt a sense of something happening, or at least about to happen. There was a vitality to the place that was almost palpable. Everyone's door was open, their jackets were off – Barry never fails to remind me that I came to the interview in a three-piece suit complete with vest – and things were getting done.

Moreover, as I soon learned, these guys were running a *business*. At my old firm, and at many like it in those days, there was a great reluctance to send out bills and otherwise be sullied by the commercial aspects of practice. Not so – then or since – at Skadden, Arps.

Peter Mullen was later quoted[*] on another attribute of Skadden that I considered very special about us in the early days, and that never changed as we grew. "When this firm was young, there were Jewish firms and WASP-ish firms, but very few firms that were all-inclusive; I think we were one of the first ones."

Up to that point in my life, I'd ricocheted back and forth between these two worlds. Brought up as a religious Christian but with a Jewish heritage, my early years through high school were spent in decidedly Jewish family and social circles. College, however, presented a predominantly Christian environment; and the girls I dated were from both sides of the aisle. The Navy was Christian, law school was mixed. My first marriage took place in a Lutheran church, my first law firm was Christian, and my adult friends were from all over. I can't ever remember feeling discriminated against by those in either persuasion; I enjoyed all groups and welcomed the variety. So I was delighted that the new firm I'd chosen went both ways.

I had a strong feeling that Skadden Arps was on the march somewhere, and that my new colleagues were people who would make the journey enjoyable. Without delay I decided to take a flyer with them. It turned out to be the most serendipitous swift decision of my life.

* * *

---

[*] *The Skadden Story,* p.174

Even though I had just three years of low-grade practice experience, I joined Skadden as the firm's senior corporate associate, making all of $10,000 annually. The prior senior corporate associate had just gone over to a client as general counsel. Skadden undoubtedly wanted someone with more credentials than mine but – truth be told – I made my Davies Hardy experience sound more impressive than it actually was.

I was in a wonderful position. Every piece of corporate business that came to the firm went to either Joe Flom or Peter Mullen, the only two corporate partners. As the senior corporate associate, I was next in line to become involved in their important matters. Later on other associates came aboard, but I'd already staked out my position.

I'll never forget my first day on the job. I had sold myself – with a touch of puffery – as an experienced securities lawyer, ready to assume significant responsibility. When I was called to Joe Flom's office, he was juggling two phone calls at once. Waving me to a seat, he let me sit there in silence for a while.

Then, during a brief lull, Joe turned to me and – pointing to a foot-high stack of papers on the outside edge of his desk – said, "It's a '40 Act problem" – and that was it. As I quickly came to learn, Joe was never one for elaborate situational expositions. A moment later, he was on to the next phone call – even then, they came thick and fast.

I picked up the stack of papers and left Joe's office. I had never even *heard* of the '40 Act! But I soon discovered that when challenged like that, I could pick things up pretty fast.

In my early years at Skadden, the firm did not have an impressive roster of clients. The largest one was probably New York Airways – a struggling helicopter line that went kaput after one of its 'copters crashed atop the Pan Am Building. Although we had some budding Wall Street relationships, there were no regular investment banking clients as such.

One of my first client assignments was representing a breeder of Angus cattle who wanted to create security interests in a prize bull's semen. As I stepped gingerly around the outbuildings of the breeder's farm in my Florsheim loafers, I couldn't help but wonder whether this was what being a Wall Street lawyer was all about.

Not only did the firm lack major clients but there were whole areas of practice we weren't equipped to handle in my early years there. Banking, bankruptcy, products liability, any sort of administrative practice other than securities or antitrust – these were all non-existent practice areas at Skadden Arps.

So, for instance, when the firm decided to move at the end of the 1960's, they assigned the job of negotiating the new lease to me, as one of the newest partners. We did not have a real estate department, and I was

very much out of my depth. So we retained a real estate lawyer, Jim O'Rorke, from my old firm for advice. Later, he became a Skadden partner, and for a time constituted the firm's entire real estate practice.

What we did have going for us was a great sense of ethics and professionalism – epitomized in Les Arps' dictum of "no cutting corners" and his insistence that we do "upper-margin" work. We also pulled together a splendid litigation team, developed an uncanny knack of attracting and retaining first-rate young talent, displayed a lot of *chutzpah* – and, oh yes, featured Joe Flom. (More on him to come.)

After arriving at the firm as an associate in 1966, I worked hard on a number of matters for Flom and Mullen. By the time I became a partner in 1968, I felt I had made up for the scant experience of those years at Davies, Hardy, had learned how to handle pressure, and was prepared for new challenges.

The Skadden tradition of working hard applied from the day I arrived and throughout the subsequent decades. As my '70s partner Morris Kramer later said,[*] "It was a whirlwind – late nights, through the nights and on weekends. This truly was a 24-hour shop. I don't recall ever being alone in the office. There was always somebody else working, too." And another '70s partner, Bill Frank, added,[**] "We were known on the outside as a sweatshop but on the inside as a very, very exciting place to work . . . .We distinguished ourselves by not only being very smart lawyers but also by working harder."

---

[*] *The Skadden Story*, p.44

[**] *The Skadden Story*, p.45

But it wasn't all work. For instance, a real morale builder was our softball team, on which I played second base. Messrs. John Feerick, Tom Schwarz, Dan Stoller, Fin Fogg, Bob Sheehan and others played alongside. Although we had fewer lawyers to draw from than others in the league, we vied for the league championship in the early '70s and ended up one year winning the title over our Paul, Weiss challenger.

My first serious writing task occurred while I was still an associate. Joe Flom was chairman of, and Barry Garfinkel a panelist on, a seminar held by the Practicing Law Institute (PLI) titled "Disclosure Requirements of Public Companies and Insiders," which focused on the leading case of the day, *Texas Gulf Sulphur*. When PLI decided to put out a hard cover edited transcript of the seminar, Joe and Barry grabbed their new associate and told me to "edit this transcript." I spent a lot of time doing just that; in many places the verbatim rendering was almost unreadable, forcing me to circle back to the panelists to make sure I was capturing what they actually said.

The resulting PLI book* gave authorship credit to Flom, Garfinkel and Freund. I appreciated that Joe and Barry put my name on the cover, rather than adhering to the more common practice of simply acknowledging thanks to their new associate. The subject matter was a hot topic, and the book sold many copies.**

I don't remember too many specifics from those first two years, but I do recall vividly one particular day in 1968. A messenger came to my office to say that Les Arps wanted to see me in his office. I went up there and when the door opened, I saw a grouping of all the Skadden partners – I think there were six at the time. Les duly informed me that I'd been made a partner, along with John Feerick and Norm Donald who were also elevated that day. It was a great feeling, featuring warm handshakes all around, and capped by Les announcing with gusto that I'd now "be liable on the office lease."

* * *

---

* *Disclosure Requirements of Public Companies and Insiders (Practicing Law Institute, 1967)*

** Still, when I list the law books I've written, I don't include this one, which really just consisted of taking somebody else's spoken thoughts and editing the words into readable form.

To explain the path I took as a Skadden partner, I need to fill in some background regarding the direction of the firm during the '70s.

Joe Flom was our unquestioned leader and in large part responsible for Skadden's rise to prominence. I'll be discussing Joe in more depth a little later, but for now just accept the fact that Joe was awesome. His performance always reminded me of the remark the legendary Bobby Jones made after watching Jack Nicklaus shoot an unbelievable round to win the Masters golf tournament. "That man," said Bobby, "plays a game with which I'm not familiar."

Still, even a virtuoso like Joe Flom needed an instrument to play on – and for Joe, the hostile-takeover movement of the '70s and '80s was pure Stradivarius. In the '60s, Joe had been engaged in proxy contests, which were the original tool for corporate takeovers. But when tender offers and such entered the picture, the field became tailor-made for Joe's talents – a sound strategic overview, inspired tactics, creative lawyering.

It required a fusing of business, financial, legal and practical concerns, calling for a field marshal with an expansive view of the lawyer's function, not afraid to tackle "non-legal" issues. That was Joe, who uttered his cogent pronouncements in definitive tones that comforted clients and colleagues.

The established Wall Street law firms were slow to enter the takeover game – even to represent victimized targets like their clients or to advise the investment bankers involved. Instead, Joe and Skadden Arps got there first. We were a major factor in unbundling the cozy relationship that used to exist between the typical big company and the single law firm that did all its legal business. Companies and investment banks began to hire us for takeover work, while keeping their usual firm for more traditional pursuits.

Skadden Arps, led by Joe, became a star in the area of hostile acquisitions, where one company (or individual) was attempting to take over another company against its will. Sometimes Skadden would represent the aggressor, sometimes the target. Either way in those early days, while a lot of strategizing and litigation maneuvers were going on, a direct negotiated solution between two firms was unlikely to occur.

I worked for Joe on some of these early contested situations and might have stayed on that path, but didn't. I wasn't comfortable representing aggressors, who forced targeted companies to accept outcomes they didn't want. It just didn't suit my personality. While this wasn't a problem when we represented the target, the opportunities to negotiate a solution there remained limited.

I found that what I enjoyed most was to negotiate deals that brought adversaries together voluntarily. The most interesting deals to negotiate were corporate mergers and acquisitions – a relatively quiet area when I first became involved. In those transactions, both parties wanted the deal to take place but needed help in reaching agreement on the business and legal terms required to make it happen. I think I can trace my interest in reaching such compromise resolutions to that class David Herwitz taught at Harvard Law School (referred to in Chapter 10).

Another weighty consideration for me was that if I continued working in Flom's area of expertise, I'd never be "the man" in major cases. Joe already occupied that spot and was likely to remain there indefinitely. I wanted to stake out my own area of achievement, independent of him.

Although there was real allure to the hostile takeover area – such as seeing your maneuvers analyzed in the financial press on a daily basis – and even though takeovers were primarily responsible for those big billings the firm was starting to realize (the income from which would presumably flow down to the responsible partners), I veered off into the more prosaic, seldom printworthy, and less lucrative field of negotiated acquisitions. I was able to make the change because Skadden Arps had attracted a group of excellent younger lawyers – especially Fin Fogg, Morris Kramer, Peter Atkins, and Roger Aaron – who formed Joe's first team. Later all of them became very successful attorneys in their own right.

This diversion of priorities was to change for me in the decade of the '80s, but I'll get to that in Chapter 14.

Although I still handled other securities-flavored assignments, my major practice area soon became negotiated acquisitions. Along with several sizeable mergers, I did a number of smaller acquisitions, which gave rise to many similar issues as those in the big deals – and sometimes quite different ones.

Take, for example, one of the first acquisitions I handled on my own. Although usually representing the purchaser, I was on the sell side this time – counseling a small company owned and operated by two men with an idea considered high-tech back then, but having little in the way of funds. A major corporation became interested in buying their business for a decent price, but for my clients the deal had to close quickly before they would run out of cash. One of them had actually scheduled his impending marriage for the day after the anticipated closing, when he would be in funds.

Less than a week before the contract was due to be signed, the key executive at the purchasing corporation – the man who had advocated the deal internally – was fired. The acquisition, now bereft of its single proponent, promptly died – and our little company, lacking an alternative angel, swiftly folded.

I was heartsick. But I do have to give the bridegroom credit – he went ahead with the nuptials on schedule. Full disclosure to the bride, not-so-full disclosure to the hotel, since he didn't have enough cash to pay the bill. *P.S.* The couple is happily married today fifty years later; we've remained good friends; and as far as I know, the hotel is still in business.

Oh, I forgot to mention one critical detail that made the deal especially painful for me. Among the investors who lost their total investment in the company were Joe Flom and Peter Mullen!

I honed some of my negotiating skills during the '70s representing two modest-sized but acquisition-minded public companies in New Jersey – Cadence Industries and Berg Enterprises. The Cadence CEO was Shelly Feinberg, a canny businessman with whom I developed a lasting relationship. The brothers Kenny and Lenny Berg who ran Berg Enterprises didn't get along too well – I often had to serve as an intermediary between them. However, I worked smoothly with Earl Bronsteen, their savvy executive in charge of acquisitions; and Earl and his sprightly wife Judy became close personal friends.

One Berg acquisition was of a mortgage banking company, whose CEO was Felix Beck, an astute and well-respected mortgage banker. Felix and I combined on a number of deals, but the story that sticks in my mind has little to do with business.

The Saab car I drove at the time (in deference to my Swedish wife) was not equipped with air conditioning and heated up noticeably during the summer. As a young partner, I wasn't exactly flush in those days and couldn't afford a proper cooling installation. I was tantalized, however, by an ad in the paper for a very inexpensive A/C substitute which I decided to buy. It consisted of a plastic unit that held a half-dozen small cylindrical cans, each containing a fluid that froze in the refrigerator's ice compartment, plus a little electric fan that ran on batteries. The idea was to freeze the cans before hitting the road, then let the fan blow across them toward the driver, thereby creating a sensation of cool air. Needless to say, it was a total flop.

One day, after we'd completed negotiating an important deal in my office, Felix had to catch a plane, and I volunteered to give him a ride to the airport. When he got in my car, he took one look at this jury-rigged cooling system and broke into raucous laughter. For years thereafter, as both my professional profile and financial resources grew, Felix delighted in bringing me back down to earth by regaling everyone within earshot about what passed for A/C in Jim's Saab during the good old days.

* * *

In the early '70s, as I grew increasingly fascinated by my acquisition practice, I felt a strong urge to write about it. I did have some background in writing – those columns for high school and college newspapers, the naval cruise book, that article about the law firm softball league, a lengthy review I'd written on five novels for the Herald Tribune's Book Week, editing the PLI disclosure book. Writing was something at which I felt competent and enjoyed undertaking. I also recognized the potential advantage to me of putting prose to work in advancing my career.

Then one day a special opportunity arose. I had begun appearing on attorney seminars to discuss various aspects of corporate acquisitions. Following one of these seminars for the New York Law Journal, Steve and Lynn Glasser, who ran the Journal's seminar and publishing operations, asked if I'd be willing to write a book on the subject.

Up to that time, the literature on corporate acquisitions had been very legalistic, concentrating on structure, principles of corporate and tax law, and such. To me, those tomes missed what lay at the heart of any acquisition – the negotiating process, which was seldom been discussed or analyzed. I told the Glassers I'd do the book, but only if I could subject the acquisition negotiating process to the same kind of scrutiny that the structural aspects had previously received. They agreed.

I worked on *Anatomy of a Merger* (while still lawyering full-time) throughout the early '70s until it was finally published in 1975.[*] I'm proud to say that it received instant acclaim as the new bible for negotiated acquisitions.[**] My partners were enthusiastic about it, and we sent copies to existing and prospective clients. The message was, *Hey, we can do mergers better than anyone, and our partner is the guy who has written the definitive book.*

Since it worked well between the covers of a book, I figured it would also play well in an auditorium. A year later, under the auspices of *Anatomy*'s publisher, Law Journal Seminars-Press, we created a distinctive two-day seminar, *How to Negotiate Corporate Acquisitions*. The initial brochure asserted that, unlike other M&A seminars that concentrate on structural elements, ours would focus on "the give and take, and jostling for position, that takes place between the parties" – and, in particular, between their lawyers.

To best convey that emphasis, I assembled a panel of experienced practicing attorneys, devised a hypothetical acquisition scenario, and led the panelists through some strenuous simulated negotiations. I encouraged by-play and disagreement – since many of the judgments were essentially subjective – and urged the panelists to stay in character, even if it meant taking controversial positions with which they didn't personally agree. (I warned the audience that everything said was off the record, subject to dramatic license, often designed to get a rise out of an adversary, and could not be used against anyone in depositions or otherwise!) The panelists followed up the negotiations with a critique of the positions taken and arguments utilized, probing the parties' motivations and anticipating the likely responses.

---

[*] *Anatomy of a Merger – Strategies and Techniques for Negotiating Corporate Acquisitions* (Law Journal Seminars-Press, 1975)

[**] Marty Lipton, a leading dean of the M&A bar (and a major competitor of Skadden), called it "a magnificent book . . . one of the rare legal texts that can be read as a novel." He said that both acquisition novices and experienced deal lawyers "will profit from the experiences of a master practitioner . . . . Anatomy is an indispensable desk book for acquisition lawyers." (*New York Law Journal*, October 10, 1975). Arthur Borden, a noted attorney (writing in *The Business Lawyer* vol.31, Jan. 1976) said, "Mr. Freund has written a unique book which will inevitably find its way onto most law firm's shelves . . . . [It] is certainly the most informative and, incidentally, enthralling account of the acquisition agreement, and how it evolves, that exists in the literature today . . . . Mr. Freund's work will long remain an indispensable guide to this tricky terrain."

Repeated at somewhat irregular intervals the first few years, the forum settled down in 1982 (under the title *Negotiating Corporate Acquisitions – Public and Private*) to a regular Fall slot, attracting hundreds of annual attendees. When I retired in 1996, we had just celebrated our 20th anniversary—having become something of an institution, and fulfilling my ambition to create a unique educational experience. It continued for years thereafter, under the able chairmanships of two close Skadden colleagues – first Fin Fogg, and then Paul Schnell.

* * *

People sometimes ask me who were my mentors and whether I had role models. I'm not sure anyone fits those precise descriptions because I liked to plot my own course, but unquestionably certain individuals at Skadden Arps were important influences on the way I practised law. Two of them particularly stand out – Joe Flom and Peter Mullen.

Joe Flom was larger than life, and the hours I spent working with him – especially in my early years at the firm – were invaluable.

I can still picture Flom in those first years as if they occurred yesterday. Joe was not only brilliant, but he was also fearless – nothing daunted him. Having Joe on our side in any legal encounter made us feel we could compete with the largest and most prestigious firms. We emulated our peerless leader by lighting up cigars almost as hefty as his, and marching with confidence into adversarial conference rooms.

Although Joe brought most of the clients into the firm in those days, he never insisted on keeping them for himself. In fact, he made a point of regularly turning clients over to his younger partners, helping us to develop our own followings.

Joe had a fresh way of looking at the situations that lawyers find themselves in – legal issues, practical problems, business judgments, and (as was often the case) a mixture of all three – a way that no one else had considered. As complex as the problem might be, his solutions and strategies were invariably simple, almost never complicated. While everyone else was wallowing in the complexity of the situation, Joe would cut through to the core of the matter. He might, for instance, take some implicit assumption the parties had been operating under, tinker with it, and presto! – the solution appeared. It was almost never predictable; it often came as a complete surprise; and yet, when you heard it, you thought, "How simple; how elegant! . . . Why the hell didn't *I* think of that?"

I recall at some point deciding to write a piece about Flom – an attempt to extract and pass along to others the secrets of his success, to transmit his insights and accumulated wisdom. So, one Saturday afternoon I sat in Joe's living room with a little tape recorder and interviewed him for over two hours. Back home, after listening to the tape and examining my notes, I realized I didn't have an article.

As brilliant as Joe was, he couldn't (or wouldn't) attempt to articulate the elements of that brilliance. He was reluctant to abstract from his performance any insights from one case that could readily be applied in other situations. It made me realize what I'd always surmised – that much of Joe's unique skill was based on sheer instinct. Certainly, he had formidable analytical skills, a stupendous memory and superior judgment; but he blended them all together in a way he declined to explain. We called it simply, "Joe going with his gut" – and what a gut it was.

Most lawyers and business people proceed in a more-or-less orderly fashion when attacking a problem – perhaps even following an agenda to guide discussion of the various subpoints under review. But not Flom. He never had an agenda, nor did he follow anyone else's. When a thought came to Joe – and they came a mile a minute – he expressed it. While others in a meeting were listening or daydreaming, Joe was thinking. The man was always one step ahead of everyone else – trying out fresh approaches and new ideas, keeping the rest of us off balance.

To be sure, not all the ideas Joe floated were notable, but everything emerging from his mouth carried with it the same level of definitiveness. There was a total absence of caveats – none of that, "Here's my tentative thinking," or "I'm not sure this will fly, but . . . ." And, although Joe was constantly refining his ideas – discarding some, improving others, using a flawed notion as a pathway to a better one – there was never any "I was wrong" admission when a concept didn't fly. This was frequently tough on the rest of us, because we were never sure when Joe had moved on in a new direction, and we often had to assume he was still enamored by the old idea he'd silently discarded.

A number of people observed and commented on the fact that while Flom was sitting in a meeting, he would create intricate small doodles on the pad placed in front of him. What was significant to me about his doodling was that although no single doodle ever filled up a whole sheet of paper, I rarely saw Joe create more than one doodle on a page. At some point, he would stop work on the doodle, tear the page off the pad, discard it, and start creating a new doodle on a fresh page. To me, this symbolized the absence of clutter in Joe's mind. It's as if his brain was proceeding down one line of thought, which he eventually rejected; from that moment on, he didn't dwell on it at all, but instead put it behind him and moved onto something else.

I always marveled at the fact that although Joe's workload was prodigious, with multiple balls in the air at all times, his desk – unlike those of the rest of us – was invariably free of paper. Joe would read a document once and then toss it into his "out" basket, with the contents fixed firmly in his mind for later retrieval and accurate reference days or weeks later.

Joe was always pragmatic and goal-oriented – thinking about how best to move the process forward. He didn't spend much time arguing over abstruse legal questions or attempting to justify actions taken – it was always, "What's the next step? What issue do we have to face up to now?"

When you worked with Joe, you learned to be crisp. He would not sit silently through a long-winded explanation of anything. If you tried to be comprehensive, he would interrupt and throw you off course. I recall so well his frequent calls from outside the office (pre-cellphone and before email) asking me, "What's up?" I learned to come to the bottom line right away if I wanted to keep his attention – something that has proved to be a useful lesson in many aspects of life.

My close partner, Fin Fogg, related something about Flom[*] that really hit home with me.

> "It was sometimes very frustrating working for him because you'd write something and he would say, 'You missed the case from the Baltimore City Court in 1936 that says such-and-such.' You'd think, Where the hell is this coming from? But sure enough, you'd go off and search and search and search, and you'd finally find the case, and it would say such-and-such, just like Joe said. He was tough as nails, not an easy guy to work for, but he certainly taught me how to practice law."

---

[*] *The Skadden Story,* p.168

At times, Joe's latest strategy or tactic would constitute a reversal of the direction he'd been heading in the day before. When I had the temerity to point that out, Joe would shake his head and say, "The trouble with you, Jim, is that you're too consistent" – and then wrap himself in the mantel of Ralph Waldo Emerson. Although Joe only cited the first line, here's more of the Emerson quote – which captures Joe's approach and should be required reading for problem-solvers everywhere:

> "A foolish consistency is the hobgoblin of little minds. . . . With consistency, a great soul has simply nothing to do . . . . Speak what you think now in hard words, and tomorrow speak what tomorrow thinks in hard words again, though it contradicts everything you said today." *

Joe may have advocated inconsistency elsewhere, but there was one professional area where he was absolutely consistent – questions of ethics. It wasn't accidental that Skadden Arps went through all the craziness of the 1970's and 1980's – smack in the center of the action, with demanding clients and lots of questionable proposals dotting the landscape – without a single black mark against our name. Joe's ethics were beyond reproach. I never heard him advocate anything that even came close to the line. And in terms of the "smell test" that good lawyers apply to complex schemes, Joe always had the fastest proboscis in the East!

One instance comes to mind from when I was a young partner of the firm. A client of mine was, in effect, being shaken down by a corrupt state official. The client was told that if it didn't take a certain legitimate-looking action that would indirectly put some money in the official's pocket, then the client would not get a government certificate that it badly needed, even though it was fully deserved on the merits. The official's scheme was ingenious and unlikely to raise any eyebrows, and the client really wanted that certificate.

My nostrils started twitching, but then, as the tale of woe unfolded and the arguments of legitimacy were pressed, I found myself beginning to rationalize. So I decided to consult with Joe (who was on the Board of the company). It took him about three seconds to reply, in that laconic, equivocal manner for which he was noted – "FUGHETABOUTIT!"

---

* But see the Freund exception when you're negotiating (later in this chapter).

Of course, he was right; and afterwards I was ashamed of myself for even bringing the official's proposal up with him. I knew damn well it should have been rejected, but I was trying too hard to see if there was a way to accommodate a client who was being unfairly treated.

The most interesting part of that story is the denouement. When I went back to the client to say that Joe and I strongly advised them not to have any part of this scheme, instead of complaining about their goody-two-shoes legal advisors, the executives involved seemed genuinely pleased that we had come out forcefully against it. They didn't like the scheme any more than we did, but they just needed to be told it was wrong by someone with moral authority in such matters. And I've never forgotten the particular lesson I learned from Joe – that this someone (in all such cases) should be their lawyer.[*]

* * *

My second major influence was Peter Mullen, who was our managing partner (and then Executive Partner) for most of my time at the firm. In the years before he devoted himself entirely to piloting Skadden, Peter was a fine corporate lawyer, doing deals and handling other business matters. Working for him initially as an associate helped me develop skills at negotiating and personal interaction.

I became close to Peter (and to his terrific wife Billie) during the early '70s when he was running the firm in between deals and with help from partners such as Barry Garfinkel, John Feerick and myself. Later, when Earle Yaffa came aboard and we became more professional about management, there was less need for my administrative services – which was okay by me, as I preferred working with clients, doing deals, writing, and conducting professional seminars.

Peter was a positive influence in several respects. He was wonderful at forging consensus in the firm. Although he had multiple projects going at any one time, he never projected a sense of being overloaded. He held his temper in check, really listened to you, and didn't feel the need to take credit for the "good idea."

---

[*] In a similar vein, as a new partner I landed as a client a would-be financial colossus who was considered hot stuff on Wall Street. I was frankly excited by the boost this was likely to provide to my stature in the firm, but the man made me nervous – not always following my advice, doing some questionable things. I went to Joe Flom and told him that my client with the big potential made me uneasy. "Do you trust him?" Joe asked. "Not entirely," I replied. Joe's response was instant and unvarnished: "Then get rid of him" – which I promptly did without any regrets.

The rise of Skadden, Arps from one small New York office practicing in just a few areas of law to a national and international presence in a great variety of legal disciplines was a Mullen-led voyage all the way. He displayed vision, remained patient when things did not go well, and always acted to foster the long-term health of the firm.

Peter was also a leader in establishing the Skadden Fellowships, by which the firm has underwritten over 850 bright law school graduates to engage in important two-year public interest projects after leaving law school. No other law firm has created anything like this, and Peter was rightly proud of it.

To grow the way we did, but without acquiring other law firms (which went against our grain), we needed to persuade top individual talent to join our ranks. The recruitment of lateral partners from other firms was a task at which Peter was especially effective. As one of them remarked to me, "Peter made the decision to come to the firm easy." To Ken Bialkin, who arrived from another large firm, Peter represented "the personality, character, conscience and moral side of Skadden, Arps. He always put matters into context and then measured them against the welfare of the firm as a whole, taking a long range view of the firm and its place in the community."

Perhaps the most important professional relationship of all for Peter was with Joe Flom. In lesser hands, this might have proved troublesome, but in their capable alliance hands it worked out well. When Joe recognized that Peter was the ideal man for the job and asked him to take over as Executive Partner, Peter said he wouldn't do it if Joe was going to second-guess him. Joe promised that he would never go around him or behind his back, but he reserved the right to tell Peter directly what he thought. That was good enough for Peter.

They functioned as a terrific team. As Joe himself said, "Peter operates beautifully by consensus. He looks like he's following, but he's leading." Peter knew when and how to tell Joe bad news and how to handle Joe's occasional venting; and he mastered the knack of taking the endless stream of ideas that emanated from Joe and making the workable ones pay off, while talking him out of the remainder.

When McKinsey, the prominent management consulting firm, took a professional look at Skadden, Arps, it concluded that Peter was "a very strong leader, with an unusual mix of humility and self-confidence, and a style that made people feel involved and part of the decision."

I was very proud of the fact that when Peter retired as Executive Partner, I gave the speech of tribute to him at our partners' retreat; and later, when Peter passed away, I delivered the eulogy regarding his professional accomplishments at the church memorial service.

I'll express my admiration for a number of other partners of the firm in Chapter 16.

* * *

Negotiating is the skill I became best known for. I can hardly remember the subject being addressed in law school, excerpt in the class taught by David Herwitz that I spoke of in Chapter 10. Little bargaining took place in my Davies, Hardy assignments. Once in practice at Skadden Arps, after the briefest of apprenticeships, I suddenly found myself in the midst of transactions which placed a high premium on this particular skill. I'm sure I floundered; I'd received no training, I had no theoretical platform to fall back on. There were no black-letter instructions to memorize. My seniors focused on substance, rarely pausing to instruct me on tactics and the like.

As I began to negotiate, I made what in retrospect were a number of obvious mistakes. I ceded points to my adversary when I didn't have to and received nothing in return. I became stubborn on issues that didn't rise to the requisite level of importance. Against patient negotiators, I wasn't as persistent as I should have been. I ignored significant clues that might have suggested paths of favorable compromise.

Gradually, though, I stopped treating negotiating as a cursory legal stepchild and began to view it as something worthy of serious consideration. Because negotiating tends to be somewhat free-form, it doesn't lend itself easily to thoughtful analysis and structured tactics. As a result, many lawyers don't bother to apply themselves to grasping how to do it well. They just plunge in, trusting their instincts. As you might expect, those with good instincts usually turn out to be competent at the bargaining table.

But the sad fact is that a large number of otherwise skilled lawyers are mediocre negotiators at best. They become so immersed in difficult substantive questions that they rarely stop to analyze how best to achieve their goals. They neglect to size up their adversary, to peer inside his mind and discover what's really troubling him. They seem to lack adeptness at devising effective compromises. Their inventiveness is reserved for matters of substance – new ways to structure a deal for tax purposes and the like – while the equally creative and necessary task of circumventing a difficult adversarial sticking point remains overlooked.

Yet lawyers are the logical choices to handle negotiations in these kinds of sticky transactions. A legal mind is invaluable for clarifying situations – for example, to identify the cause of a seeming disagreement as a simple failure to distinguish separable issues. Lawyers possess the training and experience to ask the hard questions so crucial to the bargaining process. And it's usually the attorney who realizes that the parties' minds haven't really met on an issue which is seemingly resolved.

For instance, the parties to a sizeable employment contract – the company and the executive – may *think* they've reached agreement on a cash bonus formula based on the company's net earnings. But should that bonus be based on the company's net earnings *before* or *after* the bonus itself? The parties never thought about this, but it's an important question that needs to be asked and resolved in advance. More often than not, it's the lawyer who raises the query.

I like to think I successfully mentored younger lawyers on such practical matters as negotiating tactics, but couldn't always tell since they seldom acknowledged the assistance. Well, it took 45 years, but at a recent lunch with Lou Goodman (who started out working for me as an associate and later went on to head Skadden's Boston office for many years), Lou regaled me with this reminiscence.

Back in the '70s, Lou and I were working together on an acquisition at a time when Lou was just starting out as an associate with little actual experience. Observing me negotiate this transaction, Lou had noticed that when the other side complained about certain clauses in the contract we'd drafted, my frequent response was, "Come on – I've used that clause in every deal I ever did."

At one point in the negotiation that day, I had to step out of the room to take a phone call. In my absence, the other side kept commenting on our draft, which made Lou a little uneasy, since he hadn't yet acquired the acquisition expertise he later possessed. But when the other side dared to complain about a certain arguable provision in the Skadden draft, Lou didn't hesitate with his response. "Every deal I've ever done, we've done it this way."

Lou recalls that just as he was saying this, I came back into the room and overheard Lou's response, although I had no idea what provision of the contract he was referring to. Meanwhile, the lawyer on the other side didn't argue the issue further, but just moved on to his next point.

Shortly later, during a brief break, Lou says I whispered to him, "Good boy! You handled that exactly right."

Most of what takes place in the course of negotiations can be characterized as either attempting to get a leg up on your adversary or striking a compromise between your respective positions. I firmly believe that the key to effective negotiating lies in achieving a functional balance between those two seemingly inconsistent aspects.

If all your efforts are directed toward gaining advantages over your adversary, you will undoubtedly come on too strong; and where the parties possess relatively equal bargaining power, with freedom to consummate the transaction or not, you may cause your client irreparable harm – up to and including losing the deal. On the other hand, if you don't push a little – if you never strive for advantages in drafting or stake out positions that invite rebuttal – then your client is unlikely to achieve his share of obtainable rights and protections.

There are so many ways in which my approach to negotiating differs from Donald Trump's style, but I'll just single out one of them here. Trump revels in sending inconsistent signals to his adversary, reversing directions, keeping the other side off balance.

That has never been my approach. I try to send signals of consistency to the other side, so they know which are the issues I feel strongly about – and thus are the ones where they're unlikely to move me off the posture I've taken. When you're all over the place, that message doesn't get across.

In my book on the subject, *Smart Negotiating*[*] (discussed in Chapter 16), I spelled out my concept of what kind of negotiator I was:

---

[*] *Smart Negotiating – How to Make Good Deals in the Real World* (Simon & Schuster, 1992), p.29

"Just so you know where I'm coming from, I consider myself an ethical and fair-minded bargainer. I'm opposed to misrepresentation, to the kind of dissembling that seeks to achieve an unfair advantage. I don't believe in chiseling; I scorn dirty tricks. I'm not looking to win at any cost or to make those on the other side feel as though they've lost. I like to base my arguments on reason, to have a solid rationale for my positions, and to try to be persuasive. In turn, I'm willing to listen in case the other side's rationale might persuade me; and where possible, I prefer to conduct the negotiations in an atmosphere free of rancor or personal animosity and to conclude on good terms with my counterpart.

"Nevertheless, I don't like to end up with substantially less than I consider myself or my client entitled to, based on all the factors affecting the negotiations. It's gratifying to end up with *more* than we expected, and I generally try to land in that territory if possible. But I don't look upon achieving something extra in each deal as an article of faith, as long as we get our just desserts. On the other hand, I definitely do *not* like to feel that I've been taken advantage of or jerked around; and when my antennae sense this happening, I stand up on my hind legs and let the world know about it.

"It goes against my grain to see deals muffed that should be made – whether because of intransigence, overtrading, miscalculation, misinformation, erroneous assumptions, or whatever. I recognize that some deals simply don't make sense. But when one is itching to occur, I feel a sense of failure if I can't concoct and carry out a strategy to bring the two sides together."

* * *

I'll close this section with a favorite story that sticks in my mind. It happened during a late night in my office a number of years ago. My client and I were engaged in a very tough M&A negotiation with the principal on the other side[*] – let's call him Larry – who was giving us fits.

At one point in the evening, while the outcome was still very much in doubt, Larry happened to notice on my coffee table a book I'd written on negotiating deals. He flipped through the pages and then asked if he could have a copy. "Absolutely," I said, "but not until the evening is over – I don't want to hear my own stuff coming back at me . . . . And what's more," I added, "I'll even autograph your copy."

---

[*] As was common in these transactions, where the principals were sophisticated and could be trusted not to make a move without consulting with their own counsel, each lawyer often consented to allowing his client to communicate directly with the other side's lawyer.

We continued to negotiate, making a little progress but still not getting all the way home on one key point. Then it hit me. I scribbled something on a sheet of paper. Then I wrote something else on another sheet.

I turned to Larry and said, "Look, if you see the light and come around to this very logical resolution of the issue that our side is advocating, here's the inscription I'm going to write into your copy of my book." And I handed him the first piece of paper, which read something like this:

"To Larry, a wise and consummate negotiator, who has mastered the art of extracting the essence from the situation while not letting himself get bogged down in trivia."

"On the other hand," I said to Larry, "if you stick to your absurd position, then here's what I'm going to write" and I handed him the second piece of paper, which read as follows:

"To Larry, a bumbling, inflexible bargainer who would rather stand on an invalid principle than reach out for the good deal laid at his feet."

Then I said, "Well, Larry, what'll it be?" Larry eyed me quizzically, mouthed a kind of hollow laugh, looked over at my client, and left the room to talk to his lawyer.

Fifteen minutes later, we had our deal. And all it cost – Lord forgive me! – was one little white lie about Larry's negotiating prowess . . . .

With me on this page are Joe Flom (top right), Peter Mullen (middle right), Fin Fogg (bottom right) and Barry Garfinkel (with wife Gloria below) . . . . all major colleagues in my Skadden career.

At work, in the TWA takeover (left) with TWA president Richard Pearson and Solomon Bros. investment banker Michael Zimmerman, and in the Federated takeover (right) with Skadden litigation partner Stu Shapiro (both pix from business periodicals).

At play, in Puerto Rico on our 45th birthday junket in 1979 – Fred Bacher, me, Jack Veatch, Bob Watson, George Riordan, Bob Silbey and (kneeling) Lefty Lewis.

(Above), with three of my wonderful secretaries, Nancy Martin, Chris Greges amd Ann Leyden. (Left) My big assignment during the last year at Skadden (1996) was participating in a lengthy mediation in Sydney Australia, where I got to try on this courtroom headdress.

Photos on the jackets of three of my books published in 1979, 1987, and 1990.

A copious Skadden partner turnout for the retirement dinner the firm gave me in 1996.

14. SKADDEN ARPS (#2) – DEALS GALORE

As I look back on it, the second half of the '70s was a rewarding but tough period for me.

- In 1974 my father died much too early; and in the ensuing years I felt his loss keenly, as well as the need to provide a great deal more support to my mother. This meant taking care of her business affairs, including the sale of his company, which was ailing without Dad's leadership.

- That same year I turned 40, which seemed a real milestone at the time (although less so now that so many other milestones have occurred).

- My book *Anatomy of a Merger* was published in 1975, and I was on my way as an M&A lawyer – following this up with my annual seminar, various speaking engagements, numerous writings, and going after new clients.

- I was wound up pretty tight in those days – stalking around my office waving a tennis racket, barking out actions that needed to be taken – a tough taskmaster to the associates who worked for me.

- In 1975, Barbro and I moved into The Beresford – a terrific apartment in an elegant building that we bought at a modest price due to the financial problems of NYC.

- My kids Erik & Tom – born in 1966 and 1968 – were flourishing during this five-year period, but my marriage was disintegrating (as noted in Chapter 9). The looming question of whether the marriage would survive made for an increasingly uncomfortable situation.

Against this backdrop, I loaded one more large pressure on myself – something I just couldn't resist.

I'd become increasingly aware of a big gap that exists in the education of lawyers. Law school taught us how to think and offered some legal principles; continuing legal education programs provided substantive information but limited itself to specific well-defined areas; on-the-job training helped but fell short because of its emphasis on accomplishing projects rather than how to perform the tasks; and the feedback a young lawyer should get from his or her seniors was not always available.

So I decided to write a book on lawyering – to try to analyze in depth for young lawyers the principal qualities that make up the complete attorney, including such subjects as: legal analysis, written and oral expression, diligence and due care, dealing with partners and other colleagues, handling clients, interactions with other lawyers (including negotiating); and exercising good judgment.

Since I was conducting a very active practice during those latter years of the '70s, it was almost impossible to carve out large chunks of time to work on the book. I would write bits and pieces on planes and in other places whenever I had even an hour of free time. After several years of this, I finally got all the substance down on paper; but the draft was still rough and due to the overlap of subject matter, needed a lot more organizing.

So I checked into a small Ramada Inn just north of White Plains, where I used to take my kids for weekend outings. It had a swimming pool and a modest restaurant. I stayed there alone for almost a week, limiting phone usage to the end of the day. Chapters and sections were scattered on the floor all around the room. Other than for meals, the only daily interlude I allowed myself was taking a short swim. During that week, I managed to pull it all together, polish the prose, cross-reference topics – the works. It ran to 370 jam-packed slim-margined pages.

*Lawyering** was finally published in 1979 and was very well-received in the profession.** Even today, older lawyers still tell me it's the first book they prescribe for young associates to read.

---

* *LAWYERING – a Realistic Approach to Legal Practice, (Law Journal Seminars-Press, 1979)*

** Here's an excerpt from the contemporaneous review in *The Business Lawyer* (vol.35, April 1980) by Elliott Goldstein, a partner in a major law firm: "In Lawyering, James C. Freund has written the book each of us had wanted to write – the definitive volume for associates on how to practice law . . . . The book is written as though he were talking informally to an associate . . . . The book's chief value to associates is Mr. Freund's understanding of human nature, his analysis of human behavior, and his keen enjoyment of the company of the people with whom he deals . . . . Even though the book is directed to associates, every partner should read it. It is a well written book about law practice which will help the most experienced lawyer do a little self-analysis . . . . Buy it and read it."

After the book came out, however, I experienced a real let-down. I guess I'd anticipated the same kind of enthusiastic recognition from my partners for *Lawyering* as I'd received for *Anatomy of a Merger*. After all, the new book was educational for *all* associates and young partners (not just those in M&A) and could prove to be a real selling tool for bringing in new associates.

But although Les Arps, Barry Garfinkel and a few others provided positive feedback, it didn't generate the warm reception from the firm that I'd expected. I had the unmistakable feeling that many of my partners thought I should have been spending more time doing billable work.

Then came the shocker. For a number of years, I had been grouped with two other successful partners to receive equal amounts of annual compensation from the firm. But in the year following *Lawyering*'s publication, I was dropped a few points below them – apparently due to the fact that my billable hours had been reduced by the time I spent on the book. The financial penalty wasn't that great, but the message it imparted really hurt.

As I look back now on those latter years of the '70s decade, I'm pretty sure I was suffering from a mild depression. The triple whammy of the pressure to complete the book, the negativity and uncertainty attending my marriage, the defaulted expectations and putdown message from my firm related to *Lawyering* – these marked a low point in what I had considered a booming professional career. I probably should have sought professional help, but I didn't.

* * *

Then, two things happened that broke the spell, and I was myself again.

The first of these was the sad but increasingly unavoidable decision to separate that Barbro and I mutually reached in May 1980. The uncertainty of whether this would or would not happen had been troubling me for a long while; and although resolving to part company marked a melancholy moment for us and a sorrowful occasion for our sons (see Chapters 9 and 12), it did bring clarity to my unusually indecisive state of mind.

The other occurrence qualified as serendipitous. At a seminar in San Diego's Del Coronado Hotel, a lawyer named Ed Greene and I served as fellow panelists. I knew Ed from his former days at the Wilkie, Farr law firm where we had been on opposite sides of a deal but worked well together. Since then, he'd gone to Washington to become Director of the Division of Corporation Finance at the Securities and Exchange Commission.

We renewed our acquaintance one night at dinner, and over a few drinks, I confided to him about my blue circumstances.

"Hey," Ed said, "I've got a great idea. Why don't you get out of New York City for a while – get away from the place where you've been troubled – and come to Washington as a special consultant to my CorpFin Division."

It turned out there was a program for a person with special expertise to work at the SEC for 100 days or so without having to give up his professional affiliation. It was like the venerable dollar-a-year men during the Depression and World War II – the government didn't pay you anything for your service, but you were allowed to remain on the payroll of your firm during the entire period.

I was intrigued. Since a good deal of my practice in those days involved dealing with the SEC – especially with CorpFin, the Division we had to go through on every public company merger transaction and securities offering – I thought it would be constructive for my career and for our firm for me to take this on and absorb the view from the inside. I told Ed I'd consider it.

I wanted to make sure of being able to see my kids enough during this period; and I needed the firm's blessing for me to be away for this long, as well as its willingness to keep paying me while I was gone. In addition I didn't want to go to Washington and just hang around – I needed assurance of meaningful work. Then presto! – a special idea for the proposed project occurred to me.

The year before, I had co-written with my colleague Rich Easton a long article for *The Business Lawyer* about a new trend we had seen in the M&A world of the late '70s – a multistep approach to negotiated acquisitions, utilizing techniques (such as tender offers) which up to then had been reserved for hostile deals. Given the intense competition for desirable acquisition candidates, this new method stressed speed in acquiring control of the target before someone else could poach on the deal. We called the article *The Three-Piece Suitor*.* I followed it up with a speech on the subject at PLI's Annual Institute on Securities Regulation, and I changed the format of my annual M&A seminar to feature just such a deal on the second day.

I realized that this new way of accomplishing friendly deals – often with an initial tender offer – created regulatory problems and anomalous disclosure consequences depending on how the deal was done. I had begun to ponder generating a proposal to change the way things ought to be handled. That's when I realized how much more clout I'd have with the proposal if I were working at the SEC, becoming better educated on the regulatory picture, and hopefully inducing Ed Greene as the Director of the CorpFin division to co-author the proposal with me.

Ed liked the idea, including the co-authorship. I was able to work out suitable arrangements with Barbro regarding the kids. My successful pitch to Skadden was that it would be a boon to the firm for one of us to have this experience, and I'd arranged for other partners and associates to cover for me on deals while I was away.

Thus began an enjoyable period of about a half-year in Washington. I took an apartment at an Executive Suites residential hotel, rented a piano for the duration, and looked up old friends like my college buddy Jack Veatch, now a Washington insurance executive, and Washington partners of Skadden I was keen on such as Neal McCoy. The SEC staffer assigned to me was Neal's wife, Cathy McCoy, a delightful woman and fine lawyer, who showed me the ropes. This included such menial tasks as how to make my own photocopies – a chore I'd been freed from at Skadden with its plentiful staff.

I would return to New York every week or two to see the boys, and they sometimes came down to Washington to stay with me over the weekend. I spent some time at my firm office taking care of details, although I stayed away from becoming fully engaged on any specific client matter.

---

* *The Three-Piece Suitor: An Alternative Approach to Negotiated Corporate Acquisitions* (The Business Lawyer, Vol.34, July 1979)

I spent most of the professional time researching and then writing – with helpful input from co-author Ed Greene – a substantial article for *The Business Lawyer*.* It prompted articles in other periodicals and was much talked about at the time; and although the recommendations we made were never fully adopted, elements found their way into future Federal regulations.

* * *

The time I spent in Washington proved to be a head-clearing experience for me – escaping the pressure at Skadden, and maintaining some distance from the tough aftermath of marital separation. When it ended, I returned to NYC refreshed and ready to kick my life into high gear, featuring three special directions to take.

On a personal level, I was now able to go on vacations with my sons in addition to spending weekends with them. Over the next few years, we went skiing out west several times, as well as travelling to Hawaii, Jamaica, California, Bermuda, and elsewhere. I began dating other women, eating in good restaurants, and living in a comfortable non-claustrophobic midtown apartment with daylight streaming in through glass panels, plus a terrace featuring scenic views of the urban landscape. There was also ample room for my piano, from whose keys I derived real satisfaction.

Professionally, as I dipped further into the world of multi-step transactions, it wasn't much of a step to insert myself into the hostile acquisition business. I realized that I'd been missing out on much of the excitement there. As the boisterous '70s moved into the supercharged '80s, I made my own move into the action. As before, I still never felt comfortable on the few occasions when I found myself on the side of the hostile aggressor. But the bulk of my work was representing target companies under siege, a comfortable posture for me. And so, as the '80s proceeded, I began to handle hostile deals along with the more traditional negotiated acquisitions.

I still wanted an outlet for my writing but was reluctant to do another all-consuming book. An ideal opportunity came along via my friends Lynn and Steve Glasser, who had been my publishers for *Anatomy of a Merger* and *Lawyering* at the New York Law Journal. Having moved on, they now published a monthly periodical called *Legal Times*.

---

* *Substance over Form S-14: A Proposal to Reform SEC Regulation of Negotiated Acquisitions*. (The Business Lawyer, Vol.36, July 1981)

The Glassers made me an offer I couldn't refuse – to write a monthly column on any topic of my choosing. It didn't even have to be about lawyers, although I usually tried to include at least a passing reference to the profession in each article. The column could be serious or funny, instructive or whimsical. I had total freedom to let my imagination float from the rigors of everyday lawyering to other realms – whatever came to mind.

To be sure, this assignment kept me on my toes, since I had no backlog of material or inventory of past writing. Each month consisted of a week to generate an idea, a week sketching out the article's theme, a week drafting it, and a week of re-writing. But despite the rigors of the schedule, the freedom of tone and subject matter turned this into a joyous exercise.

I wrote about such topics as decision-making, rejecting implicit assumptions, and escaping from an either/or world. There were essays on negotiating, including an imaginative approach to walking that last mile by rolling dice, and also bargaining your way out of the clutches of the KGB. I wrote about vacations with my kids, visiting a WWII cemetery, and what's worth snatching from the bathroom of upscale hotels. There were pieces on dealing with bores and the pro's and con's of embellishment. I offered aphorisms of good advice, assessed sins of omission, and sponsored an unconventional look at memory.

I was blessed with a wonderful collaborator back then (and still today – check out the cover of this memoir and the Appendix) – an illustrator named Joe Azar, who possessed an uncanny ability to capture with the deft strokes of his pen just what I was trying to get across in each article.

With the help of the Glassers, I preserved all the articles in three books of essays published between 1984 and 1990: *Legal Ease, The Acquisition Mating Dance,* and *Advise and Invent.*[*] A few years ago I released a five-disc CD album (*This Time, Just the Words*) in which I recorded myself reading the best of the essays.

---

[*] *Legal-Ease – Fresh Insights Into Lawyering (Law & Business Inc., 1984); The Acquisition Mating Dance and Other Essays on Negotiating (Prentice Hall Law & Business, 1987; Advise and Invent – The Lawyer as Counselor-Strategist and Other Essays (Prentice Hall, 1990).*

When *Legal-Ease* came out, it received a very positive review in the ABA Journal[*] that captured exactly what I was trying to achieve. Here are some extracts:

> "James C. Freund is out to demystify the practice of law . . . . [H]e has made a career of providing lawyers with insights about themselves . . . . The best thing about this book besides its good humor and its author's obvious love of life . . . [is that] it is organized to provide a wide range of lawyers with advice on everything from how to break bad news to a client to what to swipe from a hotel room . . . . [It] helps lawyers analyze what their own stumbling blocks might be. Freund's writing style is warm and witty, and he makes his points with analogies, parables, plays and poetry . . . . The reader will leave this book not only with fresh insights into lawyering, but with an appreciation for its author and his understanding that life does not end with law school."

But just to show that you can't please everyone, here's what an Idaho lawyer had to say:[**]

> "Legal-Ease is a mishmash of personal anecdotes, well worn bar and barroom stories, doggerel, parody, homilies from the inner circle of corporate practice in a New York City law firm and recollections of law school experience that would have been forgotten by anyone whose post-graduate career had more interest, substance and vitality . . . . The author has produced a pablum of prose . . . . The reader would be well advised to quit after the table of contents."

All I can say is, they take no prisoners in Idaho . . . .

In 1985, I reflected on the fact that over the past two decades women lawyers had materialized in large numbers, breaking up what was for generations a male-dominated club. But since things were still in a transitional period, with relatively few women having become major law firm partners or high-ranked corporate counsel, I tried to get a handle on the special problems facing women lawyers. I wrote in the *Legal Times*[***] about

---

[*] ABA Journal (Vol.70, November 1984)

[**] *The Advocate*, Idaho State Bar (May 1985)

[***] Contained in my book *Advise and Invent* under the heading "Women Lawyers."

a survey I'd conducted among seven (unidentified) successful women in their 30s and 40s. I posed for them a series of questions on such topics as male responses to their presence in meetings, male-female opportunities, projecting an image, sexist remarks and such.

What I received was a real diversity of reaction to the male-female issues, with some very interesting responses. I concluded that women lawyers were well on their way to solving any special gender problems. Five years later, I sent the article out to nine different successful women lawyers (again without identifying them), asking whether it seemed dated, and if the responses would be different in 1990. Once more, although all agreed on some matters, the responses to others were diverse.*

The biggest difference this time was that some of the women said I missed the boat. They wanted to discuss other issues than those I'd framed ("Your article misses what is the central gender issue of the day: leading a personal life as well as a professional one.") Some of the replies were even a little testy: "The issues you raise and the situations that the original respondents talk about are ones that I no longer care to think about . . . . The questions that I and, I think, other women are wrestling with today go well beyond this point . . . . I would hope that articles about women lawyers today would address issues at this more human level and let the male/female jockeying of prior years fall by the wayside – where it belongs."

* * *

The most exciting and productive decade of my professional life was the '80s.** I was representing a variety of major corporations – Transamerica, American Express, Gerber, Hughes Tool, Hanson Industries, Morrison-Knudsen, Albertsons, Schering-Plough, to name a few. I was mainly involved in acquisitions – some negotiated voluntarily, some under hostile pressure. In each case, I received splendid help from a plethora of Skadden lawyers (who are acknowledged in Chapter 16). There was a strong team concept that pervaded these deals, with the active participation of skilled lawyers from a variety of disciplines.

---

* Also contained in *Advise and Invent.*

** For what it's worth, I was listed in the 1982-83 volume of Who's Who in America.

Out of the resulting pack of deals, I've selected several for discussion here – some negotiated ones and others that were initially hostile. Almost every deal I did presented a special problem to overcome – virtually none were smooth sailing.

Many of the prime engagements were basically one-shot deals, often culminating in the sale of my client's company. But I also formed some enduring relationships – the most notable of which involved that venerable enterprise, Dun & Bradstreet.

Dun & Bradstreet

Over the years, I handled a number of negotiated acquisitions for D&B as their principal outside counsel in the M&A area. Paul Schnell, now a major partner at Skadden Arps, was my invaluable colleague in most of these transactions. I developed a number of relationships at the company, especially with their general counsel, Jerry Raikes, and his #2, Bill Buchanan; with business guru Dick Schmidt; with the executives handling acquisitions, Bill Jacobi, Peter Lessler, and Terry Taylor; and with three CEO'S – Duke Drake, Charlie Moritz and Bob Weissman.

I was particularly fond of Duke Drake, a marvelous CEO with whom I stayed friendly after his retirement, attending Duke's big 90th birthday bash at the spread that he and his lovely wife Patricia have in Arizona. He died five years later at 95. When I think back on Duke in his prime, an enduring picture comes to mind.

For years Duke had been trying to convince his friend, Art Nielsen (the CEO of A.C. Nielsen, the large global information source), to sell his company to D&B. At last Duke's efforts paid off, and we negotiated the terms of the deal. The final step, however, required approval by the A.C. Neilsen board of directors, the outcome of which was not a sure thing.

The D&B team assembled in a small room at A.C. Nielsen's Chicago headquarters, near the larger room where the A.C. Nielson board was debating whether or not to sell D&B the company. As the minutes passed, we became anxious that something had gone wrong.

Then the door to our room opened, and in walked Art Nielsen – a big smile on his face and his thumb up in the air. It was a delicious moment, heightened by the sight of the two CEO's so obviously pleased that they punctuated the occasion by wrapping their arms around each other in a giant bearhug. That might not seem unique today, but a hug between business executives was a rarity in those days – I can't remember witnessing a similar occasion.

I learned a lot about doing deals and also about myself in the course of representing D&B. Here's one such instance of ultimate self-knowledge that has stuck with me.

The background to this tale is that the year my college friends and I turned 45, we celebrated by taking a men-only weekend trip to Puerto Rico. (One of the wives dubbed it, "Seven assholes on a spree" and had t-shirts made up with that message emblazoned on the front.) It was such a delightful event that five years later (in mid-1984), we made reservations for a turning-50 trip to Las Vegas. We were all looking forward eagerly to this new junket.

In the weeks preceding the much-anticipated trip, I was working on a big corporate divestiture for D&B that was scheduled to be completed prior to our departure date. But as it became bogged down in technical difficulties and endless negotiating, I could see the need for expedited progress if I were going to make the spree. There was no way I'd be able to leave for Vegas if the deal were still being negotiated.

To speed up the process, I began doing things that I wouldn't have done but for the time pressure. I didn't mess anything up but I certainly wasn't operating at my best – especially in the impatience I directed at further delays and some sharp words I spoke to several innocent people. If I weren't so wrapped up in the pull of the Vegas trip, I'd have observed that the D&B executives on the deal (as well as my Skadden colleagues, Nancy Henry and Paul Schnell) were probably puzzled and put off by some of my actions.

Then one day a technical difficulty occurred that made it certain the deal would be delayed beyond our Vegas departure date. With a good deal of chagrin, I had to call my friends and tell them I'd no longer be able to join them in Nevada, a real disappointment for me.

But once I'd made that call and no longer faced the time pressure of the trip, my lawyering skills re-emerged. I was able to shepherd the deal to a successful conclusion – although not until after my friends had returned from Vegas and tried to make me feel better by saying that it wasn't the same without me.

It was a vivid lesson for me, which I often imparted to younger lawyers in the years that followed. Always check, I told them, to see if some outside factor is influencing your performance in a negative way – and if that's the case, do something about it. Your client deserves nothing but your best, even if that means missing out on a personal indulgence.

Sometimes my D&B deals worked out very well. I recall the time the company decided to sell a major subsidiary through a formal auction process. There were a half-dozen qualified bidders, but one of them came in at a price much higher than the others – really overpaying for the property. We cautiously negotiated the contract and moved gingerly toward the closing, praying that the buyer wouldn't learn of the disparity and pull his bid. He didn't.

Not every deal, however, worked out so well. The unkindest cut of all occurred in perhaps the toughest acquisition we ever had to negotiate – putting together a major D&B unit with a fierce business competitor, overcoming high levels of mutual distrust. We finally managed to pull off what promised to be a blockbuster combination, getting both sides to sign on the dotted line – only to have the FTC block the merger on antitrust grounds. Heartbreak!

I also remember the proposed acquisition of a privately-owned magazine, featuring a hard-fought negotiation which we were finally able to get resolved. Then, on the day before the agreement was scheduled to be signed, the selling stockholder (who was to remain as the magazine's president for several years) got cold feet about working for D&B and blew up the deal. To compound the adversity, the seller turned around and sold the magazine to another buyer for the exact price we had agreed to pay – and had the nerve to use our contract, word for word! I still don't understand why this happened, although we later heard that a D&B executive had inadvertently given the selling stockholder the impression that D&B frowned on having to fund *both* of his *two* lunch club memberships . . . .

* * *

An experience I recall vividly was representing Rainier Bank of Seattle. I had no special expertise in banking, but over the years managed to counsel three substantial banks – Midlantic in New Jersey, Comerica in Detroit, and Rainier. I was assisted on prior banking assignments by the very capable Rick Prins and on this one by my knowledgeable Banking M&A colleague, Bill Rubenstein.

Bob Truex, the CEO of Rainier and one of my favorite client executives, was experiencing severe health problems in 1987. Whether for that reason or other business/financial ones, the Rainier board decided to sell the bank. It selected a well-known major investment bank as Rainer's financial advisor, and us as its legal counsel.

Our financial advisor conducted a private auction of Rainer, which came down to two best-buyer candidates – Security Pacific from California and a large midwestern bank. We invited representatives of the two banks to come to Seattle with a view to our simultaneously negotiating terms with each, evaluating the results, deciding which was the better fit for Rainier, and making our final selection.

Security Pacific showed up in Seattle with its financial and legal advisors. The midwestern bank did likewise, but to my surprise, its financial advisor was none other than Rainier's investment bank.

"Hey, wait a minute!" I exclaimed to the partners of our financial advisor. "You guys are on *our* side of the deal" – not on the side of one of the two potential buyers."

"Oh, Jim, don't worry about it," they replied. "The guys representing the midwestern bank are from a completely different team in our shop than our team. We have a Chinese wall of confidentiality between us . . . ."

I wasn't buying it. Suppose we were to receive advice from our financial advisor's team that the midwestern bank was the preferred suitor (a real possibility). How could we rely on that being a disinterested judgment if we knew that our financial advisor's firm would be earning a *second* big fee for the deal on the buyer's side? In my view, our financial advisor needed to be viewed as not having any partiality as to choice of buyer. Their eye should be fixed on considerations which solely served the best interests of Rainier.

So I took a firm stand, which Bob Truex backed me up on. We would not go forward with the negotiations unless and until the midwestern bank was represented by an investment banker other than our financial advisor. I took a lot of heat from our financial advisor for this stand, and there were concerted attempts to make me change my mind. After all, I wasn't a complete stranger – I'd been on friendly terms with them for years, working side by side with their professionals on matters concerning a large client of both our firms.

I take pride in the fact that I held firm – at the distinct risk of harming my relations with this important player in the M&A area. After a short interval, the midwestern bank hired another financial advisor, thus permitting us to proceed with the competition.

Another memory from the deal has stuck with me. It was a moment when our team, led by CEO Bob Truex, was engaged in tense negotiations with one of the buyers – and just then Bob's weak health got the better of him, and he had to excuse himself from the session. The other side asked whether we intended to terminate the meeting. "No, no," said Bob – and then he added the words that thrilled me then (as they should any lawyer) and remain fixed in my mind today – "Jim speaks for me."

Rainier ended up choosing Security Pacific, in part based on receiving a recommendation to do so from our financial advisor. Would this have been forthcoming if they also represented the midwestern bidder? We'll never know, but I wasn't prepared to take that chance.

* * *

In my line of work, along with the positive qualities that many participants display, there can also be a fair number of unattractive traits – such as hubris, impetuousness, irrationality and self-pity. Here are two examples where first hubris and then those other three shortcomings came into play.

I was representing one side in a merger of two public companies roughly equal in size, but with a huge percentage of the other side's stock closely held by a single family. The president of my client was to become CEO of the combined company, but that big block on the other side (which would still remain substantial in the combined company) had me worried.

"Let me negotiate some protections for you," I said to the president. "Nah, I don't need them," he replied. I persevered, but he wasn't concerned. "They're a sleepy company, Jim – once they see me in action, they'll want me running things for life." Finally, I overcame his hubris enough to negotiate a one-year employment contract for him. A year-and-a-day later, he was out on his ear.

This next is a real-life incident that I later used in a short story.[*] I was representing a large corporation in negotiating a major acquisition of another company. My client's CEO (let's call him "Seymour") was anxious to do the deal and had taken personal charge of shepherding the difficult negotiations. But as the days wore on and things didn't get resolved, Seymour became increasingly frustrated. Everything peaked on December 23rd – a date that turned out to be significant.

We were having one of those late night bargaining sessions with the other side in the conference room of our client's office. Seymour was present – I had asked him to be available for any decisions that needed to be made, because I knew this was a crucial moment in the negotiations. The other side was resisting on several issues but I was sure the deal was there to be done as long as we stuck it out. If we didn't shake hands that night, however, I was worried that the whole thing might crater, since it had to be signed up by year-end or the numbers for the deal wouldn't work.

The negotiations in the big conference room were hot and heavy. Seymour became more and more restless and finally retreated to the confines of his private office. I went in there several times to brief him on what was happening. He was unhappy, impatient and irritable.

At about 11:00 p.m., the other side's lawyer – Steve Jacobs, of Weil Gotshal, a real pro and frequent friendly adversary – introduced a new point into the bargaining. It wasn't anything crucial, but it did run counter to a point that both sides had agreed to earlier.

"You don't want to raise that," I said to Steve, in my most menacing tone of voice. Steve knew exactly what I was getting at, but he shrugged and replied, 'Yeah, I hear you, but my guy brought it up. You've got to ask your guy for it" – which was his way of telling me, in the shorthand code we sometimes used, "Don't worry, we'll be able to work this one out."

---

[*] *The Corollary Axiom*, in my book *Smell Test – Stories and Advice on Lawyering* (ABA, 2008).

So I went into the CEO's office where Seymour was alone, pacing the floor. I began to report on this new issue that had been raised – but before I could even tell him about Steve's coded signal to me, Seymour exploded. He screamed, "That's it, the deal's off! I'm going home" – throwing a yellow pad and two pencils halfway across the room as he prepared to leave.

I couldn't believe it. "Wait a minute," I said, "we can work this out" – but he wasn't listening. "It's the night before Christmas Eve," Seymour wailed. "My kids are in from college, and I'm not home with them. I feel lousy, and these guys are jerking my chain. If I give in on this, they'll want ten more things. The hell with that – I'm history."

And with that, Seymour donned his overcoat and started to leave the premises. It's still hard for me to imagine – the head of a big public company, ready to throw away a major deal on favorable terms we'd been able to work out, in order to sing carols with his kids.

What followed was, in my opinion, one of my finest performances as a lawyer. I was calm and tactful; I was patient; I was painfully rational. I brought Seymour down off the ceiling, reminded him of how significant he considered the deal to be, brushed aside the minor point at issue, predicted the shape of the ultimate compromise, convinced him to stick around just a little while longer – and then I marched out into the next room and bargained vigorously with Steve to get the final terms we needed to sign the agreement. It worked – my client's wonderful deal was saved.

I was so proud of my performance that I thought I'd be Seymour's attorney for life. But as it turned out, he never used me again as his lawyer . . . . In light of the results I'd achieved, I can think of no other reason than that I had seen him at his absolute worst – impetuous, irrational, self-pitying. My surmise was that he'd never feel comfortable with me again – he just didn't want me around as a reminder of that evening.

It's a lesson I passed on to a lot of lawyers in the succeeding years – if you can help it, never let yourself see a client at his worst.

The academic model for a negotiated acquisition may contain an implicit assumption that the bargaining takes place on a level playing field. But in most of my deals, the existence of positive or negative leverage was the order of the day. As a consequence, tactics applicable to a level playing

---

279

field were often not well-suited when one side is in a stronger position than the other.[*]

It's a difficult situation for a lawyer when the leverage is working heavily against you. Two of the toughest situations I encountered on the sell side of acquisitions were representing clients who were running out of funds or were otherwise in danger of imploding.

Remember the People Express airline? In its headiest days, it was the most exciting new innovation around – low cost, no frills travel – and its founder and CEO, Don Burr, was on the cover of Time magazine. But, for various reasons, its early success didn't last. When I came on the scene, People Express was running out of funds and needed to be sold to avoid bankruptcy.

All the potential buyers were identified – including United Airlines, which was interested but ultimately declined to bid. In the end, only one buyer was available – Texas Air (which owned Continental Airlines), headed by Frank Lorenzo. Frank knew he was the only game in town and the negotiations were agonizing. Eventually we got a deal done before disaster could strike, but at a cut-rate price.

E.F. Hutton found itself in real trouble after the '87 stock market crash and had to be sold quickly before imploding. We went into an auction mode but it was a very difficult environment for brokerage firms. We managed to get the Shearson firm, which coveted the Hutton retail system, to preempt the auction with an ironclad bid at a good price – something I considered a major achievement.

* * *

Let me turn now to hostile deals – an area where Skadden's reputation during the '80s was quite remarkable. To give you some idea of our prominence, here's a true episode I'll never forget.

---

[*] I wrote about this in *When the Playing Field Tilts: Negotiating Leverage in Acquisitions* (Insights, July 1987), incorporated in my book *The Acquisition Mating Dance and Other Essays on Negotiating.*

One day, two gentlemen came to see me in a conference room at the Skadden office. I didn't know them and can't remember how they happened to get in touch or who referred them. They told me they wanted to do a hostile takeover of a certain company. I don't recall the specific details, except for one key item that emerged as I quizzed them on the situation – namely, that another unaffiliated group already controlled more than 50 percent of the company's stock.

"That, of course, is a major obstacle to your seizing control," I told them right off the bat. "In fact, it's likely to be insurmountable."

"We realize that," they said. "But we thought that, given Skadden's famed reputation, you might have some ingenious idea as to how it could still be accomplished."

I questioned them further about a variety of details to get a better understanding of the situation, the people involved in the company, and the issues. I did see one possible path to pursue that might offer a chance – albeit, a slim one – of achieving their goal. So, when I finished questioning them, I summed it up along these lines:

"As I said before, this is a very tough situation for you to gain control of the company. Offhand, I can think of only one possible way you might be able to do that, but it's definitely a long shot – a real uphill slog."

"So there *is* a way!" the senior of the two men exulted. "What is it?"

I chuckled politely and said, "Well, you're not even my clients at present. I wouldn't share that kind of information with strangers."

"Okay," he said, "then let's become your clients. What do we need to do?"

"Well," I said, "I have to tell you that when we are about to get into anything involving a prospective corporate takeover, the firm has long required the new clients to pay our standard up-front non-refundable retainer."

"How much is the retainer?" he asked.

My recollection is that this was when the amount of our standard retainer was at or near its peak. "It's $250,000," I said.

I could see they were taken aback by the number, which was pretty hefty back in those days. After a brief pause, the senior man said, "Give us a few minutes to confer." The two of them went outside the conference room. A few minutes later, they came back into the room. Without further discussion, one of them took out his checkbook and wrote a check to Skadden for the full $250,000.

I wish I could tell you that my idea proved to be successful and that they gained control of the company. But as I had warned them, it was no more than an uphill slog. They were intrigued by the possibility, so we tried it – but sadly, we didn't prevail. To their credit, though, they never complained – they'd paid for their long shot and felt they had gotten full value for it.

* * *

In the hostile takeover arena, I usually represented the target company. At times this presented a wonderful opportunity to negotiate. The best kind of situation was an informal private auction, such as when our client Richardson-Vicks, which was under siege by Unilever, decided that the company had to be sold. We invited three well-heeled and eager purchasers to the party – Proctor & Gamble, Pfizer and Colgate. Significantly, Richardson-Vicks was indifferent as to who won. (The dynamics can be different when the target has a preference.)

We set up the three buyers in separate conference rooms and conducted a veritable shuttle service, letting them present and then improve their proposals, each attempting to prevail with the best price and terms. Their offers became increasingly favorable to our client as we played the contenders against each other.

I can recall, for instance, telling the lawyer for one of the bidders something along these lines: "If you wish, you can insist on inserting that negative provision in the contract that you're waving at me, but I must tell you that the guys in the other two rooms have not insisted on it. Think how your client is going to feel if he loses the auction – even though he was offering the best price – because his lawyer insisted on including a contract provision that no one else even cared about." As you might imagine, such nudging had a positive effect. P&G eventually took the prize on excellent terms for our client.

One memorable moment for me occurred at the Boise, Idaho headquarters of Morrison-Knudsen ("M-K"), a major engineering and construction company. A foreign investor had recently snapped up enough M-K shares to constitute a real threat to its continuing independence. I had been brought in for advice by my good friend, Sam Crossland, M-K's worthy general counsel.

In a scene that might have been staged for a Hollywood movie featuring a replica of Gregory Peck, M-K's CEO, Bill McMurren, stood atop a dining table in the center of the huge M-K company cafeteria and, with evident personal emotion, told the hundreds of M-K employees crowding the room that he'd be damned if he would allow anyone to take over his company without a real fight.

It was a thrilling performance, which inspired us to take a very hard line with the foreigners. Ultimately, we were able to negotiate a standstill agreement that restricted their stockholding to the status of an investment.

There were other times, though, when we ended up behind the eight ball, such as when I represented National Can. An upstart Triangle Industries, financed by Drexel Burnham junk bonds, started a hostile tender offer for National Can. This was in the days before the protection of poison pills was available, so we lacked effective defenses and were in danger of Triangle seizing control. Our CEO, however, said, "Let's wait – I don't think it's that big a problem."

In those days, though, when tender offers moved so quickly they were sometimes pejoratively referred to as "Saturday Night Specials", we were facing a desperate situation; and we finally managed to convince our client that finding another competing bidder was the only possible solution.

Our investment banker then initiated a search for a so-called "white knight" – another company to intervene on our behalf. But none showed up. So, just two days before Triangle was positioned to buy a majority of our shares under its tender offer, we ended up negotiating weakly with Triangle – hoping to get a few extra dollars for National Can stockholders in return for dropping our opposition to the tender offer. It was a losing proposition, though, especially since the very shrewd Drexel Burnham firm was calling the shots. The Triangle team kept saying, "Hey, we'd love to oblige, but Mike won't let us." Mike Milken, of course, was Drexel Burnham's major Wall Street operator at the time, before winding up in prison for securities law violations (before being recently pardoned by President Trump).

By the way, finding a white knight to rescue the target of a hostile takeover didn't always signify an easy negotiation. We represented a company named General Steel, whose management was willing to do almost anything – such as restructuring or a possible leveraged buyout – to stay out of the clutches of a certain hostile bidder it despised. Although nothing of that kind worked, we were able to buy sufficient time through litigation to locate a tolerable white knight willing to enter the bidding. Its proposal was more attractive to General Steel than that of the hostile bidder, but appeared to be only marginally profitable for the white knight. Its management was decidedly risk-averse, very hard-nosed, and aware that it was the only possible savior for General Steel. It was a very painful negotiation – but at least the white knight's offer prevailed, and the company didn't have to face life with that despised hostile bidder.

* * *

One of my specialties was writing articles about new developments as I saw them occurring. Once an article was published, I would then include the subject matter in one of my professional seminars – devising a hypothetical situation and asking a panel of top-flight M&A lawyers to simulate for the audience the maneuvers involving the new tactic that were actually taking place at that moment in conference rooms all around town. Since this technique had rarely been tried before, I felt I'd made a real contribution to continuing legal education.

By way of example, I became fascinated in the mid-'80s by the intricate cat-and-mouse choreography that had become a feature of the negotiated merger scene. I called it "The Acquisition Mating Dance" in a 1985 article I wrote for *Legal Times,*[*] and then used the situation in subsequent seminar settings.

In this scenario, the target company doesn't want to be acquired by another menacing company. The target's management, however, recognizes its fiduciary duty to scrutinize any offer for its stockholders. The would-be buyer would prefer not to make a hostile bid although isn't averse to exerting pressure if needed to get management's attention. But this is easier said than done. The essay explored the tactical maneuvering – the approaches, the responses, the countermeasures, the various considerations – that the parties were employing in these corporate courtship dramas.

---

[*] *Friendly Deals Require Acquisition Mating Dance* (Legal Times, November 1985), later incorporated in my book *The Acquisition Mating Dance and other Essays on Negotiating.*

What made the maneuvering tricky here was the paradox of pressure. The more pressure the purchaser exerted, the less likely the target's ability to sweep the purchaser's proposal under the rug, but the more likely it would engender a hostile reaction. Conversely, less pressure might lead to greater receptivity but also to an increased likelihood that the takeover proposal would never see the light of day. So the ideal mix for the purchaser who hoped to get a negotiation going was to generate enough potential pressure that the target couldn't ignore him, but not so much that the target stopped talking and started to fight. The target in turn had to try to counter this with whatever leverage it could generate.

One of the features in M&A practice that appealed to me was the need for a lawyer to be multi-faceted in order to excel. In addition to being a good transactional lawyer and negotiator – traditional roles you might expect – there were other less customary functions that were often requisite for success. I wrote an article about these skills, titled "Wearing Many Hats".* Here's a brief runthrough of ten such additional roles.

- <u>Financial Whiz</u> – since many key decisions and negotiating issues were financial or numbers-driven, they couldn't just be left to the investment bankers, business executives and accountants.

- <u>Public Relations Expert</u> – because what appeared in the newspapers could have a major impact on contested acquisitions, declining to comment publicly on developments was an inadequate posture.

- <u>Writer</u> – since you often had to justify why your client took the action he did, or draft a document that called for subtle composition.

- <u>Psychologist</u> – inasmuch as predicting reactions, persuading people, and understanding their motivations and hot buttons were constant elements in any negotiation.

- <u>Moralist</u> – because Solomon-like judgments were often called for on slippery ethical issues.

---

* National Law Journal, June 1986. This can also be found under the title "The Many Faceted M&A Lawyer" in my book, *The Acquisition Mating Dance.*

- <u>Employee Benefits Consultant</u> – since attorneys were often caught in the middle when employment agreements were being negotiated between top executives and their companies.

- <u>Stock Market Analyst</u> – because so many of the moves in a public acquisition were geared to their effect on the market.

- <u>Businessman</u> – inasmuch as the distinction between legal and business issues was rarely clear-cut, lawyers had to structure sensible business transactions that would withstand legal attacks.

- <u>Generalissimo</u> – since aspects of contested takeovers could be analogized to conducting a military campaign, it was vital to have an effective commander.

- <u>Seer</u> – because we often had to take stabs at solutions that might have unforeseeable consequences.

* * *

The biggest takeover I worked on – under the leadership of Joe Flom – was representing Federated Department Stores.[*] It was the parent company of an impressive roster of the nation's premier department stores – Bloomingdales, Filene's, I.Magnin, Bullocks, Foley's, Lazarus, Burdines and Rich's. On its board were such titans as former Secretary of Treasury Mike Blumenthal and former General Electric CEO Reg Jones. But the market decline of October 1987 dropped Federated's stock price from the mid-40s to the low 30s, and six potential bidders for the company then surfaced: KKR, the Pritzker brothers, the Simon Property Group, the Dillards of Arkansas, Robert Campeau of Canada, and Donald Trump. The idea of being acquired did not appeal to the Federated Board and its management, so we mounted our steeds to do battle.

---

[*] A vivid chapter on the Federated takeover can be found in John Close's book, *A Giant Cow-Tipping by Savages – The Boom, Bust and Boom Culture of M&A* (Palgrave Macmillon, 2013), ("Cow-Tipping")

Trump had bought five percent of Federated's shares in the market, probably violating an SEC reporting requirement. I called him and delivered a tough message, saying in effect, "Get rid of those shares, or we're coming after you" – at which point Trump backed off and wasn't heard from again. *

In January 1988, shortly after the Federated stock sank to $33, Robert Campeau bid $47 per share for the company. Campeau, a combustible Canadian advised by First Boston investment banker "bid-'em-up" Bruce Wasserstein, had acquired Allied Department Stores a year earlier through a hostile takeover.

Over the next month, after much maneuvering, Campeau raised his offer to $66 per share, much higher than Federated could reach with its own competitive restructuring proposal. We hoped to be rescued by a desirable white knight, the highly regarded May Department Stores, but their management ultimately deemed the transaction too big a risk and passed on it.

The seemingly climactic evening occurred on February 25 in a Skadden conference room. Joe Flom wasn't there, so I was on my own. Campeau's advisors were sure he'd be the highest bidder if he bumped his bid to $68, but they couldn't locate him to do so. In fact, during the entire three months of the deal, we never laid eyes on him. John Close quoted me about Campeau's disappearing act: "We never knew where he was or whether he'd show up . . . . In fact, I never actually met him." **

Finally his team tracked Campeau down to a restaurant near his Austrian chalet and persuaded him to agree to pay $68. Here is John Close's description of the rest of the evening.

"Wasserstein was elated. He urged Federated to sign up the deal that night. He had not reckoned with Skadden's Jim Freund, adviser to the Federated board. "That was my finest hour,' Jim says. 'I really just refused. Bruce went crazy. He was ranting and raving, pressuring us and yelling at us. 'Campeau will go away,' Bruce said.

---

* As related in *Cow-Tipping*.

** *Cow-Tipping*, p.286

'The offer will go away. You can't risk this. We've got a deal. We've got a deal.' I just took a very strong position – 'Nope. We'll talk to you after the weekend.' Oh, Bruce was upset. He wasn't happy with me. We were never really friends after that. But it was the right thing to do'."

The reason I held firm was that during the same time period we had also been talking to Macy's, which Federated's management and board of directors much preferred to Campeau as a purchaser. A few days later, on March 1, Federated and Macy's signed up a $6.1 billion deal. (With all the astronomical numbers floating around today, that might not seem so large; but back in the '80s figures like this were rare indeed.)

I have a poignant memory from that day. The deal was signed by the two parties in their separate lawyers' offices in New York City. The Federated team promptly jumped on a plane to return home to Cincinnati, leaving me to deliver the signed papers to Macy's. When I arrived at their lawyer's office, the Macy's CEO, Ed Finkelstein, was seated alone in a darkened conference room.

He had just signed an agreement which was the presumptive capstone of his career – one of the biggest and most celebrated deals of the decade – and he was undoubtedly expecting a CEO-to-CEO celebration, with flash bulbs going off and champagne corks popping. Instead, he had nobody to share the moment with but me, the second-tier outside lawyer for the seller. I did my best to congratulate him on his achievement, but I could see how bitterly disappointed he was at how he'd been treated.

There was still a lot of work to do that night to be in a position to publicly announce the deal the next morning. Many years later, I was the dinner speaker at a tribute to Joe Flom sponsored by the University of Miami Law School; (which speech was later printed in its Law Review[*]). After touting his many abilities, I added the following caveat:

---

[*] *University of Miami Law Review* (Vol.54, 2000)

"Not that anyone would have mistaken Joe for compassionate. He may have mellowed some now, but in the good old days he was one tough cookie – although there was one moment, in all those years we were together, that he let his guard down just a little and showed me another side of himself. It happened at a crucial juncture in the Federated fight, when we had just reached a deal with Macy's. I had stayed up all night to get things buttoned down; now it was the next morning, and Joe and I were in a cab heading down to Herald Square to meet with the executives of Macy's. As the cab pulled away from the curb, Joe turned to me and must have observed the ravages of an all-nighter on my face. He said – I can still hear the words clearly today, it came as such a shock – 'If you want to take a snooze, Jim, I'll wake you up when we arrive.' That was about it for compassion."

This wasn't the end of the fireworks, however. Campeau and Bruce didn't stop, and the bidding war continued – Campeau up to $73, Macy's to $74.40, Campeau to $75. Finally, Joe Flom – who was worried that Federated would go belly up with all the debt they'd need to take on to fund the acquisition – advised the Federated board to halt the auction and reach a three-way settlement. Campeau got Federated for $73.50 cash per share, while Macy's would buy three West Coast divisions from Campeau for $1.1 billion.

It had been a hectic deal which absorbed the entire first quarter of 1988. My office was Ground Zero to company executives, stalwarts from three different investment banking firms (Tom Hill of Lehman, John Golden of Goldman Sachs, and Tully Friedman of Heller & Friedman), as well as countless lawyers (including my indispensable Washington partner, Mike Rogan).

As we were getting ready to close over a weekend, I told Joe Flom – who wouldn't be there for the actual closing – that the lawyers for Campeau had asked how much we were going to bill for the deal. This was a matter of clear financial interest to their client, since the money would be coming out of the company that Campeau was about to own.

Joe examined our time charges, thought for a few moments, and then stated, with an aura of finality that only he was capable of, a number that seemed huge to me. Clearly, we had done an excellent job; and in M&A deals, this typically led to substantial premiums over our hourly fees. But this was much higher than any of the firm's fees I'd been aware of – a hell of a premium. I must have given Joe a skeptical look, because he repeated, seemingly without a care in the world, "Go ahead, Jim – tell them that's our fee."

So the next day, when the senior partner of Campeau's law firm posed the question, I managed, with some trepidation, to spit out our hefty number. "Oh, he replied quickly, "that's fine" – and ended the conversation. It only hit me a little later that it was "fine" because now – with our fee giving him ample cover – he knew exactly how much to bill for his own services! I'm sure this was why Joe, shrewd as ever, seemed so relaxed about the whole thing . . . .

15. SKADDEN ARPS (#3) – THE TWA TAKEOVER

To complete this compilation of what I did for a living in that overcharged decade of the '80s, I would like to take readers on a more extended tour through the highlights of an actual takeover deal in which I was centrally involved.

The deal I've selected is, for a number of reasons, my favorite of all those I participated in – the 1985 brawl over TWA, initiated by Carl Icahn's bid to take over the airline.

TWA wasn't one of those faceless giant companies that crowd the financial pages. Its lineage dated back to Charles Lindbergh and Howard Hughes; its theme song, the Fifth Dimension's *Up, Up and Away*, was instantly recognizable; it touched many lives and was one of the best-known companies in the U.S.*; it had a blue ribbon board of directors including Robert McNamara, Peter Ueberroth, Arjay Miller, Lester Crown, and Jack Valenti; and the consequent rapt attention the deal received from the press and other media made everything more stimulating.

It was a rollercoaster of a deal, with many ups and downs and some real surprises. The adversaries we faced – especially the raider Carl Icahn, and to a lesser extent, the so-called white knight who emerged, Frank Lorenzo – were colorful characters, thus ensuring never a dull moment in the negotiations and byplay. Each adversary was represented by a first-rate lawyer – Steve Jacobs of Weil Gotshal for Icahn, Dick Katcher of Wachtell, Lipton for Lorenzo. The three of us respected and trusted each other, which made the pressure of events more bearable.

More than anything, though, it was my favorite deal because of the role I was able to play. As contrasted with, say, Federated Department Stores (also a remarkable deal, but where Joe Flom was the *eminence grise*), I was the lawyer in charge of the TWA defense. To back me up, I had a skilled colleague, Rich Easton, with me every step of the way, plus Bob Zimet leading a full team of dedicated litigators, and a number of capable corporate associates.

---

* Well-known, to be sure, but perhaps not so universally loved. As Steve Jacobs, Carl Icahn's lawyer, later pointed out, TWA had been "miraculously transformed from being the third-least-respected company in the United States into a national treasure." See the Case Study of a Contest footnote near the end of this chapter.

TWA's investment banking advisor was Saloman Bros., represented by Michael Zimmerman. Zimmy and I became real friends as we worked closely together on all the major developments, and his intelligence and good judgment were essential during the entire assignment.

The key here was that TWA's board and management delegated to Zimmy and me authority over almost all of TWA's tactical maneuvers, conduct of negotiations, adversarial understandings, and public communications. Of course we reported periodically to the board and management– furnishing information, outlining their choices, presenting our recommendations, and so on – and we received the necessary authority to proceed. But, as Zimmy puts it, management "was not equipped for a wartime command, and no one on the board, despite their pedigrees, was anxious to show real leadership." It wasn't a case of the two of us hijacking control of the process; we did what we had to do because we were not being piloted from within.

Michael Zimmerman has suggested to me that I remind readers of "how different the M&A world was 35 years ago. The business was evolving and there was a need to innovate along the way that would be more difficult today. The community was smaller, the relationships more intense and personal." Michael says that he "wouldn't want to suggest it was better then, but it was certainly more fun."

In addition to all the contemporary press coverage the deal spawned, including long pieces by Carol Loomis in *Fortune* and Connie Bruck in *The American Lawyer*, the TWA contest was later featured in two books on the subject – one in 1986 by Moira Johnston[*] and the other more recently by John Close.[**] After the dust cleared, I spoke extensively to these writers and will refer often to their observations – especially to the text of Moira Johnston's book, in which she really made an attempt to get inside my head.

---

[*] *Takeover – The New Wall Street Warriors: The Men, the Money, the Impact.* (Arbor House, 1986)

[**] See footnote on *"Cow-Tipping"* in Chapter 14 regarding the Federated deal.

Here's the way Moira framed the subject at the outset:

> "[TWA] is the deal that demonstrates that although takeovers may be cold-blooded asset plays driven by balance sheets, they are still unmapped frontiers in which the behavior and personalities of individual men determine the shape and outcome. TWA became a crucible that tested three of the principal players, Icahn, lawyer Jim Freund, and Captain Harry Hoglander – as they had never before been tested."

* * *

Could I handle this?

I had just begun to represent TWA in the spring of 1985 when Carl Icahn first expressed interest in controlling the airline. "He behaved himself at the first two meetings," I told Moira. "He was very low key. But we disliked his game plan because it would bust up the airline." Carl wanted to close down or sell off all the domestic routes, peddle the facilities, lease the TWA planes, and employ other cash-generating tactics.

Icahn wasn't just musing about the *possibility* of going after this particular prey. We were shocked to learn that before filing any formal documents announcing his intention to control the company, he had already accumulated over 20 percent of TWA's stock in open market purchases. As I put it to Moira, "All the talk of Carl holding back went out the window. Once we saw the numbers, we knew he would go for control. Everything else was wishful thinking. The fat was in the fire."

Moira seemed fascinated by the ironic fact that I – whom she described as the guy who "had veered away from hostile takeovers and created his own niche in the area of negotiated mergers" – was leading TWA's defense.

> "Freund's professional profile had been shaped by more than the need to escape Flom's awesome shadow. Freund believed he had more a bargainer's than a warrior's temperament. It's not that negotiated deals were a love fest. It has hard confrontational stuff. But the parties had a common goal. 'And I didn't like the idea of forcing my will on someone else. I like a win-win situation . . . .' Freund said, as he faced the most significant hostile deal of his career with Skadden Arps."

Moira got it just right. After almost two decades, I was "restless for change" and had begun "to nibble at the edges of the hostile action." She linked all this to "a broader transformation" in my life – pointing out the energy boost I received from my courtship of and marriage to a much younger Barbara Fox, my musical interests, and interactions with my teenage sons. "As he had neared fifty," she said, "he had intuitively begun to strip passive activities from his life."

Still, Moira managed to pose the pertinent question about me: "[As] the crises came thundering into the boardroom over the next weeks and months, would he have the decisiveness and judgment all-out war requires?" In fact, I was concerned about just that challenge. As I told her later: "In defending a takeover, most of your clients have never been here before. They've had little preparation. They don't just want you to spell out the options and alternatives . . . . They want your *views*."

Having a strong point of view was something that came hard for me. Here's how I put it to Moira: "We were the silent generation. We missed all the wars – World War II, Korea, and Vietnam – and the activism of the 1960s. We matured in the fifties during the Eisenhower years. The Age of Conformity. We were noncontroversial and I was always uncomfortable with strong opinions."

There was no escaping the fact that an absence of strongly held views had been the story of my young adult life. In my own words that she quoted: "I went through Princeton acutely aware of shades of gray. And that was compounded at Harvard Law School, where you argued fifteen points of view and professors who were models for *The Paper Chase* turned us into judgmental eunuchs. I went through my entire three years of law school without forming a view of whether any of the court opinions we had read were right or wrong. I just focused on the issues." And I observed that lawyers were often "shackled by caveats, concern for nuance, and the desire always for more raw facts." That was why I often qualified my opinions with caveats such as "subject to a number of other relevant considerations," or "one might think," or "it can be argued that . . . ."

Now, however (as Moira aptly put it), "There was no time to be indecisive."

Taking a stand

Settling into my role as TWA's outside counsel, I soon realized the airline lacked any of the defensive weapons that companies who fear a takeover had recently been adopting. There were none of the usual "shark repellants" – no poison pill, no special voting stock, no staggered board. TWA had been spun off a year earlier by its parent conglomerate, Trans World Corporation – "Kicked out of the nest," in John Close's colorful verbiage, "and it fluttered to the ground, a broken-winged bird helpless before the ultimate corporate predator, Carl Icahn."

The fact was that the TWA management and board of directors had never expected the company to be the target of a takeover. Why, they asked, would anyone want an airline? Fuel costs were more and more expensive, powerful unions kept driving wages and benefits up, and deregulation exposed them to open competition in the marketplace – bruising price wars with aggressive cost-cutting airlines, resulting in reduced revenues. The TWA stock price reflected all of this, trading at around eight or nine dollars per share.

We considered employing some of the standard defenses – a stock buyback, greenmail, a poison pill – but for a variety of reasons I won't get into, rejected them all. This left the TWA board quite vulnerable – in fact, Icahn could remove "without cause" all 19 directors in one fell swoop, just by getting written "consents" from a majority of the shareholders. And in the share department, having acquired 24% of the stock by now, Carl was already almost half-way there. Clearly we needed to buy some time to come up with a good defensive plan.

So we adopted a variety of defensive maneuvers – a lobbying blitz attacking Icahn's moral and professional fitness to run an airline, asking the Department of Transportation to investigate whether TWA could operate under Icahn's control, making appeals to friendly congressmen, and bringing litigation in two separate courts seeking a preliminary injunction against Carl's further stock purchases.

Although we realized that the litigation might not ultimately halt him, we did get some temporary relief from it. Icahn agreed not to buy additional shares prior to the crucial TWA board of directors meeting we would be holding a week later. The lawsuits also had a second important function, related to the board's view of TWA as a national institution that ought to survive. In the litigation, we accused Icahn of having plans for liquidation, lay-offs and dismantling of routes. This forced him, in order to counter those accusations, to take positions committing himself to the long-term interests of the airline.

Prior to the TWA board meeting (and to the court ruling on TWA's preliminary injunction motion), Carl delivered a merger offer to the TWA board – $18 a share in cash for all the TWA stock he didn't own. This was no love-letter from Carl, since with a merger proposal, he could continue buying stock on his way from the 24 percent he already owned to the 51 percent assuring control. Adding to the ominous pressure being created, his letter stated that he'd already commenced the consent procedure to remove the TWA directors and replace them if they didn't allow shareholders to vote on his offer.

According to John Close, "Jim Freund and his team knew that the board had to take a stand and respond to Icahn's offer, which Freund called Icahn's 'I'll take the high road, but I may take the low road' approach'."

Although the $18 offer was substantially above where TWA's market price had been, our investment advisor Salomon considered it inadequate – not reflective of the true value of the airline's assets. This opinion allowed the Board to turn down Carl's offer. But if they did, he would then presumably buy up to 51 percent, throw out the board, and install new directors to approve the offer and present it to stockholders, who would likely leap at it.

Putting TWA up for sale

So Salomon (through Zimmy) and I concluded that if we lost our injunction motion in federal court, the only real alternative to maximize value for shareholders was to put the company up for sale. Lightning struck during the board meeting when word came in that we had, in fact, lost on the injunction. Now Carl was free to buy stock again, which I'm sure he'd already started doing as soon as the injunction was rejected (and while our board meeting was still in process).

Zimmy and I told the board that unless we did something, the company would be lost to Carl at an inadequate price. The only move that made sense was to sell the company to a third party in a deal that was better financially than Carl's and would also keep TWA from being dismantled. But in order to have time to find a buyer, we needed to keep Carl from buying his way into control and implementing his throw-out-the-board strategy.

So, at our urging, the TWA board committed to Icahn that if within 60 days we were unable to achieve anything better than his offer, we would submit his proposal to shareholders along with the board's view as to its merits. Our idea was to tie him up for 60 days, while leaving the door open for the board to recommend rejection of his offer if we still disapproved it.

Here's Moira Johnston's interpretation of my performance:

> "Freund knew that some of the board would resist anything that seemed to validate Icahn. Some would fight it. To sell his strategy to the board would require a formidable display of decisiveness. A loaded gun was at the company's head and they were still woefully unprepared for war. They must expand their options and buy more time, and as Freund presented his ideas, he found himself increasingly convinced that the correct route for TWA lay in his strategy. He found himself making strong statements, expressing his personal *views*, with all the force and confidence he had feared he might lack in the heat of war. As the vote was taken, Freund glimpsed the shaking off of an old albatross from the Age of Conformity, and he began to feel confident that he could handle the hostile takeover."

The board unanimously approved our package to put the company up for sale. We also added a sentence in the press release that we expected Icahn not to use the consent procedure to throw out the board, because it might thwart the best interests of shareholders.

Icahn didn't reply directly to us, and he sputtered about the deal to the press. "But (Moira quotes me as saying) Carl never did the consent thing . . . . [and] that strategy is one of the things I'm proudest of in the whole deal."

Dealing with Carl and Joe

Dealing with Icahn, according to some people, consisted of asking themselves "What did Carl really say?" – like reading the entrails of a pigeon. I had my own metaphor here, which I reported to Connie Bruck for her article:

"Freund says that over time he became less discomfited by Icahn's idiosyncratic ways. 'On the chess computer I have, you see all the moves the computer is contemplating. It's like that with Carl. He thinks out loud, and he's trying a lot of things out to see how you react, to see how he feels. Things may seem widely disparate. It's not all random either – he's thinking out loud, but also with a purpose.'

" 'And the most important thing he says in any meeting, I've learned,' Freund continues, 'is the last thing he says. It's like the computer – at the end it goes click, click, click, and it makes its move.' "

I have a confession to make. At various times during the TWA deal, Joe Flom would see me in the hall of our office and say, "Hey, Jim, how's TWA going?" In the past, I would have gladly acceded to an invitation from Joe to discuss something I was working on – he was, after all, the guru. But with TWA, I confess to just responding "Fine, Joe," and briskly moving on. I was frankly worried that if the TWA board heard Joe was interested in the deal, they'd want to be briefed by him – and, selfishly, I wanted this one for myself.

The white knight enters

Over the next two weeks, Salomon approached a hundred potential suitors about acting as a white knight. Only two stepped up – a casino operator who wasn't swimming in cash, and Frank Lorenzo of Texas Air, owner of Continental Airlines, who was willing to go to $20 per share to acquire TWA.

Then, in a surprise move – but one that's typical of the man – Icahn sent a signal that he might be willing to be a seller, if we could work out a deal with Frank that didn't discriminate against Carl. Fearful that $20 wouldn't cut it with Carl, Zimmy worked hard to get Lorenzo's sights up into the $23 area.

The teams for Lorenzo, TWA and Icahn met in New York on the night of June 12 – except that Lorenzo, whom we knew was in town, never did show up for the crucial meeting. As for Icahn, he finally arrived at about 2 a.m., after having taken an evening cruise around Manhattan.

We negotiated all night and by daybreak reached tentative agreement on a satisfactory deal merging TWA with Lorenzo's Texas Air, which would make Frank (in conjunction with the ownership of Continental) chairman of the nation's second-largest airline system. Stockholders (including Icahn) would get $23 per share. Carl would get an additional $16 million to walk away from his takeover bid. His profit on the deal, almost $100 million, would be the largest profit he'd ever made on a single transaction up to then.

But then the dramatics started. Dick Katcher and Leon Black (Texas Air's financial advisor) left the room to put in a wake-up call to Frank Lorenzo. When they returned, they told Zimmy and me (but not Icahn or his team) that Lorenzo had reacted to the intricate deal we'd negotiated by saying, "Carl's a pig. Let him have the airline." We all decided not to tell Carl this, however, in hopes that Lorenzo could be persuaded to approve the deal after Dick and Leon went to see him in person.

Moira quoted me on what came next:

" 'It was now 6:00 a.m. We went to the Brasserie for breakfast. We were all dragging, but Carl was ebullient – feeling terrific. He won't get the airline. He's a seller. But he's perfectly satisfied. I'm listening to Carl reminiscing about other deals, and feeling a sense of dread because I know we have a problem with Texas Air.' "

I bought a shirt and razor to clean up before the TWA board meeting scheduled for that morning. Leon and Dick then came back to report that Frank still wouldn't buy the deal. As I told Moira:

" 'That was the night a deal should have been struck. But it wasn't. There was a gap – and it wasn't closed. If they had communicated, it might have been settled. But you were dealing with two massive egos, and there was an awful lot of macho wrapped up in this.' "

"A man of his word"

Predictably, Icahn blew up when he heard what had happened. But Zimmy and I sat down with Carl and his lawyer Steve Jacobs and managed to reach an informal understanding. Carl agreed not to be a spoiler – he wouldn't buy more shares if he didn't have the best bid on the table, *unless*

– and this is the *unless* that would haunt us for the next month and a half – unless Lorenzo started accumulating stock himself, or unless TWA changed the status quo, such as by issuing some kind of special treatment "lockups" to Lorenzo. Icahn agreed to put out a press release to that effect.

We reported to the board what had been going on in those crazy last hours. We still considered Carl a loose cannon but Lorenzo's $23 deal (now $19 cash and $4 preferred stock) was our best course. Carl (who by this time owned 33%) took no position on it, reserved the right to make a counter, but said he wouldn't prevent TWA shareholders from taking advantage of the highest available bid.

It was as good a deal as we could have made under the circumstances. But what we didn't anticipate was the depth of anti-Lorenzo feeling existing in the TWA unions.

According to the head of the pilots union, Harry Hoglander (as paraphrased by Moira), at some point over the summer Icahn had fallen in love with the idea of owning an airline. He changed from thinking he could make the most money *selling* it to thinking he could make the most money *running* it.

So (according to Moira) Carl began negotiating with the TWA pilots. They hated the idea of working for Lorenzo, who had a reputation from prior dealings as a union-breaker – someone who (in Hoglander's words) would "knock labor on its ass." Icahn was angling to get wage concessions for the pilots that would enable him to pay more than his $18 bid for the company.

Here's Moira's take on Icahn at this time:

> "It did seem as if a new dimension was coloring and shaping his moves. The man who loved to say, 'If you want a friend, get a dog,' was using words like *loyalty* and *moral obligation*. Even in his first agreement on July 1, he had committed to keeping the airline intact, sacrificing the raider's prerogative to dispose of assets as he wishes. Was it possible that Icahn was doing the thing Freund was convinced he never did – getting emotionally involved with the property?"

And Carl, appearing before Congress to counter TWA's efforts to claim he would damage the airline, emphasized in response that he was "a man of his word":

" 'This would make me both a liar and a fool, and I am neither. I am in a business where my word is my bond. I buy and sell increments of hundreds of thousands of shares, solely by oral agreement. My reputation as *a man of my word* [my italics] is something that I would not risk for any transaction.' "

Heading toward the denouement

Meanwhile, through June and July, Lorenzo was pressing TWA to give him so-called "lock-ups" to strengthen his position and discourage Icahn. These included super voting preferred stock, as well as the option to buy key TWA assets (known in the trade as "crown jewels") – the transatlantic routes and the reservation system. We refused to grant them, unless and until he had all his financing in place and was willing to make a substantial bump to his $23 price – neither of which was yet happening. As John Close put it:

> "For TWA to grant any special treatment to Lorenzo would be what Freund called waving a red flag in front of a bull. What's more, the bull had given his word not to buy more stock as long as his offer was not the best bid on the table. Icahn had issued a public statement promising that he would not use his TWA stock to prevent the other shareholders from getting the benefit of the best available offer. He would keep his word, he told Jim Freund, as long as 'Lorenzo isn't buying stock and there are no shenanigans between you and Texas Air'."

After checking with the TWA board, Zimmy and I told Lorenzo's people that he would have to increase his bid by at least $2 per share for us to consider lockups. Frank wasn't willing to do that – in effect, betting that Carl wouldn't be able to make his deal with the unions and come up with a better price.

But Icahn did get the financial concessions he wanted, not only from the pilots but also the machinists. He then sent a letter to the TWA board raising his bid to $24 – which became the best bid on the table – and noting that he now owned over 40% of the stock. The stage was set for the deal's frantic denouement.

In the press and the market, Icahn was suddenly perceived as the heir-apparent to the chairmanship of TWA. But we discovered a technicality that temporarily halted Icahn from buying more stock and going over the top to absolute control. In Moira's words:

"It was a small pocket of time . . . . But for Freund, buying time had become a way of life. The entire battle had been marked off by these narrow, desperate envelopes of time. The incredible pressures of the deal had been contained and intensified within them. Freund's role had been to create or identify them, then work like hell to expand or exploit them to their fullest."

There was one offbeat incident during this period that I recalled vividly and told John Close about, which he included in his book.

" 'In the midst of the takeover, Jim Freund, while on a TWA flight, struck up a conversation with a stewardess. 'Her last name began with a Z. Let's say it was Zim. It turns out her father and I were at Princeton together, and we got to talking, and in the midst of it I said I was representing TWA in the Icahn thing. She says, 'Oh, we're so worried about this. All the girls are so worried about this. There's rumors that he's going to lay off flight attendants, and it's terrible. We'd lose our jobs and everything.' So I don't know if I said, 'I'll see what I can do' – I don't know. But the next time I saw Carl, I said, 'Hey, Carl, there's a stewardess named Elaine Zim, who's the daughter of a friend of mine, and she's worried that if you get control of this airline, you're going to lay off stewardesses and she's going to lose her job. Is there anything I can tell her that would make her feel better?' He says, 'Tell her if I lay them off, I'm going to start with the A's.' And that's why, although he was a tough adversary, he was never dull to do business with. We had so many laughs."

Negotiations between Lorenzo and Icahn for Lorenzo to exit the deal broke down over Carl's refusal to pay any breakup fee to Frank. Then Lorenzo bumped his bid to $26, making Carl's $24 the second-best bid on the table – and leading to what I still consider a choice bit of repartee in the deal. Moira tells the story.

"Freund met with Icahn to try to get him to raise his bid to top Lorenzo's. It was their most intense and abrasive meeting. Gentlemanly quests to maintain a level playing field had been reduced to the exhausted bickering and dogged trench warfare of the endgame. Stress and frustration were taking their toll on them all. But Freund was feeling confident about taking a decisive role. 'I've never worked over anybody like that in my life,' says Freund of the meeting with Icahn. 'It went on for hours, trying to get more dollars out of him.' Freund challenged Icahn: 'You said you wouldn't stand in the way of the best bid, and Texas Air has the best bid. You should either go along with this $26 dollar bid or match it.' Icahn burst in, 'Bullshit! It's a spurious bid because Texas Air can't possibly win. I'm not going to raise my bid, I'm going to buy stock . . . .'

"Finally, Freund struck where he knew it would hit home. 'You always like to say you're a man of your word, and if you do this – if you block the best bid for shareholders – in my book, Carl, you're only 50 percent a man of your word.'

"Icahn blazed back, indignant, 'Wait a second, wait a second. Didn't I say that I wouldn't buy more stock if Lorenzo didn't buy more stock? Didn't I keep my word there?'

" 'Yes, Carl, you did,' Freund admitted, as Icahn recited a litany of kept promises. 'Okay, okay, Carl, let's say you're a 75 percent man of your word, okay?' Freund offered reluctantly.

"Then Icahn paused and smiled the slightly sheepish smile of a man who knows he's been caught. 'Hey, I'm at least 80 percent. Jim, give me 80,' and the ten men in the room broke up laughing."

The board meeting to end all board meetings

It was all building to an incredible conclusion, which would take place in the TWA boardroom on August 20. At 11 a.m. TWA would be free to issue the super voting stock lockup to Lorenzo that would likely gain him the deal. At 1 p.m. Icahn would be free to start buying again, and could presumably gain majority control within hours.

Carl mused over all this, leading Moira to conclude:

"But as a chess player, he saw the endgame now nearing checkmate. Whatever option carried the day, it was time to end the war. Ultimately, he believed that 'the smart thing, instead of fighting, is to try to make peace.' He was closer to Freund's philosophy than perhaps even Freund knew."

On August 20, Moira reported, people began gathering for a meeting that would be, for Freund, the most dramatic event of twenty years of law – 'the best show in town. We could have sold tickets.' "

Frank Lorenzo came on first, taking a high-road quiet approach – but he didn't come up with any concrete proposals of how to deal with the unions.

Icahn was next, and initially he didn't shine. Here's how Moira described my reaction.

> " 'He's not doing well,' Freund thought, 'not as well as Lorenzo. He's being more of a blusterer, threatening 'you do this and I'll do that.' He was acting, it seemed to Freund, 'like a guy who sees something behind every rock and who, for all his bravado, knew the lockups *could* happen. If it was going to be a personality contest, so far Lorenzo would win.' "

But then Harry Hoglander, resplendent in his pilot's uniform, gave an impressive performance as a man who was willing to take big pay cuts because, as Moira reported, " 'the TWA pilots do not care to work for Lorenzo.' " And then came the lawyer representing the machinists, who (in Moira's words) "compounded the threats of strikes, warning that being sold into bondage to Lorenzo would provoke nighttime trashing of airplanes and other sabotage."

In a few short minutes, the board had heard threats of lawsuits, formal strikes, and sabotage. Nobody likes to be threatened, I knew, but the reality was there – a fact that had to be considered in selecting the best offer made for TWA. None of us knew whether such a dire prediction would actually come to pass, but I had to assume our board had little doubt that people with such strong feelings were capable of doing just about anything.

And then Carl resumed his presentation, much better now. When Icahn was asked how he was going to run the airline, he said "I'm not going to run the airline. I'm going to hire the best talent I can find to run it – men like your own Dick Pearson." Pearson, the new president of TWA, had replaced Ed Meyer in the middle of the struggle. For me, there was this irony in Carl's words (per Moira):

> "Earlier, Icahn had told Freund and Zimmerman, 'I hear good things about him [Pearson]. I'd like to talk to him. But Pearson has said some terrible things about me – and I've never even *talked* to him.' He paused, then added, 'At least Ed Meyer *met* me!', as Freund and Zimmerman cracked up."

It was close to noon when Icahn ended his presentation to the board. There was a wall of reporters and TV cameras outside. I asked Carl to go back and relax in his office, and I'd call to let him know what happened – and in the meantime, he shouldn't buy any stock. Here's how he replied: "Come on, Freund, you got your guy in Delaware, I got my guy on the floor of the exchange. At one o'clock, he buys everything in sight."

TWA did, indeed, have a lawyer poised at the office of the secretary of state in Dover, Delaware, ready to file the charter amendment creating the preferred stock for Lorenzo's super-voting stock lockup if the Board went that way. Likewise, Icahn had all his stock purchasing lined up.

Moira did such a skillful job on what then transpired at the meeting that I'll just quote her verbatim.

"Freund, in his old mode of presenting all sides, summarized what he thought the two men had said and what the implications were. He felt strongly that it was not his job to tell the board what to do; they must decide. But he knew that, if he could vote, it would be against issuing the lockups. It would be for Icahn. 'Let's look at the upside of Lorenzo. He's offering $2 more per share than Icahn, and the airlines would be a good fit. But let's look at the downside: Carl's $24 seems much surer than Frank's $26. And it would happen much sooner. There's no way to predict whether the lockups – which Carl would surely challenge – would stand up in court. If they did *not,* Carl would get the company and feel free to force a much lesser deal on the TWA shareholders.'

" 'And waiting for completion of Lorenzo's deal there could be labor unrest,' Freund warned. Hoglander's intensity had cast the specter of strikes, slowdowns, trashing of airplanes, lawsuits – anything. And, Freund posed, would Drexel's financing [for Lorenzo] hold together? There was a clause in Drexel's contract with the committing group that if TWA's financial condition was 'severely adversely changed,' investors could back away from their commitments. Over the next six months, 'severe adverse changes' could well occur. An unknown, threatening prospect.

"Freund believed he knew the way voting would go, but that, in a close vote, Pearson would be the linchpin. 'Pearson had more to gain from Lorenzo' . . . . Pearson spoke very quietly. Very controlled. And he voted against the lockups. The board went with him unanimously, and Icahn had won the day.

"Freund picked up the phone and called Icahn's office. How cool could you be! He wasn't back yet. He left a message, then prepared to put out the press release. He had written two press releases the night before – one for each outcome.

"As he waited for Icahn to return his call, Freund felt the tension of the morning released. He believed the board had reached the right decision, and he was pleased with the role he had played. Yes, and pleased, too, to discover that working on hostile takeovers wasn't just lobbing mortar shells back and forth between an irreconcilable raider and target. More subtle skills – strategizing, negotiating, persuading – did come into play. In the ten years since he'd written *Anatomy of a Merger*, the two strands of hostile and friendly had fused. The dichotomy had evolved into a continuum."

When I reached Icahn to tell him the TWA Board had gone his way and wasn't issuing Lorenzo any lockups, I'm told that Carl gave his group a "thumb's up" sign, a grin spread across his face, and he said, *"We've got ourselves an airline."*

Post-mortem

Moira liked a post-mortem story I told her about a subsequent contact I had with Carl, so she included it in her book.

"Jim Freund spotted Carl Icahn in his center court box at the U.S. Open in Queens in late September, watching a tennis match between [John] McEnroe and the Swede, [Joakim] Nystrom, as intensely as Icahn had negotiated for the airline. It was the calm of armistice after the wars; they were settling with Lorenzo that weekend, and to all intents and purposes, the fight for TWA was over. As McEnroe overwhelmed the Swede and got into an angry fight with the umpire, images of Icahn flashed through Freund's mind. On the phone to Icahn a few days later, Freund tried out his analogy.

" 'Carl, I saw you at the tennis matches, and it struck me that there was a real parallel between you and McEnroe. I don't mean the screaming at the umpire part, but his *play*.' He had Icahn's attention. 'There are lots of good tennis players around, but some balls they hit are apparently without purpose. Any shot that McEnroe hits always has a plan, a design. That's the way you are in the game.'

"Icahn murmured a little approval, as Freund built his metaphor.

" 'McEnroe hits some shots with great power, and that's you going out and buying 2 million shares. He hits others very deftly – little unreturnable drop shots – and you can play it deftly, too. You don't stay at the base line.'

" 'Yeah,' Carl agreed with a grin. 'I like to go to the net. But not all the time, not all the time.'

"Freund didn't mention the final parallel between the two. But as Icahn got louder and more intense, recalling the fury he'd felt when Lorenzo had, by his judgment, reneged on agreements, he suddenly stopped and laughed. 'And when that happened, I got *angry* . . . . just like McEnroe!' To Freund's delight, Icahn himself had completed the metaphor."

After Icahn took over, things went bad for TWA. I'm not going to get into that whole story, but John Close gives us a glimpse of a moment at the outset.

"The first quarterly report after the deal showed a drastic loss. Carl demanded to see the TWA executives responsible. 'Carl was furious,' Freund remembers. He said, 'Get those guys over here.' He says, 'I'm coming over to your office, and I'm going to give them hell.' So we arranged a meeting, and Carl came in waving this thing about the quarterly earnings down. And then one guy turns to Carl and he says, 'Hey, Carl. Welcome to the airline business.' It was such a great remark. Welcome to the airline business.' "

The *Fortune* article by Carol Loomis, one of the best writers on financial subjects, is entitled "The Comeuppance of Carl Icahn." It gets into the negotiations Carl and I had that led to a new complex deal (about which Loomis says, "It took an artfully crafted 11-page TWA press release to explain these provisions . . .").

But Carl wasn't accepting this treatment in the press and wrote a letter to *Fortune* that concluded: "Lastly, I strongly disagree with the title of the article. Comeuppance is defined as 'just desserts' [sic] and at TWA I have not yet even reached the main course."

Anyway, all that is a story for another day. But I do want to pass along one of the telling anecdotes from those bad days for Icahn, as related by Moira.

"During one of the bleakest hours, late at night at Skadden Arps, Icahn was walking down the hall with Freund. They'd struck some friendly bonds. The 'sweater joke' had become a trigger for laughs: at an endless night meeting, Icahn had been cold and Freund had lent him his cashmere sweater, and he'd worn it home. At a subsequent meeting, when Icahn had again borrowed the sweater and was taking a very tough negotiating stance, Freund broke the tension by quipping, 'Hey, Carl, give me back my sweater.' They were comfortable trading frank talk, and Icahn said to Freund now, 'Jim, sometimes I think I was a *schmuck*. In a way, I'm in this mess because of my loyalty to the pilots, my *moral obligation!*' For Freund, it was a wonderful moment. The rock-hearted man of commerce who loved to say 'If you want a friend, get a dog,' was admitting to being in a pickle. Because he'd been nice."

My poetic tribute

The year after the TWA deal, I chaired a panel at a PLI seminar entitled *Case Study of a Contest: TWA*,[*] in which Steve Jacobs, Dick Katcher and I reprised our roles as the three lawyers involved – something that had been done only rarely before (if at all) on other notable transactions. Our review of the dynamics of the deal gave a real sense of the takeover process, and it was well-received. At the conclusion I read to the audience a poem I'd written about the deal, which sums up its entire scope in ersatz Ogden Nash couplets. It went like this:

THE BALLAD OF FRANK AND CARL

Here's a Halloween tale, but it's not about witches,
It concerns Carl and Frank – two smart sons of bitches –
And their unwary prey: TWA.
Carl decided the time was right, before he developed a receding hairline,
To take on an airline.
An airline? What kind of target is that?
Is this aggressor spastic? No – just Icahnoclastic.
By the way, TWA was not a stranger to the blues;
Its former owner was Howard Hughes.

---

[*] *Case Study of a Contest: TWA* (Practising Law Institute, 1986)

So Carl began to purchase stock, using loopholes in the law, until
    finally, when he had to disclose the total extent,
    the man had acquired 20 percent.
"You're not welcome!" bellowed TWA –
    but Carl's just like a large, mean whale,
    who won't take greenmail.
The airline's defenses were really laggard.
Even lacking a board that's staggered.
TWA tried Icahn to thwart in Congress, DOT, and court.
But Carl flinched not, and his lawyer was imperturbable –
    not like some lawyer-golfers who get mad and even break clubs:
None of that for Stephen Jacobs.
Then Carl made an offer of $18 in cash, noting that,
    if the TWA directors failed to find themselves in sweet accord,
He'd kick out the board.
That left them 'twixt a hard place and a rock;
They decided the airline must go on the block.
The State of Missouri attempted to help, with legislation dutiful,
Held: unconstitutional.
But a St. Louis court then addressed the complaint,
And issued a key temporary restraint.
Now enter Frank, and Drexel, his bank;
Plus a lawyer of stature, doughty Dick Katcher.
Lorenzo saw no fatal barriers to linking up these common carriers.
And where was the dough for this costly event? Drexel's "highly
    confident."
A deal was done at 23, with Carl the only absentee.
"I won't be a spoiler," Icahn remarked in his best Business
    Roundtable manner – "and I don't intend to provoke any fights;
But remember this, boys, I'm reserving my rights!"
Carl could have quit and just pocketed his winnings,
But he put the game into nine extra innings.
Trading his lucre for the ultimate euchre.
Instead of brandishing a sabre, he just went and talked to labor.
And while Texas Air put its case to the DOT, in a number
    of rather lengthy sessions,
    Carl obtained some real concessions.
It seems those pilots would walk the plank
    to avoid having to deal with Frank.
Not that the unions thought Carl was a doll;
But in a pinch like this, I guess their sense of dread mellows;
Takeovers make for some really strange bedfellows . . .
So, before anybody could close the barn door, there was Carl at 24!
And just in case Frank couldn't see his defeat,

———
309

Carl now proceeded to sweep clean the Street.
But Frank was determined to have the last licks, and so he went
    to 26.
For TWA, the issue here was very squarely joined: What now,
    Mr. Freund?
Negotiations then became complex and and quite clandestine,
Could a lock-up work on Carl? remained the burning question.
Each man made his presentation; the board retired for deliberation.
The messenger was down in Dover. File that preferred, and Frank's
    in clover.
Icahn's man was on the floor, set to buy up shares galore.
Carl's 24 was a bird in hand; Frank's 26 was sculpted in sand.
The board went with Carl, but don't pity Frank;
He's chuckling all the way to the bank.
And just a final word to Carl;
    Remember, it's a far, far better thing
    to be vilified, sniped at, and even sued,
Than to have to eat that airline food!

16. SKADDEN ARPS #4 – THE CHALLENGING '90s

Back in those days, a lot of criticism was aimed at the '80s – at junk bonds, at corporate greed, and such. I'm sure much of this was deserved; but for guys like me, as hectic as those years were, it was one helluva decade! In fact, I used to keep a little printed sign on my desk that read, "What was so terrible about the '80s anyway?"

In my view, the symbolic high moment of the decade for us was the party Skadden held in 1988 to celebrate the 40th anniversary of the firm's founding. The location was the Temple of Dendur at the Metropolitan Museum of Art in New York City. We were all dressed up, the food was superb, the setting exquisite – it was truly one "for the ages." All of us had this feeling of having finally arrived at the top of the legal heap; the hubris we exuded that night was almost tangible.

But life moves on, and as the decade wound down, a weak economy and the end of the robust M&A market signaled the demise of those heady booming '80s. As business contracted, previously growth-oriented law firms like ours were forced to pull in their horns. In 1991, for instance, almost half of the nation's top 250 firms shrunk in size; and even Skadden was forced for the first time to lay off competent lawyers.

For a couple of years, the firm's new associates were feeling decidedly uneasy about the future. All of them were wondering whether the current climate was a blip or a more permanent blight? Were they in danger of being released at some time? Would there be partnership slots open for them when they'd served their time?

* * *

One of my proudest duties at the firm was to give the annual keynote speech to the new class of entering associates, which I did for over a decade right up to my retirement. Each year I tried to sound a different theme appropriate for the occasion. Here's a brief survey of these themes during the '80s:

- 1986 – What Skadden was like 20 years earlier when I arrived, how we grew, and what distinguished us from the herd.

311

- 1987 – (against the backdrop of a recent stock market crash) Easing the tension the newcomers felt by providing my personal Ten Commandments of what kind of lawyering succeeds at the firm and what falls short.

- 1988 – (against the backdrop of the collapse of the large Finley Kumble law firm) Why this couldn't happen to the institution we had built at Skadden.

- 1989 – (as we passed the 1,000 lawyer mark) No matter how large the firm might get, it would always consist of a series of small groups, each working on a single matter – and that's why each lawyer at every level represents the firm and bears a measure of responsibility to its clients.

Now, as the heady '80s turned into the negative early '90s, I needed to temper my pep talks to buck up the spirits of the associates:

- 1990 – Bad times, relatively speaking, had jolted the firm and the rest of the legal profession. Don't focus on that, I said; concentrate on what it takes to do things right; and learn to make do with excellence instead of blindly seeking unattainable perfection.

- 1991 – Against the backdrop of a weak economy, the M&A market in tatters, and the firm's shrinking size, I tried to assure them that they had chosen the right firm, while admonishing them to work hard to be well-positioned for when things would go our way again (as they did, not too long after).

By the next year, things had settled down sufficiently that I could return to more traditional themes:

- 1992 – I offered new associates a starter set of "Unconventional Wisdom" that might prove useful over the years – such as how the bug of self-interest (that we think we're impervious to) can infect us all, especially when our work product has been questioned.

- 1993 – This took place against the backdrop of Lincoln Caplan's book on the firm,[*] aspects of which had bothered many partners. Since I felt that our new lawyers should hear what we stand for from us, not Caplan, I offered my list of what I called *The Defining Dozen* – twelve qualities that made Skadden special.

- 1994 – My theme was the "ethical instinct" – the need to get things in decent shape ethically, and then to stand up for what's right.

- 1995 – I talked about going with your gut – giving appropriate weight to your initial response to people and to decision-making, plus what to do when sober second thoughts run the other way.

- 1996 – (my swan song prior to retirement) I reviewed my past dozen themes, offered an ode to two qualities so crucial to a lawyer (good judgment and intensity), gave some tips on how to avoid screwing up, and reprised *The Defining Dozen* from 1991.

Speaking of *The Defining Dozen,* here's a listing of the elements that back then I considered most important about the firm. It was my own list, and I made it clear that other partners may well differ as to which factors they would choose to emphasize. The twelve basic traditions and attitudes that I felt made up much of the composite culture of Skadden were:

- *One Firm.* Clients have always been clients of the firm, not meal tickets for individual partners. Different practice groups and far-flung geographical offices work in tandem for the common good.

- *Meritocracy.* It's performance that's rewarded – how well you've handled your responsibilities – not who you are, or who you know, or how you did at law school or at another firm. In short, we recognized talent.

---

[*] *Skadden* – Power, Money, and the Rise of a Legal Empire (Farrar Straus Giroux, 1993)

- *Diversity.* Our individual lawyers come from different social, economic, religious, geographic and ethnic backgrounds; we differ politically; we went to a slew of law schools; and we practice individual styles of lawyering throughout the large scope and sweep of our practice areas.

- *Growth.* This has long been an article of faith at the firm – not growth for its own sake, but occurring as the natural result of our good efforts, in order to provide better service to our clients and more opportunities for our lawyers.

- *Running a Business.* We've always had a healthy regard for the commercial aspects of practice. We've stressed prudent fiscal management – keeping indebtedness to a minimum and creating reserve funds for future needs and rainy days.

- *Collegiality.* We pride ourselves on the sense of community in our halls, reflected in the teamwork we bring to projects, and the informality of an open-door kind of firm.

- *Service to Clients.* We're in the ultimate service business, and it's only through extra special service to clients that we can hold on to what we have and gain significant new business.

- *Quality Work.* We've always been fanatical about putting out "upper margin work" – the work that first-rank firms do – even back when we were far too small to be considered a first-rank firm.

- *Hard Work.* The price to pay for high quality work and special client service is that we have to put in long hours to do our damnedest all the time.

- *Integrity.* We've instilled in our lawyers the need for ethical vigilance of the highest order as they operate in areas that continually test character – applying a strict "smell test" to everything we touch.

- *Assertiveness.* We got where we are by being assertive, taking on the competition, both in terms of the business we go after and the type of law we practice – that's just good stand-up lawyering.

- *Problem-Solving Attitude.* We always wanted to be viewed as constructive, not nit-picking – as makers, not breakers of deals. We sized up the situation, appreciated the practical elements, understood the business realities, came up with solutions and helped the client implement them and solve his problems.

To me, these weren't just carefully chosen words; they represented what I'd witnessed and been part of during my three decades – the growth of Skadden from a small firm to the behemoth it was when I retired. Though I haven't been directly involved in the operations of the firm for the past 23 years, my hope is that this *Defining Dozen* still persists to this day.

* * *

Although the economy bounced back after a few years, and the firm's practice eventually resumed its high growth, I had pretty much burned out in the '80s and never fully regained my prior intensity. Other M&A partners coped much better than I did – turning themselves into bankruptcy counsel or international lawyers – but for me, approaching the sixth decade of a strenuous life, the transition was less than satisfactory.

To be sure, I wasn't completely immobile during the '90s and did do a few deals of note. One was a successful mid-decade acquisition by GenRe, the large reinsurance company. The technique I used in that deal became the model for advice I gave other lawyers in a booklet[*] I had printed and distributed just before retirement, which analyzed acquisition practice from the days when I'd written *Anatomy of a Merger* through what was currently being done.

In competing for a desirable acquisition, it had become harder to get an advantage in the face of a leading court decision that reduced the ability to obtain effective lockups. I advised acquirers that if the prize is so strategic you can afford a blowout bid to preempt the process, then take the plunge. Otherwise, the key advantage to seek was a short exclusive negotiating and due diligence period. To get this, I cautioned, you will probably have to put on the table early a number that's close to your top dollar and be prepared to move fast – there's no time for a lot of marginal tire-kicking. But if you get the exclusive period, then once you've satisfied yourself on the major

---

[*] From There To Here – Reflections on the Past Two Decades of M&A Practice (1996)

issues and have a fully negotiated agreement you're ready to sign, you've made yourself into a desirable bird in the hand – which the target's board won't find easy to relinquish for what might be out there in the bush.

When the management consulting firm of Bain & Co. came under some financial pressure amid disputes between its partners, I represented Bill Bain, the firm's founder and lead partner. This had all the makings of a chaotic situation, involving bank loans, cross-claims, potential litigation and such. But then Mitt Romney, who headed up the separate Bain Capital firm, stepped into the breach, playing a mediator-type role that greatly aided us in resolving all the conflicts peaceably. I recall being very impressed at the time with his problem-solving ability.

My favorite deal during this period was the sale of my client Neutrogena, in which a private auction generated a blockbuster bid from Johnson & Johnson that resulted in a very successful transaction. But the most interesting part for me was how I got into it in the first place.

Neutrogena was a successful public company based in Los Angeles, controlled by a man named Lloyd Cotsen who owned roughly half of the stock. When he decided to sell the company, my friend Bob McCabe, who was on the Neutrogena board, suggested to Lloyd that since his company's regular lawyer was not an expert in M&A, I would be the right guy to represent Neutrogena on the sale. Lloyd said he'd like to make my acquaintance, and Bob advised me to make the trip to the West Coast, which I did.

I spent hours with Lloyd that day. Frankly, I was selling myself and my firm pretty hard. I trotted out all the statistics and war stories of what we'd done; I touted my books, articles and seminars, my knowledge of "the territory," etc.

When I got back to New York, I called McCabe to ask how I'd done. His response: "Terribly." I was taken aback. "How could that be? "I gave Lloyd all the pertinent information . . . ." Bob scoffed. "He didn't want to hear about your skills and triumphs; he wanted to know if you were the kind of guy he would feel comfortable working with – the sort of personal stuff he could relate to."

I was stunned. "What should I do? I'd really like to land this assignment." Bob replied, "Get back on the plane to L.A. and meet with him again." Which I promptly did – only this time the discussion was all about my family, my hobbies, memories from Princeton (where Lloyd had preceded me by a half-dozen years), and so on. (If there had been a piano in the room, I would have tickled the ivories.) It must have worked, because I got the assignment and felt I did a good job in seeing it through to accomplishment. Lloyd and I remained friends until his passing a few years ago; and I'm still in contact with his lovely widow, Margit.

It was a real lawyering lesson for me – albeit occurring at the end of my career – namely, that you should assess your prospective client's personality right from the start and then figure out what lawyering approach would work best.

* * *

My literary achievement during those tough '90s years at Skadden was *Smart Negotiating – How to Make Good Deals in the Real World.*[*] This was my first attempt at presenting a definitive style of negotiating – contrasting my own views in a number of respects with those in the popular *Getting to Yes* books by Roger Fisher and his colleagues. It was also my first effort to address my advice on negotiating to the general public, my prior works having been aimed primarily at lawyers.

---

[*] Published by Simon & Schuster in 1992. See what Simon & Schuster said about it at the time:

"If you've ever tried to make a deal, reach an agreement, close a sale, or negotiate in everyday business, *Smart Negotiating* shows you how to avoid the pitfalls and achieve your goals. James C. Freund is a skilled, seasoned lawyer who negotiates for a living, and the techniques he presents in *Smart Negotiating* have been proven effective in real-world bargaining situations. Freund emphasizes basic negotiating skills – how to use leverage, how to get the information you need from the other side, how to build your own credibility, and the importance of good judgment. He then shows you how to design a winning game plan: how to develop realistic expectations on key issues, choose the right starting position, plan your concessions in advance, and anticipate the final agreement. Fresh, clever, practical – and packed with vivid real-world examples – *Smart Negotiating* will help anyone succeed at negotiating a deal."

I'm very proud of the book, and it was well-received. Marty Lipton called it "must reading," written by "a grand master negotiator." John Feerick said, "This beautifully written book is a gem . . . ." And Judge Simon Rifkind, then the senior partner of the Paul, Weiss firm – and against whom I had a very tough negotiation to settle a bitter intra-family conflict (which we were successful in accomplishing) – wrote: "Anyone who has read *Smart Negotiating,* whether he be novice or expert, will conduct his next negotiation differently and, I believe, more successfully. It is an indispensable book by a great master of the art of negotiating."

The negotiating approach contained in the book became the basis for a variety of seminars I conducted, lectures I gave, and articles I wrote in subsequent years.[*]

It was also in the '90s that I first got involved with mediation, which was to become my principal professional function during the otherwise "retired" years following Skadden. I'll be examining this subject in Chapter 19.

* * *

My last significant assignment at Skadden was to spend 40 days in Sydney, Australia in February-March 1996, working with my longtime partner and friend Tom Schwarz, plus our talented colleague John Gardiner and Australian counsel, to successfully settle through mediation a huge multi-party case that was a major priority for Skadden. It turned out to be a real accomplishment; and when I returned I gave a speech at my last annual partners' retreat (my prospective retirement later that year being public knowledge), which touched on various aspects of the experience.

The case was being conducted in a Fellini-esque courtroom setting – 18th century wigs and gowns juxtaposed against giant modern computer screens. The big question for us was whether to try the case or to attempt to settle it through the mediation that was being conducted by a retired (and not terribly effective) Australian jurist. I made up my mind which way to go soon after arrival Down Under. Here's how I described that decision to my partners at the retreat:

---

[*] But see "Sign No.3" in my article about retirement (reproduced in Chapter 17) as to what the book *didn't* lead to that I'd hoped for. (The senior partner referred to there is, of course, Joe Flom.)

When my kids were small, I once took them to an animal farm. The keeper showed us around, commenting knowledgeably on the creatures. He came to an odd-looking, ostrich-shaped bird called the emu. This animal, he told my boys, is so dumb that if you stretched a wire across its cage at a height of one foot and the emu tripped over it, he would keep tripping over it again and again as he paced around the enclosure, never realizing it was an obstacle to be stepped over. When I walked into that Sydney courtroom with Tom Schwarz the first day to see justice dispensed, my first glance was at the judge (who turned out to be a superb jurist), perched high on his bench, under the state symbol of Australia – the royal seal flanked by a kangaroo and an emu! I grabbed Tom and said, "Let's settle this goddamn case!"

I told my partners of a personal reason for being glad we were able to work out a settlement when we finally did. Back in February, when Tom asked me to join him in Sydney for two weeks, I very much wanted to participate; so I begged my wife's indulgence and took off. When the two weeks turned into three, I felt a little guilty, so I bought Barbara a lovely piece of Australian costume jewelry. When the three weeks turned into four, I stepped up to a silver necklace. When number five rolled around, I turned to gold. By the sixth week, I found myself in the most exclusive South Sea pearl shop in town . . . If this mediation had lasted another month, I'd have been totally broke!

After making a number of points about legal matters generally applicable to the practice of law, I closed my remarks at the partner retreat by focusing on four thoughts that I considered worth passing along to younger generations of Skadden partners. The four had a common denominator – perhaps attributable to the sober realization that I would never again be as good at anything else as I was at what I was giving up by retiring. All had to do with a lawyer's ego.

1. *Don't let yourself be deluded into believing you're indispensable.* You may be missed, but you can be replaced (as I knew was about to happen to me, without "a single ripple in the water") Some ramifications of this include:

   - Take the goddamned vacation.
   - Don't take clients for granted.
   - Get out of the habit of always "doing it yourself."

319

2. *There's truth to the old proverb, "There's no limit to what can be accomplished if you give someone else the credit."* Don't suffer from the N.I.H. malady – "not invented here" (i.e. if it's not my idea, it can't be any good).

3. *In dealing with colleagues and subordinates, be less quick with your criticism and more generous with your praise.* Revel in each other's success and reinforce positive accomplishments with sweet words of praise.

4. *But don't let your self-esteem be dependent on the praise or positive reactions of others.* Don't overrate yourself on the basis of extravagant praise or underestimate yourself on the basis of criticism – or even on the absence of an anticipated favorable reaction when you think you've done something well. Judge for yourself how you're doing. As Shakespeare put it: "Go to your bosom / knock there / and ask your heart what it doth know."

Others in our Skadden crew

I wrote in Chapter 13 about my two strongest influences at the firm, Joe Flom and Peter Mullen. Now I'd like to pay tribute to a number of my other colleagues who helped make my years at Skadden such a positive experience.

Barry Garfinkel, a superb litigation partner, was instrumental in persuading me to join the firm, and then took me under his wing when I first arrived, even though we were in different departments. In later years, Barry encouraged me to get into alternative dispute resolution – both arbitration and also mediation, the latter then becoming my new post-retirement specialty.

More than any other partner, Barry symbolized the attribute of dedication to the firm that infected us all to various extents – the team spirit, not just individual effort, that was at the heart of how we practiced law. In earlier days, Barry was the firm's assignment partner, and I can vividly recall associates hunkering down on Fridays so they wouldn't end up with Barry snaring them for a big job to do over the weekend.

Every year for over a decade, Barry and his wife Gloria invited my family (along with Fin Fogg and his family) to their weekend home ("Redbrick") in the Catskills for the long Thanksgiving weekend. It was always a wonderful and heartwarming get-together away from the pressure of the office. Having recently celebrated his 90th birthday, Barry – as sharp as ever – is still going at it full tilt.

If it wasn't for *Les Arps* (and, to a lesser degree, Marshall Skadden and John Slate), there wouldn't have been a Skadden Arps. (Marshall Skadden was already deceased when I arrived at the firm, and John Slate passed away soon after.)

Les played a key role during those critical years of the late '60's and '70's, when Skadden, Arps made its rapid and heady transition from small to major firm. In the early years, Les and his wonderful wife Ruth really fused the firm together, highlighted by a warm annual party they gave for all in their apartment, and also through Ruth involving our spouses in her activities for the Legal Aid Society.

Les set an endearing tone of total informality; the door to our senior partner's office was always open, whether to discuss a problem with him or just to visit. Even to the youngest associate, Mr. Arps was always just "Les" – there was no aura of self-importance with which prominent members of the legal profession are so often afflicted.

Les had superb ethical judgment and deserves a lot of the credit for our avoiding any breath of scandal. Whenever one of us faced a client situation involving the canons of ethics, the word would go out – often initiated by Joe Flom – "Let's run it by Les," and he never let us down. In my eulogy to Les at his funeral in 1987, I spoke these words to my partners: "In the years ahead, when ethical issues arise, we could do a lot worse than ask ourselves the question, 'How would Les have reacted to this one?'"

John Feerick was already a fixture at the firm when I arrived, and we became partners at the same time in 1968. After building up the firm's labor and employment practice for about a decade, John left to become Dean of the Fordham Law School, where he served with distinction for several decades – plus becoming president of the New York City Bar Association and handling numerous important assignments of a public service nature.

In addition to being a good friend (which has persisted to this day), John opened my eyes in two important respects. One was that you could be a lawyer and still write. His excellent book on presidential succession[*] was written while he was an associate at Skadden, and it inspired me to meld these two disciplines. The other eye-opener was John himself – a genuinely good guy, in both his personal and professional lives. He showed me that you didn't have to come across as tough as nails to get your point across or your influence felt, and that there was room for compassion and other decent qualities in a lawyer's makeup.

Last year, *Fin Fogg* – the man I long considered my closest friend at the firm – was stricken with a brain tumor and sadly passed away. My special kinship with Fin dated back to the mid-'60s, when I helped recruit him from law school to be an associate at Davies, Hardy & Schenck. Six months later, I left there and joined Skadden. Within another six months – not from pangs of guilt, but because I already knew what a good guy and fine lawyer he was – I persuaded Fin to join us at Skadden; and we worked side by side for the next three decades.

Part of my special feeling for Fin (and his family), as I mentioned before, is that we shared a house with them – along with my high school/college buddy Dick Kluger and his family – for two summers on Fire Island, where our two-year-old sons caused us palpitations by wandering off unattended. Later the Foggs and we had those wonderful Thanksgiving family weekends with the Garfinkels in the Catskills.

After retirement Fin served for over a decade with real distinction as Chairman of the Board of New York's Legal Aid Society.

I feel close to *Paul Schnell*, now a major Skadden partner, whom I mentored many decades ago when he worked with me on D&B and other deals. I sense that Paul very much shares my approach to lawyering and negotiating deals, and he's the lawyer I'd want to represent me if I needed legal help on a commercial matter.

---

[*] *Failing Hands: The Story of Presidential Succession* (Fordham University Press, 1965)

Tom Schwarz was a first-rate litigator for clients, as well as handling litigious matters that directly involved the firm. We knew each other from summers on Fire Island, where Tom eventually became mayor of Ocean Beach – and I, as his law partner, had to sign a written pledge that I would not solicit legal business at the beach! In 1996, as you just read, we spent 40 days together in Australia settling a major case. For most of the past two decades, Tom served admirably as President of Purchase College, State University of New York.

While interviewing law students one year, I encountered a bearded young man who looked familiar. It turned out to be *Hank Baer*, who had been my (beardless) high school classmate, and had switched to law after years in business. I helped persuade Hank to come to Skadden to work with John Feerick, where he turned out to be a first-rate lawyer, heading up the labor/employment department after John left for Fordham.

Bill Frank came under enemy fire in Vietnam, emerging safely to ultimately become the leader of Skadden's litigation practice and my friend for many years.

My clubmate at Princeton, *Bob Del Tufo* – a terrific guy who sadly passed away several years ago – was U.S. Attorney for New Jersey and the New Jersey Attorney General before joining Skadden.

My friend *Ike Shapiro*, whose adolescence was spent in Japan during World War II, became a top-flight international lawyer who was a leader of the firm's expansion overseas.

In addition to being a tennis buddy and long-time friend, <u>Rich Easton</u>, a talented corporate lawyer, worked closely with me on the TWA case (Chapter 15) and *The Three-Piece Suitor* article (Chapter 14).

I like to think that I played a significant mentoring role in helping *Brian McCarthy* develop into the fine lawyer he is today – a mainstay of the firm's Los Angeles office.

Greg Milmoe, successfully crossed over into a notable corporate restructuring practice when M&A deals turned sour in the early '90s, and ably headed up the section of my annual M&A seminar devoted to such matters – plus which we've shared the piano at the firm's Christmas party.

Ed Robbins, in addition to being of counsel to the firm, was also its client, for whom I did some work in the early days. His good judgment on firm matters was helpful during those significant years.

I worked with a number of excellent litigators over the years, especially *Jon Lerner*, who in addition to his considerable litigation skills was also Skadden's post-Les Arps ethics guru; *Henry Wasserstein* and *Ed Yodowitz* who gave me valuable input on cases I was involved in and critiqued the references to litigation in my writings; *Mike Mitchell*, who specialized in hostile takeover litigation; and *Doug Kraus,* who was the litigator for several of my important clients.

I have great respect and affection for two men who were not attorneys but who played key roles at Skadden, both during my time there and since. *Tony Arbisi*, who started out as Joe Flom's secretary, managed many aspects of our office, making everything run as smoothly as possible. In the early years, he and I formed the committee that planned the firm's annual parties (and were charged with the decision of whether or not to erect a tent in case there should be a summertime sprinkle).

When *Earle Yaffa* headed up a management consultant review of the firm by Ernst and Young, he recommended that we recruit a financial VP-type of person. We were not excited by the candidates he proposed, however, and I discussed with Peter Mullen the possibility of enticing Earle himself to take the job, which is exactly what we did. Earle's excellent judgment and oversight helped turn Skadden into a well-run modern-day enterprise.

I note that all the people I've mentioned so far are male. When I arrived in 1966, there was only one female associate. But over the years, women have flourished at Skadden, and a number of excellent female lawyers have left their marks on the firm. As to their feelings about Skadden, here are the comments that some of the successful women partners of the firm made on that subject in *The Skadden Story:*[*]

> *Phyllis Korff:* "From the moment I arrived, I never felt I was treated differently because I was a woman. All they cared about was whether you were working hard or whether you were good."

> *Eileen Nugent:* "I have never had an issue here with being a woman . . . I honestly believe that the firm is very supportive of anyone who is smart enough, wants to work hard and wants to be a part of it."

---

[*] *The Skadden Story* pp.158-159

Nancy Lieberman: "Everything is based on ability. It doesn't matter if you're male, female, orange or purple. All anyone cares about is whether you can do the work."

Successful lawyers have their own version of "the woman behind the throne." Over the years I was blessed with seven of the most competent, caring, and supportive secretaries anyone could have asked for:

Shirley Mucatel, the first one, fresh out of steno school, improving every day.

Sue Tholl, bright, efficient, did it all while earning her Master's degree and attacking her Ph.D.

Susan Mackin, very good, but already had her Master's and longed to return to acting.

Rebecca Pikus, who held things together during a difficult period for me, got her B.A. and started on her Masters at night.

Nancy Martin, a college graduate with writing skills and extensive administrative experience, very hard-working, and with an upbeat attitude.

Chris Greges, extremely competent, helped keep my head above water in those tough years of the early '90s.

Ann Leyden, Ireland's gift to America, stupendous skills, enormous drive, made me laugh, and took great care of matters that related to my Mom.

Pauline Cella, joined me part-time after my retirement and has been very helpful in the years since.

In each of the M&A deals I've been discussing, I was ably assisted by a variety of good lawyers. Some were younger partners or associates from the M&A group; others were lawyers from other disciplines – such as tax and litigation – whose special expertise contributed mightily to what we were trying to accomplish. In most cases, the association went beyond the professional interaction to positive personal feelings on my part.

There is a listing of such people in the Appendix, as well a number of people who impressed me with their acumen as they went about their business enhancing Skadden's stature, plus some other people who, for one reason or another, I've had special feelings for; and then a lot of other admirable Skadden people I've known and worked with over the years.

17. SKADDEN ARPS (#5) –
THE DECISION TO RETIRE EARLY

In 1996 I retired from Skadden Arps at age 62. When I told Barry Garfinkel of my intention to do so, the senior partner couldn't believe it and demanded rationale. I pleaded a current lack of zest for the work; he countered that, although five years older than me, he couldn't wait to get started every morning.

Retirement at 62 was very unusual in those days. There was no attractive financial package offered to induce early retirement as there is now (when 62 seems to have become the "voluntary" retirement age of choice for Skadden lawyers). I was among the very first Skadden partners to retire, which elicited surprised reactions at my decision from the partners and a big firm party to mark the occasion.

To best capture my reasons for doing so, I've included in the following pages the entire article I wrote in 1997 for the American Bar Association's periodical, *Business Law Today** which sums up in detail the thought processes I went through to arrive at that decision. I put aside all the huffing and puffing of my years of practice and confided my inner thoughts to a broad audience.

Over the years I've received more favorable comments about this piece than about any other article I've written. So many lawyers have told me they keep a copy of it on their desks, checking off each of the "surefire signs" of readiness to retire as they occur. I consider it equally applicable (with some minor changes) to non-lawyers contemplating retirement from whatever lifetime activities they've been involved in.

* * *

A TIME TO REAP
(published in 1997)

I've just retired as a partner at a major law firm. I enjoyed a long and successful career practicing law and still retain strong affirmative feelings toward my firm, but I finally decided I'd had enough of lawyering.

---

* A TIME TO REAP . . . . A dozen surefire signs that you're ready to retire. *Business Law Today* December 1997

Every lawyer leaves active practice at some point, but I didn't have to retire when I did. At 62, I was eight years short of the firm's mandatory retirement age.

This decision wasn't made suddenly – it was the product of much reflection over an extended period. I retired because I observed a number of signs that collectively signaled me it was the right step to take. I heeded these signs – listening to the rumblings of my subconscious for once, rather than issuing myself rigid fiats about what to do or avoid. I hesitate to rush to judgment, but so far I'm quite comfortable with the decision and very positive about my new life.

This is a decision that most of us will face at some point. Like deciduous trees shedding their leaves in the autumn chill, we sense ". . . the days grow short / when you reach September . . . ." So, while recognizing that each individual situation is different, I thought you might be interested in the dozen signs that led me to retire.

Two caveats. This article won't address the separate question of giving up the practice of law for something else (such as investment banking) – a genuine change of career. Some of the 12 signs may have relevance to that decision, but I've never been tempted to try something else professionally. And though I intend to pursue a number of interests, I don't envision turning any of them into a second career.

I'm also steering clear of the issue of finances. If your resources are skimpy and you're dependent on legal fees or other compensation for your daily bread, you probably shouldn't be thinking about giving up your main source of income. Or perhaps your means are adequate but making a lot more money remains a high priority item – then early retirement makes little sense. My working assumption here, however, is that you have the financial wherewithal to pull this off and aren't money-driven, so that the issues you face arise in different spheres.

* * *

Sign No. 1. *On weekday mornings, you stay in the shower a few minutes longer than usual. You linger at the breakfast table over coffee and the daily newspaper. Just transferring the stuff from the pockets of yesterday's suit to today's becomes a time-consuming chore. Instead of arriving at the office at 9 or 9:30 a.m., as you once did, it's now more often in the 10 to 10:30 range.*

When I told one of my senior partners that I intended to retire, he first expressed disbelief and then said, "You know, Jim, I get up every morning, and just can't wait to get to the office and start my day." Although he's older than I am, he wasn't kidding – I know this is exactly the way he feels. But when you find yourself lingering at home many mornings – putting off the moment of re-entry into the working world – then your body is telling you something significant. What it told me was that the zest I used to feel about tackling the day's challenges – the enthusiasm with which I tried to approach each new project or problem – wasn't there any more and, moreover, seemed unlikely to return.

Sign No. 2. After an hour of hard negotiating with the other side, you settle the major issue between the parties. Although a number of less significant questions still remain unresolved, you excuse yourself from the meeting, leaving your younger colleague to handle the rest. When later that week your colleague brings you the draft agreement, rather than read it through, you ask her to point out the sections that resolve the disputed issues, and you scan only those portions.

One of the most important qualities for any lawyer to possess is intensity. It's a mélange of various attributes – the willingness to work long hours, thoroughness in approaching any task or document, self-discipline to avoid slipshod work, and the estimable ability to juggle conflicting time demands, seize the initiative, churn out work, meet deadlines, handle pressure and rise to the occasion.

These aspects of intensity may not be the most glamorous aspects of legal practice, but lately I've come to understand the importance of their composite product. Can you guess why? The answer is simple – because I began to realize I didn't have that high degree of intensity any more. I had it in spades for a long time, and then in recent years it waned. The many years of intensity ultimately wear most of us down. "Life," it's been said, "is one long process of getting tired."

A friend of mine who's an orthopedic surgeon about my age recently told me he had stopped operating on patients – formerly his principal professional activity. "How come?" I asked. He replied, "Well, Jim, I can still operate at a high level today. But frankly, I've seen too many instances where doctors in their 60s call the hospital to reserve two hours of operating room time – and the hospital give them three. I didn't want that to happen to me."

That's the way I felt, too. I wanted to go out while I was still in the two-hour bracket. My brain was all right (with perhaps an asterisk for shrinking memory), my judgment remained reasonable – but without intensity, which accounts for so much of our effectiveness, I realized I had become less of a lawyer than I once was.

Sign No. 3. You daydream about what you would like your practice to be. For example, you fantasize about a day at the office that consists of eight different clients coming in to see you for one hour apiece. Each asks for your help on some question of strategy or judgment call or decision they have to make, or seeks advice about a negotiation in which they're engaged. In each case, you absorb the pertinent facts, ask some pointed questions, and then give the advice. Your younger colleague, who's been sitting in on the meting, then goes out and takes care of implementing your advice for the client . . . .

Well, that was my pipe dream; and if that were my typical day. I'd probably stay in practice past 90. But lawyering isn't like that. Clients want you to deal with their problems. They don't want you just to tell them what to do; they want you to do it. No matter how exalted your billing rate has become, you have to be willing to get down there in the trenches to handle whatever is needed.

Several years ago, I wrote a book I was quite proud of called Smart Negotiating. I recognized that many people wanted to conduct their own negotiations; but I thought that even those people, after reading the book, would come to me for behind-the-scenes negotiating advice and strategy. I remember relating this expectation to my senior partner who, in his instinctive wisdom, replied. "Forget it – you'll never see them." And he was right; with few exceptions, that kind of business didn't materialize.

I'm not knocking advice, and providing large doses of it represents one of the most significant roles we play as lawyers. But you also have to turn out the product, get the job done. And when you're no longer keen to do that, you've got a real problem.

Part of the difficulty, I think, is the accumulation of stress we've been living with for so many years – the rigors of confrontation, the burden of responsibility, the attention to detail. Like a boxer who has absorbed too many blows – no one of which was enough to knock him out – the cumulative effect can finally take its toll. You find yourself longing for a stress-reduced environment that little short of retirement will provide.

*Sign No. 4. You're telling your client how to handle something –
explaining why the course you recommend is preferable, although it's not
the precise path he wants to follow. But the client doesn't seem to get the
message – "Why do I need to do all that unnecessary stuff . . .?" – and is
resisting your repeated advice. All of a sudden, you find yourself blowing
up at him. "Goddamit, how many time do I have to tell you the same
thing . . . !"*

*In my book Lawyering, I began the chapter on handling clients with
the heading: "Clients" Color them Indispensable." Let's face it,
I counseled, we can't function without them. You don't pay your bills
solving hypothetical problems. If you dislike working with clients, then the
practice of law – whether in a firm or a corporate setting – may not be for
you.*

*Moreover, as a lawyer, you must be constantly available. The client
may want you to answer questions, to reassure him that what he's doing
makes sense, to serve as a sounding board – or even just to hold his hand.
But that's what he's paying you for. He's entitled, even if you think it's not
the highest and best use of your valuable time. You have to adapt yourself
to his idiosyncrasies, satisfying each client on his own terms even when he's
unrealistic or stubborn.*

*And, by the way, it's not just a matter of indispensability. When
you're functioning effectively as the counselor to whom the client turns for
advice on his problems, you can experience personal satisfactions
equivalent to the pleasure of devising a creative solution to a complex
substantive issue.*

*I first wrote those thoughts 18 years ago, and I stick by their thrust
today. Still, the problem I gradually began to experience was putting such
words into practice – I found it harder and harder to follow my own advice
all the time. Yes, I blew up on occasion; and even when I controlled myself,
I probably treated a few clients with less respect than they deserved. In
retrospect, I think I finally became a little tired of pursuing other people's
agendas – which is the very essence of what we, as lawyers, are supposed
to be doing.*

*Sign No. 5. At a cocktail party, you're introduced to a CEO, two
presidents and three general counsel of Fortune 500 companies. You spend
the bulk of the next hour discussing (1) with the caterer, recipes for Tuscan
pasta, and (2) with the pianist, whether Richard Rodgers did his best work
with Lorenz Hart or Oscar Hammerstein.*

New business is the lifeblood of a lawyer's practice. There was a time when we could tell ourselves, just keep your head down, produce superior work, and clients will come to you. But what has become increasingly apparent in the competitive '90s is that you can't rely entirely on building the better mousetrap. Rather, you have to go out and fight for new business. Making a cold call may still be anathema, but when you're presented with opportunities to strut your stuff and you take a pass, something's awry.

I will confess that hustling legal business was never my favorite pastime, but I did my share over the years. Lately, however, even though I fully understood you have to "ask for the order," I found it harder to prod myself to make the effort.

Here's another ominous sign in this same vein. Say you're in a beauty contest, competing for some new business; or you've been selected to represent someone, but there's a potential conflict that has to be cleared. And you find your mind churning along these lines. "It would be great, of course, to land this business. On the other hand, if I do, then things are really going to be hectic for the next few months. That probably means no trip to Anguilla . . . . And I can see that the client's deputy general counsel is going to be tough to deal with . . ."

***Sign No. 6**. The business page carries an item about a new initiative being taken by a company you used to represent. Hopeful that you may be able to land some of the legal work, you place a call to your former contact at the company. You're put through to someone who stops humming the theme from "The Lion King" long enough to inform you, in a voice reeking of adolescence, that your contact "uh, like, retired a while back – know what I'm saying?" having been replaced by guess who? – the young man on the phone, who turns out to be good friends with your most junior partner.*

Even when you get the urge to solicit business, it's not so easy any more. The area I specialized in, for example – mergers and acquisitions – tends to be a young person's game. At the investment banking firms that. I once looked on as a major source of business, my contemporaries have either retired or are ensconced in management positions far away from the actual deals. Their younger colleagues, the ones in a position to hire lawyers, aren't that interested in dealing with an aging fogy – even if the name is hazily familiar. Quite properly, they're busy establishing reciprocal relations with their contemporaries – your younger partners. They don't want to hear war stories about the deals you pulled off in the '80s – ancient times, to their way of thinking. They want the word on the latest fad or fashion from someone who's currently out there on the firing line.

I suspect that most of us – even lawyers who might be willing to concede they've lost a little in the way of intensity – are embarrassed to admit they've noticed this kind of thing happening; but I'm willing to wager I wasn't the only fogy around. Let's face it, there's a little Willy Loman in all of us. And while there's no need to take out a full-page ad in The Wall Street Journal to inform the world, we ought to face up to it squarely in the privacy of our deliberations.

Sign No. 7. *You have always prided yourself on being a mentor to younger lawyers. Gradually, however, you realize that the young associates you mentored have all matured into accomplished lawyers, doing their own deals and uncomfortable with you looking over their shoulders. Meanwhile, the younger lawyers who need the mentoring still seek it – but from that first group who were once your protégés! They wouldn't think of bothering you . . . .*

Well, this may overstate the case somewhat – and it's another kick in the shins that's not easy to acknowledge – but my observation is that as you age, there's less opportunity to perform the kind of mentoring role you found so rewarding in earlier days. And, if you're like me, while making clear to others your availability for this function, you don't like to go around asking people to seek your counsel. But then, as your coaching hours decline, another worthwhile aspect of legal practice is diminished.

Sign No. 8. *You have a healthy ego, taking pleasure in the plaudits you receive from others for your achievements. Recently, however, you notice that the bulk of the kudos coming your way relate to past accomplishments. "I really enjoyed that book you wrote 10 yeas ago . . ." "I remember what a great job you did on that Buggy Whip takeover back in the '80s . . ." And now, in lieu of praise, some of the remarks contain a little zinger. "You must be involved in that big airline deal I read about the other day . . . ." (but you're not); "Are you representing Charlie again in his suit against the power company?" . . . . (No, Charlie went out and hired new counsel this time); "So, what major tomes have you written lately . . .? (don't ask).*

In addition to the money, one of the many reasons that we practice law (or that other folk design buildings or give advice on business strategy) is for the ego gratification. When that diminishes, and rebuffs to the ego occur more frequently, one of the compelling reasons to remain at your desk becomes neutralized.

That is another delicate topic for many of us to confront, but I consider it central to the retirement decision. No matter what interests you intend to pursue in retirement, this much is clear: You're voluntarily giving up the one thing you're best at and best known for. If the ego gratifications of continuing in practice are undiluted, this is hard to do. When the bag is mixed, you're more likely to stand down.

Sign No. 9. *You hear a currently faddish phrase whispering in your ear as you undertake each new assignment: "Been there, done that." Moreover, the list you used to keep in your wallet – a catalog of things you wanted to accomplish as a lawyer – has finally been discarded, with a check mark next to each item listed.*

Those of you with mountains yet to climb in your practice have a good reason for sticking around. But if you're like I was – having done what you set out to do, and now simply repeating yourself with no particular heights to conquer – then the reason drops away. Alternatively, the mountain may still be there, but the time has come to acknowledge that if it hasn't happened by now, the climb is unlikely to occur. Or, as Thomas Mann put it:

> *At ten, a child; at twenty, wild;*
> *At thirty, tame, if ever;*
> *At forty, wise; at fifty, rich;*
> *At sixty, good, or never.*

Sign No. 10. *You wake up in the morning with fragments of stories running through your head. You catch yourself humming snippets of tunes at odd times of the day. You walk down the street consumed with visual images. The left side of your brain seems to have gone into hibernation....*

That's what happened to me. I've had a number of interests outside law – principally as a writer, musician and photographer – which for years have been scrapping for limited shelf space in my law-centered world. I finally decided that I wanted to give them fuller vent than they've enjoyed up to now. Significantly for me, each of these pursuits held out the promise of self-improvement – in contrast to law, where I had clearly peaked.

334

Now, depending on what your other interests are, the signs you receive will be different ones. What's important, however, is that you do have other interests to which you can – and would like to – devote yourself. These can be of any kind or variety – as far removed from the practice of law as cooking or gardening, and as close to it as teaching a law school course or acting as a part-time arbitrator or mediator (which still entices me).

I would add this caveat, though. Since you've presumably been achievement-oriented so far in your life, your interests should include something at which you can improve measurably, in order to feel that familiar sense of accomplishment. And your prospects for getting better at something are far brighter if you take it up in earnest in your early 60s, rather than a decade later when you might just be hanging on for dear life.

The flip side to this is that I wouldn't advise going naked into voluntary retirement, with nothing to sustain your attention other than a stack of unread books and the prospect of doing some laps in the pool. (Or, as one wag described retirement days, "You wake up in the morning with nothing to do, and by evening you're half-way finished.") The shock of decompression might be just too unsettling. Amid the luxury of leisure, you need to be busy – because, as Cicero reminded us, "When one has much to put into them, a day has a hundred pockets."

__Sign No. 11.__ Breaking your decades-long habit of turning first to the business section of the morning newspaper, you find yourself making a quick perusal of the obituaries. You've developed a new interest in the reported ages of the principal decedents. When the range is from 89 to 95, you relax. But your day is off to a bad start when four of the five obits are of individuals in their 60s.

I don't want to be melodramatic here, but even when you're enjoying good health (as I am – knock wood), intimations of mortality can start to creep in once you pass 60. There's nothing like attending the funeral of a high school classmate to make you sit up and take notice – not that there's much you can do about it. Schopenhauer had it just about right: "In the morning of life, work; in the middle, give counsel; in the evening, pray."

A sense of the days dwindling down can weigh heavy in your decision to call it quits if there are things outside the law that you want to undertake or accomplish. There's a concern that if you wait, you may never get around to doing what you've long planned – such as taking that trip around the world. And this can chafe at you. Who was it who said, "We are but older children, dear / who fret to find our bedtime near" . . .?

Sign No. 12. You meet a lawyer who has recently retired and ask him how he likes it. Before he can answer, you whip out a yellow pad and No. 2 pencil and begin to take voluminous notes – interrupting only to inspect his AARP card and ask how to spell "elder hostel" . . .

That's it; you're ready!

* * *

Let me attempt a brief summation here. When you get right down to it, there are only two good reasons for a lawyer to take voluntary early retirement (other than for matters of health or to move onto another career):

- *You no longer get a kick out of what you're doing.*
- *There are other things you would much prefer to be doing.*

The best case for early retirement is when both of these reasons are applicable. If neither apply, you won't (and shouldn't) retire. If you're no longer professionally motivated but have no other resources, retiring early is dangerous. I would like to think that just being bored is insufficient to take this step – you'd have to be thoroughly unhappy. When you're happy in your work but have strong pulls elsewhere, that's the toughest call. My general advice would be to keep working if you can give partial vent to those other interests at the same time (as I did for many years).

If you do decide to retire, you might try the method I chose, which worked well for me. I made my decision at the close of 1995 to retire at the end of 1996. I told the firm of my decision in December 1995. This suited my style of not rushing into things abruptly and gave both the firm and me a year to get used to the idea. It also allowed me to put my affairs in order, finish certain projects, turn over clients to other partners, make my farewells, and so on.

As the months of 1996 passed. I kept my eyes and ears open to test whether I'd made the right decision. For example, I worked on several interesting deals and also participated in some significant dispute resolution matters. The question was, would these beguile me into staying at my desk? The answer proved to be "no." I was glad to have been involved and thus to exit on a relatively high note, but I wasn't tempted to stick around. If I had been, though, the decision to retire could presumably have been deferred or even reversed.

At any rate, I'm now at home, enjoying myself thoroughly. The first chore I set myself was to write this piece – to close that long chapter of my life while the experience was still fresh. My second project is to compose a song on the subject of retirement, which I'm in the process of doing. The working title is "Every Day is Saturday."

* * *

As I re-read my decision-to-retire article, I find it accurately covered my rationale 23 years ago. There are just two points noted in the article that I'd like to enlarge on here.

Many of my best corporate clients had been acquired by other companies in the '80s. Typically in any such case, the law firm representing the acquiror replaced Skadden Arps at the combined company. As a result, I had a much-diminished base of clients to rely on; and (for reasons noted in the ABA article) I was reluctant to pound the pavement in attempting to attract new business.

One major consequence of this was that in the '90s I didn't bill as many hours as other partners. This was reflected in a diminution of the income I received from the firm. At the beginning of that decade, according to Lincoln Caplan's book *Skadden*, I was among the firm's top ten moneymakers; but this ranking dropped off rather sharply as the decade moved ahead.

This was not, however, the same kind of blow to my ego as it would have been in earlier years. I was objective enough to realize that I couldn't argue with the logic of my diminished income, since I wasn't giving the firm the kind of sustained effort I'd provided in the previous decades. Moreover, I later came to realize that this downgrading made it easier for me to walk away from the firm voluntarily "before my time," since I was no longer earning at a level that would have been very difficult to surrender.

The other point involves an aspect that I think influenced my decision to retire early more than it does most other 62-year-old lawyers. It was that I really wanted to spend a serious amount of time on my non-legal interests – particularly music, photography, and writing (especially fiction). Over the years, many lawyers contemplating the possibility of retirement in their early 60's have admitted to me that they've been too busy lawyering to develop any other serious interests. As I noted in the ABA article, retiring early can be dangerous for those who can't lay claim to any other desirable pursuits. Fortunately for me, as you'll see in Chapters 19 and 20, that wasn't my problem.

18. MY WIFE, BARBARA FOX

Whenever my wife, Barbara Fox, and I go out to dinner with a couple we've recently become acquainted with, one of them will invariably ask us, "How did you guys meet?" We happen to have an interesting answer; and since my role in it predates Barbara's, I usually relate the story. Here's the condensed version, shorn of the elaboration and hyperbole that often accompanies the actual narrative.

I went to high school in New York with a guy named Joe. We knew each other but weren't particularly close. He graduated a year ahead of me, and we lost touch completely.

Ten years later – after college, the Navy, and law school, and during the early years of my first marriage – I landed back in New York as an associate in a law firm (Davies, Hardy & Schenck) where, lo and behold, Joe was one of the other associates. But after a year or so, Joe left to pursue a career in real estate, and we once more lost touch.

Fast forward to a Manhattan street corner almost two decades later. My career is in full swing at Skadden, Arps, but my first wife and I have been separated for a few years. On the street one day, who do I bump into but Joe, who has become a very successful real estate broker and now has a young wife and family. It's the kind of chance New York encounter that happens from time to time, and generally nothing comes of it. But we break the rule and make a lunch date.

At lunch, Joe and I find ourselves reminiscing about the good old days at that first law firm. It's been years since either of us has seen a number of the men we knew (women lawyers were scarce back then). Wouldn't it be fun to have a reunion? It's a thought frequently expressed by old acquaintances but almost never implemented. Wonder of wonders, Joe decides to hold a cocktail party reunion in his new apartment. He tracks down a number of lost souls and sends out invitations.

Late in the afternoon of reunion day, Joe's vivacious wife, Marjorie – who was well on her way to a prominent career as an interior designer – calls her younger sister on the phone. The sister, who lives in New York, has recently concluded a long-term boyfriend relationship. "You've got to get over here without delay," says Marjorie. "Joe has invited a bunch of old farts for a reunion, and I'm about to be bored to death. I need support."

The sister grumbles but dutifully complies. And so, while I'm sipping a beer in Joe's parlor, the door opens and in walks this vision – who, our dinner companions have guessed by now, is Barbara. I sidle over to the Fox, and the rest is, as they say, history. . . .

Each time I relate this tale, I'm struck by how many coincidences and other events outside my control had to occur in order for that fateful encounter to take place. What are the odds of Joe Hilton and I starting our careers in the same law firm? Of our bumping into each other two decades later on a street corner? Of converting that chance encounter into a lunch? Of Joe organizing a reunion? Of Barbara and I both being unattached at the same time? . . . . Even after 35 great years of marriage, I still consider the whole thing just *sheer happenstance*.

* * *

Before waxing eloquently on the considerable merits of this woman, let me provide a brief rundown of her life before we met in December 1982.

Barbara Fox was born in Rocky Mount, NC and lived there through her high school years. She was very close to her parents, Al and Anita Fox, and to her older sister Marjorie (the party hostess noted above), and they had strong family ties in various other mid-Atlantic and southern cities.

Barbara's parents instilled in Barbara and Marjorie a strong work ethic. Al Fox owned and operated a successful furniture business that took up most of his time. In fact, following dinner with his family, he would often head back to the office to catch up on paperwork. Anita was the credit manager for the business and integral to its success. Later, when Al sold the furniture business, Anita opened an antique store in downtown Rocky Mount; and after Anita passed away, Al ran it for a number of years.

From all accounts, Barbara had a happy childhood and adolescence and made a great many friends. Encouraged by her mother after high school, she was anxious to try life up north. She matriculated at Centenary College, enjoying her two years in New Jersey, with frequent visits to NYC where Marjorie was an undergraduate. She then transferred to the University of North Carolina in Chapel Hill NC – in large part because her boyfriend, David Dove, was attending nearby North Carolina State.

David graduated in 1969, and they got married in September of that year. He was studying for his masters in aerospace engineering at MIT, so

339

Barbara moved to Boston, where she attended and graduated from Boston University. While there, she worked for a while at MIT and then as a claims adjuster for an insurance company.

The marriage didn't work out. By 1972 they were divorced, and Barbara moved to New York City, where she had always wanted to live and work. Her first employment was at Town & Country magazine, her second at Doubleday, working with the editor of children's books. She got restless, though, and wanted a job where she would be her own boss. As she later said in a professional interview, "I had fire in my belly, and I didn't want to be constrained."

She decided to go into real estate – first working part-time with a commercial realtor, and then (on brother-in-law Joe Hilton's advice) transferring into the residential sector. Her initial employment was basically answering the phone for Alice Mason, a major broker at the time, from whom she says she learned a great deal. When that proved to be tiresome, she went to work at Whitbread Nolan, where she became a successful broker. But the firm had some financial troubles; and when brokers Elizabeth Stribling and Connie Tyson left to form what became the successful Stribling firm, Barbara joined them as their first vice president.

After a few years, Barbara left New York to be with a boyfriend, Harlan Kleiman, who had moved to Los Angeles to pursue a career in film-making. She worked with him out there but was unhappy in L.A. and missed New York. She had retained her Manhattan apartment for regular visits, as well as making intermittent trips to Rocky Mount. After a year, she left Harlan and came back to New York.

While in Los Angeles, Barbara heard that Cross & Brown, a major New York commercial real estate firm, had started a fledgling residential division and was looking for someone to head it up. Through Joe Hilton, she was introduced to the C&B president, Richard Seeler. At 28 years old and with no administrative experience, Barbara created a business plan, sold herself, and took over as the head of a four-person firm. With Dick as her mentor, she was very successful at Cross & Brown – growing the residential firm to its ultimate size of 60 brokers.

While this was happening, I came into the picture at the end of 1982.

* * *

When Barbara and I began dating in early 1983, both of us had already ended previous romantic relationships. Our focus on each other quickly became paramount. Although we lived apart in NYC, we spent a lot of time together that first winter and spring, including taking a ski trip to Massachusetts and enjoying a casino weekend in Atlantic City.

Barbara had previously rented a house in Easthampton for the summer, so we drove out to enjoy it every weekend except for a few in August which we spent at my house on Fire Island. We had a wonderful time in Easthampton. One highlight: when I rented a piano, she decided to take up the drums, which she played surprisingly well. For our duets, I even changed the lyrics of Ellington's famous tune to, "She's beginning to get the beat . . . ."

Having fallen in love, we wanted to continue spending weekend time together outside the city, so we rented a house that fall in Carmel, NY. It worked out, but Barbara was inclined to be nearer her family (who had a place in Wilton, CT), so we rented a house in nearby Westport. When the boiler there blew up, we moved to a rental in Weston.

Barbara was so upbeat about life that just being around her roused my spirits immeasurably. At this time, although my law practice was still hectic, I no longer felt the pressure of the '70s when I was working on my two big books. Instead, I was writing essays on any subject that interested me, published in *Legal Times* each month (as noted in Chapter 14).

About the time the 10th anniversary of the publication of *Anatomy of a Merger* neared, we were out jogging one day. In a burst of my new zeal to tackle any problem – I said, "You know, I think I'm ready now to revise *Anatomy* – bring it up to date on all the new developments during the past decade."

Barbara stopped jogging, looked fiercely at me, and said something like, "You idiot! Just when you've got everything working fine, you're talking about taking on a huge project that will screw everything up!"

I grasped at once that her words were totally realistic, and I acted accordingly. Instead of the revised book, which would have been a monster task, I wrote a pamphlet about the decade's changes – not too difficult to do – which received wide circulation. The woman saved me from the very hubris that she herself had aroused!

The measured progress we were making toward an ultimate union was accelerated by two events in 1984. The first came on my 50th birthday. Without any involvement by me, Barbara and her sister moved the living room furniture in my apartment to the nearby quarters of my friend Bill Silver, brought in low tatami tables and a chef from Nippon restaurant, and turned it into a Japanese paradise for a memorable evening.

The second 1984 event was a trip to Europe. Bill Silver and I, a couple of inveterate World War II buffs, went over to the Ardennes to celebrate the 40th anniversary of the Battle of the Bulge. Then we joined Barbara for a few days in Paris, where I bought her a pair of sleek red leather pants. One sight of her in that outfit with the Eiffel Tower as backdrop clinched it for me.

Barbara found a place for us to live together at 55 West 73rd Street – the first 2 floors of a townhouse co-op with six tenant-shareholders on the three floors above. Since neither of us had ever lived in a house like this, we worked out a deal to lease the premises with an option to buy the unit if we liked it.

We finally got around to talking about marriage in the fall of '84. I was all for it, but wasn't in a hurry – I figured we could wait until the following June ("a popular month for marriage," I argued), which would give me time to acclimate my sons to this change of life. But Barbara – a skilled student of negotiating leverage – refused to move into our new digs until we were married.

A negotiation took place. If you want to know how it came out, just read the words of my dedication to her contained in the book *Smart Negotiating*:

> "To my wife, Barbara Fox, a world class negotiator. In fact, to this day, I still don't know whether she was bluffing on the "now or never" position she took seven years ago over the issue of whether our wedding would be in January or in June. But if it was a bluff, I wasn't willing to call it – which is surely one of the smartest negotiating decisions I've made in my life."

In reflecting on our courtship, I realize that my darling Barbara played me like a Stradivarius. She knew just how to handle her man – not exerting overt pressure but insuring enough good stuff came my way that I found myself inexorably drawn toward this delightful coupling.

We had a small private wedding ceremony for family and a few close friends in a lovely suite at the Carlyle Hotel in NYC. Then we hosted a large reception back in our new (not yet furnished) townhouse apartment. After a honeymoon on St. Martin, we held a second reception in the apartment for other friends.

We were married by a New York judge, Mike Dontzin. Both of us remember his reading from "On Marriage" by Kahlil Gibran, which goes as follows:

"You were born together, and together you shall be forevermore.
You shall be together when the white wings of death scatter your days.
Ay, you shall be together even in the silent memory of God.
But let there be spaces in your togetherness,
And let the winds of the heavens dance between you.

"Love one another, but make not a bond of love:
Let it rather be a moving sea between the shores of your souls.
Fill each other's cup but drink not from one cup.
Give one another of your bread but eat not from the same loaf.
Sing and dance together and be joyous, but let each one of you be alone,
Even as the strings of a lute are alone
though they quiver with the same music.
"Give your hearts, but not into each other's keeping.
For only the hand of Life can contain your hearts.
And stand together yet not too near together:
For the pillars of the temple stand apart,
And the oak tree and the cypress grow not in each other's shadow."

We thought at the time that this was an exquisite way to put the matter and perfectly epitomized our personalities. We've been following that advice to splendid effect ever since.

During the ceremony, I gushed about my wonderful wife-to-be and the special knack she had for handling me, which I illustrated by telling this story. At the last minute the prior Christmas Eve, I decided we ought to have a tree. So we went to a place where a few remaining evergreens were for sale. We picked out the best one, and I asked the attendant for one of those metal stands on which to mount the tree trunk. "I'm sorry," he said, "but we're all sold out of those." I grimaced. "Well, how will I be able to make it stand up straight?" He thought for a minute and then suggested some two-by-four planks of wood he had, which could be sawed and hammered into a makeshift stand.

I quickly realized, however, that as straightforward as it might have seemed to him, this task went well beyond my limited carpentry skills. "I can't do that," I confessed to Barbara sheepishly. Seeing the forlorn look on my face, she smiled, patted my cheek, and offered this condolence: "That's all right – he can't do a merger!" And that, I told the wedding guests, was the moment I knew that only insanity could prevent me from marrying this woman.

There was a grand piano in the suite, and after the service, I played and sang in Barbara's honor two of our favorites – *Two for the Road* and *Just the Way You Are*. We toasted each other and the guests with caviar and champagne and were then transported back to the house for our reception, arriving five minutes before the first wedding guests.

* * *

On January 12, 2020, Barbara and I celebrated our 35th wedding anniversary. A lot has gone on in our lives since our marriage – most of it positive, such as the successful growth of Barbara's business (detailed later in this chapter), and some distressing, as in the loss of our parents. I believe it's safe to say that for each of us, this marriage has formed the bedrock of our lives, the fulfillment of our hopes and dreams. My task here is to give the reader some idea as to the countless contributions of my wonderful wife to our decades of happiness.

A good place to start is acknowledging her central roles in the geography of our married life. For instance, those two bottom floors in the west side townhouse expanded over the years under Barbra's stewardship into ownership of the entire building as we systematically bought out each of the six other shareholder/tenants. We spread out over the five floors – putting in a gym, and installing a huge, (but rarely-used) bathtub. My stuff resided everywhere. There was a lot of climbing and descending stairs, but we rationalized that this kept us in good physical shape. While I don't recall the two of us spending any substantial reflective time in the garden, there was a lovely meditative quality to our own modest greenacre (and our cat frolicked there daily).

It was a wonderful house to party in, and thanks to Barbara who was so skilled in putting these gatherings together, we enjoyed plenty of celebrations. There were a number of birthdays and anniversaries, including several marking other people's occasions. A highlight was that remarkable 50th anniversary of my 6th grade graduating class (see Chapter 2). Each year we gave a party for the panelists (and their spouses) from my annual M&A seminars (see Chapter 13).

Some of these parties were quite large, spreading over the two lower floors and into the garden. Perhaps the biggest was the 60th birthday celebration Barbara threw for me in 1994. A friend of mine, visiting from the West Coast, came to the party, but claimed he never got to see me at the second floor spot where I was holding forth because the first floor (where he entered) was so packed with people.

At the parties, Barbara handled everything. My principal contribution was musical. The second floor housed my Steinway B piano, a set of drums, a bass and a vibraphone – plus a lot of small rhythm instruments. We liked to get everyone singing and/or banging away on jazzy popular tunes.

Weekends were a different matter. Unless we had a commitment in the city or elsewhere, we spent every weekend of the year at our home in Easton, CT. The circumstances of how we acquired this retreat have achieved legend status in our family.

After a search in that general Westport area of Fairfield County, we came up with this odd coupling of a house in the nearby town of Easton – an 18th century structure, which had been taken down to the rafters and fireplace by the owner, who then proceeded to engraft a singularly-shaped modern edifice on top of them (with the original rafters fully visible). The house was surrounded by six lovely acres of land in a semi-rural community that had no business center but was home to several working farms.

When she first saw it, Barbara especially liked the kookiness of the house and designated me to negotiate with the owner. He was proud of what he'd fashioned and was asking a price that, while not exorbitant, was clearly more than was justified by the then current market. I tried various negotiating strategies to get him down on price but to no avail.

After some days of this, I said to Barbara, "I'm heading up to Easton today to give this one final try. What are my negotiating instructions?" Without hesitation, she replied in no uncertain terms: "COME-BACK-WITH-THAT-HOUSE!!"

It was crystal clear. I drove up there, made a few more vain attempts to secure a better price, and finally – following instructions – capitulated and accepted a deal at his price. Although it was early in our marriage, there was little question who was calling the marital shots on anything significant.

Next to deciding on wedlock, this purchase turned out to be the best negotiating decision of our lives. Sure, we overpaid somewhat, but we quickly forgot about that and just fell in love with the place. We'd never have gotten it if I hadn't thrown in the towel on price. Both Barbara and I have used this as a persuasive argument to our buyer-clients who get a case of chintzy cold feet at the last minute and are about to pass up something they prize – a useful way of convincing them to walk that extra mile.[*]

We view our house in Easton as a retreat from the turmoil of New York City. We drive up in two cars – Barbara plus seven dogs in one car, me with one cat and our commuting possessions in the other. We seldom invite friends or even relatives to visit us there, and we haven't tried to make new friends in the town of Easton – all our socializing takes place in NYC, while the Easton house remains our private preserve. It's our go-to place on weekends year-round as long as we don't have some conflict that keeps us in the city or we're not away on a trip. In addition to weekends we stay up there for a week over July 4th, Labor Day and Christmas/New Year, which is very relaxing – we just wish the weekends were longer.

I play a fine Yamaha piano there (plus we have a set of drums and a vibraphone); the surrounding area is a rural photographer's dream; and Barbara has assigned a snug room to me for writing. I have regular tennis partners, singles and doubles, in the nearby towns of Weston and Westport. Barbara is in her glory here with her dogs running around the fenced-in fields, tending her gardens (both vegetable and floral), and shopping for food, clothes and other stuff in the nearby towns. She cooks an excellent meal for us every Saturday night, and tasty French Toast or scrumptious scrambled eggs for Sunday breakfast.

Barbara takes lessons on our court from a local tennis pro – her backhand has become superb, and we often rally with each other. I can't get any of my old fogy friends to venture onto our court because (unlike the Har-Tru they favor) it's a hard surface that they claim hurts their knees. I have an outdoor hot tub that I enjoy using (except in the rain or on too cold winter days) – taking a harmonica out there to play while soaking – but Barbara won't have anything to do with it.

---

[*] In this regard, see my article on the point entitled, "Who Wants the Deal More" in the book, *THE ACQUISITION MATING DANCE and Other Essays on Negotiation* (Prentice Hall Law & Business, 1985).

Although we don't often entertain in CT, our house was the scene of a wonderful outdoor 75th birthday celebration Barbara organized for me. Back in NYC, she has overseen many parties in our home and also in public spaces, such as for my 80th birthday, for Tom's NYC wedding reception, and upon publication of several of my books.

Once we entered the 21st century, Barbara was anxious to sell our West Side townhouse and move to the East Side. But we needed to remain a certain number of years to resolve a potential tax problem related to its co-op status. The day the period ended (about a dozen years ago), Barbara swung into action, located the 180 East 79th Street penthouse (with its wraparound terrace for the dogs), supervised a gut renovation, and presented me with the finished product.

Our two city dwellings couldn't have been more disparate residences. The townhouse provided us with plenty of room to spread out but ranged over five floors, and we spent a lot of time on the staircase; by contrast, the penthouse is rather small, although all on one floor. The penthouse and its terrace offer good urban landscape views in all directions, while the townhouse, although it had a nice garden, was very insular view-wise.

Then there's the issue of the West Side vs. the East Side. I've been a fan of both areas, but Barbara was delighted to evacuate the West Side townhouse (where she chafed at playing a janitorial role that I eschewed) and move over to the East Side, where she feels she belongs. It's nearer to her family and work, and she doesn't have to take care of the plumbing.

Truth be told, although I complained about moving, the years on the stairs had taken their toll; and considering the probability of reduced mobility in the years ahead, I acquiesced. After all, I liked the new building, its location and terrace. The airy non-claustrophobic feeling of Barbra's renovation suited me fine. My only concern was a lack of space for all my stuff. Barbara rectified this a few years later by purchasing a small apartment on the ground floor for me to use as an office. I commute each day to my office by elevator!

Barbara took total charge of our move, which as usual she handled quite ably. I'll pass along just one anecdote. In the midst of the move, I had an alumni meeting at Skadden one Saturday which was scheduled to last until late afternoon but ended early. I telephoned Barbara to say I'd be back before she expected me. I can still recall her chilling reply: "Take your time coming home."

I immediately hailed a taxi and raced to the townhouse. There, outside my home-office, was a giant garbage receptacle (a sort of moderate-sized dumpster), which now contained many of my most precious items, such as the notes from my Contracts class the first year in law school. I quickly interjected myself into the proceedings, demanded removal of the dumpster, attached over my office door some of that yellow tape the police use to seal off crime scenes together with a giant "No Admittance" sign, and managed to save a few items that now safely reside in a spacious storage facility I rent monthly.

On a typical week, our Monday through Thursday meals in NYC usually include one or two dinners out with friends, one meal cooked by our beloved housekeeper Gloria, and fine take-out fare on the other nights. Most Fridays, we head up to CT and dine on a roasted or barbecued chicken purchase. She cooks up a treat on Saturday in the Easton kitchen she prefers to the smaller NYC version. After driving back to the city Sunday night, we usually order in – often Chinese food or pasta.

I think a word is in order here regarding our dogs. I swear that the subject of canines never came up in my conversations with Barbara prior to marriage, let alone being singled out in our pre-nuptial agreement. But in recent years, Barbara has fallen in love with the critters. At present we have six full-time dogs (and one cat), at least five of which sleep between us on our king-size bed. I'm relegated to a small sliver at one edge, which requires me to sleep on my side since there's no room for a full body profile. On weekends, a golden retriever that we're co-parenting with our niece Alexis joins the other six in the car with Barbara to drive up to CT.

The practicalities of the matter are that I've got to live with this woman (who's otherwise flawless), so the only thing I'll say about our animals is that they're basically a decent bunch. I do my share of petting and awarding treats, I've managed to develop some promising relationships with several of them, and I genuinely mourn their inevitable passing.

During our marriage, Barbara and I have taken a number of trips together, although these have diminished in recent years. In the old days, we visited England, France, Italy, Japan, Hong Kong, and various Caribbean resorts. Our international trips since my retirement include South Africa, Italy, Paris, Mexico, Vancouver and the Caribbean. Domestically, we've hit Napa, Southern California, Hawaii, New Orleans, Taos/Santa Fe, Las Vegas, Little Rock, Rocky Mount NC, Charleston SC, Boston, Washington DC, Maine, Atlantic City and Princeton. We've skied out west in Montana, Colorado and Wyoming, but with the Deer Valley

Resort in Park City, Utah as our favorite spot by far. I happen to think – and I hope Barbara feels the same way, albeit missing her animals – that we're at our best when away from the cares of NYC/Easton.

Anyway, with all that real estate to our name and delightful travel junkets to look back on, when the time came to greet the new century at midnight, we were marooned in our car between Fairfield County destinations, exchanging hugs in a small parking area off the main road.

* * *

Career-wise, Barbara successfully built the residential business of Cross & Brown up to 60 brokers, as I previously mentioned. But as the decade of the '80s was coming to a close, Met Life bought Cross & Brown, and corporate types replaced her mentors. The new relationship didn't work out, and she was not unhappy to leave in 1988.

Barbara had been spending a lot of time that year in North Carolina as her mother's health declined. Then, sadly, Anita Fox passed away. When Barbara returned to New York, I urged that she take a year off from work to refresh herself. But within a week – going stir crazy sitting around our house – she was back in gear with a new concept.

Barbara reasoned that since everyone in her family owned businesses, it would be natural for her to have her own. It didn't concern her that early 1989 was a terrible time in the Manhattan real estate market. Barbara was – and still is – a risk-taker. With some help from my ex-shipmate Jim Messing, she came up with a business plan for a new residential real estate brokerage firm of eight to ten people. Six brokers from Cross & Brown came along; and fortified by her own savings (plus modest financial help from her father and husband), Barbara opened the doors of Fox Residential Group in January 1989.

Over the years since, Barbara has built her company into one of New York City's finest boutique real estate brokerage firms with up to forty brokers. (It's worth checking out her firm's fine website, **www.foxresidential.com**.) She has become one of the most successful women on the New York residential real estate scene.

When asked a few years ago by an industry magazine what distinguished her from other successful women in her field, she replied: "Almost all the others are either first-class transactional brokers or top executives involved in firm management. What distinguishes me, I think, is that I try to excel at both of these pursuits. The firm I founded 27 years ago and actively manage today, Fox Residential Group, has grown from four to forty brokers, and I like to think of it as a successful extension of myself."

Then, when asked how her firm differs from other brokerage companies, she replied: "It's what I call our customized concierge service. Don't get me wrong – I'm not saying that other firms don't treat their clients and customers well. It's just that with us, it's a passion. Right from the start, I knew this was what we needed to do to set us apart from the larger, more corporate firms. I've instilled in our brokers the determination to provide our buyers and sellers with solutions tailored to their individual needs, to whatever problem they might encounter throughout their transaction."

In addition to the success of her firm, Barbara has been a major force in the residential division of the Real Estate Board of New York (REBNY), the trade organization that oversees the industry. In addition to a term on the overall REBNY Board of Governors, she was a founding member of REBNY'S Residential Committee, a member of the Residential Board of Directors, and also of a number of other committees dealing with the education of brokers and the ethics of the profession. She has chaired for over a decade the REBNY Committee that plans and oversees the huge annual Residential Deal of the Year Charity and Awards Gala benefiting its Members-in-Need Fund.

Barbara has received two of the highest honors her industry grants. One is the Henry Forster Award, the lifetime achievement award given to the most outstanding figure in residential real estate that year (1997). The other is the Kenneth R. Gerrety Humanitarian Award, given to REBNY members (commercial or residential) who provide exemplary service to their community. In Barbara's case, it was for years of dedication to improving her industry through REBNY, as well as for her non-real estate extracurricular activities (notably her animal rescue work (described below). The Gerrety award was presented before 2,000 attendees at REBNY's annual banquet in 2015. Barbara was the only female in the group of six honored, and also the only honoree from the residential side of the real-estate business.

Another noteworthy activity is Barbara's animal rescue organization, WOOF DOG RESCUE, that she founded, runs and has been its principal funder for the past 15 years. Each year WOOF rescues up to 75 dogs and cats from being euthanized in the NYC shelter system. Here's what Barbara has to say about this.

"A special feature of WOOF is that each animal is placed directly into a foster home to receive needed medical care, resocialization and training – and in many cases, love and security from the fear and anxiety to which these animals have been previously subjected. After rehab, WOOF finds them loving new homes. Each animal we take has its own special needs.

"For example, Stevie, a precious young terrier mix, was with WOOF for over seven months, recovering from a nasty skin infection which had never been addressed before we took him into our care. In addition to consulting all the New York City vets, we also contacted New Jersey and Long Island specialist vets to help Stevie recover. After many months and many relapses, Stevie is now doing incredibly well with the wonderful family that adopted him – but Woof is still helping the adopters work through his health issues.

"This kind of care requires many thousands of dollars – even for just this one dog – and most of them we later have one kind of problem or another. I'm proud of the fact that WOOF stands by each of the animals we rescue until they're ready for prime time!"

* * *

I want to conclude this chapter on Barbara by enumerating some wonderful qualities of hers, plus a number of ways in which she endears herself to me.

Here are the attributes:

- Her outstanding qualities as a businessperson, entrepreneur, and leader of a commercial enterprise are awesome!

- I'm also amazed by what she has done to benefit animals – not just those in our home but through her wonderful WOOF! Organization. The woman's patience here is astounding.

- Barbara has such a strong sense of family – always there for her kin, very much part of their lives, helpful, supportive, great with the kids.

- Barbara is cool under fire – decisive, not afraid to act, dauntless in the face of adversity.

- She looks great, takes good care of herself, is in fine shape, dresses well, and has boundless energy and enthusiasm.

- With a terrific sense of humor, Barbara doesn't just flash that million-dollar smile – she isn't afraid to laugh out loud. So often we find ourselves laughing together at the same things.

- She is a wonderful conversationalist in groups small or large. That includes talking, asking pertinent questions, and actually listening to others. While I wouldn't say she's humble, her considerable self-confidence is low-key, with no bluster or braggadocio.

- She is consistent. There are few mixed messages emanating from her – you know where she stands.

- She has good judgment that keeps her (and me) heading in the right direction.

- She's expert at handling our family's interactions with tradespeople, displaying an easy camaraderie but taking a hard line when necessary.

Here are the ways that she gets to me:

- She's my best friend – we love to be together, we laugh a lot, we confide in each other, she's my supportive audience.

- She knows how to give me space (as Gibran advised at our wedding), which I need so badly at times.

- She's great to travel with. We have such fun when the pressure is off. And she's an irresistible dancer.

- She's always in my corner – enjoys my writing, music and photography, gives me lots of positive impact, although not hesitant to speak up when she believes something of mine falls short.

- She handles her many business and social relationships with both men and women in flawless fashion.

- When she feels I can be helpful, she seeks out my judgment on matters or negotiating advice or writing facility.

- We share attitudes toward money, so it has never become a big issue between us.

- She's the best hostess for parties big and small.

- I relish her Saturday night home-cooked meals.

- (In the same vein as that *My Fair Lady* song, *I've Grown Accustomed to Her Face*), I adore the sound of Barbara's voice.

And that's all I'm going to say right now about the love of my life!

Laughing in big sister Marjorie's arms; the beachgoer (with our first dog, Lucy), and lovely adult; my model for waggish pix in Pisa and Florence; world-class shopper; hosting REBNY's annual industry-wide fundraiser; and tennis enthusiast.

Barbara's mother (Anita) at two times of life, then at our wedding with Barbara's father (Al), who lived into his 90s to the delight of Barbara and sister Marjorie.

With Barbara here: sister Marjorie, brother-in-law Joe, nieces Alexis and Alison, plus Alexis's children Kate and Charlie and close friend Michael.

(Above) The family at Ali's wedding to Josh Friedman in 2014 – Joe, Marjorie, Josh, Ali, Alexis, Kate, Charlie, Barbara and Jim. (Below) Ali and Josh's son Willie, from baby to Pre-K.

Family photos from our wedding on January 12, 1985 at the Carlyle Hotel in NYC. I played Two for the Road and Just the Way You Are in tribute to my adorable wife.

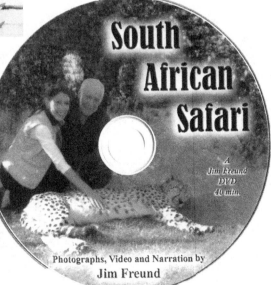

*Together for 37 wonderful years
and counting . . . .*

South African Safari

A
Jim Freund
DVD
40 min.

Photographs, Video and Narration by
Jim Freund

Here's Barbara: with Marjorie and eleven (count 'em!) dogs; holding Buffy; with Winky (the cat), Lucy, Buffy and me, and attending a major reunion of her graduating class from North Carolina's Rocky Mount High School.

19. RETIREMENT (1997-PRESENT) (#1) – ADJUSTING TO THE NEW LIFE

As of January 1, 1997, I was no longer a partner of Skadden Arps, where I had practiced law for the preceding three decades. I was designated "Of Counsel," but that really didn't have much meaning – no work would be coming my way from the firm, and the only financial tie between us related to past events.

I'm pleased to report that being retired from the firm didn't mean I'd retired from life. The 23 years that have elapsed since then have been enjoyable and productive for me. So enjoyable and productive, in fact, that I'm dividing up the narration on my retirement years into three chapters.

- Chapter 19. *Retirement (#1) – <u>Adjusting to the New Life</u>*
  This contains my general observations about being "out of a job", the teaching and mediating I've done to make some use of what I absorbed during the three prior decades, my belated introduction to serving the public interest, and certain other activities I've been involved in.

- Chapter 20. *Retirement (#2) – <u>The Three Challenges</u>*
  This is about three pursuits that have absorbed so much of my time these past several decades – music, photography and writing –new challenges to replace the ones I faced in my professional career.

- Chapter 21. *Retirement (#3) – <u>The View at Age 85</u>*
  This conveys my current thinking as to where I now stand, having crossed the age 85 milestone.

* * *

I'm grateful that things have worked out well for me because this isn't automatically true for everyone who retires. In fact, retirement is what might be termed a "package deal" – a balancing of pro's and con's, somewhat akin to what you achieve in negotiating a compromise resolution of issues in an adversarial transaction or in maintaining a sensitive personal relationship. For almost every positive, a correlative potential negative lurks around the corner.

Take, for instance, the sense of relief that washes over you when you're no longer under the gun. For a lawyer, not being beholden to demanding clients is sweet indeed. But it's counter-balanced by the abrupt realization that you weren't indispensable. Even if you're missed, you'll be replaced. The awareness that people no longer depend on you – or, for a lawyer, seek your advice – creates a troubling void. You've gone from a position of importance to one of relative insignificance. If your mama taught you that "Absence makes the heart grow fonder," just forget it. More often it's a case of "Out of sight, out of mind." How quickly they forget. . . .

Sure, your time is your own – there's a wonderful sense of freedom as you realize you can do whatever you want with your waking hours. But the flip side is that without any structure to your day (as there usually was for a lawyer), you have to schedule your activities each morning from scratch, which can be a little daunting.

The absence of stress is delightful – no more of those bruising confrontations, no burden of responsibility, no required attention to detail. But a concomitant of this is that you spend a lot of the day alone. (For a lawyer, that means that no one is any longer chomping at the bit for an hour of your time.) You have to learn how to be good company for yourself.

Sure, you can now hop on a plane to see the grandkids, travel to exotic spots without a cellphone, tool around in your spanking Mini-Cooper convertible. But even if you're well-positioned financially for retirement, it's still something of a shock to watch dollars flowing out while little is coming in. As for any illusions you may have harbored about embracing frugality, allow me to confess how hard it is to relinquish creature comforts that you and your spouse enjoyed when you were earning enough to afford them.

Perhaps the biggest mental challenge about retirement is that you are voluntarily giving up the one thing you're best at and most known for. Even for those of us who feel secure in our identity apart from our profession or business, this represents a major jolt that shouldn't be minimized as you face up to the end of a career. Little adulation – even for past glories – comes your way in retirement. Your self-esteem will definitely be tested.

One issue I hesitate to get into – although I recognize its significance – is the retiree's personal financial situation, which involves two interrelated considerations:

- How are things going right now? Am I able to do what I want (within reasonable limits), or do I feel uncomfortable constrictions?

- How will things be for the remainder (duration uncertain) of my (our) years?

Barbara and I would give generally positive answers to these questions – we're comfortable (although far from opulent). As far as I can tell, this also seems to be the case with most of our friends. But I realize how much this factor can affect one's views on the subject – how difficult it would be to feel positive about the future if you're under (or foreseeing) considerable financial pressure.

* * *

Because of my widely-circulated article about the decision to retire (see Chapter 17), I've been asked from time to time to write or lecture about how I've actually coped with retirement. In particular, people seem interested in any advice I can offer on how best to fill one's time. I recognize how difficult it is to generalize on the subject, since individual interests vary so greatly. Still, taking into account what I've experienced myself, and at the risk of oversimplification, my basic formula to get the most out of retirement is to have something going in each of four general areas:

Having Fun. The first category is just kicking back and having some fun. Travel, sports, reading, entertainment – the whole litany. We worked hard all our lives, so now we're entitled to some enjoyment. People who pack their post-working days so tightly with demanding activities that the fun segment is ignored have negated one of the major arguments in favor of retirement.

"A Little Lawyering." Second, my advice to lawyers (although this recommendation holds true, I think, for retirees generally) is to keep something on their plate that calls into play skills developed during their productive years. (For non-lawyers, this translates to activities linked to the way they made a living.) This shouldn't take up a major portion of one's time – otherwise, what's the sense of retiring? – but it does feel good to know you've still "got it".

Public Interest. Third, I suggest that everyone (including lawyers) ought to do something in the *pro bono* or public interest area. The reward here is that you can feel good about doing good – benefitting others without considerations of self-interest.

363

The Challenge. The fourth category, harder to pin down, has been for me the most crucial factor in making retirement rewarding. I believe that people who leave behind challenging careers need to find something to replace the sense of accomplishment and periodic acclaim that previously came their way. For maximum fulfillment, I'm convinced that a retiree needs to become immersed in at least one activity with these sort of characteristics:

- Ideally, it should be something you can do primarily by yourself, without the need of a supporting cast.
- It involves a skill that requires some effort on your part to become proficient at, while holding out the prospect of continued improvement.
- It produces something you can view with pride and perhaps show off to others.

In my own case, I've become enmeshed in three such activities, as delineated in Chapter 20.

* * *

Here's a report card on my pursuit of "a little lawyering" – through time spent teaching and mediating.

Teaching

During my active years at Skadden, much of the non-client work I'd been doing involved legal education. In addition to books, articles, seminars, and instructional videotapes, there was also some teaching at law school.

After my *Lawyering* book came out in the late '70s, Bob Mundheim, who was then Dean of the University of Pennsylvania Law School, persuaded me to teach an evening course there based on material in the book. I did so in the early '80s – the theme of the course being to look beyond the law school curriculum to what a young lawyer needs to focus on in order to succeed in the practice of law. I think the students found it interesting – I know I did. I applied the school's honorarium to hiring a limo service that took me down to Philadelphia and back once a week.

In the early '90s, when the *Smart Negotiating* book was published, my former partner and good friend John Feerick, who was then Dean of Fordham Law School, enticed me to teach an evening class there on negotiating. The class was large – about 60, I recall – and made up mostly of students who (like me) held day jobs, and so, by the time the class started, were a little fatigued (like me). I found the in-class experience worthwhile, but the preparation (including the need to create and grade problem-solving exams) took up a lot of time. On top of that, I felt uncomfortable leaving the office at six in the evening – when active deals were being processed and needed my attention – to cross town and teach. After several years, I gave it up.

But Dean Feerick remained persistent, and right after I retired coaxed me into teaching a smaller class of about 20 third-year students during daytime hours. I also was able to access Fordham's clinical facilities, which enabled me to coach individual students on negotiating tactics while viewing with them the televised sessions I'd arranged for them to conduct.

I taught that way for a number of years, enjoyed it thoroughly, and believe it served to keep my mind sharp in the early years of retirement. Mentoring young lawyers at the firm was an aspect of practice I'd always savored, and imparting some insights to this still younger generation was very satisfying. It did require a lot of work, though, and I got a little jaded repeating myself each year. After a good run, I called it a day.

Around the time of my retirement, I made a six-hour boxed set video course for the Practicing Law Institute called *Smart Negotiating for Lawyers*. Based on the material in my *Smart Negotiating* book, but now tailored to lawyers and the negotiating problems they face, it featured simulated lawyer-to-lawyer and lawyer-client exchanges, punctuated by my commentary on how to make a deal. The box included a copy of *Smart Negotiating,* a training manual for discussion leaders to use for in-group sessions, and an interactive video enabling viewers to test their evaluation of how effectively the actor-lawyers were negotiating against my own in-depth analysis. The course was well-received by leading lawyers.[*] Several years ago, it was reissued in digital format and is still being marketed by PLI.

---

[*] A "remarkable tool" / "a super way to develop and define negotiating skills" / "the best course on negotiating I have viewed on the subject in any medium" – but I'm afraid it didn't quite live up to one reviewer's comment that it "will help revolutionize the way young lawyers are trained in the art of negotiating."

For many years after retirement, I conducted an annual series of negotiating seminars for Skadden associates in multiple domestic offices. I also gave special negotiating seminars for a number of law firms, investment banks, and business groups. At the suggestion of my wife, I concocted a presentation that applied *Smart Negotiating* advice to the specific tactics and decisions facing residential real estate brokers, which generated a number of speeches I made to large and small groups of brokers over the years.

Mediating

My principal professional activity after retirement from the firm has been mediating commercial disputes. I'd started on this in my last years as a Skadden partner, and I wanted to do more of it once retired. Truth be told, though, I was initially hoping that another more lucrative area of practice would work out for me.

Here's what I envisioned happening at comfortable intervals. A sizeable company would be hit with an unsolicited takeover proposal. The company's long-time outside counsel firm was not expert in M&A takeovers, but the company might be reluctant to bring in an M&A firm like Skadden to take charge. However, I surmised, they may like the idea of enlisting an unaffiliated guy like me – with gray hair and considerable expertise in the area – to work alongside their regular counsel.

Sure enough, during my first year of retirement, I received just such an assignment from a sizeable company, which was the subject of an unsolicited, unwelcome takeover offer of about a half-billion dollars. Right up my alley, I told myself.

I can still picture the scene on the day when I was addressing the company's assembled board of directors. I did it on a hands-free conference call from my study at home, dressed in sweats, feet up on the desk – and the words I was spouting were very much the way I found myself talking to target boards in similar situations over the years.

"You can tell the raider to shove it with his chintzy half-billion offer. Your investment bankers peg your company at a much higher value and have opined that the offer is inadequate. You have no obligation to negotiate with the raider for a higher offer . . ." and so on.

When the call ended, I suddenly realized that there was something different about this situation from the ones I'd handled before – and it wasn't just me wearing the sweats. At Skadden, I enjoyed the protection of a very sizeable malpractice insurance policy in case anything went astray. But for a lawyer on his own, the maximum insurance you could then purchase had a limit of $1 million – and here I was, feet up on the desk, advising the board to reject a half-billion dollar offer that might no longer be available once they'd followed my advice!

Suffice to say, I maintained a much lower profile for the balance of that deal, and never took on another matter involving advice in a contested M&A situation. Actually, I haven't taken on many client matters of any kind in retirement – most of those I've done have been for friends. I did serve as an expert witness in several substantial arbitrations.

I've acted as an arbitrator on a few occasions, but that just hasn't been my cup of tea – probably because arbitration is so akin to litigation, which is not where I came from. An arbitrator (or arbitration panel), after reviewing all the evidence and assessing the arguments of the parties, renders a verdict on the merits that binds the parties.

Before I contrast mediation with that, though, I must mention one particular assignment I had in retirement. Two giant companies, who were entering into a sizeable joint venture, were concerned that legal squabbles between them could become a drag on the active pursuit of available business opportunities. So they agreed to appoint what they referred to as a "wise counselor" (in effect, a standby arbitrator) to whom disputes could be referred. The agreement spelled out an expedited basis to speed up the decision process and provided that the wise counselor's decision on the merits would bind the parties (without recourse to appeal) for judgments up to half a billion dollars.

I was named the wise counselor and paid a hefty annual sum just to stand by. Over the duration of the joint venture, although some disagreements did arise, no dispute was ever referred to me. The parties managed to work everything out without resort to seeking a decision from the wise counselor. I'm convinced that my principal contribution to this desirable state of affairs was that neither side wanted to have to abide by a decision emanating from someone (namely, me) who knew a lot less about their business than they did.

In contrast to arbitrators, mediators do not render a verdict that binds the parties. Even when a mediator offers a proposed resolution of the dispute, it's just a recommendation that neither party is obliged to accept. To have any effect here, the mediator has to persuade the parties to buy into a proposed resolution – which I found to be very much in line with what I'd been doing in the dealmaking area for the prior three decades.

Being a professional mediator also didn't carry the same malpractice risk as advising on mergers, so I embraced this activity. I want to pause here to pay tribute to a prominent mediator at the time, Marguerite Millhauser, who furnished me with wise counsel on the subject, co-authored my first mediation article, and has still been providing me (although now as the author and educator Marguerite Millhauser Castle living in Israel) with valuable insights into a variety of issues

I mediated some interesting cases – mostly concerning M&A deals that had later turned sour one way or the other – and wrote some lengthy mediation articles for *The Business Lawyer*. My best-known of these articles, *The Neutral Negotiator*[*] (written shortly before I retired from Skadden), was awarded the 1994 First Prize for Professional Articles by the CPR Institute for Dispute Resolution.

The nation's financial debacle in 2008 changed the landscape for me. When financial behemoth Lehman Brothers declared bankruptcy, multiple disputes arose involving how much the firm was owed on its countless contracts involving derivatives. The parties (and their "experts") were usually miles apart on this issue – a result of ambiguous provisions in their underlying contracts and quarrels over the applicable provisions of bankruptcy law.

The bankruptcy court in New York appointed me as one of three mediators to try to resolve these Lehman cases without resorting to litigation. Over the succeeding half-dozen years, I handled about fifty such disputes. This was demanding work – I'll never forget one of my earliest cases where the bid and asked was one million dollars and 100 million dollars! But it engendered a real sense of satisfaction when I could help the disputants reach a reasonable compromise resolution (as I did in the case just cited). In the early years, I was able to accomplish this most of the time. It grew more difficult later on, dealing with the tougher cases that had resisted resolution. During the busiest years I probably spent an average of

---

[*] The Neutral Negotiator – Why and How Mediation Can Work to Resolve Dollar Disputes (Prentice Hall, Law & Business, 1994).

about thirty hours a month on this work – nowhere near full time, but a significant time commitment that resulted in substantial fees.

During this time, I wrote a book on the general subject, entitled *Anatomy of a Mediation – A Dealmaker's Distinctive Approach to Resolving Dollar Disputes and Other Commercial Conflicts,* published in 2012 by the Practicing Law Institute (PLI). The book received fine reviews.[*] It was the dispute-resolution bookend to my acquisition deal-making *Anatomy of a Merger,* written almost 40 years earlier. I don't know of anyone else who has so directly addressed in print these disparate issues – making deals and resolving disputes – but that was my pitch in the book. When you get involved in a dispute, you need a mediator who knows how to make a deal, and that's what I've been doing for so many years.

I won't go into detail here about my mediating style. Let me just say that unlike many seasoned mediators who limit their involvement to playing a facilitative role between the parties, I take an unabashedly activist and evaluative approach. I prod the parties toward a feasible settlement; and if that proves unavailing, I try to persuade them to come to terms based on a resolution of the dispute that I propose.

Public Interest

I did virtually nothing of a public interest character in my years as a lawyer and prior to becoming one. I did perform some useful services – such as teaching other lawyers at seminars and my experience at the SEC in Washington – but frankly, these were all in pursuit of my career, not out of the goodness of my heart.

Nor, truth be told, did I consider engaging in some public-spirited activity as a goal when I retired. Nevertheless, I've performed two principal activities of this type over the past two decades, each of which came into my life more or less accidentally. They have provided me with a sense of satisfaction different from any I previously experienced.

The first of these – singalongs for senior citizens – I'll discuss in the music section of Chapter 20. The second consists of awarding public interest fellowships.

---

[*] "A joy to read" / "A clinical tour, by a very wise guide . . . canny, shrewd, pragmatic and cerebral" / "The book is great". My most prized comment came from Charles B. Renfrew, Chairman Emeritus of the Board of the CPR Institute for Dispute Resolution, and a former Federal Judge: "A superb job . . . the best analysis emphasizing the positive role of an evaluative mediator . . . . I have seen no book about mediation which compares to it."

Awarding Fellowships

This came about as a result of a continuing interest in Princeton-related activities. In the late '90s, my class of 1956 had formed a public service entity named ReachOut56, to serve as a conduit for classmates to participate in community service projects. It got off to a slow start. After my retirement, I was asked to join in. I can't say I was initially enthusiastic about doing so, but it seemed like something I ought to try.

We were meeting one day to discuss possible ways to expand our reach when an idea came to me. For a number of years, Skadden Arps had been sponsoring a highly successful program called the Skadden Fellowships. Each year, the firm selected 25 highly qualified law school graduates to practice two years of public interest law under grants provided by the firm. It suddenly hit me – why couldn't the Class of 1956 try to do something along public interest lines for seniors graduating from Princeton?

Well, there was one big difference right out of the box – Skadden had lots of money to finance its program, while ReachOut56 had very little. We realized we'd have to launch a series of annual campaigns among our classmates to raise the funds necessary to sponsor any ReachOut56 Fellows we selected.

But the leaders of ReachOut56 – Dan Gardiner, Jack Fritts, Slade Mills, Mort Chute, Fraser Lewis, among others – liked my idea and had the courage to move ahead. I've overseen the project since its launching in 2002, but it would never have been consummated without their leadership and the generosity of over 100 alumni, who enabled us to award two fellowships – now worth $30,000 each – in every year since.

Candidates (graduating Princeton seniors) have to perform their own research to find an underfunded public service organization that makes a position available for an important project or function devised by the applicant for the year of the award – something that this organization desires to have done but lacks the funds to hire someone to accomplish it.

Originally both fellowships were awarded for domestic projects but in 2010, through the generosity of our '56 classmate Ladi Pathy, the 1956 ReachOut International Fellowship was created. Funded by Ladi's foundation ever since, the Fellowship has sponsored projects performed all over the world – Sierra Leone, South Africa, Nigeria, Turkey, the West Bank, Nicaragua, Canada and Mexico. Happily, Ladi has also become a close friend of mine in recent years, and we get together whenever he comes down to NYC from Montreal.

370

We've had programs centered on aid of children, medical activities, law for the disadvantaged, civic engagement, teaching – the list goes on. The forty Fellows we've sponsored over the years comprise a cadre of the finest young people you can imagine – bright, articulate, energetic – with a real passion for public service and the creative talent to embark on impressive charitable projects. Interest at Princeton has grown over the years; competing for the two 2019 openings, for instance, there were over 20 fine applicants.

Some years ago, then Princeton President Shirley Tilghman wrote to congratulate us on this initiative with these words:

> "You have chosen wonderful students who exemplify the Princeton motto. The class has every reason to be proud of this project, which provides recognition and opportunity for students who have been committed to public service. I know a fair number of your fellows, and they are among the best we have."

As our class aged, we recognized the desirability of partnering with younger alumni. In 2008 we formed an alliance with the class of 1981 (who graduated the year we celebrated our 25th reunion). Then in 2011 the class of 2006 joined with us (they had graduated while we were saluting our 50th). The inter-generational partnership is now called ReachOut56-81-06. In the succeeding years, three wonderful women from 1981 (Jean Telljohann, Sarah Lederman, and Tracy Pogue) joined me as co-chairs of the Fellowship Committee. They have performed splendid work and assumed a good deal of the responsibility. Marty Johnson and Jon Wonnell from '81 are now co-chairman of ReachOut. Slade Mills and Arthur Eschenlauer from '56 are very active in ReachOut activities.

In addition, ReachOut has a very active college awareness program, which sends Princeton undergraduate volunteers to mentor disadvantaged students in urban high schools on how to cope with the challenges of getting into and graduating from college. We've also sponsored a social entrepreneurship program featuring business plan competitions for undergraduates.

There's one other educational activity I've been involved in during retirement – serving on the Board of Governors of The New School Jazz College. During the past year, the Jazz College has melded together with two other New School units – Mannes School of Music and the School of Drama – to form the College of Performing Arts, on whose governing board I now sit.

Having Fun

The first of my prescriptions for a worthwhile retirement was to have some fun, and I've fared pretty well on that score. Much of my fun has come through the three prongs of my "challenge" – music, photography and writing – which are discussed in Chapter 20, so I won't say more about them here. But there have also been plenty of other sources of enjoyment.

People

The most fun for me in retirement has stemmed from the good people with whom I interact. In that regard, the principal source of my everyday happiness is my wife, Barbara Fox. She's my love, and my best friend. It's hard for me to imagine life without her. There's a special place for her in this memoir (Chapter 18), to which I refer you for the details; but in case you missed it, I'll offer here just my bottom line.

Barbara Fox and I celebrated our 35th wedding anniversary this January – and all I can say is that it gets better each year. The woman is a real dynamo – managing her real estate brokerage firm and handling major residential transactions, rescuing abandoned dogs and cats while tending to her own menagerie, nourishing her family, playing tennis with me, and so on indefinitely.

With all that, she takes loving and unbelievably supportive care of her guy. The Fox is so consistent – none of those highs and lows that may bedevil other unions – I always know where she stands. And such fun to be with – we're laughing together and reminiscing and strategizing all the time. And she's in such good shape. . . and I find her so attractive. . . . Negatives? Well, I'm not happy about her predilection for throwing out my old magazines. . . . Anyway, you can bet that Barbara is going to do her best to keep me youthful – she simply won't allow me to wither.

Prominent for me in the fun category of my retirement are my two sons, Erik and Tom, and my granddaughters, Delilah and Paige. I've discussed my relationships with them in Chapter 12, but suffice to say here that I'm always very happy when we get together. Unfortunately, it's not as often as I'd like, given the geographical, work and educational constraints. The few trips I've taken with the boys during these years – to Napa, Tahoe, and Atlantic City – have been very happy times; and the trip the six of us (with Barbara, Delilah and Paige) made to Deer Valley several years ago was splendid.

Retirement also gave me a lot more time to spend with my mother until she passed away in 2013 and to appreciate her special qualities even more. Detailed remarks about this are contained in Chapter 3.

I've spent time with other members of my family. Periodic lunches with my cousins Judy and Joni, and attendance at the numerous jazz concerts Pat sponsors, have been enjoyable. I also have a high regard for Judy's daughter Michelle, her son Michael and his family, and for Judy's granddaughters Hannah and Laura.

The family I've spent a great deal of time with has been Barbara's – in particular her sister Marjorie and brother-in-law Joe, her nieces Alexis and Alison (with husband Josh), grandniece Kate and grandnephews Charlie and William. This Fox-Hilton family has accepted me completely as one of theirs, and I've been very happy getting close to them and enjoying their kindnesses to me.

As for friends, I feel blessed. They form a disparate but indispensable multitude. Some of the closest date back to high school and college, with the relationship refreshed each year. Others have been more recent additions – many of them through Barbara's contacts. Also I've been a member of San Francisco's Bohemian Club for a number of years and annually attend the Bohemian Grove, its summer encampment in the California redwoods, where I have made a number of friends.

Included in my wide variety of friendships are a healthy mix of men and women, contemporaries and younger folk, New Yorkers and geographic outliers. (I've listed many of them in the Appendix.) When we get together, we pick up right where we left off months before. I make a real effort to reach my friends through the annual year-end package of writings, music and photography I send out to 800-plus recipients. While many of them don't always acknowledge the outreach, I'm hopeful that it nevertheless serves to keep the relationship alive.

Finally, a word about those special people who have been helping me thrive in retirement. Gloria (with assistance from Henry) has been a stalwart to Barbara and me taking care of our homes and the menagerie. Sweet Gloria keeps the dogs quiet while we record in the living room, selects what tie I should wear, packs for my occasional trips – she's helpful in so many ways, with a wonderful attitude. I'm also appreciative of the support that Barbara and I receive from the skilled and congenial building staff of our Manhattan residence at 180 East 79th St.

Gent, who drives (and does many other things) for Fox Residential Group, has helped me a lot as I've became less inclined to take the wheel for long distances. He's a splendid chauffeur and good companion on trips to Princeton, as well as when I'm visiting various sites for my photos or just getting around this turbulent city.

The person I owe the most to by far is my assistant Raymond, who has been with me for the past 15 years. There's no way I would have been able to turn out the recordings, the photography folios, and the writings without his invaluable help. He's kept me sane in terms of finding everything I misplace, putting together my gear for weekends and other trips, dealing with all the electronic gizmos I find so difficult (but imperative) to use. He was especially invaluable in helping to take care of my mother, and he's become the go-to guy for Barbara and others in her family for electronic expertise or when something needs fixing. He handles this all with such aplomb and courtesy. Raymond has played an essential role in making my retirement such a positive experience.

Athletics

My principal athletic activity during retirement has been tennis. I never played much as a kid – too wrapped up in team sports – and not at all in the decade of college, Navy and law school. But I started playing in earnest when I got back to NYC, both in the city and during the summer on Fire Island, and I've been at it steadily ever since.

At my best, I was a decent player, with some shotmaking and court coverage ability, but always inconsistent, and seemingly unable or unwilling to put in the effort to gain more consistency, even when I had the time to do so in retirement. Still, as a former athlete, I've been happy to be doing something athletic; and I manage to feel better about the good shots I make than to be frustrated by the numerous errors I commit.

In NYC, I've been a long-time member of Town Tennis Club, and play there once (or occasionally twice) a week from May through November. My long time playing partner has been Al Eden, a pediatrician now in his 90's, who not only still plays a good game of tennis but also keeps regular office hours. Our singles games have now morphed into doubles, for a while with my friend Fred Bacher when he was around, and now usually with one or two pros at the club who keep the ball in play and make the competition enjoyable as we oldsters struggle around the court.

I mentioned in Chapter 18 the tennis court on our property in Easton, where Barbara and I have rallied a lot over the years. (We also try to find a court when we're on vacation.) I play in Connecticut on Saturdays from spring through fall in a doubles game with various local players, arranged by my friend Gerson Pakula. On Sundays all year round I engage in the friendliest of rivalries with my close friend Dick Eisner, who with his lovely artist-sculptress wife Carole has a weekend house in Weston, CT. Dick and I have been going at it since we were nine years old, playing pingpong in the 3rd grade at Walden School. Nowadays, with both of us somewhat slowed down, we play points instead of games; but we're still striving to hit winners, and we make sure to vocally applaud our opponent for each good shot.

Until recently, Barbara and I took one or two ski vacations out west each year. We were very compatible skill-wise on the hills – avoiding big moguls and really enjoying ourselves whipping down moderate slopes. On occasion we'd be joined by one of my sons – excellent skiers who were kind enough to ski a run or two with us before disappearing to seek out more challenging venues.

After experiencing some weakness in my left leg several years ago, I found that I really couldn't handle the slopes. Having proved to my granddaughters in person that I could still ski (barely) into my 80's, and increasingly fearful of injury, I've given up the sport. Barbara would still like to ski, but she needs to find a new downhill companion.

The other way sports come into my life is through watching games and matches on TV – I don't attend many events. My favorites are football, tennis and playoff basketball. Barbara frets continually over this, but so far I've been holding firm.

Eating

A real pleasure for me during retirement has been food. I like almost every kind of victuals, sometimes in copious quantities. New York restaurants are splendid – even the modest ones in our neighborhood. Our housekeeper is a fine cook, and the East Side takeout is delectable. As I mentioned, Barbara cooks a variety of interesting meals when we are in CT, displaying the same talent in the kitchen as elsewhere.

Most of the things in life I want to accomplish I've been able to do. But there's one frustrating item that has so far proved too formidable to conquer – namely, losing 15 pounds, the bulk of which is located at present in the familiar rubber tire locale.

For one of my birthdays several years ago, Barbara's present was to underwrite my first visit to a diet doctor. (It reminded me of the proverbial husband-to-wife anniversary gift of a vacuum cleaner.) Although I went to see this guru regularly and tried to follow his regimen, the advances I made would invariably be followed by setbacks.

It's not that I'm ignorant of what I should be eating, and I don't gorge myself with sweets and such. But I seem to lack the necessary willpower to pass up tasty slices of bread, reduce consumption of wine, eat smaller portions of steak – those kinds of temptations. I am in the thrall of an "I'm entitled" attitude that became magnified as I passed 80, to wit: at this advanced age, why should I deprive myself? I find I'm frequently giving myself "a treat" for finishing a project or starting a new one or celebrating some event. Many of the resultant treats find their way into my mouth, from whence they journey south.

I make all the usual pep talks to myself – thinner is healthier, I'll look better, be more agile on the tennis court, those old trousers banished to the rear of the closet will once again fit. But when I'm sitting in a first-class Italian restaurant, waiting impatiently for the appetizer to be served, that basket of fresh bread is simply irresistible.

If I were relegated to eating institutional food (such as we had at school or in the Navy), I'm sure I could take off some weight through an absence of temptation. With these tasty morsels on my plate, however, how can I send half of it back to the kitchen uneaten? (I know, you can take the other half home in a doggy bag; but the delayed gratification of day-old pasta just doesn't compare to the initial surge.)

I realize what I need to do – persuade myself of the tremendous sense of accomplishment I'd feel having shed the weight and kept it off. So far, this hasn't happened, and 85 seems a tough age to succeed in substituting deprivation for rewards.

New York City

Living in NYC is great, so many terrific attractions. I take in a few regularly, such as *Lyrics and Lyricists* concerts at the 92nd Street Y and periodic jam sessions by the jazz band of the New York Youth Symphony. Some I do irregularly, like the many sporting attractions – basketball at the Garden, tennis at the U.S. Open.

I have to admit, though, that for the most part we don't take advantage of the tremendous cultural offerings NYC provides. We're out of town on weekends, and during the week Barbara works hard and is disinclined to go to shows and such on weekday evenings. I take in a Wednesday show matinee from time to time; but as regards the theatre, ballet, philharmonic, opera and plethora of museums, we're not taking full advantage.

We do enjoy movies, but seldom go out to the cinema. Instead we watch them at home on DVD's or through streaming. Barbara's favorite TV shows have been Law & Order and Blue Bloods – usually programs I've pre-recorded, so we can fast forward through the ads – which we watch a lot, particularly during dinner and often stretching into the rest of the evening.

Books

I enjoy reading books and also listening to them audibly while driving up to CT, but there's a catch. When I'm asked how I manage to get so many things done, one reason I've often given is that I simply don't read as much as I should.

For many of us, reading a book is the most pleasurable of pursuits, demanding little from the reader except his attention. And if what you're reading is worthwhile, you don't get tired of it – you can go on for hours. I've concluded that in order to accomplish stuff in other more demanding (albeit less pleasurable) activities such as writing, you have to ration the time devoted to reading so as to free up the necessary hours. Until recently, I've been able to do just that – to keep myself on what might be called a "reading diet."

But now at 85, and with this book near completion, that may be changing for me. Any past success I achieved limiting my reading did not reckon with this gizmo called Kindle.

I'm the kind of reader who seldom stays exclusively with one or two books. Rather, I dip into one, read a few chapters, then switch over to several others for a similar brief stint, then back to the first one for a further dip. Over the years, I've bought my share of hard cover books and paperbacks as they were published or came to my attention, even though I knew deep down how unlikely it was I'd get around to reading them. Mostly, they piled up on my bookshelves, requiring later effort to find them again. It served my subliminal intent of wanting to own each book, but didn't motivate me to take the time to read it right then.

Then along came Kindle – beguiling me with two irresistible features. First is the instant gratification of reading the review of an interesting new book and then – in less than a minute after a few taps on the screen – having it appear on my Kindle ready for perusal. Second it's the delight of knowing I can stockpile dozens of books that I'd like to read in this one small portable unit I can tote anywhere. That's just what I've started to do in earnest – leaf through a chapter here, a section there, switch between fiction (novel, short story, play) and non-fiction (history, biography, "how to" books) – it's exhilarating. I've also taken to listening to audio books.

I hope the left side of my brain doesn't discover I'm taking covert pleasure in such breaches of my reading diet. It's too early to tell, but this may be one of the ways that turning 85 will affect me going forward – more input, less output. We'll see.

Puzzles

I may sound like a person who fills every waking hour with productive activity, but let me now confess that I spend five to ten percent of the time doing puzzles. I've always done crosswords and acrostics; in recent years, I became enamored with ken-ken, sudoku, kakuro and solitaire. Lately I'm a great daily fan of a word-forming game on the NY Times app called Spelling Bee.

I know my limitations – I steer well clear of The New York Times crosswords on Thursday, Friday and weekends. But I'm good enough to take on some difficult stuff and sometimes succeed – as with those daily Spelling Bee puzzles, where in a burst of initial energy, I achieved the first or second highest-rating status for over 100 consecutive days. I often start off the day spending 20 minutes or so in mental warm-up exercise – ten with a logic puzzle to get the left side of my brain functioning, and ten with a word puzzle to jostle my vocabulary. The added element here is that in a world of increasing complexity, where definitive results are hard to come by, it's reassuring to tackle something that has a successful outcome — satisfying when achieved and not devastating when you come up short.

My favorite table game is backgammon, though I must confess that my usual adversaries are the computer and iPad. I sense I'm improving and can usually hold my own against the highest level of the machines, but I've lacked opportunities to take on skilled human opponents who would clarify where I really stand. What I like best about the game is its combination of strategy, tactics, and gambling with the cube, but all of it subject to the vagaries of the dice — unlike chess, which is so sober, relentless and unforgiving of mistakes. Oh yes, I'm also keen on the fact that, unlike card games such as bridge, you don't have to memorize anything — it's all spread out there on the board in front of you.

Jokes

One of the real enjoyments of retirement was putting together a 64-page booklet entitled *JIM'S CHOICE JOKES — 90 Rib-Ticklers to Regale Your Friends*.

Let's face it — this is one tough world out there today. All that stuff going on in Washington and around the country, all the violence, all those international brouhahas. Well, one antidote for this is humor, which can make the negative stuff temporarily palatable.

In addition to jokes that have long been favorites of mine, I combed through countless selections from joke books, and finally selected 90 that made me laugh. Much of the humor I find amusing is edgy, waggish, mischievous, and irreverent, while a number of the situations are sexual; but hopefully, there's nothing in there that would make anyone cringe.

My selections include jokes involving animals, lawyer, accountants, doctors/nurses, psychiatrists, men of the cloth/religions, heaven, genies, "dumb" jokes, getting back, nationality, cannibals/savages, police, golf, oldsters, husbands and wives, family and some others. I especially like husband-wife jokes — and here, as a sample, are four of them from the book.

A shipment of husbands arrived in heaven. To speed up the processing, St. Peter said, "I want all the husbands who acted like mice in their homes on earth to form a line on the right. Those who were kings in their own castle, step to the left."

The men went to their places. The line of henpecked husbands stretched beyond the horizon. Only one man stood in the other line. St. Peter asked, "Are you sure you belong on the macho line?"

"I don't know, but this is where my wife told me to stand . . . ."

* * *

A married couple, both 60 years old, were celebrating their 35th anniversary. During the party, a fairy appeared out of nowhere to congratulate them and grant each of them a wish.

The wife wanted to travel around the world. The fairy waved her wand and Poof! – the wife had tickets in her hand for a world cruise.

Next, the fairy asked the husband what he wanted. He said, "I wish I had a wife 30 years younger than me."

The fairy picked up her wand and Poof! – the husband was 90.

* * *

An old couple die in an accident and are transported to heaven. The wife is amazed at the beauty of the place, and the peace and the contentment she feels. Her husband, on the other hand, is furious.

"What's the matter?" she asks. "Don't you like it here?"

"Of course I like it," snaps the husband. "And if it wasn't for your damn health foods, I'd have been here twenty years ago."

* * *

A pair of newlyweds are arguing on their honeymoon.

The couple had promised to be open and honest to each other, but the husband still won't tell his inquisitive wife how many sex partners he's had.

"Look," he says, "If I tell you, you'll just get angry."

"No, I won't," she says, "cross my heart and hope to die."

"Okay, then," says the man. "Let me think. There was one. . . two. . . three. . . four. . . five. . . YOU. . . seven. . . eight. . ."

We haven't traveled overseas in recent years, but had some fine visits earlier. Here is England's town of Oxford (top left), Paris at night (above), and the unusual trees (top right) that adorn the French wine country.

A view of Capetown, South Africa is on the right; closer to home is Vancouver's nearby Grouse Mountain; and below is the stony beach of Cabo, Mexico (that's Barbara dwarfed in the middle)..

Our favorite country to visit has been Italy. Venice is home to the gondolas, Milan the Cathedral, and the Dolomites the glacier.

Our favorite retirement trip was to South Africa and especially the Singita animal preserve, where we got up close (but not too personal) with lions, a cheetah, several leopards, intertwined giraffes, elephants (parent and baby), a close-knit pair of cape buffalo, an itchy wildebeast (gnu) and some very tough hyenas.

382

I'm a big fan of visiting zoos and photographing the occupants. Among the most active performers is this Central Park Zoo sea lion. I'm alert to shows of affection, as between these honeybears, turtles and giraffes. Check out the unusual albino peacock (ready-made for black &white prints). The other birds below are a penguin and pelican. (Top) The elephants perform in a circus, and the gull – envy of all – flies free.

We're not traveling as much as we used to, but certain U.S. venues still stand out such as Las Vegas (although the glitter is sometimes now eclipsed by security measures) and Taos, NM, a photographer's delight. In Washington DC, there's an interesting view of the Capitol from the notable train station,

I'm also intrigued by the unadorned train station in Rocky Mount NC, Barbara's home town. In Boston, the dome of the statehouse looms from behind the steed. The view in Chicago looks out toward Lake Michigan. Here's Atlantic City's famed boardwalk, and the bustling waterfront street of Portland ME.

My favorite state to visit is California. During retirement I've been out there at least once a year.

(Above) Along the Pacific coast – From the air, alongside the rocks, above the curved road, and behind Carmel's famed lone cypress. California's photo jewel is hilly San Francisco, with fog separating Fisherman's Wharf and the Golden Gate Bridge. Barbara and I enjoy Napa with its vineyards and fine hostelries. Further north is this mystic island and the timeless sign.

One of my favorite U.S. cities is New Orleans. I used to go there often until hurricane Katrina hit in 2005. I made a DVD tribute to the city when that occurred but didn't return until 2017. Here's an aerial view from my plane, a typical latticework terrace, a showboat on the Mississippi River, Jackson Square, the Andrew Jackson statue, a plane in the marvelous WW II Museum, Robert E. Lee (about a week before he was knocked off his pedestal), a neighborhood grocery, and a blues guitarist.

"*New York, New York, a wonderful town . . . .*" *The top three photos were taken from the wraparound terrace of our apartment. The city plays host to plenty of political street demonstrations. As a photographer, I enjoy juxtaposing two unlikely images in the same frame, as in this shot of the intrepid kayaker paddling alongside the carrier USS Intrepid.*

Pictured in the bottom row are two of NYC's grand venues – Lincoln Center (the night I saw Gershwin's "Porgy and Bess") and Grand Central Station. The third shot made it onto the page because the building that's two-to-the-right from the white monster is 300 Riverside Drive, where I spent my formative pre-teen years.

New York City abounds in compelling photographic images, as with mother and child absorbing the cool sounds of a Fifth Avenue jazzman, homelessness in front of Bendel's, and an elementary school class viewing my favorite statue in Central Park's Conservatory Garden.

(Above) This is a view of downtown at night from a high perch. (Right) Here's Central Park when it snows. (Below) The newest notable structures in NYC are the Vessel at Hudson Yards and the Oculus at Westfield World Trade Center.

(Top) Two views of our weekend home in Easton CT. (Above) One of the many impressive metal sculptures by Carole Eisner arrayed on the grounds of the Eisners' Weston CT home, and two spots near our home where the water flows. (Right) Easton's annual celebration of Memorial Day. (Below) Of the countless trees in this neck of the woods, here are my two favorites.

I attend at least one Princeton football game each year – usually either the Yale or Harvard matchup. (Top) Here's a view of the team playing, followed by the ritual at the end of every game, win or lose, of singing (with accompanying rhythmic arm waves) the alma mater. (Above and below) For so many years now, our class has held its own delicious tailgate before every home game, organized by Tom and Joanne Meeker and featuring an appearance by the University Band. Here is an overview of the site, Tom raising money for the band, and a group of '56 classmates.

(Top half) The class at our 60th reunion, and some scenes from the Reunion P-Rade. (Bottom half) The gathering at the annual Alumni Day and the very capable women's basketball team that plays a home game in the evening.

A number of us from our Horace Mann class meet for lunch quarterly at a Manhattan restaurant – or on occasion, at Porter Miller's apartment (top). At our 65th reunion, Mickey Littman, Alan Sklar and I met with Head of School, Thomas Kelly. Every spring over the last decade, Ed Aronson, Alan Sklar, John Flaxman, and I (plus Paul Margulies prior to his passing) have been meeting for lunch at a cozy inn on the shore of Lake Waramaug, CT.

The scene below is from a seminar at my 55th Harvard Law School reunion.

I'm proud of the work I've done spearheading the public service Fellowship awards of ReachOut56-81-06. Above is a montage of the Fellows between 2002 and 2015; the first Fellow (Aili McConnon Adamson) and a recent one (Natalie Tung); and members of the committee that interviews applicants annually. For a number of years, I led (on behalf of ReachOut)a phtoographic trip in Central Park for students at Brooklyn's Paul Robeson high school.

*(Above) A recent Hilton family snapshot and the Hilton's
50th Anniversary party*

*(Left) Joining me
at the piano are
relatives Laura
Roland, Michelle
Sussmann,
Hannah Roland,
and Paige
Freund; joining
me in Easton are
Michael
Sussmann and his
three children,
Paul, Margaret
and Rose. (Right)
Here's the entire
Sussmann family
celebrating Judy's
recent birthday.*

*John Doyle, Jack
Veatch and Fred Bacher
join me two years ago
in our last meeting with
Jack before his passing;
and here's Jack with
his family.*

*I was so inspired by Kit Watson's courageous fight against ALS,
which included leading Team Watson in an ALS Walk in Santa
Rosa, CA (that's Kit herself walking on the right). Below are
photos of the Bachers and me with the Watsons, and of Bob,
Kit and their daughters, Daphne, Whitney and Amanda.*

That's the personnel of Fox Residential Group, celebrating its 30th anniversary; Barbara with our wonderful housekeeper Gloria Parrocha; and Barbara at an animal shelter for her rescue organization, WOOF.

After many invaluable years, John Doyle and Judy Crawford "retired" Crawford Doyle Booksellers in 2017.

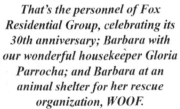

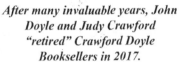

20. RETIREMENT (#2) – MY THREE CHALLENGES

I turn now to my three "challenges" – music, photography and writing. These three areas may appear to be quite distinct – after all, one is directed to the ear, one to the eye, and one to the brain. But for me, they share a common linkage.

To my mind, playing the piano, taking photos, and writing prose share the following characteristics:

- Each calls for a singular, activist approach to creating something new – often from scratch.

- Each can be performed solo – collaboration with or assistance from others is not necessary.

- The finished products can be shared with others.

What I find meaningful is that each allows me to accomplish something that's *sui generis*: a Jim Freund production, if you will. Other people undoubtedly derive satisfaction as music enthusiasts, lovers of fine photography, or devourers of good books. But I experience gratification from producing and performing in my chosen areas.

Take photography, for instance. I recognize and appreciate the expert work of professional photographers but rarely go to photo shows or museum exhibits, nor peruse books containing their finest images. My skills might well be bolstered if I were more attentive to these images, but what galvanizes me is being out on the street or in a park with my camera, snapping away and producing my own images. Although they may not compare with those in exhibits or professional books, it's satisfying to know that these images are mine – and that, if I desire, can be shared with others.

I listen to a lot of enjoyable music at home or while driving, and on occasion played live. (A favorite, of course, is the music composed, recorded and performed by my son, Tom.) But for most of my life, when arriving home after a day's work and wanting to relax, I don't turn on my CD player or (nowadays) ask Alexa to play a few of my favorites. Instead I head for the piano, uncover the keyboard, and plunk out my own lesser versions of those songs. And to boot, while I'm completely satisfied to play alone, it also works well for me when others listen in, or I'm accompanying singers or playing for an audience.

I consider reading the ultimate luxury, and enjoy it thoroughly (including audio versions of books read by capable narrators). But when I'm engaged in any sort of writing project, I don't hesitate to put my current reading aside in order to concentrate on what I'm trying to convey. I also savor the effort to craft a readable sentence, perhaps consulting a thesaurus to uncover the most fitting word or phrase to express my intention. I usually share what I write with others and, like most writers, am gratified when it's well-received.

At times, I've been able to combine these pastimes into a single package. For instance, a DVD I made of my black & white photos contains a full-blown narration I wrote and delivered. In a CD album where I read my early essays, each is introduced and concluded by one of my musical interludes.

Excluding the legal and professional writing I've done over the years, each of these activities I've described is simply an avocation for me. I would like to improve my skills but don't feel a need to excel. The pressure I experienced in the professional world does not exist here, nor do I expect to ever be as competent in any of these efforts as I was at my profession. The key for me is enjoyment, which is something I've found in abundance.

Music

My first musical memory is of attending an after-school music class in the third grade – clashing little cymbals and tinkling metal triangles, then graduating to the instrument called the recorder, advancing from the shrill soprano model to the better-modulated alto. After a year or so, my mother decided I should learn to play the piano.

My parents bought a Baldwin Acrosonic spinet (which still adorned my mother's living room 65 years later), and I began to take piano lessons from private teachers. It did not go well. I failed to connect with the classical repertoire they taught and displayed little talent on the keys. It wasn't just the agony of having to practice when I wanted to be outside playing ball or my lack of interest in the involuntary repertoire I was tackling. I was also rebelling against the notion of having to play a particular note at a given time with a prescribed fingering and in an insistent meter.

Mom wanted to show her nascent virtuoso off to my parents' friends, but I would not cooperate. Nor do I recall ever playing for my school buddies. Anyone evaluating my situation back then would have predicted that I'd ultimately join the vast majority of American kids who take a decade of classical piano lessons and emerge into adulthood unable to play a note. I'm often heard pontificating about this as one of America's major wasted resources – all those years of keyboard torture with nothing to show for it.

The transformative moment occurred for me when I was 13 and in the seventh grade at P.S. 6. It came at one of those early boy-girl parties, taking place in the apartment of classmate Bill Kaufmann. At one point in the evening, and without any trace of parental urging, my friend Bill – who, as far as I knew, hadn't shown any musical talent or even interest – walked over to his living room piano, sat down on the bench, and began to play. The technique was minimal, but emerging from the keys were the unmistakable strains of that year's popular song, *Near You*.

A surprising development, to be sure, but what really captured my attention was how all the little girls at the party – including the one I had my pubescent eye on – swarmed around Bill at the piano, singing the familiar words and applauding loudly when he finished. Bill took in the acclaim, then stood up and strode over to the fruit punch table, trailed by his harem of female worshippers.

I cornered Bill alone later in the evening and questioned how this musical metamorphosis had occurred. "No big deal," he replied, "I just got a guy to teach me how to play it, real simple – it's the only song I know . . . ."

I had my marching orders. Invading my piggy bank for the needed resources, I went out the next day and bought the sheet music for *Near You*. At my next regular lesson, I handed it to the teacher and told him this was what I wanted to learn. I remember his reaction – spoken in an agitated Germanic accent –something to the effect of, "No, no – you learn Mozart – not that junk!" But I persisted – spurred on by the image of Bill's smitten girl-pack – and made him teach me the song.

The result? – I was able to play *Near You,* but it sounded like third-rate Mozart! I soon realized that this mating of teacher and repertoire wouldn't work. But for the first time I found myself excited about caressing those Baldwin ivories in our living room – to play in tolerable fashion the popular songs I liked, not the classical pieces that were giving me such a hard time.

I revisited my piggy bank and bought a simple booklet on how to play popular music using just the melody line and chords, and what the chords consisted of. I also managed to obtain one of those fake books (then illegal) containing the melody lines and chords for a number of popular songs. I convinced my mother to let me give up the classical lessons by promising to pursue this alternative route assiduously, and I was off to the races. I never took another lesson – a source of pride for me as being largely self-taught. Unfortunately, it also accounts for a number of my musical weaknesses.

I played all through high school, college, the Navy and law school – not with any particular distinction, but the tunes were recognizable and served to get a group together around the piano. (Anecdotes touching on this are contained in the chapters dealing with those periods.) I was never keen on practicing, working out arrangements, fingerings, etc. – I just liked sitting down, deriving the basic information from the fake book, and pounding away.

In contrast to my son Tom – who showed real musical aptitude as a teenager, so that for him to pursue his successful musical career made a lot of sense – the gods saw to it that I didn't play any better than I did. As a result, I wasn't tempted to take up music as a career. For me, it has never been anything other than a valued avocation. This was confirmed by the candid words of a professional jazz pianist, spoken loudly to me and the audience after I performed before a large crowd at a 92nd St. Y jazz master class: "Jim, don't give up your day job."

During my lawyering years, I continued to play the piano, although the opportunities weren't plentiful. It was a real tonic, though, to be able to spend some time at the keys after a tough day at the office. Unlike a pastime such as painting (where you have to mix colors before getting started), it's so easy to swing into action on the piano – you just open the keyboard cover and you're ready to make music. I also own an electronic model, so that if the hour is late, I can muffle the sound by playing through earphones.

Speaking of my "day job," I did have one recurring piano gig at Skadden – playing carols and seasonal songs at the annual Christmas party, along with my partner and friend Greg Milmoe. A faithful core of lawyers and staff – some with fine voices – would gather round, and we'd spend a few hours running through the whole repertoire. Also, when Skadden was smaller, the firm's partners put on comical plays at retreats for which I provided the musical accompaniment – and then played in the hotel lounge for singalongs into the wee hours.

My big night came when celebrating my 55th birthday in 1989. Barbara and I had previously thrown an 85th birthday party for my uncle Milton (the father of my cousin, jazz producer Pat Philips). In return, to recognize the occasion, Pat booked a hall (actually, an upscale Chinese restaurant called Fortune Garden Pavilion that welcomed jazz artists). She introduced me to a guitarist and bassist for accompaniment – the guitarist being John Pizzarelli (son of jazz legend Bucky Pizzarelli), who has since gone on to fame in the musical world. After some practice sessions at my house, we played three sets of vocals and instrumentals at Fortune Garden that night, which I appropriately led off with Joe Bushkin's standard, *Oh, Look at Me Now*. The joint was packed with relatives, friends, and a bunch of Skadden colleagues, including senior partners Joe Flom, Peter Mullen, and Barry Garfinkel.

USA TODAY took note of the occasion with a feature story (plus photo) in its Money Section under the heading, "From Law Bar to Piano Bar." Here's how it began: "It's summertime and the livin' is easy on Wall Street. So hotshot lawyer Jim Freund, who orchestrates corporate takeovers and defenses by day, made different music Monday night . . . [making] his professional piano-playing debut at a Manhattan jazz club." And the article closed on this note: "Freund won't trade the legal bar for a piano bar. 'People might say, this lawyer can really play the piano,' he says. 'As long as I'm judged by that criteria, I'll be OK.'"

In my last decade of legal practice, I formed a singing group for public performances. We did a number of sessions at a midtown club, The Red Blazer, as the intermission entertainment for the first-rate big band swing orchestra of my Princeton friend, Stan Rubin. We also played at various senior centers and other places – including performing a medley of Irving Berlin songs (plus my narration) at the Lower East Side's venerable Educational Alliance.

As I've mentioned, my son Tom is a professional musician – a singer-songwriter who plays a number of instruments in a variety of modes. My son Erik is an accomplished amateur drummer. Although the boys have lived in a variety of locations all over the country, we've managed to get together musically from time to time. In addition to jamming in my home and on one upbeat studio recording session, we played some pleasurable gigs at major Princeton reunions and the annual "Battle of the Alumni Bands" traditionally held that weekend. I've continued entertaining at Princeton reunions – in 2019 I played at the 60th, the 65th, and my class's 63rd – and at the "Battle," where the host introduced me as the oldest person ever to participate.

Along the way, for a little variety, I learned to play two other instruments – the vibraphone and the harmonica. The metal tone plates of the vibraphone lay out in the shape of a piano keyboard, so it feels comfortable for a pianist. I had some initial help here from world-class vibist, Warren Chiasson, although I've never come close to manipulating four mallets simultaneously as he does with such aplomb. I was, however, able to make a CD album (*Duets*) which features me playing both vibes and piano in unison.

The harmonica first appealed to me decades ago when I realized you couldn't tote a piano down to the beach. It has become a prime tension-reliever for me over the years as I play it solo on beaches, in hot-tubs, or riding a ski area chair lift. When we're together, son Tom's guitar and my harmonica accompany his late night vocals. Barbara and I serenade relatives and close friends on the telephone with a vocal and harmonica rendition of "Happy Birthday" whenever their big day arrives. I'm even able to generate some singalong with it, as when I played *Dixie* for a rousing chorus of Princeton alumni on a sightseeing bus in a southern city.

* * *

Shortly after my retirement, I decided to try becoming a real jazz pianist – a calling dependent upon the ability to improvise skillfully. I invited a professional jazz pianist friend of mine to our house to give me lessons. He asked me to play something for him, and when I finished, he said, "Well, that's okay, Jim, but you need to limber up those fingers in order to make the runs that are at the heart of improvisation. So here's what you have to do." He sat down and proceeded to play a variety of scales with both hands, first steering them in the same direction and then away from each other, then in different keys and modes, increasingly swifter and more complex.

"I can't do that," I protested – realizing that not only was I incapable of it technically, but that the task would likely bore me to tears. "Well, then," he said with frosty finality, "you'll never become a real jazz pianist."

(There's an epilogue here. A few weeks later, a *New Yorker* profile on Hank Jones, a leading jazz pianist, revealed that Jones – then well into his 80's – still practiced scales for two hours every day . . . .)

Well, I didn't do it, and as a result, I can't say I'm a real jazz pianist. I do try to inject a jazz feel into my playing – I guess you could call my playing "jazzy" – and I never play a song the same way twice, often take some melodic liberties, and can "swap fours" with the bassist or drummer. Knowing my limitations, I seldom impose my more ambitious improvisations on listeners, concentrating instead on how best to present the melody and harmonic structure that the composer wrote. I would still relish being able to improvise with distinction; but I realize that unless I'm willing to devote more time and attention to it than I'm presently prepared to offer, this isn't going to happen.

* * *

I've referred at several points earlier to my belief in *sheer happenstance* and its effect on major developments in one's life. In the years subsequent to my retirement from legal practice in 1996, three such music-flavored events occurred that proved meaningful to me.

The first happened one warm night in the summer of 1997, when Barbara and I were taking a post-dinner stroll on Columbus Avenue near our home – something we rarely did. We passed by a bakery we had never entered. (Barbara doesn't eat sweets, and she exercises food-police discipline over my intake.) Much to our surprise, live sounds of jazz flowed out the front door into the street. Tantalized – why was the bakery open this late and what's with the music? – we went in.

There were no other customers at that hour, but two young men were in a corner, creating a classy duet of guitar and bass. They sounded so good that we sat down on some folding chairs arranged for the occasion, tapping our feet to the beat.

When they took a break, we went over and spoke to them. Dmitri Kolesnik and Andrei Ryabov turned out to be delightful fellows from St. Petersburg, Russia, who had come to NYC to break into the jazz scene. We told them we sometimes hosted private parties at which they could entertain, got their contact info (I don't remember them even having business cards), and said we might give them a call.

Shortly after, I was listening to some early recordings of Nat King Cole and his trio. Not everyone is aware that Cole was a marvelous jazz pianist before he became a popular crooner. While I obviously could never match his chops, this was just the kind of group sound I wanted to strive for. Nat's piano was accompanied at that time by a guitar and bass. I ruminated, and then – light bulb flashes! – I remembered Dmitri and Andrei.

Within a year, The Jim Freund Trio, featuring Andrei and Dmitri, recorded its first album and had a weekly gig at a fine Manhattan venue – the large attractive lounge of midtown's Lombardy Hotel.

Ultimately, however, I didn't find such gigs satisfying. While they sustained professional musicians who needed to put bread on the table, I already had other bread sources. I found it disconcerting to be giving my all to the music while many of the lounge's clientele were eating, drinking and conversing, with only passing attention given to the trio. I felt the need for a musical outlet that featured more interaction with the audience. It was time for a second *sheer happenstance*.

As Christmas neared, I was walking on a side street near my home – a street I had seldom traversed before. Half-way down the block, I saw a sign over a door that I'd never previously noticed – it read, "Hamilton Senior Center." I wasn't even sure what a senior center was. Were the denizens ambulatory or infirm? Did people live there or just pay visits?

Perhaps sparked by a holiday wreath on the door, a thought hit me. I had always enjoyed playing the piano to accompany friends and colleagues singing Christmas carols and seasonal popular songs. Maybe the seniors would enjoy having someone do the same for them.

I went inside and asked the person in charge if the Center had a piano ("yes") and would they like a pianist to come and help celebrate Christmas ("yes" again). I fixed a date, several people (ambulatory and quite tuneful, it turned out) showed up, and we had an enjoyable session.

From that beginning over two decades ago, I now play in all seasons about 70 free sessions of popular standard singalongs every year at Hamilton and two other Manhattan senior centers – Goddard-Riverside and JASA. I also have a regular monthly piano engagement at the American Cancer Society's residential Hope Lodge establishment. This musical activity, along with the awarding of fellowships to graduating Princeton seniors (described in Chapter 19), infuse my retirement with a very fulfilling public interest component.

Singers come in from all around the city – (one fellow even used to travel from Philadelphia) – for these senior singalongs. Some have fine voices and offer solos, a couple of them dance, and everyone sings with enthusiasm. We've made two compact disc recordings (referred to below); I churned out a documentary video about the whole senior singalong experience, and pulled together video clips to honor certain centenarian singers and others who had recently passed away; and I've recorded CD's of solo vocals by two of the group's finest singers, Norma Villafuerte and Anita Sim. The seniors give me concurrent feedback, convey affection, and let me know how important this is in their weekly lives – as it is in mine.

When I began these senior singalongs, I was the youngster in the room; now I'm one of the oldsters. I've developed a healthy respect for people who are coping with advancing age as they try to inject some joy into their everyday existence. Unfortunately, the singalongs also serve as a reminder of our mortality – a regular doesn't show up for a while, and then we get the bad news of his or her demise. Although there's a continual flow of new voices, they have yet to fill all the places of those missing in action.

* * *

What I'm proudest of musically are the 30 CD albums I've made over my 20-plus retirement years. These contain well over a thousand songs (or about 1,300 if you include duplications from album to album). Although they sound to me as if they were done in a studio, all were recorded in my living room through the magic of microphones plugged into something that's plugged into a laptop computer, operated by my talented assistant Raymond.

Most of these have been strictly piano albums.

- *Round Midnight* – 26 of my favorite ballads, from the '40s and adjacent decades, played in a quiet reflective mood.
- *34 from '34* – as my 75th birthday approached, a look back at 34 fine songs from the year of my birth.
- *Both Sides Now* – 31 songs played in slow or medium tempos from the prime musical decade of the '60s.
- *The Way We Were* – 31 sensuous songs from the romantic '70s.
- *Bring Him Home* – 28 songs from the '80s (including one written by my son Tom).
- *Autumn in New York* – my 35-track tribute to songs about the Big Apple, recorded right after 9/11.
- *The Joint is Jumpin'* – three dozen up-tempo tunes for your next party.
- *Once Upon a Time* – 29 melodious ballads from six different decades.

- *Rodgers (without Hammerstein)* – 25 ballads from *Oklahoma, Carousel, South Pacific, The King and I, Sound of Music*, etc.
- *Loewe (without Lerner)* – 39 songs from *My Fair Lady, Camelot, Brigadoon, Paint Your Wagon*, and *Gigi*.
- *In a Mellow Tone* – a two-disc, 40-song piano tribute to Duke Ellington.
- *A Salute to Ragtime* – excerpts from 39 of Scott Joplin's euphonic melodies.
- *Old Folk* – a 72-song (my age at the time) piano tribute to America's rich folk song heritage (with some harmonica cameos).
- *Wearing of the Green* – 36 authentic Irish (not American-Irish) tunes, old and new, vigorous and plaintive.
- *Carols Galore* – 58 Christmas carols.
- *Chestnuts Roasting* – 30 popular yuletide standards.

There were three special piano albums.

- *It's Three-Quarter Time* – a four disc cornucopia (192 tunes including medleys) of popular American waltzes through the years.
- *Happy Anniversary* – my piano versions (on two discs) of 50 of Barbara's favorite songs, on the occasion of our 25th anniversary.
- *Duets* – the album cover reads, "Jim on Vibes and Freund on Piano" – playing duets with myself on 17 songs from the '30s and '40s.

On two albums, I featured the combined choruses of Hamilton and Goddard-Riverside seniors (recorded at their centers), with booklets of the lyrics attached.

- *Songs of the World War I Years* – 33 songs from the years 1914-1918, sung lustily by the two choruses, with my narration interspersed.
- *Young at Heart* – two discs (one sung, the other solo piano) of 80 songs from my college years (1952-1956) for our 50th Princeton reunion.

On one of my first discs, I sang all the songs with my trio's backing.

- *When I'm 64 – m*y age back then, singing 21 upbeat songs, with great backing from Andrei Ryabov on guitar and Dmitri Kolesnik on bass.

* * *

Here's my third musical *sheer happenstance* tale. For many years I've been a regular subscriber to the annual program of the 92nd Street Y called "Lyrics and Lyricists." At each session, a narrator and a half-dozen talented professional singers pay tribute to a certain lyricist or genre or period. I have two season tickets but Barbara isn't an avid fan, so I usually invite a relative or friend to share the evening.

On this particular night, the guest was my friend Gene Young – a lovely woman (recently deceased) who knew the words to every great song written during popular music's halcyon years. At one point, a female singer I'd never heard before was singing *The Thrill is Gone*. I found her voice so compelling that it raised goose bumps.

When she finished, I turned to Gene and said, "I love the way that woman sings. I would really like to accompany her on the piano. You've got to help me. Find out her name, get her phone number, call her and make a date for us to get together."

"What?!" said Gene, incredulously – she'd never heard me speak in that vein before (and neither had I!).

"I want you to act as my intermediary so she won't think I'm up to no good. You're a woman – you can vouch for me."

Gene gave me a look like "this guy is nuts", and no more was said on the subject. But the next morning at precisely 9 a.m. (I later found out) – having discovered the singer's name (Annette Sanders) and somehow located her phone number – Gene called Annette and put the proposition to her. Within a matter of days, Annette and I had launched an enduring musical partnership.

Annette is a superb professional vocal stylist. Over the years she has performed with Benny Goodman, Lionel Hampton, Stan Getz and other greats, while recording with top jazz instrumentalists. She hits every note on the nose, keeps me relatively calm, and avoids the least vestige of diva.

In addition to becoming good friends, Annette and I have since made seven albums together, frequently accompanied on bass by Dmitri (Andrei having returned to Russia). The three of us have also been entertaining in recent years for various classes at their 60th and 65th Princeton Reunions, and a few years ago we performed a special Irving Berlin tribute at the 92nd Street Y.

Here are the albums Annette and I have made:

- *Thanks for the Memories* – my 79th birthday present to myself, 40 songs on two discs, Annette and I singing solo and in duets, and featuring my friend, retired federal judge Lee Sarokin on drums.
- *Accentuate the Positive* – 52 buoyant *glass-half-full* songs to lift spirits throughout each week of the year, reflecting my generally optimistic attitude toward life, and including *Jim's Rose-Colored Riff* which contains a rhyme for each tune title.
- *The Dream Album* – 19 songs, mostly from the Depression and World War II years, that have some variant of "dream" in the title.
- *The Passage of Time* – 23 popular standards dealing with various elements of time, and also featuring my son Tom singing James Taylor's *Secret of Life* (which is, according to James, "enjoying the passage of time.")
- *Vacillating Rhythm* – 20 songs, each of which is performed both as a ballad and in a more up-tempo style.

Annette and I also did a pair of two-disc two-name albums:

- *Play it Again, ~~Sam~~ Jim* (my piano stylings of enduring melodies) and *Long Ago and Far Away* (Annette singing 36 of the beguiling ballads of the '40s).
- *Just Friends,* consisting of *'Deed I Do* (our duets on ballads and "list" songs) and *Sensuous Scats on Timeless Tunes* (Annette's marvelous improvisations atop my three dozen keyboard ballads).

Finally, upon becoming an octogenarian, I made an effort to sum things up.

- *Jim's Retrospective at 80* – five discs of my piano and vocal favorites (129 songs in all): 1 – My vocals with the jazz trio; 2 – My duets with Annette; 3 – Rhythmic instrumentals with Dmitri and others; 4 – Solo piano on standard ballads; and 5 – Solo piano on folk and rock tunes of the '60s and '70s.

* * *

Here's a brief pianistic self evaluation. *Weaknesses*: I can't move my fingers nearly as fast as the professionals. I'm not skilled at playing tunes by ear. (If someone requests a song I don't know by heart and don't have the music handy, I may fool around with it, but I'm rarely satisfied with the result.)

I can play a song in all the keys when the music is before me (albeit somewhat less sure-handedly when the number of sharps or flats in the given key increases beyond three). But I have a problem if I'm playing a song in one key, and the singer asks me to transpose it to a lower or higher key. I could take it home with me and laboriously perform the needed transposition, but I'd make a mess of it on the spot. So I just ask the singer to make do with the key noted in the sheet music before me.

When I read from a fake book (which has just the melody line and the chords), I am in a sense improvising. I choose which notes of the chord I'll use, in what inversion, and whether played in unison or rolled – plus similar issues for the melody, such as choosing the register, the tempo, the kind of beat, single notes or chords in the right hand, etc.

What's significant to me here is that my style overcomes the aspects of classical music I rebelled at seven decades ago – the need to play a particular note at a given time with a prescribed fingering and in a fixed meter. This freedom to play the song any way I want and rarely the same way twice is very fulfilling, but it isn't the kind of improvising that jazz musicians speak about, and – as I noted earlier – that's something I haven't attained.

In recent years I've found it increasingly difficult to memorize songs. There was a time it wasn't so hard, which is why (when I have no sheet music in front of me) I tend to play the old favorites that have carved out a permanent niche in my head.

Better aspects: What I'm adept at is reading songs from a fakebook without having to check whether my fingers are doing what they're supposed to do. This distinguishes me from many amateur pianists who can play the hell out of a few songs but not much more. As long as I have the sheet music or a lead sheet, I'm able to play the songs I like and honor reasonable requests of listeners.

I pride myself on having good taste in popular and jazz standards, but I'm not up on what's been written in the last 35 years. My best efforts are swing-flavored numbers and ballads from the '30s, '40s and '50s. Although it required a shift in style to adjust my playing to rock and folk rhythms, I now enjoy playing songs on the softer side from the 60s, 70s and 80s – but little from the last three decades. I feel capable of bringing out the best in a tune – melody, chords, rhythm – and can go back and forth between ballads, swing, gentle rock, Latin, folk and ragtime.

I have endurance. Even at 85, I don't feel any discomfort in playing continuously for well over an hour without a break. I make few mistakes when recording, so we seldom have to do retakes.

I'm getting better at playing behind a vocalist (such as Annette). It calls for a certain restraint, close attention to the singer's phrasing, and using notes and chords that add to but don't interfere with what's being sung. As for my own singing, well, it's serviceable, and at least you can hear what the lyrics are meant to convey.

What I'm best at is playing for groups of people to sing along. I can generate real enthusiasm in a group, such as the ones I play for in those senior singalongs. It may not be the highest form of the art but it brings joy to the people who join in, and I find it eminently satisfying.

Finally, I do take the time and trouble and absorb the expense, of preserving and distributing my best musical moments in album form.

I'll close this section with a personal confession. I get a big ego boost out of the fact that what I do with this avocation is something that very few people I've run into (excluding professional pianists) can do. They may take photos and write essays (as I do), but they don't make music. This gives me a mental leg up that comes in handy for my psyche, especially when other things aren't going so well.

Photography

Unlike my affinity for music, which commenced at a relatively early age, my affair with photography began a lot later.

I don't remember taking photos as a youngster or in high school. I carried a primitive movie camera along on that cross-country trip in 1952 (recounted in Chapter 5), but the film quality is spotty and I have no photo images of the great sights we saw. I can't recall shooting pictures in college (which, given our hi-jinks, was probably just as well). In the Navy, I did take some snaps in the Antarctic and at New Zealand ports of call but then put my rudimentary equipment away during law school and the early years of legal practice (even, sadly, during that memorable European excursion in the summer of '59, described in Chapter 9).

I unpacked both my still and movie cameras when my kids came upon the scene in the late '60s, but the pictures were mainly of them with little attention paid to the surroundings. For several months each year, Fire Island summers whetted my appetite for surf and sand. My first real photographic impetus, though, came in the mid-'80s when Barbara and I bought our weekend house in Easton, CT.

Having grown up as a city lad, I was accustomed to a world of concrete and glass. But having a place in the country opened my eyes to the joys of nature. I became mesmerized by the trees, the foliage, the quiet lanes, the change of season, the play of light and shadow – riding my motor scooter over the back roads, seeking out fresh vistas. Each year I entered my work in a local photography contest and was encouraged through receiving several awards. Some of my pictures hung in the Easton town hall, and in 1997 I had a show of my photos at the Easton Library.

Along the way, I began to experiment with black & white film. When we made some renovations to our house in 1995, I had a darkroom installed. I spent some delightful hours there printing 8x10 black & white images, while still using commercial photo labs for larger prints and color pictures. In the fast-evolving world of computers and other advanced technology that I had difficulty confronting, my traditional darkroom exuded a workaday low-tech atmosphere – World War II equipment, old stuff chemistry, straightforward variables such as lens openings and exposure time. It became a real refuge. To emphasize these roots, I'd play Glenn Miller and Tommy Dorsey recordings on my cassette deck, while watching the prints slowly emerge from the chemical solution.

Nevertheless, my heart was still in New York City, where we lived a half block away from Central Park. We New Yorkers are lucky to have this great treasure in our midst. For cramped apartment dwellers, it's literally our own backyard. Central Park isn't a private preserve, restricted to the wealthy or a social elite, nor a tourist haven shunned by locals; rather, it beckons all to roam its pathways and enjoy the beauty of its settings. In one of the priciest cities, where most things are prohibitively costly, this one is free.

After my retirement in 1996, no matter what I'd planned for any particular day, if the morning light was sparkling and I knew there were buds on the trees or snow on the ground, I'd grab my cameras and head out to the Park for a few choice hours. I was fascinated by the blooming flora, the multiple fauna, the architecture, the waterways, the craggy rocks, the remarkable statuary. And all this played out against the kaleidoscopic background of the changing seasons – verdant spring, lush summer, colorful fall, and snowcapped winter. I saw beauty and starkness, humor and pathos, activity and quietude – a little bit of everything.

Over the years, I accumulated quite a few pictures of Central Park, and in April-May 2000 exhibited the best 225 of them in a show entitled *A Park for All Seasons*, presented by the Parks Department of the City of New York at the Arsenal Gallery adjacent to the Commissioner's office (near Fifth Avenue and 64th Street). NY1, the cable network, broadcast a special feature on the show just before the opening, and a large crowd assembled that evening – a real highlight of my retirement life.

I collected the photos from that exhibit, together with my commentary, in a book entitled *CENTRAL PARK – A Photographic Excursion* (Fordham University Press, 2001), which drew favorable comment from the then President of the Central Park Conservancy, Regina Peruggi.[*] I was thrilled to see the book featured in the window of the Barnes & Noble bookstore near Rockefeller Center during the Christmas season.

Central Park remains my favorite venue and one I enjoy sharing with others. For a number of years, through ReachOut56, we supplied disposable cameras to a group of students from Paul Robeson High School in Brooklyn,

---

[*] "There is no park quite like Central Park and there is no photographer quite like Jim Freund. Combine the two and you have a rare gem! A passionate lover of the Park, Jim Freund unveils its many secrets through his glorious photographs. His wit, wisdom, talent, keen eye and sense of wonder come through on every page. "

whom I then led on a tour of the Park. I arranged to have their films developed and printed, together with enlargements of each student's best shot. We awarded a prize in person to the overall winner, and I made a montage of the photos for the wall of the school.

In the years following the Park show and book, I broadened my scope onto the avenues and cross streets of my home borough, Manhattan, in search of new photographic subjects and locales. An exhibit *Slices of the Big Apple*, consisting of 150-plus shots in both color and black & white, was held in June 2003 at The National Arts Club near Gramercy Park. I collected the photos from that exhibit, accompanied by my commentary, into a book entitled *SLICES OF THE BIG APPLE – A Photographic Tour of the Streets of New York* (Fordham University Press, 2004), which attracted some favorable commentary from Walter Cronkite[*], Ed Koch[**] and Hal Prince.[***]

In the 16 years since *Slices*, I've continued to build on this photo experience with the welcome aid of the tremendous boom of digital cameras and the computer "darkroom." The usefulness of being at able to see what you just captured, the little card that replaces film and holds a thousand shots, the ability to shoot color and black & white with the same camera and card while adjusting the "film" speed to accommodate indoors and outdoors lighting, the improvements that can be achieved in the computer – the progress has been unbelievable.

Before we consign the past to oblivion, however, let me relive a scene I've never forgotten. Back in the pre-digital days, I was in Florence, Italy, standing with my film camera in the alleyway that runs from the Arno River to the square that features a replica of Michelangelo's statue of David. I was trying to use the alley as a frame for a view into the square that

---

[*] "Jim Freund is a superb photographer but he also is a philosopher and a humorist. In this volume – so much more than a picture book – his camera captures the images of the people of Manhattan; his commentaries explore their hearts and souls."

[**] "James Freund takes us on an absorbing photographic tour of the streets of New York. The photos and text in Slices of the Big Apple are terrific, and the book is well worth your time."

[***] "This is James Freund's love letter to New York. Like all artists, he charts the majesty of its architecture in contrast with the ironies and contradictions in the life that swarms and collides in its streets. The Big Apple is all muscle, difficult and exciting. And celebrating its poetry is no mean task. Freund has nailed the city I love – and pretend to know."

featured David, but one thing bothered me – a naked light-bulb hanging from a wire strung across the alley. If I stood way back to get the desired picture, the bulb and wire ruined the scene. If I moved up underneath the bulb, then I wasn't getting the picture I wanted. Walking backwards to find the best place, I suddenly bumped into an unnoticed man behind me – an artist with portable easel and oils, observing the same scene. He laughed and said to me in English, "*I'm* not having any problems with the light bulb and wire."

With digital you can now get rid of such pesky little objects that undercut your picture. It's very convenient, and doesn't really do violence to the main aspects of the scene. Understand, I'm not advocating the old Russian trick of deleting a deposed commissar from the photo to change historical reality. This is strictly for small stuff – like an annoying light bulb.

Remember the darkroom in our Connecticut weekend retreat? As the digital age gained traction, Barbara suggested converting the darkroom into another bathroom. I held my ground. I'd long envisioned taking grandchildren into "my place" and introducing them to the miracle of developing photographic prints.

But the last time I used the darkroom, instead of marveling at the image slowly coming to life in the pan, I found myself tapping my foot and mumbling, "This . . . is . . . taking . . . a . . . long . . . time . . . ." As for my granddaughters, they've never set foot inside the room – and if they did, instead of gazing with awe at the print taking form in the chemicals, they'd probably be saying, "Hey, Jimpa, why are you going through all that? We can do this in two minutes – and with better results – on our computers."

They would be right. I was never that proficient in the darkroom anyway; and the computer's ability to remove shadows on faces and other foreground objects, to brighten the image, to eliminate red eye (and pesky light bulb wires), to straighten the horizon, and effortlessly crop or enlarge what's vital to the picture – that's what's magical.

Still, just in case some family member has a change of heart and decides to show a little interest, I'm not giving in to Barbara's unreasonable demand to install an extra toilet.

Black & white photography has long fascinated me and was certainly heightened by my darkroom experience. Perhaps this has to do with my strong continuing interest in history (my college major), which so often harks back to a day when color photography didn't exist. Black & white also confers a certain artful gloss on a photo that color does not. A further appeal is that most amateur photographers seem absorbed in color, so my emphasis on black & white stands out by contrast.

In 2014, I made a video entitled *EIGHT HUNDRED FIFTY SHADES OF GREY – Jim's Black & White Photography Retrospective at 80* – containing my favorite black & white photos (850 of them!) of animals, cities, people and landscapes I've encountered, plus a personal narration and my piano soundtrack. I'm very proud of this one.

I followed up that video the last two years with portfolios entitled *Black & White Photos 2015-2018* and *Black & White Photos 2019* – pictures taken in New York City and a number of other U.S. venues, depicting scenic views, people, animals, structures, sports, light and shadow, family, and so on.

Just as I've sought out variety in musical and writing endeavors, I have also experimented in photography. In recent years, for instance, I've been adding a touch of color to an otherwise black & white photo. It's not so difficult to accomplish, especially with the help I receive from my valued assistant Raymond. I take the original photo in color, then make a black & white copy, and then (in Photoshop) "paint in" the underlying color to the chosen subject on the black & white copy. This works best when the spot of color calls the viewer's attention to a significant aspect of the photo. Lately, Raymond and I have been printing these in a large format, which definitely enhances the concept.

For the last decade or so, I've been assembling portfolios of my yearly pictures and sending them out to friends as part of an annual mailing of new writings, musical albums, and a calendar encircled by pint-sized color photos from the past year. One of these portfolios contained only photos taken on, and edited in, a cellphone. I'd initially been dismissive of cellphone photography, but it has certainly come into its own in terms of quality. Now you always have your camera with you when you run into a noteworthy sight; you can crop, brighten and perform other helpful edits right in the phone; and the finished product can then be emailed without delay to family and friends.

Photographs are wonderful for capturing the look of a place, or a moment in time, but it's not always easy to tell a coherent story through them. Since I like the idea of telling a story through visual images, I turned to shooting video, which also allowed me to include a narration for added depth, plus a musical soundtrack from my own recordings. I did an 80-minute DVD addendum to the *Slices* book, attempting to capture some of the sights, sounds and attractions of a vibrant New York City in action. I made a video of the 2005 exhibit in Central Park entitled "The Gates" – a sculptural display by Christo and his wife of multiple vinyl "gates" along 23 miles of pathways.

Although we haven't left the country recently, Barbara and I have traveled to some good international venues over the years, as mentioned earlier. My favorite photo trip was the South African safari we took in November 2007 – a three day visit to the Singita game preserve adjacent to Kruger National Forest. Our first (and only) time "in the bush" proved to be a terrific experience, as it seems to be for almost everyone who makes the trip. We took countless still pictures and video, and I pulled them together (with accompanying narration and an African musical soundtrack) on a 40-minute DVD of our journey. I also had three public exhibits of the enlarged photos.

I've taken photos in the many interesting U.S. locales listed earlier. The city of New Orleans had been a favorite destination of mine, so I was distressed at the damage inflicted by hurricane Katrina and the resulting floods. I paid a tourist's tribute to America's unique city in a DVD combining video and stills of pre-Katrina New Orleans, adding a soundtrack partly of my own music and other excerpts from recordings by various musicians identified with The Big Easy.

I put together both videos and portfolios of Princeton and the Class of 1956, which were distributed to classmates at major reunions. I've had exhibits of my photos in various libraries (including three public showings of Singita animal enlargements) and many of the pictures can be found on my website, **www.jimfreund.com**.

* * *

As for evaluating myself as a photographer, my skills here lag behind those in writing and piano. This is another area where I'm self-taught. When I started to get serious about taking pictures, I did read a few books on the subject which were helpful, but no one has given me formal instructions. There are undoubtedly many fine points of the craft that I've missed. For what it's worth, my technique is pretty much instinctive.

In terms of certain aspects of photography, my performance reflects both a weakness and a positive attribute. For instance, I lack the patience that a really good photographer exhibits. I find it hard to wait for the perfect shot. I seldom use a tripod unless shooting at night. But I am pretty quick at getting a decent (if not the optimum) hand-held shot, which can be important when one's time in the area of the image is limited.

Friends who observe me in action sometimes chide that I'm not enjoying the scene because I'm too busy snapping away. I respectfully disagree. I think that when I'm photographing, I scrutinize the surroundings more thoroughly than they do, and appreciate the scene even more. I also end up with a permanent record of what we both saw.

I like the horizon in my photos to be level – seeing things the way a human standing upright sees it. If I don't always achieve that in the shot, I usually fix it in the computer. I happen to consider that to be a positive trait, but gifted photographers have told me that I'm not adventuresome enough – my pictures are too static, not sufficiently angular or daring.

In photographing people, I'm aware of often failing to get as close to them as I could. For some professional lensmen, the issue of getting up close is solved only by doing just that – getting right in the subject's face with a wide angle lens – which undoubtedly introduces a sense of immediacy. I'm a little shy about doing this and, in New York especially, there's also an element of resentment or even danger involved. I tend to stand a distance away, using a telescopic zoom lens to focus in on the people – a method many experts undoubtedly deplore. Actually, though, one advantage of this technique is that the subjects, being unaware that their photo is being taken, often have more natural expressions and postures than someone reacting to a camera thrust in his or her face.

When you first look at a scene to be photographed, your eyes take in even more than a wide angle lens – with everything in focus and no differentiation between what is important to the scene and what isn't. To my mind, the key to shooting pictures is figuring out what's significant in that total picture your eye sees, and then homing in on it. In a similar vein, my favorite photographic activity on the computer is cropping, which I consider basic to good composition. The family and vacation photos I see in other people's homes are often uncropped, leaving lots of non-essential or distracting stuff in the picture. Getting rid of the dross almost always creates a better result.

I'm at my best in recording juxtapositions – especially when I shoot in New York, a jumble of a city in which innumerable disparate elements manage to co-exist. Many of my better images result when I've been able to juxtapose two (or more) of these seeming contradictions within a single frame – for instance, a stretch limo parked in front of a hot dog stand – which I then crop to eliminate distracting elements. The tone of such pictures is often ironic – the offspring of an incongruous pairing.

Sometimes the coherent story I seek can't be captured in a single photo. I've been a fan of creating photo montages, containing smaller photos of the several elements. I consider this a strength, but I've been told by some professionals that I should instead concentrate more on singling out the best picture and blowing it up larger. I can accept that critique when the photos aren't closely related; but when they are, I'm more interested in portraying the complete picture.

Summing up, I think I have a pretty good eye and adequate technique. I like the idea of not limiting myself to one thing, but rather experimenting with various aspects of photography. Perhaps best of all, I'm "out there" with the product – not like so many other capable amateurs whose photographic output lies moldering in a desk drawer or consigned to a life sentence in the owner's cellphone.

Writing

The third big challenge I've been undertaking in retirement is writing. More of my time has been spent at this than anything else, and I've actually been quite productive – penning 40 or so essays, 31 short stories, six books (including a novel and this memoir[*]), a play, a long poem, a spoken CD of my earlier essays, and a joke book – most of which have been sent out to my friends in annual compilations. Here's a recap of my retirement writing, starting with the essays.

---

[*] Two of my other books were discussed in the photo section of this chapter, one in the discussion of mediation in Chapter 20, and one collection of short stories and commentary under "Fiction" in this chapter. My dozen books divide neatly into six written while I was busy lawyering and six during retirement.

About 10 of the essays are professional in nature, appearing in various periodicals such as *The Business Lawyer*. Several were reflections on my former M&A practice – including my *Ten Commandments for Negotiating Deals* – but most related to mediation, my primary professional activity during retirement. I explored how to handle a mediation that contained both deal and dispute aspects, focused on mediations involving more than two parties, encouraged deal lawyers to get more involved in resolving disputes, summarized my distinctive approach (as a former corporate dealmaker) to resolving dollar disputes, predicted the odds of whether particular mediated cases will settle, and compared mediating commercial disputes to the much more challenging attempts to settle global conflicts.

A half-dozen essays addressed serious non-professional topics of a more general nature:

- *Putting in a Good Word for Compromise* was aimed at countering the extremists in our public life who have lately been making so much noise and taking such all-or-nothing positions;
- *Good Judgment* explored this quality, making an effort to understand why otherwise intelligent people often exhibit poor judgment, and offering a few tips to improve decision-making.
- *The Sensitivity Valve and the Ambiguity Filter* was an attempt to deal, first, with verbal slip-ups that can be harmful, and second, with oral ambiguities from which inaccurate inferences are often drawn.
- *The Case of the Triple Duty Boat* cautioned that when we aim at doing something designed to appeal to a number of varied constituencies, it may well flunk on all fronts.
- *Sheer Happenstance* explored the voluntary decisions we make in life (some of which have been reported in prior chapters), which propel us in directions leading to relationships and outcomes that wouldn't occur without those choices, but can make all the difference in terms of our future years.
- We oldsters all have our *Senior Moments*, but the question I researched and then explored was how concerned we should be about this, given the increased incidence of dementia that affects so many of our friends and acquaintances.

The other essay topic I've been writing a lot about in retirement relates to retirement itself. My first such venture was the piece in *Business Law Today* that I included in Chapter 17 – *A Time to Reap . . . . A dozen surefire signs that you're ready to retire*. I followed this up nine years later with a piece called *A Retirement Scorecard*, which dealt with how to spend one's time after you've taken the step.

I wrote a series of essays in *Business Law Today* dealing with such subjects as a lawyer's ego, the refuge of age, hurdling the credibility gap in negotiations, acting as a part-time professor in law school, and an eye-opening experience at a tennis "fantasy" camp featuring legends of the game. Then in 2015 I circulated a compilation of eight essays (the *Octogenarian Octet*), which included:

- *An Ex-Navigator's Lament* for items that used to be readily available but are in scant supply nowadays.
- *Tales with a Kicker*, designed to make your advice to others more trenchant.
- *Dastardly Decibels*, the curse of dining out in Manhattan.
- *Pure Fiction*, detailing the tribulations of writing a short story.
- *Sins of Omission*, the everyday annoying stuff you forget (or deign) to accomplish.
- *Playing Favorites*, the lingering effects of my childhood compulsion to identify personal preferences.
- *Bite-Size Wisdom*, morsels of useful advice culled from the prolific pen of a man named H. Jackson Brown, Jr.
- *Sheer Happenstance Revisited*, an updated look at the voluntary decisions we make and actions we take that can lead to meaningful relationships and outcomes.

I wrote a number of essays celebrating the passage of time:

- For my 50th college reunion, I focused successively on health, wives, retirement, pro bono give-backs, wise/smart, assumptions, risk-reward, resolving disputes, self-esteem and the ages of man.
- Turning 75, which dealt with the big plus/big minus of three score and fifteen, plus retirement activities (notably, "the challenge"), and salutes to my amazing wife and mother.
- Turning 80, which had major segments on mortality and health before examining retirement, the elusive tummy diet, and what lies ahead.

- Our 60th Princeton reunion, which frankly had more octogenarian negatives then positive stuff.
- *The 65th Horace Mann Reunion Lament: What the hell are we callow high school lads doing here at this venerable juncture?* contained more of the same.
- *85 and Counting* . . . – the essence of which can be found in Chapter 21.

In addition, there was a multi-disc audio CD, in which I read favorite essays of mine that I'd written in the early '80s.

I encourage readers – especially those retired – to try writing essays on topics that excite your interest. For those who might undertake this task, let me pass along a few thoughts about my own approach, which may prove helpful.

I'm a great believer in the adage that the key to good writing is rewriting. For my money, you can only achieve the necessary specificity, root out redundancy and ambiguity, and concentrate on what's truly significant after several go-arounds.

My first step in writing an essay is to think through its structure in general terms, recognizing that this is subject to change as content is added. What I like to do next is to get bits and pieces of my thoughts on the subject down on paper (usually handwritten). For me, these morsels become more productive (in the sense of leading to other thoughts) and more malleable into a coherent whole when reduced to writing, rather than remaining stored away in the crevices of my mind.

I find the key at this stage is *not* to refine what is said, *not* to struggle to find the best word – in some cases, *not* even to worry about completing sentences. I don't concern myself with paragraph structure; I don't worry about the order in which the thoughts tumble out. If along the way I recognize that elaboration will ultimately be necessary, or an example would be appropriate, then I'll simply put down ["elaborate"] or ["give example."] All I'm interested in at this point is getting the thoughts down in front of me in a typed transcript, where they can be worked into something meaningful.

When this has been typed (not by me!) in double-spaced mode, I revise it, concentrating on structure, order and overall design. Then I take the retyped revised version (again double-spaced) and hone in on the *substance* of what I've written, probing deeper this time – looking for nuances, analogies, additions to (and often deletions from) what I've said – so that when I've completed this step, everything I want to say about the subject is down on paper, and in the order I want to say it.

It's only when this has been completed that I feel ready to do the necessary polishing (of the final double-spaced draft) to achieve effective prose – eliminating ambiguities, sharpening the wording, assessing the grammar, injecting some humor, substituting better words for those previously used, etc. So, as you can see, each step has its own purpose and priorities, each one building on the step before . . . . And now, finally, it can be single-spaced.

Fiction

I take some pride in the fiction I've written in retirement, inasmuch as I'd never done anything previously in that genre.

My principal fictional milieu has been short stories – a format I've come to feel comfortable in pursuing. At the outset, I wrote about the subject I knew best – lawyers. Still, I tried hard to focus on issues readily accessible to non-lawyers – especially those with a foot in the business world – and took pains not to let a lot of "law" intrude on the action.

My major short story achievement is the book *SMELL TEST – Stories and Advice on Lawyering,* published in 2008 by the American Bar Association. It consists of ten short stories about lawyers, in which much of the lawyering involved was praiseworthy, a portion was questionable, and some of it stunk. So I wrote a commentary to each story, aimed at focusing readers on the actions taken, decisions made, and rationalizations offered by the fictional attorneys. "How'd they do?" – that's the recurring question I posed to readers in these commentaries, before offering my own views on both the specific instance and broader related issues. The book was very well-received.[*]

---

[*] "Only a lawyer of Jim's wide experience, great judgment and keen sense for avoiding problems could write this book. Only a person with Jim's sense of humor and story-telling skills could combine fiction and practical advice into the compelling "read" that is *Smell Test*." (Martin Lipton, one of the nation's top lawyers). "*Smell Test* is a masterful achievement that should be read by lawyers, young and old." (Former Federal District Court Judge Vaughn Walker) "Leave it to Jim Freund to both entertain and educate us through a series of amazingly realistic short stories that illustrate the challenges confronting deal lawyers." (Well-known lawyer, Franci Blassberg) "This is a hugely entertaining and enlightening collection that will appeal not only to lawyers but to the general reading public as well." (leading short story author, Bruce Jay Friedman).

The topics explored in these stories arise from a variety of conflict-prone relationships. In some cases, there's an ethical issue at the core – a law firm deciding whether or not to take on questionable business (*The Smell Test*), a lawyer who discovers he may be sponsoring false testimony (*You Gotta Get Me Off!*), an attorney directed by his client to perform a distasteful action that raises ethical questions   (*The Reluctant Eulogist*). Wrestling with the implications of telling the truth is a recurrent theme – most notably in *Partnergate* (vis-à-vis one's partners) and *Sex, Lies and Private Eyes* (in dealing with a client).

The lawyer-client relationship also abounds with other issues, such as the client who doesn't level with his own lawyer (*On-the-Job Training*), and the lawyer who has the misfortune to see a client at his worst (*The Corollary Axiom*). In *Negotiating 101* this relationship is viewed from the vantage point of a client under pressure, who is concerned with the soundness of the lawyer's advice he's receiving.

Partners in a law firm can sometimes find themselves at cross-purposes with their colleagues over issues like taking on new business (*The Smell Test* and *On-the-Job Training*) and making new partners (*Partnergate*), while intergenerational tensions can undermine collegiality (*The Reluctant Eulogist* and *The Smell Test*). Partner-associate relations may also become strained, as detailed in *Awash in Associates*, *Partnergate*, and *Sex, Lies, and Private Eyes*.

The subject of negotiating deals takes center stage in *Negotiating 101, Awash in Associates, and On-the-Job Training*. Family connections that impinge on legal practice are explored in *The Smell Test* and *The Corollary Axiom* (spouses), and in *Father's Day* (parent-child).

Following that experience, I was intrigued by the idea of grouping several short stories around a common issue, which I then applied to stories about seniors, photography, tennis and high tech.

I called the grouping about seniors *DEFYING DOTAGE – Six Short Stories Starring Sprightly Seniors*. It consisted of:

- *Assisted Living*, in which romance flourishes in a senior setting, although having to overcome some obstacles not faced by younger swains;

- In *The Fab Four*, a fantasy buddy caper, a quartet of oldsters pool talents to demonstrate their ingenuity, while engaging in some geezer high jinks in pursuit of a shared goal.
- In *Three Beeps Redux*, a bed-ridden old-timer regales his great-grandsons with a stirring tale from his earlier days, while pondering whether to include a certain troubling aspect.
- *Four Hours* is a humorous take on a risqué subject, as this randy oldster copes imaginatively with an unforeseen affliction.
- In *Marital Maneuvers,* husband and wife each try out a variety of gambits to make the other over in the prankster's image, while kindling the curse of unintended consequences.
- The ninety-plus narrator of *Nonagenarian Musings* attempts to cope on his own with both a serious medical condition and a plethora of personal and family demons that tend to impair his judgment.

Then there was *SNAPSHOTS – A Quartet of Short Stories with Photography Themes*, which included four photographers who run into troubles stemming from:

- An effort to influence viewers' reactions to his framed photo (*Perseverance*);
- Attempting to squeeze two incongruous images into a single frame (*Gotcha!*);
- Submitting a composite photo in a contest that disallows such entries (*Just Tinkering*); and
- Depicting a resilient older woman as weak and pathetic. (*A Photographic Eye*).

Next, I turned to *TENNIS ANYONE? – Three Short Stories That Feature the Net Game . . . and Illustrate The Adage," Be Careful What You Wish For."* To wit:

- In *Singles*, the issue is how to deal with a player who consciously makes bad line calls to help himself win;
- In *Doubles*, the issue is how to handle one member of a long-time foursome whose game has badly deteriorated in recent years;
- In *Mixed Doubles,* the issue is a romance that develops between a married man and the single woman on the other side of the net.

More recently, *THREE FLIGHTS OF HIGH-TECH FANCY* had me peering into three different fantasy futures:

- *GPS With a Twist* features a navigational aid that offers some unique routes to take, which lead to surprising outcomes;
- *Home Movies on Demand* spotlights the means to revisit moments from one's distant past, plus a special aspect; and
- *Iris in Bloom* introduces a cellphone that provides glimpses into the mindsets of friends, colleagues, and adversaries.

Three other short stories, otherwise unrelated, all probe the grandfather-grandson relationship:

- In *But The Melody Lingers On*, the grandfather makes a deathbed confession to his grandson about a dishonest transaction he was involved in, causing an unusual effect on the grandson;
- In *Blue Moon*, a humorless daughter-in-law comes between the grandfather and his adored grandson, which calls for some strategic responses on the old man's part; and
- In *The Name of the [Blasin]Game*, the grandson is called upon to deal with his accounting firm's attempt to remove the name of his retired grandfather from the firm's title.

The final two short stories share a quality of unreality that appeals to me.

- *Is There A Lawyer in the House?* is a Walter Mitty-esque adventure, where things go awry in an unexpected fashion.
- *Fortune Cookie* – the first story I wrote and my favorite of them all – explores the magic of communications emanating from a dessert confection, as filtered through the brain of an otherwise realistic lawyer, leading to some high-stakes consequences.

In 2012 I wrote something a little different – a one-act play titled *Montana Murder Mystery* – which represented my initiation to both the drama format and the mystery genre. A young woman is murdered in a western ski resort, her sister undertakes the principal detective work, a fierce killer is on the loose – and it wraps up in a way that should (I hope) surprise most readers.

In 2017 I self-published a novel titled *THREE'S A CROWD*. It was a real challenge, and occupied a lot of my time over portions of three years. It received some generous written reaction on its back cover and on my Amazon page.[*]

To give you a taste of the plot, here's the "ad copy" I wrote to accompany its slot on Amazon:

"During ten eventful days in March 1996, the myriad problems that engulf New York lawyer Ben Fletcher ("Fletch") all seem to come in triads
.

- *He's attempting to mediate a compromise to a bitter dispute among three self-righteous antagonists, none of whom is giving an inch – and with reason to believe that failure to break the deadlock will jeopardize Fletch's future.*
- *He's on the verge of being ousted from his law firm partnership by a trio of senior partners who don't have Fletch's best interests at heart.*
- *He's beset by a triplet of family problems that greatly add to the professional pressure he's experiencing – a mother suffering from dementia, a ne'er-do-well brother pressing him for money, and a daughter on the verge of linking up with a man Fletch deems unworthy of her.*

"What exacerbates his situation is that Fletch can sometimes be his own worst enemy – with an unruly temper, an inability to cope with pressure and handle criticism, and too many moments when he exercises poor judgment.

"On the plus side, Fletch is fortunate to have a triad of supportive allies – a thoughtful wife he sometimes doesn't deserve, a female law partner who has his back, and a wise buddy who provides useful advice.

---

[*] "Fascinating and helpful insights into the complexities of negotiation and strategies to reach an acceptable settlement" / "I highly recommend Three's A Crowd. It's both educational and entertaining" / "Freund did a fantastic job of keeping me in the know, on top of the story until the end." / "One of the country's best-known negotiators comes up with an entertaining thriller I could not put down" / "An endearing, fascinating and beautifully written story."

"In this exciting and sophisticated legal thriller, Three's a Crowd guides the reader through this flawed lawyer's gradual awakening to his shortcomings. But will it be in time to resolve the thorny and fascinating mediation dispute, maintain his partnership, and cope with the family difficulties?"

Writing the novel was a real challenge, both to the intellect and to the imagination. There were moments I regretted having taken on this kind of weighty assignment (although not strongly enough to give it up). There were also moments of real excitement at having solved a structural problem or inserted some good words in a character's mouth. The freedom of having complete control of the subject matter was exhilarating, but it led to the problem of where to stop – you can always think of another way things might be handled. As Nell Scovell put it (in *Just the Funny Parts*), "When I write, I feel like an optometrist, flipping between lenses and asking, 'Is this better? Is this?' " Anyway, at 85-plus, I doubt I'll take on another novel, but I'm glad I completed at least one.

* * *

Here's my brief evaluation of myself as a writer. I'm well-pleased with the professional books I've written, which I consider right up there with the best instructional books written for lawyers, negotiators and mediators. My essays are in general very good – not world class, such as those by E.B. White and Charles Krauthammer, but usually pithy and entertaining, dealing with interesting topics, and containing some fresh thoughts on a variety of subjects. I also think highly of my audio reading of the earlier essays.

My fiction is a cut below – interesting, I hope, but not compelling. I have some real shortcomings – not going deep enough into character, dialogue that is sometimes stilted, failure to provide good descriptions of people, their characteristics, and the settings. But I'll settle here for my fiction being "a good read," and I'm pleased that my friends seem to have enjoyed the stories and the novel.

I do like the fact that taking up fiction demonstrates my versatility – not only writing short stories but also a novel and a play, alternating between realistic and fanciful situations, weaving instructional material (such as about mediation) into the story, and coming up with various plots that contain drama, comedy, romance, a little sex, and lots of family.

* * *

426

Just in case anyone might be interested in my personal tastes regarding the professional worlds of music, photography, and writing, here's a partial listing.

First, music. On the piano, I like to listen to Teddy Wilson from back in the '30s, Nat King Cole through the '40s, and Oscar Peterson from the '50s onward. Two saxophonists top my instrumental list – Paul Desmond on alto and Lester Young on tenor. On the vibes, there's my mentor, Warren Chiasson, and on bass, my invaluable rhythm section, Dmitri Kolesnik. I'm partial to many female vocalists, such as Lee Wiley from the old days and Judy Collins of more recent vintage, but my recording buddy, Annette Sanders, now tops my list. The male vocalist I listen to most is Frank Sinatra. One of my favorite recordings is by the vocal duo of Sarah Vaughan and Billy Eckstine singing the melodies of Irving Berlin. As for big bands, none of them compares with Count Basie and Duke Ellington. My choice composer of popular standards is Jimmy Van Heusen. Among singer-songwriters, while I have real regard for Paul Simon, James Taylor, John Prine, Tom Paxton and John Denver, the guy I listen to most today is my son, Tom Freund.

I'm much less involved with top photographers, although there are some whose work I find notable. With landscapes, for instance, Ansel Adams is still the touchstone. Among the leading (post-Matthew Brady) war photographers are Robert Capa, Margaret Bourke-White and James Nachtwey. For street scenes and human interest, there are those "decisive moments" of Henri Cartier-Bresson, plus fine work by W. Eugene Smith and NYC's own Boogie. As for photos of musicians, I've looked to Jim Marshall, who did the shots on my son Tom's first album (and also took a fabulous snap of Tom and me playing a bass-piano duet).

Turning to writing, I consider Peter Baker of The New York Times the top current journalist. The essayists I favor are E.B. White and Charles Krauthammer. I enjoy the non-fiction of William Manchester; the poetry of Ogden Nash, the fiction of Bernard Malamud and Philip Roth, and my favorite detective is Harry Bosch from Michael Connelly novels.

My runaway favorite author of fiction, both short stories and novels, is Bruce Jay Friedman, who sadly passed away just weeks ago. I became friendly with Bruce in recent decades, and he's the one writer I return to over and over – rereading much of his work (and recently devouring his play *Steambath* for what seemed the tenth time). I'm well aware of how tough it is to write humorous prose, but he always made it seem easy.

I invariably break out in a grin – and often laugh out loud – at his outrageous humor, offbeat plots, and politically/socially incorrect observations. But underlying the comedic touches lies a core of solid insights into people, especially their foibles and follies. Bruce was a singular voice – someone I'll sorely miss.

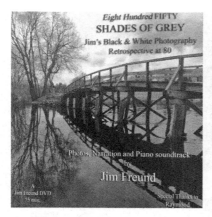

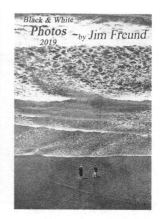

I've bcome fascinated with black & white photography during retirement. (Top) I made a DVD of my best b&w work in 2014, following it up with portfolios covering 2015-2018 and 2019. Here are a half-dozen of my favorite b&w shots.

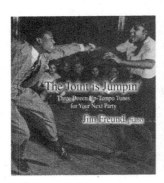  

Here are the front covers of a dozen of the 30 CD albums I've made in retirement.

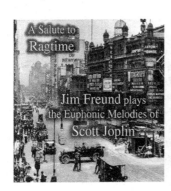  

These are eight covers (seven from the pen of the very talented Joe Azar) that adorned my writings in recent years. The top three are fictional short stories. *Montana Murder Mystery* is a one-act play. My joke book is just that. The bottom three are essays, including one that's age-appropriate and another that takes a comical/serious look at our increasing senior moments.

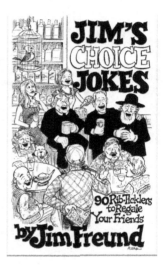

431

The Jim Freund Trio featuring Annette Sanders and Dmitri Kolesnik; and Annette with Tom, Erik and me playing at Princeton reunions. The singalong group at Hamilton (plus my Mom next to me) a number of years ago. The annual Xmas caroling session at Goddard Riverside – reaching out to aging occupants of the building.

(Above) the poster for the exhibit of my Central Park photos, held at the Park headquarters in the Arsenal building with a fine turnout for the opening. (Right) poster for the showing of my NYC photos, held at the National Arts Club. (Below) covers of the books that resulted from the two shows. (Bottom right) Barbara and I at the 2017 book party for my novel THREE'S A CROWD.

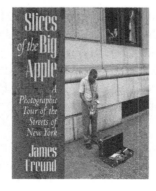

21. RETIREMENT (#3) – THE VIEW AT AGE 85

85! – and I ask myself: What the hell is this erstwhile callow lad doing here at this venerable juncture?

Well, I reply, better to be an old codger than the alternative . . . . Anyway, here are some ruminations on what it feels like to hit the big 8-5.

First, let me try to put this in perspective. In 1934 (the year I was born) someone 85 would have been born in 1849. Remember 1849? – the height of the California gold rush – when Zachary Taylor succeeded James Polk as President and Dolley Madison (who had been born in 1768) died.

Attitude

Much can be said about this situation that probably comes off as sounding dark (and I confess in advance to a few downbeat tones in this chapter). Still, I'll begin with the one indisputable plus for me and others of us arriving at this particular milestone: WE MADE IT! The painful reality that a growing number of our brethren haven't made the cut reinforces our achievement.

If you don't consider this a feat to celebrate, I bet you haven't looked recently at what the Old Testament has to say on the subject. It starts out very matter-of- factly – "The days of our years are three-score years and ten." That, for non-math majors, comes to 70. Then the prophets appear to throw the elderly a bone: "or even by reason of strength four-score years" (that gets us to 80) – but then it's quickly snatched away with this bleak caveat: "yet is their pride but travail and vanity; for it is speedily gone, and we fly away."

Not me, baby! Sure, those of us at this juncture may have encountered some of that travail – as Bette Davis remarked, "Old age ain't for sissies" – but at 85, we still retain our pride . . . . The sense of satisfaction (not of vanity) we ought to feel at having survived sometimes gets obscured when we wallow in the downsides of aging. But we should not let it diminish what we've accomplished.

For another view, check in with Shakespeare and his seven ages of man (from the "All the world's a stage" soliloquy in *As You Like It*). I'd like to think that at 85 we're hanging on to the end of the fifth age ("the justice, in fair round belly with good capon lined. . . full of wise saws and modern instances"). But I'm afraid that, in the Bard's mind, we've eased into the "slippered pantaloon" of the sixth age, whose youthful hose is much too wide for a "shrunk shank." (I refuse to even acknowledge the seventh age – "second childishness. . . sans everything.")

In an upbeat piece I wrote upon turning 50, there's one segment I'd like to retract – my comparison of a man's age to the calendar months. I had June down for the good stuff that comes in your 30's, I awarded the prime month of August to the 50's, and so on. I'm ashamed to say, however, that I coupled the early 70's to November – a month to which, back then, I ascribed a "penultimate feeling" (when, in the songwriter's words, "the days dwindle down to a precious few"). I then compounded the insult by comparing 75 with December – "the final chapter," I called it, although with the throwaway caveat that "there may be plenty of good times to come." I didn't even mention 80, to say nothing of 85.

Hey, Mr. Freund-at-50, I don't feel a bit penultimate today. If I could go back, I'd renegotiate the month allocation with my younger self – asking for the 80's to be October, although probably accepting November by way of compromise.

I walk around nowadays wearing a black baseball cap that bears the letters "ndy" on its front. "What does that mean?" people ask. Whereupon I flip the cap around to display these dauntless words on the rear: "Not Done Yet". To say nothing of the sanguine implication contained in the title I selected for this memoir . . . .

However you slice it, though, there's one indisputable minus to reaching this survival plateau, namely: PSYCHOLOGICALLY, IT SUCKS! How did I get to be this old? Where did the years go?

Mortality

For me, the biggest difference between achieving octogenarian status over five years ago and prior milestone birthdays was summed up in a quote from Gloria Steinem (a contemporary) that I saw at the time – something along the lines of, "80 isn't about aging; it's about mortality."

435

Ugh! But much as I try to disregard such commentary, it's a reality that hovers out there, refusing to be ignored – even when I'm feeling full of beans.

I think a college classmate of mine put it best. Several years ago, our class lost three prominent members in the span of about a month. Standing outside the church after the service for the third one, I asked my classmate, "What's your take on all this – what does it mean for the rest of us?" His answer was prompt and very much to the point: "Well, we may not be in the batter's box, but we're sure as hell on deck."

It's not just the quantity of the losses, but the quality too. A few years ago I had the sad task of delivering a eulogy (something I do nowadays with increasing frequency) at the funeral of Bill Silver, a life-long friend. We'd been together in the fourth grade, and he'd become an integral part of our family over the years. Nowadays we often find ourselves bemoaning his loss – especially when something comes up that we know he'd have been fascinated by, or some question arises that he (with his encyclopedic knowledge) could have answered in a flash.

It's also about losing shared memories. Each of us has many vivid recollections from prior years of events that were shared with just one person who was also present; and when he or she goes, so does the sharing – and perhaps, ultimately, the memories. I became most aware of this when my first wife, Barbro, passed away several years ago. The tensions of our divorce had softened into an amicable relationship; we met for lunch periodically, where we had begun to share some pleasant memories that only we two could recall. Now, I have to revisit these past times on my own.

I try to deal constructively with the passing of others. For instance, I come in touch with mortality all too often at the three senior citizen centers where I play piano for weekly or monthly singalongs. From time to time, one of the regulars doesn't show up for a while, soon followed by the sad news of his or her passing.

Mortality, however pertinent, is a topic I find quite difficult to deal with. Relevant issues like whether or not to pull the plug, or burial vs. cremation, or what comes after, are just not my cup of tea. I'm roughly in the same camp as my son Tom was at age 12 when I asked him how he was doing in terms of his spiritual education in Sunday School. "Dad," he said, "when they start to talk about those things, I've just got to get up and walk around."

My friend from Horace Mann and that post-graduation cross-country trip, Paul Margulies, believed in reincarnation and told me several years ago that he was actually "looking forward" to his passing – which sadly occurred too soon thereafter. It seemed like an enviable way to approach the subject, and I'm also sure many readers find comfort in the teachings of their religion. For me, though, so far it's still a matter of getting up and walking around – I've obviously got some work to do here.

Meanwhile, buoyed by the fact that my mother, Marcy Freund, lived to 105, I like to put off having to deal with any morbid stuff by asserting, "Hey, I've got 20-plus good ones left in the genes" – ignoring my father's untimely demise at 67. I'm poised to arrive at the 86 average of their two lifetimes on my next birthday, but I am sticking with my mother on this score.

I did find myself treating 80-plus as a sufficient milestone to pull together some of the things I've been doing over decades past, as I mentioned in Chapter 20. I made a five-disc CD of the best recordings I'd done in prior years. I made a DVD of 850 of my favorite black & white photos. I collected all my articles and stories for publication in two books in the near future. And finally, not really knowing what lies ahead and wanting to get the job done while I still have all my marbles, I decided to write this memoir about *The First 85* . . .

* * *

A recurring issue as the years pass – but with extra resonance over 80 – is whether or not to reveal one's age to others. Attitudes on this range across the spectrum – from those who don't give an inch ("It's none of their goddamn business") to those who flaunt their longevity for all to see. Or a third way, courtesy of Lucille Ball: "The secret of staying young is to live honestly, eat slowly, and lie about your age." And see Chapter 3 for my mother's evolving take on the subject.

I'm not embarrassed to say that I've been volunteering the information to my friends and acquaintances. (I am not, however, stopping strangers on the street to report the news.) As for why I'm doing this, I suppose it's that I'm proud to be belying my age by engaging in various activities associated with younger men.

In terms of the reactions I receive, everyone purports to be overcome with disbelief. "You, 85? No way!" After I verify the number, they say something like, "Well, haven't you heard? – 85 is the new 65." I'm flattered by these responses but realize they may stem less from genuine surprise than diplomatic nicety – mindful of Washington Irving's wisdom here: "Whenever a man's friends begin to compliment him about looking young, he may be sure they think he is getting old." (If I had any doubt that everyone already knows my age, it was dispelled when the phone rang recently and a voice greeted me with, "Hello – you've been selected to receive a medical alert device. . . .")

Although signs at airport security assure me that at my age I'm entitled to keep on my shoes when passing through the checkpoint, I often take them off and deposit the pair in a bin for x-ray inspection. I tell myself that the reason for this is that if I were to be questioned about my footwear, the I.D. containing my proof of age would still be wending its way through the x-ray machine. But I suspect the real reason, deep down, is that I resent the implication of the age exception – namely, that someone of my advanced years is too old to be dangerous.

Health

As outgoing alumni president of my Princeton class, I wrote a piece for our 25th Reunion book containing my personal ten commandments – a variety of lessons of adulthood that I wish someone had offered me at graduation. Twenty- five years later, in writing an essay for the class's 50th Reunion book, the first topic I turned to was health – after noting that it was a subject I didn't even allude to once in the 25th book. But for the 50th – with most of us having entered our 70's – times had definitely changed. "With age," I wrote, "you gain a true appreciation of the importance of good health. . . . Everything else – money, status, whatever – takes a back seat."

This is certainly true in spades now in our mid-80's. It's dangerous to start a conversation with a contemporary by using the standard greeting of, "How ya doin'?" It used to evoke a "Fine – how're you?" response, at which point the two of you could get down to business. Nowadays however, it can lead to an interminable medical/therapy interlude. Ditto for the invariable exchange of bodily info during the initial 15 minutes of a dinner out with senior friends, which one wag dubbed "the organ recital."

Unfortunately, much of how we deal with life after reaching 80 has to do with the issue of health – an unsurprising observation perhaps, but one that was brought home to me with some force when I was on the verge of octogenarian status.

In January 2014, I felt on top of the world, exuding lots of energy. My contemporaries may have been ailing in various respects, but I was full of physical vigor, still skiing and playing a lot of tennis. For many years I had been diligently trained several days each week under the expert guidance of Eric Ludlow and Val Kacik, who had managed to keep me in reasonably good shape. Whenever trouble beckoned, I turned for helpful support to my effective physical therapist, Lior Cohen. My attitude toward the impending eight-o was really quite positive.

Barbara and I had scheduled our annual ski trip for early March and were looking forward to it. Envisioning long days ahead on the hills, I decided that my quads could use a little strengthening. So one unsupervised day in February I got on two machines I'd never used before at the gym – the kind where your legs push and lift against resistance.

Big mistake. . . . By the next day, my lower back had gone into spasm, the pain shooting down through the buttocks to my left leg. I had to use a cane to get around and was in such discomfort I could barely sleep.

I went to have an MRI. (It was done, by the way, at a so-called "stand-up" MRI facility – although in fact I was seated – which is much better for those of us subject to claustrophobia than the lying down variety.) It showed all the historical disc bulges, spinal stenosis and scoliosis that, like locusts, make a painful reappearance every 17 years or so, when I do something stupid like get on those unforgiving machines.

(I must pause here to voice a complaint against the terminology used by doctors. If there's one phrase I hate, it's that I have a "degenerative" disease. It sounds to me like an indictment – the depraved patient having committed some immoral act that goes much deeper than a merely aggravated physical condition. . . .)

Anyway, I went into physical therapy, chugged some pills stronger than Advil, and gradually recovered. We had to cancel the ski trip – it was the first winter we missed – and I stayed off the tennis courts for several months. But after a while I became free of pain, pretty mobile and sleeping well – hopeful that the problem would go underground for at least another decade.

But here's what I took away from the experience. Not only was my mobility affected while ailing, but I found it hard to sustain all the non-physical activities I'd been doing. My prime focus was on getting into as comfortable a position as possible, which interfered with trying to write, take photos, or play the piano. With discomfort rampant, I realized anew that once we hit 80 good health is the most essential of all positive attributes.

My back problem doesn't compare in seriousness to the ailments that so many of my contemporaries have suffered – strokes, heart attacks, cancer, spine surgery, joints that need replacement, the onset of dementia, and so on. But even though I put it behind me, it produced an increased self-awareness of the fragility of my ongoing physical well-being. The prideful hubris of the prior January had departed; I was painfully aware that a medical episode can rise up and bite you any day. And questions arise, such as how hard should I run for that ball my tennis opponent has angled toward the sideline? Health trumps all – which is probably why it's the dominant topic of conversation when we fellow geezers get together.

Not much later, shortly before embarking on a much-anticipated trip to the West Coast, I twisted my left knee during a routine tennis outing. It swelled up, producing weakness and a reduced range of motion. I found myself shuffling along and dependent on a cane. Still, I was determined to proceed with my planned excursion and did so.

Bottom line, it worked out all right, but I had trouble adjusting to the role of a partial invalid. Everything appeared more complicated and time-consuming than usual – I seemed to be operating in slow motion. Staircases were a problem, uphill climbs a real chore.

What most fascinated me was how much I came to resemble an old-fashioned 80-year old (you know, the kind that existed before 80 became the new 60). When you shuffle along tapping a cane, people feel sorry for you. They get out of your way, they encourage you to "go first", they offer you their seat – and if you should chance to drop something, they jump in and pick it up. I couldn't recall having experienced this type of thing previously and found it somewhat off-putting. *Don't they know that I'm really a splendid physical specimen with only a minor temporary patella problem?* When anyone who knew me asked what was up – and in some cases, even before they inquired – I was quick to implicate tennis as the culprit. I guess this was my way of underlining how fit I *usually* was and implying I'd soon be that way again.

I can't deny, though, that my cane caper led to perks and prerogatives that were not to be sneezed at. The best moments took place at the airports, where I was whisked in a wheelchair from curbside check-in to the departure gate – including a go-to-the-front-of-the-endless-line shortcut through security. At first, I wondered whether the authorities might be suspicious that I was faking it – the cane being just a useful prop to justify riding in style. But no – and here's where being over 80 and looking the part came in handy – my bona fides were never questioned. I'll always remember the stout lady across the plane's aisle who, without my even asking, offered to lift my heavy carry-on bag into the overhead rack – an offer, I'm ashamed to say, I gratefully accepted without hesitation.

On my most recent solo airline foray, I wasn't tapping a cane, but people just seemed to know when I needed help. The escalator wasn't working; I would have to lug a heavy carry-on bag down a long flight of stairs; presto! my savior materialized, hoisted the bag and deposited it at the foot of the stairs. I must look old and helpless for that to happen. I'm glad people are helping, but it's a bit of a shock to the system that I appear so vulnerable.

Here's what I can't help noticing at 85. It's tougher walking any extended distance, or at any speed faster than sluggish. It's even tough standing in one place for a long time, as at a cocktail party. Your body wants to slope forward – it's real work to keep it upright. And getting out of the back seat of a NYC taxi is pure torture.

Still, in the last few years, I rate my health as good. I did have a recent hernia operation which was done laparoscopically with minimal disruption and no negative after-effects. I realize each day is a potential challenge, so I'm not relaxing about it. I have, however, developed a simple defense mechanism. When something bothers me, I try to make it pale into insignificance by comparing it to the much greater problems that many contemporary friends are going through.

As my buddy Fred Bacher puts it (with respect to finances, but equally applicable to health), it's not how much you've lost – it's how much you have left. I also like this take on the subject by Bob Mack, a friend and contemporary: "I'm glad I'm old enough to have the problems I have [none significant]. We're blessed if we're here."

* * *

How about memory? My sense is we overdo the significance of memory lapses that are such a common source of complaints in our senior years. Most of us can remember what's really significant (like the name of our spouse), even if our minds take a hike on names, phone numbers, and the location of car keys.

One aspect of this keeps getting worse, and I addressed it two years ago in a poem titled *The Noun Nemesis*. I started off by complaining about "The way you feel so damn absurd / when you forget a chosen word" . . . . "You're vexed at the lack of text / irate at your empty plate / dismayed by the dumb blockade." Then, after analyzing the problem, I arrived at this conclusion: "When a verbal abyss casts you amiss / (so you feel like a clown, face wreathed in a frown) / the word that's escaped you is usually a noun."

After illustrating why this was so, I contrasted a noun with its cousins. "Each other form of speech conceivable / is much more readily retrievable." I assessed each of them, e.g.: "With an adverb I'm superb"; "with a participle I'm no cripple"; "I can run errands with gerunds / and encounter no curbs with verbs." But sadly, I was forced to conclude, "I'm not aces / with nouns, names and places."

Not long ago, I wrote an article on this subject called *Senior Moments* – all about those pesky brain freezes that many of us experience with age. The good news is that we're not alone – and the article contains many humorous examples of others who have failed to cope – but I also tried to distill some of the sobering (albeit conflicting) views on whether we should be worrying about this phenomenon.

I have to admit that some of my findings were disturbing:

- 40 percent of us oldsters have a little bit of Alzheimer's in our brain.
- All memory loss should be taken seriously because it could signal a higher risk of dementia later on.
- Clues can start emerging up to 12 years before diagnosis of dementia.
- There's a pesky MCI intermediate stage that increases the risk of later progressing to dementia.

Still, as a lifelong optimist for whom the glass has always been at least half-full, I've concluded that this is no time to waver. I'm a disciple of the adage, "Worry is the interest paid on trouble before it's due."

Besides, I've got this little gizmo I carry around, that I speak into whenever I want to remember something I need to do, and it records my exact thoughts . . . . This leaves me with only one problem – remembering to play back what I've recorded when I need the information.

On a lighter note, my favorite joke about recall is one I've used to break the ice when I stepped up to the lectern – pleading my imperfect memory to justify referring to notes for my speech.

My wife and I are dining at another couple's house. After dinner, the wives repair to the kitchen, with the guys still at the table – and I'm complaining to my buddy about my failing memory.

"Oh," says he, "I had the same problem, but my wife got me a great book that explains how to deal with it – by making image associations and such."

"Great," I say, "I'd like to read the book – what's the title?"

My friend's brow furrows, he thinks for a moment and then says, "What's the name of the flower you give to someone for a special occasion?"

I don't answer right away, so he continues, "You know, the one that's red and has thorns on the stem."

"Do you mean a rose?" I offer.

"That's it!" he says. Then, turning toward the kitchen, he yells, "Hey, Rose, what's the name of that memory book you gave me?"

* * *

An especially troublesome and sad condition is coping with Alzheimer's or some other form of dementia. At my age, it's impossible to deny having wondered whether this might be in store – especially right after I've forgotten something I should have remembered, or repeated myself, or lost my way, or misplaced my possessions.

When my wife Barbara comes into contact with someone who's deep in the throes of Alzheimer's (the real thing, not just imagined), she'll often say, "If I ever get that way, just take me out in the backyard and shoot me." To which I reply with something inane like, "There's no backyard in our apartment," and we move on.

For me, the ultimate issue is less clear-cut. I enjoy living so much that it's hard for me to envision situations dire enough as to make me want to bow out voluntarily. But, then again, I realize that if I went way downhill, I wouldn't be in the best position to decide whether I'd had a change of heart on the subject.

This was brought home to me recently when a good friend, who had been experiencing a protracted run of serious health issues, said to me, "I'm now in an assisted living facility. I'd rather be in an assisted dying facility."

So I've devised my own test, which I have conveyed to my wife on more than one occasion. "If I'm really losing it, Barbara, seat me at the piano and place my hands on the keys. If within 30 seconds you hear something resembling those two B-flats that kick off *Blue Moon*, then keep me around." (By the way, I'm charging my readers with the sober responsibility, assuming I pass the *Blue Moon* test, of not letting her take me out into the backyard – assuming we have one – at least for a while.)

Some Octogenarian Negatives

Even though we surviving octogenarians have a number of reasons to be happy, there are also some negatives aside from health – and these are actually more fun to write about. I'm sure each of us has his own list, but let me offer up a few of mine that I have a hunch some of my peers may share.

One of my biggest bugaboos is a seeming inability to locate specific possessions of mine at the time I want them to appear. Nothing has been the cause of more self-flagellation in recent years. The objects in question are rarely lost, usually turning up hours or days later, when they're no longer in such immediate demand. But if someone out there has a surefire panacea for this, please let me in on it before I go over the edge.

Have you noticed – or is it just my problem? – how everything seems to take a lot longer to do nowadays? I'm not talking about major projects – just mundane stuff, like getting ready to go play tennis in the country on Saturday morning. So many little things to accomplish before stepping out the door. . . .

Excess noise levels – ah, there's one that I'm more cranky about with each passing year. At weddings and other celebrations, the amped-up dance music drives me out of the room. At trendy New York restaurants, the cacophony of voices not only impedes conversation but undercuts enjoyment of the food (although not enough to diminish my diet-breaking intake!). I'm grateful that my hearing remains relatively unimpaired at 85, but I can't abide the frequent assaults on its well-being.

I seem to be more impatient now (or was I always that way?). I find it tougher to roll with the punches. Some people (e.g., my wife Barbara) get impatient with the pace at which other people (e.g., me) are operating. My primary impatience, though, is directed at machines and other artifacts of life that refuse to operate as they should, thereby evoking from yours truly a lusty string of Anglo-Saxon epithets aimed in their general direction.

I'm too crotchety, as Barbara often reminds me. I frankly don't see this trait improving appreciably in the years ahead. (As for my lack of patience when it comes to the relentless barking of four-legged critters around the house, I'm going to remain silent, thereby preserving amicable relations with my canine-rescuer wife.)

Something I notice frequently nowadays is how often I'm the oldest guy in the room. This was always the case when I attended my wife's high school reunions, but lately I'm noticing it more and more – at parties, sporting events, lectures and so on. Now that I think of it, this isn't really a negative – sometimes, as on a tennis court, I even take a quiet pride in the realization.

By the way, I haven't failed to notice how easy it is to claim my senior discount at the movies and sporting events. You may consider that a positive, but I'm apt to wonder why the ticket-taker doesn't mumble, "Hey, this young-looking stud is definitely faking it" – and demand to see a birth certificate.

One sober disadvantage of being 85 is the diminution of your visibility to those who used to seek and value your views, opinions and judgments. To the extent your contemporaries are still around, they're no longer in positions of influence where such views might be valuable; and the people one and two generations removed who now occupy those positions have their own contemporaries and incipient seniors from whom to seek guidance. It's perfectly understandable, but notwithstanding, I miss the opportunity to do some serious thinking about pressing issues and to hold forth on how I would recommend solving a knotty problem.

The Years Ahead

In the many months I've been laboring on this memoir, here's the mantra I've often recited to myself – "After the memoir, no more major projects, and *no pressure*." My mind keeps lingering over an idyllic post-memoir octogenarian life – watching all those grand old movies I've recorded but haven't yet viewed; reading a bunch of the hundred-plus good books I've assembled on Kindle but have scarcely dented; taking in more Broadway matinees; visiting a few special museum exhibits – or even just goofing off.

It's a comforting agenda, but I have to admit I'm skeptical about actually following this course. Granted, I'm unlikely to take on a major project, such as another novel. But I doubt that the recurrent need I usually feel to accomplish something will simply dissipate. Rather, it's likely to lead me into smaller creative activities – but hopefully without me being subjected to the kind of pressure I've imposed on myself to complete this memoir, or to finish that novel a few years ago, or to get *Anatomy of a Mediation* published a while before that.

I have two projects that do lie ahead, but they aren't very demanding and don't require much creative thought. I intend to collect all the short fiction I've written – 31 stories, plus a play – into one published volume; and then I'm going to assemble the 40 or so essays I've written since my Skadden retirement into a second published book. But what else?

Frankly, I wouldn't mind taking on a major mediating assignment, but that requires being hired by the disputing parties – so I'm loath to factor into my plans something that's out of my control.

One thing I could see myself doing is to write some songs – both the words and the music. I did a little of this years ago – you can hear my favorite, *The Claustro Rag*, on the album titled *When I'm 64* – but I've been silent on this front in recent times. I'd enjoy being able to sing, play, and record my own new music.

In terms of concept albums, although I've recorded many songs from the '40s, I've never done an album devoted solely to the memorable songs of World War II, although I've long wanted to do so. As for timeliness, I can't help noting that 2020 is the 75th anniversary of the war's end, while 2021 marks the 80th year since the December 7th Japanese attack on Pearl Harbor.

When I've had a few drinks at our CT home, I often sit down at the piano and sing out lustily on a few of my favorite folk-rock tunes. I've recorded piano versions of many of these, but I'm tempted to take this a vocal step further. I also like the idea of recording my other two instruments – vibraphone and harmonica – in a trio setting with the piano.

There's an app called iReal Pro that I access through ear-pods, which plays accompaniments (bass and drums) for all my favorite standards. In effect, I have my own private rhythm section. With the beat thus taken care of, this has expanded my ability to do more interesting things on the keys; and I'm sure I'll make a recording one day employing this feature.

There are two musical projects I'd like to accomplish – improving my jazz improvising and committing to memory more tunes to play without consulting the sheet music – but these would take some real work to accomplish, so I'm not optimistic about success.

I'm sure I'll keep shooting and editing photos, and I have some ideas for new directions to move in, too nebulous to talk about now. I was hoping to make more documentary videos, but the time commitment for the novel and memoir got in the way, interrupting a video project devoted to Barbara's rescue organization, WOOF – I need to get back to that.

As for writing, I'm sure I'll do some, but don't know what just yet. Will I still be attracted to short fiction? What subjects will move me enough to justify an essay? Might I want to write about what it feels like to approach 90? How about composing humorous poetry – Ogden Nash style?

All these things and more are possible – so the recorded movies, the Kindle books, the matinees and museums (to say nothing of just goofing off) may have to continue taking a back seat . . . .

* * *

At 85, I'm maintaining a very positive outlook and am well-satisfied with what I've accomplished up to this point. Once having completed this memoir, I don't have a bunch of things to fulfill going forward. I feel comfortable about my health and state of mind, although recognizing there may be real challenges ahead.

I'll close with a negative and a positive. The negative involves that new phone app that shows you what you're going to look like some years in the future. I made the mistake of taking a peek. That's my face – I know it's me – but with such wrinkles that I expect to have a tough time facing a mirror.

The positive occurred in a restaurant recently, when I ordered a beer. The waiter (I swear to this!) asked for some proof of age. I couldn't believe it, stammered out something about being 85, pointed to my white hair – but he didn't back off, and I had to produce my license. Now, I know that he must have been told by management to card *everybody* that walks in the door, but still I'm taking it as a positive sign for the decade to come . . . .

22. OVERVIEW

So, that's my story. I'll just conclude with several observations about what I've learned about myself in the process of penning this memoir.

First of all, although it was a major effort to undertake, I'm glad I took on the project. At 85, it's a worthwhile task to pore over the old days. It really doesn't turn on whether anyone reads it although I hope many do – I just find it very gratifying to have surveyed my whole life story (albeit recounted by an observer who isn't exactly unbiased).

I've been asked by several people whether, in the course of the assignment, I discovered anything about myself that I didn't already know. The answer, truth be told, is not too much – mainly because I've been keeping in close touch with myself for the last 40 years or so. Still, some things stand out more clearly now, given the perspective that time affords.

Chief among these items of added clarity is the realization that those aspects of my life I deemed least palatable while enduring them proved to be more constructive than I realized at the time. So, for instance:

- I was an unhappy man while in the Navy, but it was my court martial experience on the ship that turned me on to a legal career, while my ship's home port of Seattle led directly to meeting my first wife (and from that, to the pleasure of fathering two wonderful sons).
- If anything, I was even more unhappy at law school, but – in addition to honing my analytical chops – I did come to grips with the concept of deferred gratification, an appreciation of which has been so basic to some of my major achievements in later life.
- I felt unfulfilled at my first law firm, but the stint there did position me to be in the right place at the right time to join Skadden Arps, to say nothing of it leading (albeit in deferred fashion) to meeting the nonpareil Barbara Fox.

How about regrets – did I find a lot of them lurking about? Not many, but there were a few, such as:

- Not being a more attentive son during a difficult period in my father's life.

- Not being a more attentive father during a difficult period in my sons' lives.

I still retain the regret I've felt for over 65 years of having quit the Princeton football team rather than toughing it out. It's partially offset, though, by the lessons imparted – namely that good things don't come easy and persistence is an essential virtue.

On a less personal level, I do regret not having a good camera along on those '52/U.S. and '62/European excursions . . . .

For our 25th college reunion, I wrote a piece about the important lessons we'd learned since graduation – serious stuff like appreciating significance, rejecting inertia, not providing yourself with excuses for failure. But here's the epitaph I concluded the listing with:

"And while you hold these precepts dear
Through mire and through muck,
Don't underestimate the need
To have a little luck."

In that regard, although my wife will chide me for saying so, I do believe I've been quite fortunate in most aspects of my life. (According to Barbara, if you dare to say you're lucky, a run of bad fortune is likely to seek you out.) This includes:

- Having two fine parents
- Attending excellent schools
- Fathering two great sons
- Meeting Barbara
- Having lots of good friends
- Enjoying sound health (and hopefully inheriting maternal survival genes)

Bottom line, I'm comfortable with myself and the way things turned out. (This is a good way to feel at 85, because if you're not comfortable, it would probably be difficult at this late juncture to do much about it.) Here are some specifics of why I feel this way:

- I think I have good judgment, at least most of the time – appreciating significance and not majoring in minor things.

- I like my addiction to multi-tasking – being pretty good at a variety of things. I recognize that I could be better at any one of them if the others were eliminated, but that's not a trade-off I'm willing to make.
- Professionally, I'm gratified that I became skilled at both making deals and resolving disputes – the yin and yang of negotiating – and that I wrote books about both endeavors.
- Although I'm basically cautious, I do take some chances and accept certain measurable risks.
- I generally call things as I see them – likes and dislikes, what I can do well and not so well.
- I'm happy with my positive attitude – for me, the glass is always at least half-full.
- I am comfortable with a plethora of different people, without feeling restricted by gender, age, religion, ethnic affiliation, etc.
- I have some wonderful friends – both long-time and newer ones – and few enemies. I generally like people, albeit some more than others, and there are very few people I actively dislike. I'm pleased that I keep in touch with friends through hefty missives I send out to them each year.
- I'm glad that while still in my early 60's I recognized that my constructive time at Skadden had ended – leaving me plenty of energy still to expend.
- I'm pleased that I have the energy at 85 to get out on the tennis court and the aplomb not to be overly embarrassed by my ebbing competence.
- Perhaps best of all, I've managed to do just about everything I wanted to do – I have no pressing bucket list.

Well, so much for the first 85 years. As for the future, I'll be interested to see how it works out . . . .

AFTERWORD

Having completed the memoir, I've pondered whether there was anything further to say. Two subjects come to mind.

- In the memoir, I wrote about what seemed important to me. The flip side – what I left out – includes some subjects worth mentioning, and I'll tell you why I avoided them.

- As the title of the memoir suggests, I aimed to conclude this narrative around the time of my 85th birthday in July of 2019. Almost a full year has now passed – and what a fractious time it has been! so I've added a few words about this.

Omissions

In reviewing the text of the memoir, I realized I've almost totally omitted personal commentary on what has been going on in the world during my adult years – dramatic times, to say the least. Consider the cold war, Vietnam, Watergate, the civil rights movement, Clinton's impeachment, 9/11, natural disasters, the 2008 recession, the wars in Iraq and Afghanistan – the list goes on. I steered clear of discussing these events, and I largely refrained from comment on the statesmen and politicians who directed the nation and generated the critical issues that have polarized public life over these decades.

Since I seem to have opinions on almost everything else, readers may wonder why I've been so silent on this score. It's a fair question. It is *not* that these issues don't interest me – they very much do. And it's not that I haven't formed personal opinions concerning what's been happening, as well as about our leaders – I most certainly have done that. Rather, I think, my silence reflects an amalgam of two concerns: *pertinence* and a certain facet of my *personality*.

The *pertinence* factor can be simply stated. This book is a memoir about me. These issues, while vital to the nation and central to its citizens, haven't directly impacted me that much. They have not altered the directions I've taken nor usurped my attitudes toward the matters I've dealt with. Because these are complex issues that shouldn't be addressed with a lick and a promise, I've excluded them on the basis of relevance.

The *personality* aspect is more complicated. Throughout my life, I have consistently restrained from voluntarily expressing my views on such hot topics, either orally or in writing. I don't suffer from the delusion that everyone is anxious to know my opinion about these matters. Even if asked, I regard the query as a reflection of politeness, an overture to include me in the conversation.

Having a strong point of view was something that always came hard for me. A quote I gave author Moira Johnston for her discussion of the TWA takeover (Chapter 15) made the point: "We were the silent generation. We missed all the wars – World War II, Korea, and Vietnam – the activism of the 1960's. We matured in the fifties during the Eisenhower years. The Age of Conformity. We were noncontroversial and I was always uncomfortable with strong opinions."

In reflecting on the reasons for such restraint, I recently re-read an article I wrote close to four decades ago (included in my 1984 book, *Legal-Ease,* under the title, *A Matter of Opinion*). At the time, I had recently met Barbara Fox and was under her spell. I was especially taken by her ability to express "an unhesitant opinion on a subject which she'd never previously faced; and when it turned out to be based on a false premise, she reiterated her view – and was right!"

I contrasted my hesitation (shared by many lawyers) with Barbara's intrepid approach. With lawyers, I wrote, "a veritable penumbra of caveats surrounds each minor pronouncement." We lawyers abound in elegant phrases like 'it can be argued' and 'one might think' and 'subject to a number of other relevant considerations'." I reflected how often I found myself "tentative on stuff (foreign policy, movies, personalities) when a matter of opinion is called for. Our Mideast policy may be a 'positive shambles' to the guy on the next barstool; for me, there are 'some considerations I feel the policymakers may have overlooked'."

Much of my caution may stem from law school, where the Paper Chase professors "managed to turn us into something resembling judgmental eunuchs." Why it still persists for me decades later and carries over to other parts of life seemed to me "largely a matter of not having the requisite knowledge." I felt that we lawyers need "raw facts for rational judgments. The absence of a sufficient data base makes us uncomfortable," as is the case when "we don't have a feel for the nuances of other matters," which are "often determinative." I noted that "I rarely have a strong view on foreign policy issues. I'm getting my information second-hand from newspapers and magazines. I can't possibly have the feel for a situation that the guy at the State Department desk has."

And that's the way I felt about things until the fateful presidential election of 2016 . . . .

Since my 85th birthday last July, the two most mesmerizing events have been the impeachment of President Trump and the scourge of the coronavirus.

[Just as I'm turning in this memoir to be printed, news has broken of the appalling "I can't breathe" murder of a black man by a white policeman in Minneapolis, followed by widespread protest marches, violence, and the Administration's controversial response. This has given rise to abounding critical issues of ingrained racism, "black lives matter," police brutality, lawful protests, dealing with destruction and looting by troublemakers – issues that I (in common with most people I know) have strong feelings about. Still, this is too complex a subject for me to summarize my views in a few paragraphs, and it's unclear where this is headed in the months ahead. Right now, my need is to complete this book, so I'm going to refrain from delving into it further in these pages.]

With regard to President Trump, my feelings about the man who presently occupies the oval office are so relentlessly negative (as is my dismay at the complicity of Congressional Republicans) that were I to express those views, you wouldn't recognize me as the same careful and measured attorney I've tried to be in years past.

Still, unlike many acquaintances, I tend to keep my views to myself and those closest to me. You'll note that, except for one peripheral point about our differing negotiating styles, I didn't voice any of my anti-Trump opinions in the memoir. Since politics has not been a major factor in my life, it seemed inappropriate for me to inject that strain into what is essentially a personal reflection on myself. Moreover, so many better-qualified observers have occupied this territory that there's little reason for me to lob in second-hand opinions on what, in my view, is such an open-and-shut case of malfeasance, misfeasance and nonfeasance.

But if anyone is really interested in how I feel about this (not that I think you would be), give me a call . . . .

* * *

Turning now to the coronavirus, as I write this (in June 2020) the country and the world are deeply damaged by this terrible plague which first appeared earlier this year. The human cost increases daily; the quarantines and other steps we've taken – not only to protect ourselves, but to contain the virus and avoid added problems for health care workers – have altered our daily lives immeasurably; and the negative financial impact on the nation's economy and individual livelihoods is almost incalculable.

I have seen some welcome words of wisdom on this – such as a piece by Bill Gates that was circulating about all the positive things the virus is reminding us of (which we've been ignoring for too long), beginning with:

> "It is reminding us that we are all equal, regardless of our culture, religion, occupation, financial situation or how famous we are. This disease treats us all equally – perhaps we should too. If you don't believe me, just ask Tom Hanks."

Still, other than acknowledging my fears about the virus – especially since it's unlike anything we've faced before in its multiple implications – I'm not going to comment on it generally. This is partly because so much else has been written about it that I'm not sure what I could add, and partly because I hesitate to pontificate now while we're still uncertain and fearful of where it's going to lead us. To be perfectly frank, it's also because I've been paying almost as much attention to how it has been mishandled by the administration as I have to its overwhelming potential ramifications – which is not the personal face I want to put on something so vast while it's still being combatted. I leave that to the electorate and to historians.

While others may equate and contrast the virus with earthquakes, hurricanes, wars, 9/11 and such, my reference point is polio. This scourge was a terrifying challenge, especially for youths, until Jonas Salk's vaccine came along while I was in college (1955).* Polio was most active in the summer months, then would go away and reappear the following spring – paralyzing an average of 16,000 people and killing nearly 2,000 each year. We learned to avoid public pools and other potential triggers. The heavy metal braces were artifacts we dreaded; even worse was the horrific iron lung respirator for those needing artificial breathing support.

---

* See the article by Marco Della Cava in *USA TODAY* 3/21/20. By the way, with all this talk going around nowadays about quick vaccine relief for coronavirus, Salk spent seven years seeking a cure for polio before his vaccine materialized.

As I noted in Chapter 4, polio hit the Horace Mann football team my junior year, killing one boy and injuring two others. We went into quarantine for several weeks, fearful that more of us would be stricken. I don't retain many specific memories of this, but I'm sure there must have been a good deal of fervent prayer around our household.

On a personal note, Barbara and I have moved up from NYC to our Easton CT home, where we've been hunkered down since early March. My approach has been extremely conservative – only rarely venturing off the property, avoiding all physical contact with other people, eschewing shops, etc. Barbara had been our lifeline to the outside world – fetching food and other essentials, cooking up superb nightly meals (often successfully experimental) plus maintaining virtual links with her real estate responsibilities and caring for seven dogs, one cat, and a needy husband.

I'm embarrassed to admit, however, that while fully aware of the carnage beyond my doors, and feeling genuine concern about family and friends, I'm not finding it personally uncomfortable being isolated here in our rural outpost. I've spent much of my time completing the memoir. Many hours have been consumed organizing extensive pages of photos that I feel provide an added dimension to what's being discussed in the text.

I've also recorded fifty songs on the piano for a planned "Sheltering-in-Place Songbook" album. Barbara and I play tennis on our court; I luxuriate with my harmonica in the hot tub; we watch cinema on the tube as well as home movies of former days; Barbara devised a digital feed enabling us have physical workouts with our NYC trainer (Eric Ludlow) several times a week; we enjoy virtual cocktail hours with close friends; and so on.

The best I can offer on the situation is the short wisdom I've seen to the effect that, "It's going to be a bumpy ride, but we are going to get through it together."

There has been one highlight for me during this shelter-in-place response to the pandemic, Princeton had to cancel its traditional alumni reunions weekend, but decided to substitute a virtual version. I had been scheduled to play at reunions for three classes, so I was asked to perform from my home for a virtual Saturday cocktail hour accessible by all classes.

I decided to use my 90 minutes to put a positive spin on these troubling times – to look for silver linings with an "accentuate the positive" choice of buoyant songs to lift everyone's spirits. (Many were taken from the album of that name that I made in 2011.) I wanted to encourage listeners to sing along on songs like "You'll Never Walk Alone," and "Bridge Over Troubled Water," so I fed them the words slightly ahead of the notes I played on the piano.

From the reaction I received via the chat room on the Zoom screen and by email, it worked well (although there apparently were some technical difficulties meshing the volumes of the piano and the voice). People seemed quite enthusiastic over the session, and I was pleased at what I'd managed to accomplish at a challenging time.

APPENDIX

Listings of Other Friends and Colleagues

In the course of writing this memoir, and calling to mind multiple recollections from these past eight decades, I have tried to focus on specific events that had special meaning to me. In doing so, I've identified many of the friends, colleagues, and other individuals who populated those events.

What has become apparent to me, however, is that many of the people with whom I interacted in a positive way over the years don't appear in those specific recollections – yet in the aggregate they played major roles in different periods of my life.

So I'd like to pay tribute to them by listing their names in this appendix. (In many cases, I've also been friends with their spouses, even if I haven't included their names.) There are undoubtedly others who should appear on these listings but aren't named due to my imperfect memory; and I apologize in advance to them for any such omissions.

Proceeding chronologically, I'll start with friends at Horace Mann School that I haven't focused on previously. As I noted in Chapter 4, many of us from the Class of 1952 still get together quarterly for lunch in Manhattan, thanks to Alan Sklar's organizing efforts. Frequent members of this group are: Jay Jacobson, Mickey Littman, Alan Patricof, Sirgay Sanger, Carl Seligson, Burt Siegel, Burt Strauss, Porter Miller, Joel Block, Harry Lipton, Bob Belfer, and Jay Haft. Also attending often are members of the class of 1953; Lew Lowenfels, Lou Rabinowitz, and Mike Koplik – and of late, Joe Diamond. Some other good friends from Horace Mann days are: Ed Aronson, the family of Dick Eisner, Dick Kaplan and family, Herb Kutlow, the family of Paul Margulies, Harvey Pollak, Ted Weill, and Ed Nordlinger.

Turning now to Princeton, here's an alphabetical list of friends from my Class of 1956 that I haven't focused on previously (a number of whom are now deceased): Bill (and Penny) Agnew, Bob (and Sandy) Aldrich, Steve (and Rita) Alfred, Ted (and Polly) Bellingrath, Pierre (and Cheryle) Bennerup, Jim (and Margo) Bennett, John Bodman, Pete Briger, Pete Buchanan, Bobby Clark, Denny Crimmins, Bos (and Gerry) Crowther, Russ (and Gay) Culin, Dick DeCesare, Collins (and Anne) Denny, Jack (and Rita) Doub, Jim Duffy, Dick Dzina, Charlie Elliott, Frank Embick, Arthur (and Janet) Eschenlauer, Mac (and Ross) Francis, Jack (and Anne) Fritts,

Dan (and Joyce) Gardiner, Pete (and Scotty) Gillette, Arch Gillies, Larry (and Myrna) Goodman, Marc Grassi, Bill (and Sue) Grassmyer, Ed Gray, Joe (and Vivian) Grotto, Jon Hammer, Svend (and Debby) Hansen, Doug Harding, Jim (and Toots) Henderson, George (and Shay) Hirsch, Fritz (and Connie) Hollenberg, Kirby and (Judy) Holmes, Bill (and Marilyn) Horner, Boyd Hovde, Bob Hut, Dave (and Jean) Jordan, Frank Klapperich, Joe (and Jane) Knox, Jack (and Betty) Kraus, Ken Lange, Bill Lawlor, Fraser (and Maxine) Lewis, Bevis (and Clara) Longstreth, Gabe (and Terry) Markisohn, Lou Masotti, Craig (and Alice) McClelland, Bob (and Dina) McCabe, Lenny Meyers, Sandy (and Joan) Millspaugh, Bob Morgan, Joe Nishimura, Sid (and Cathy) Pinch, Fred Poole, Tom (and Winnifred) Quay, Marty Raymond, Major Reynolds, Fritz Riedlin, John Rutgers, Bill (and Phyllis) Rosser, Neil Rudenstine, Bob (and Sue) Rodgers, Fred Sater, Gordie (and Shelley) Schwartz, Bick (and Barbara) Satterfield, Peter Sellon, Jim Schisgall, Ken (and Mary) Snedeker, Ben (and Jo Ann) Spinelli, Walt Stapleton, Paul Shein, John Steel, Neil Steibigel, Art Szeglin, Bob (and Flora) Varrin, T.K. Vodrey, Joe and Patty Walsh, John Hill (and Sandy) Wilson, Ross Wilson, and Toby (and Karen) Wise.

There are also a number of Princetonians from other classes (or otherwise associated at some point with Princeton) that I'd like to mention: Nate Bachman, Bill (and Mary Ellen) Bowen, Philip Cannon, Marcia Cantarella, Hodding Carter, the family of Mort and Jane Chute, Janet Clarke, Paul Dunn, Steve (and Fredi) Friedman, Gerry (and Glenda) Greenwald, Mike Iseman, Marty Johnson, Dan Kelly, Katie Kutney, Sarah Lederman, Bob (and Patty) Mack, Eldon (and Betts) Mayer, Aili McConnon, John (and Judy) McCarter, Rich McGlynn, Jessica Munitz, Jon Murphy, Frank Ordiway, Nancy Peretsman, Ev Pinneo, Tracy Pogue and family, Dave and Susie Rahr, Tina Ravitz, Bob Rawson, Denny Rice, Charlie Rockey, Dick (and Inez) Scribner, Eliot Spitzer, Jean Telljohann, Dorothy Werner, Jon Wonnell, and Tom Wright.

Numerous people from my three decades at Skadden Arps haven't been previously mentioned but played definite roles in my life back then. Let me start with some of the people I worked most closely with and have held in high regard over the years: Phil Adams, Rich Grossman, Dan Kurtz, Bruce McGuirk, Dan Stoller, Milt Strom, and Charlie Ufford.

A number of people at the firm – some now deceased – impressed me greatly with their acumen as they went about their business enhancing Skadden's stature. Here's a partial listing: Roger Aaron, Peter Atkins, Ken Bialkin, Sheila Birnbaum, Mark and Helene Kaplan, Judith Kaye, Morris Kramer, Neal McCoy, Bill Meagher, Greg Milmoe, Mike Mitchell, Frank Rothman, and Bob Sweet.

There are some other people who, for one reason or another I've had special feelings for over the years, including: Hunter Baker, Eric Cochran, Lynn Coleman, Mike Diamond, Dana Freyer, David Friedman, Mike Goldberg, Ken Gross, Linda Hayman, Alf Law, Jim Levitan, Nancy Lieberman, Ray Roche, Irene Sullivan, Jeff Tindell, Tina Tchen, and Tony (and Vivian) Zaloom.

Finally, here's an alphabetized partial list of other admirable Skadden people I've known and worked with over the years: Rand April, Cliff Aronson, Steve Banker, Bob Bennett, David Brewster, Bruce Buck, Jerry Coben, Mike Connery, Ben Crisman, Gary Cullen, Susan Curtis, John Donovan, Don Drapkin, John Fricano, Eric Friedman, Mitch Gitin, Frank Gittes, Joe Giunta, Jeff Glekel, Fred Goldberg, Shep Goldfein, Les Goldman, Peter Greene, Henry Hacker, Joe Halliday, Phil Harris, Michael Hatchard, Nancy Henry, Sally Henry, Jerry Hirsch, Carrie Hirtz, Sam Kadet, Rich Kalikow, Stacy Kanter, Jay Kasner, Tom Kennedy, Peggy Kerr, Lou Kling, Kurt Koegler, Phyllis Korff, Ted Kozloff, Mike Lawson, Jim Lyons, Matt Mallow, Martha McGarry, Chip Mullany, Alan Myers, John Nannes, Peter Neckles, Ben Needell, Tim Nelsen, Eileen Nugent, Jim O'Rorke, Barney Phillips, Bob Pirie, Ken Plevan, Rick Prins, Matt Rosen, Steve Rothschild, Irving Shapiro, Stu Shapiro, Mike Schell, Wally Schwartz, Bob Sheehan, Scott Simpson, Mark Smith, Mitch Solomon, Mary Lou Steptoe, Laura Ward, Rod Ward, Michael Weiner, Ed Welch, Wayne Whalen, Vaughn Williams, Peggy Wolf, Bob Zimet and David Zornow.

Here are some people I interacted with professionally or otherwise during my Skadden years although they weren't colleagues at Skadden: Bill Achtmeyer, Bill Allen, Susan Antilla, Francie Blassberg and Joe Rice, Bill Buchanan, Maryellen Cattani, Bill Chandler, Dick Cheney, Joe Connors, Charles Craver, Bill Crerend, Sam Crossland, Judy Dart, Rebecca Davies, Nat Doliner, Jimmy Finkelstein, Louis Fishman, Arthur Fleischer, Fred Gerard, Peter Goodson, Fred Gould, Gershon Kekst, Jerry Kohlberg, Larry Lederman, Alan Levenson, Don Mandich, Deryck Maugham, Cathy McCoy, George Montgomery, Chuck Nathan, Jerry Raikes, Marti Robinson, Victor Rubino, Carl and Mary Ellen Schneider, Bruce Slovin, Al Sommer, Evelyn Sroufe, Stephen Swid, Mort Weiner, Linda Wertheimer, and Michael and Barbara Zimmerman.

Finally, here in alphabetical order are my past and present friends, and special acquaintances, not connected to any of the prior institutions, whom I haven't previously focused on. This list contains those whom we socialize with frequently today, others less often, and some professional or business associates. A number of those named are now deceased. I haven't tried to divide this up further, but please know I have friendship and admiration for all of you.

Annie and Hank Alprin, Carol April, the family of Fred and Claudine Bacher, Tom Barton, Dick Bass, Rosemary Bella, Marshall Berman and Karen Kaplan, Kim Birbrower, Joni Blackstein and family, Russ Bleemer, Dick Bodman, Taylor and Willa Bodman, Abe Borenstein, Joel Braun, Earl and Judy Bronsteen, Clark Callander, Wilson Chu, Alex Ciarnelli and Jessica Elbaz, Andre Coetzee, Joel and Lillian Cohen, Lester and Linda Colbert, Margit Cotsen, Ronnie and Howard Cowan, Bill and Dolores Crerend, Melissa Cross, the family of Sam Crossland, Don Emelio de Lemos, Michael Dennis and Kathy Wenning, Cam and Bobbie Devore, Bobbi Devore, Rich Dooley, Jim and Susan Dubin, Karen Duncan, Al Eden and family, David Elinson, Diana Elton, Steve Epstein, Jack Esher, Mark and Donna Evens and family, Dick and Ann Fabrizio, Dino and Pat Fabrizio, the family of John and Emalie Feerick, Betty Feinberg, Harvey and Audrey Feuerstein, Joan Finkelstein, John and Judy Flaxman, Ruth Flaxman, Louis and Carla Fishman, Greg and Melissa Fleming, the family of Fin and Diane Fogg, Linda Frankel and Bob Werbel, Arthur Friedman, Joel Friedman, Irma Friedman and family, the family of Barry and Gloria Garfinkel, Peter and Barbara Georgescu, David Geronemos, Lou Gerstner, Ron Gidwitz, Laurie Gilkes and George Maniscalco, Rhoda Glass, Sondra Gilman and Celso Gonzales, Arthur Goldblatt, Larry and Myrna Goodman, Gerry and Glenda Greenwald, Dick Greiser, Peter and Carin Gruenberger, Rich Guggenhime, Maeve and Andy Gyenes, Ken Hagen, La Tanya Hall, Bill and Sally Hambrecht, Linda and Mitch Hart, Sandra Heath, Dennis and Huguette Hersch, Dalma Heyn and Richard Maryk, Fred Hills, Kate Hughes, June Iseman, Dana Jackson, Deke Jackson, Amanda Silver Jaffa, Claude Jarman, Bill and Dominique Kahn, Stephanie Kanner and Ronny Kreisman, Joan Kaplan, Neil Karnofsky, Vanessa Kaster, Ronnie Katz, Bill Kaufmann, Ellen and Rick Kelson, Greg Kennedy, Tom Kiernan, Jacqui Klinger and David Price, Charles Koch, Anthony Korf, Harvey and Barbara Kurzweil, Ann Kwan, Sacha and Rebecca Lainovic, John Larson, Jerry and Nancy Lawton, Fred and Sandy Levin and family, Jay and Sharon Levy, Anna Lew, Keyman Lew, Lefty and Joyce Lewis, Penny and Jay Lieberman, Leni Liftin, Michael Lubell, Ralph Mabey, Bob and Patty Mack, Dick Madden, Barry and Sally Mandel, Bruce and Naomi Mann, Fred and Barbara Marcus, the family of Paul Margulies, Andy and Terri Marks, John Marquis, Nick and Mary Marshall, Reba Miller, Greg and Laura Milmoe, Marty and Mendelle Milston, Margo and Tom Mohr, Michael Mondavi, Norman Moss, Paul Moss, Tony and Alice Moss, Dede and Bob Moss, David Muller, Dick Myers, Sheldon Nadler, Brian Newfeld,

Susie Noddell, Nancy Noddell, Tom Okin, Donna and Peter Olshan, Suzi and Marty Oppenheimer, Jason and Dori Ortmeyer, Tanya Oziel, Gerson Pakula and family, Tim Parrott, Regina Peruggi and Jerry McCallum, Fred and Alexandra Peters, Tracy Pogue and family, Carmen and Gail Policy, Val and Marty Pollner, Tim Porter, Sylvia and David Posner, Rick Prins and Connie Steensma, Jen Raikes, Rayna Ragonetti, Albert Reff, Charles Reich, George and Ann Riordan and family, Fred Roberts, Seth Roland and family, Betty Rollin and Ed Edwards, Marcia Roma, Phyllis Roth, George Rothman, Ernie Rubenstein and Tova Friedler, Victor Rubino, Ernie Ruehl, Ernie Ruehl Jr., Lee and Margie Sarokin, Barbara Savinar, Ed and Betsy Schiff, Judy Schneider, Joey Scott, Dick Seclow, Steve and Joan Selig, Karen Shapiro, Stan and Sydney Shuman, Bill Silbey, Mark Silbey, Bob and Esther Silbey, Bernice Silver, David Silvers and Joan Binstock, Michael Silver, Nita Sim, Joanna Simon, Alan and Anita Sklar, Barbara Sloane and Sidney Winawer, Dick and Teressa Snyder, Gloria and Bill Sokolin, Charles Solomon and Diane Gallagher, Rocky Spane, Dante Sta Cruz, Carol Sterling, Hank Stern, Ettore Stratta and Pat Philips and her extended family, Roz Strizver, Charles and Barbara Strouse, Jim Sullivan and Ray Flautt, Marjorie Sussmann, Stephen and Nan Swid, Bob Taisey, Arthur Taylor, David Tendler, Paul and Susan Tierney, Michael Torkin and family, Bob Towner, Allen Unger, Jay Urstadt, David and Lisa Van Zandt, Norma Villafuerte, Vaughn Walker, the family of Jack Veatch, Burt Waggott, Linda Wank, the family of Bob and Kit Watson, Jill Windwer, Judy Wong, Judy Woodfin, Cathy Younger, and   Alfred and Patti Youngwood.

Photos of Friends and Colleagues

Given some reflection time by the need to shelter-in-place at our CT home, I've rounded up from my computer and the internet a number of photos of friends and colleagues. (Other individuals would have been included, but I lacked access to photos of them that are housed on discs in my NYC apartment – my apologies.) These appear in thumbnail size and in totally random order on the following pages, plus some duos and larger groupings. I've decided to omit any identifying names – if your picture is included, you'll recognize the face, while the identity of other particular subjects can be turned into a guessing game.

First, though, there's a page devoted to the dogs and cats that have occupied our quarters over the past three decades (lovingly cared for by Barbara and our housekeeper, Gloria), and a page of striking illustrations by Joe Azar that accompanied my past articles and stories.

Buffy   *Smudgie*   *Stella*

Macee   *Annie*   *Laddie*

**Our
Present
Menagerie**

Harry   *Sydney*

Those who have left us . . .

Lucy   *Winky*   *Molly*   *Laddie*

Over the course of the past four decades, my writings have often been accompanied by illustrations from the fertile pen of Joe Azar. In addition to the covers of seven of my books, he has done close to 200 skillful sketches that illuminate in vivid pictorial terms the points I'm trying to make in the text. I've selected five of my favorites on this page.

* * * * *

The article here, entitled "Balls in the Air," posed the question of how to make the best use of our limited leisure time. Joe chose to illustrate one possible approach – namely, trying to fit them all in simultaneously.

Here's how Joe illustrated the different approaches my wife Barbara and I take to problem-solving (referred to in the Afterword) – me tied down by "a veritable penumbra of caveats," Barbara unhesitant about expressing firm opinions on weighty matters.

To accompany my short story The Smell Test, Joe focused on the aging protagonist as he wrestles with an ethical question – recalling how his senior partner used to react to any resolution that didn't pass the smell test.

For this article about negotiating deals, When the Playing field Tilts, Joe captured my comment that in lieu of the proverbial level playing field, the existence of positive or negative leverage had become the order of the day.

Joe Azar

Perhaps my most popular essay was about lawyers on the road, staying in good hotels, and facing the tricky question of what you're permitted to take with you from the bathroom upon departure – the lawyer Joe featured having adopted an expansive view of the issue.

473

Made in the USA
Middletown, DE
14 November 2021